Children's Rights: Reality or Rhetoric?

THE UN CONVENTION ON THE RIGHTS OF THE CHILD: THE FIRST TEN YEARS

Hey Gill ; Ben

look my book!

♥ Sarah x

The International Save the Children Alliance

Citation: Children's Rights: Reality or Rhetoric?
Editor: Sarah Muscroft

ISBN 2 940217 09 2

Designed by River Design
Printed and bound by Impressions
Printing costs kindly donated by Virgin Healthcare Foundation

For more information please contact:

The International Save the Children Alliance
275-281 King Street
London W6 9LZ United Kingdom
+44 (0)20 8748 2554
E-mail: info@save-children-alliance.org

Photographs

Part I	Sarah Muscroft
Chapter 1	Save the Children Sweden (Rädda Barnen)
Chapter 2	Dave Stewart-Smith, Save the Children, PhotoDisc
Part II	Save the Children Sweden (Rädda Barnen)
Chapter 3	Save the Children Sweden (Rädda Barnen)
Chapter 4	Julio Etchart, Save the Children
Part III	Jenny Matthews, Save the Children
Chapter 5	Julio Etchart, Save the Children
Part IV	Penny Tweedie, Save the Children
Chapter 6	Liba Taylor, Save the Children

Contents

Preface i

Forword ii

Acknowledgements iii

Glossary iv

Part 1 The Context 1

Chapter 1 Introduction 4

Chapter 2 Rights of the Child 12

Part 2 The Global Issues 39

Chapter 3 Child Soldiers 42

Chapter 4 Child Labour 64

Part 3 The Country Analyses 83

Chapter 5 Country Reports 86

Part 4 Conclusion 281

Chapter 6 The Challenge Ahead 284

Annexe 1 The UN Convention on the Rights of the Child 296

Annexe 2 The International Save The Children Alliance 313

'Children have rights. We have a right not to fight. We have a right to an education and to health'.

Stephen, age 17 - former child soldier, Liberia

Preface

Children's rights are human rights.
This may sound like a statement of the obvious. Yet for millions of children around the world, this one simple undeniable fact is being overlooked, time and time again.

The United Nations Convention on the Rights of the Child is ten years old. It is the most widely ratified human rights convention and the first international instrument which covers the full rights of an individual. It was designed to create a common legal framework through which to increase governmental accountability, bring about legislative reform and ultimately create a better worldwide environment in which all children can develop.

A decade is time enough for governments to put their promises into practice. Yet, in reality, have children's lives improved since ratification? In a world where children continue so visibly to suffer, it is difficult to believe that adequate steps have been taken to ensure rights are a reality for children.

In this revealing publication, *Children's Rights - Reality or Rhetoric?*, Save the Children poses these exact questions and draws out the undeniable, disturbing conclusions.

In this provocative analysis of the first ten years of the Convention, Save the Children makes an analysis, before looking elsewhere, at the actions of governments of its own Members. In addition it offers a penetrating view of the emotive issues of child soldiers and child labour - two complex subjects, which are constantly under scrutiny in the international arena thanks to organisation like Save the Children.

For the sake of generations to come, recognition of children's rights can not afford to be merely academic; it must take the form of practical and applied action. Save the Children works in over 100 countries around the world, striving to implement a child's rights based approach in everything it does, with activities integrating key principles of the CRC. It urgently calls upon Governments, NGO's, and civil society equally, to do the same.

Every child has the right to survival and protection and a secure and happy childhood. It is not a moment too soon to now take stock and face the fact that we are simply not doing enough collectively, to ensure the delivery of promises and better lives for children.

I congratulate Save the Children for this highly perceptive critique of the first ten years of the UN Convention of the Rights of the Child, and wish them every success in continuing their invaluable work with and for children.

Graça Machel
Expert of the UN Secretary-General on the impact of armed conflict on children

Foreword

Children's Rights: Reality or Rhetoric? is a publication which is not so much designed to celebrate what we collectively, have achieved for children, but rather to identify important areas where we have failed and where there is still much work to do.

The International Save the Children Alliance is well positioned to carry out this critique as an organisation which witnesses at first hand and works to relieve the suffering of children while also fighting to bring about a change in overall attitudes and behaviour towards children. We aim in this publication to show the reader how complex the challenges of realising children's rights are, and to inspire the sheer hard work which is needed to deliver on our promises to children.

John T. McCarthy.
Chair of the International Save the Children Alliance

Acknowledgements

The International Save the Children Alliance Secretariat would like to thank all those who have been involved in this project and the preparation and production of this publication.

Principal Writers: Bill Bell, Rachel Brett, Rachel Marcus & Sarah Muscroft.

Editorial Board: Bill Bell, Diana Dalton, Burkhard Gnärig, Sarah Muscroft, Angela Penrose, Stephen Segal & Carl Von Essen.

Editing Team: Annie Jackson, Charles Harrowell, Diana Dalton, Mike Gidney, Craig Baxter, Nancy Terry, Karen Morgan, Gary Willis, Sophie Ganevitch, Ian Munt & Jonathan Tuchner.

Advisors: Lisa Woll, Chris Smith, Johan Stanggrens, Simone Ek, Annika Malmborg, Aina Bergstrom, Sigurd Johns, Anna Groesland, Elizabeth Jareg, Tone Lauvdal, Helena Karlen, Celia Petty, Lennart Reinius, Frances Ellery & Maeve McAnallan.

Research Team: Federica Donati & Jean-Pascal Obembo; Andrew Johnson, Save the Children Australia; Sarah Stevenson & Daryl Keating, Save the Children Canada; Kirsten Holm-Peterson, Ellen Hoeedt-Rasmussen & Neils Hjortdal, Save the Children Denmark (Red Barnet); Mirja Winter-Helkila & Eija Kempii, Save the Children Finland (Pelastakaa Lapset Ry); Isabelle Moreau, Save the Children France (Enfants et Développement); Christina Marouli, Save the Children Greece; Angel Gaytan, Save the Children Guatemala (Alianza Para El Desarrollo Juvenil Comunitario); Mariano Planells, Save the Children Honduras (Asociacion Salvemos Los Niños de Honduras); Sveinbjörg Palisdöttir & Kristen Jonasdöttir, Save the Children Iceland (Barnaheill); Atsuko Tsuruta & Miho Wada, Save the Children Japan; In-Sook Kim, Save the Children Korea; Nevena Serafimova & Maria Stambolieva, Save the Children Macedonia; Graciella Bonilla & Jesus Vega, Save the Children Mexico (FAI); Mathieu Hermans, Save the Children Netherlands; John Bowis & Beverly Turnbull, Save the Children New Zealand; Turid Heidberg & Lisa Bang, Save the Children Norway (Redd Barna); Raluca Slamnescu & Anca Suciu, (Salvati Copiii); Manuel Posso, Save the Children Spain; Simone Ek, Save the Children Sweden (Rädda Barnen); Lisa Harker Save the Children UK; Corrine Woods, Renee Wessels & Marianne Levert, Save the Children US.

Production Team: Antony Lawrence, Judi Turner, Colin Smith, Louise Roberts, Lucie Brooks, Louise Statt & Martine Felthouse, River Design; Clare McKenna, Atlas Translations; & Stuart Traynor, Impressions.

The International Save the Children Alliance would like to express special thanks to the Virgin Health Care Foundation for its donation, which has assisted in the printing of this publication.

Finally, my particular thanks go to Bill Bell, Angela Penrose, Diana Dalton and Charles Harrowell, for their unfailing commitment and efforts, which extended well beyond the call of duty.

Sarah Muscroft, October 1999.

Glossary

Additional Protocols to the Geneva Conventions
The four Geneva Conventions are the principal instruments of international humanitarian law. The two additional protocols of 1977 refer to: 1) strengthening the protection of victims of international armed conflict and 2) strengthening the protection of victims of non-international (internal) conflicts.

African Charter on the Rights and Welfare of the Child
A charter adopted by the Member States of Organisation of African Unity in 1190 which aims to add an African specificity to the provisions of the UNCRC.

Beijing Rules
The United Nations Standard Minimum Rules for the Administration of Juvenile Justice.

Civil society
Non governmental actors in society who are organised to act in the pursuit of various interests.

Globalisation
Most often used in the in its economic context (pan-national economics which is accompanied by huge immediate capital flows of the global electronic economy). Globalisation is also a set of interrelated political, technological and cultural processes.

ILO
The International Labour Organisation - a UN affiliated body.

ILO Worst Forms of Child Labour Convention
A new convention adopted in June 1999 and awaiting ratification. It seeks to prevent work that, 'is likely to harm the health, safety or morals of children.

International Criminal Court
In July 1998 the International Criminal Court came into being in order to prosecute and punish, 'persons responsible for crimes such as genocide'. Unlike the International Court of Justice at the Hague it prosecutes individuals rather than dealing with cases between states.

NGOs
Non-governmental Organisations.

North
A loose grouping of the 'developed' nations which are mainly located in the northern hemisphere.

OECD
Organisation for Economic Co-operation and Development

Optional Protocol - (to Article 38 of the UN Convention on the Rights of the Child)
The optional protocol on Article 38 seeks to raise the legal age for recruitment and participation in hostilities to 18 years of age.

Riyhad Guidelines
The United Nations Guidelines for the Prevention of Juvenile Delinquency.

Sexual exploitation
In this publication this refers to all forms of sexual abuse whether committed for commercial profit of individual gratification.

South
A loose grouping of the 'underdeveloped' nations which are mainly located in the southern hemisphere.

States Party
A nation that ratifies the Convention becomes a 'states party' to it.

CRC
The United Nations Convention on the Rights of the Child.

UNDP
The United Nations Development Programme.

UNHCR
The United Nations High Commission for Refugees.

UNICEF
The United Nations Children's Fund.

UNWRA
The United Nations Relief and Works Agency.

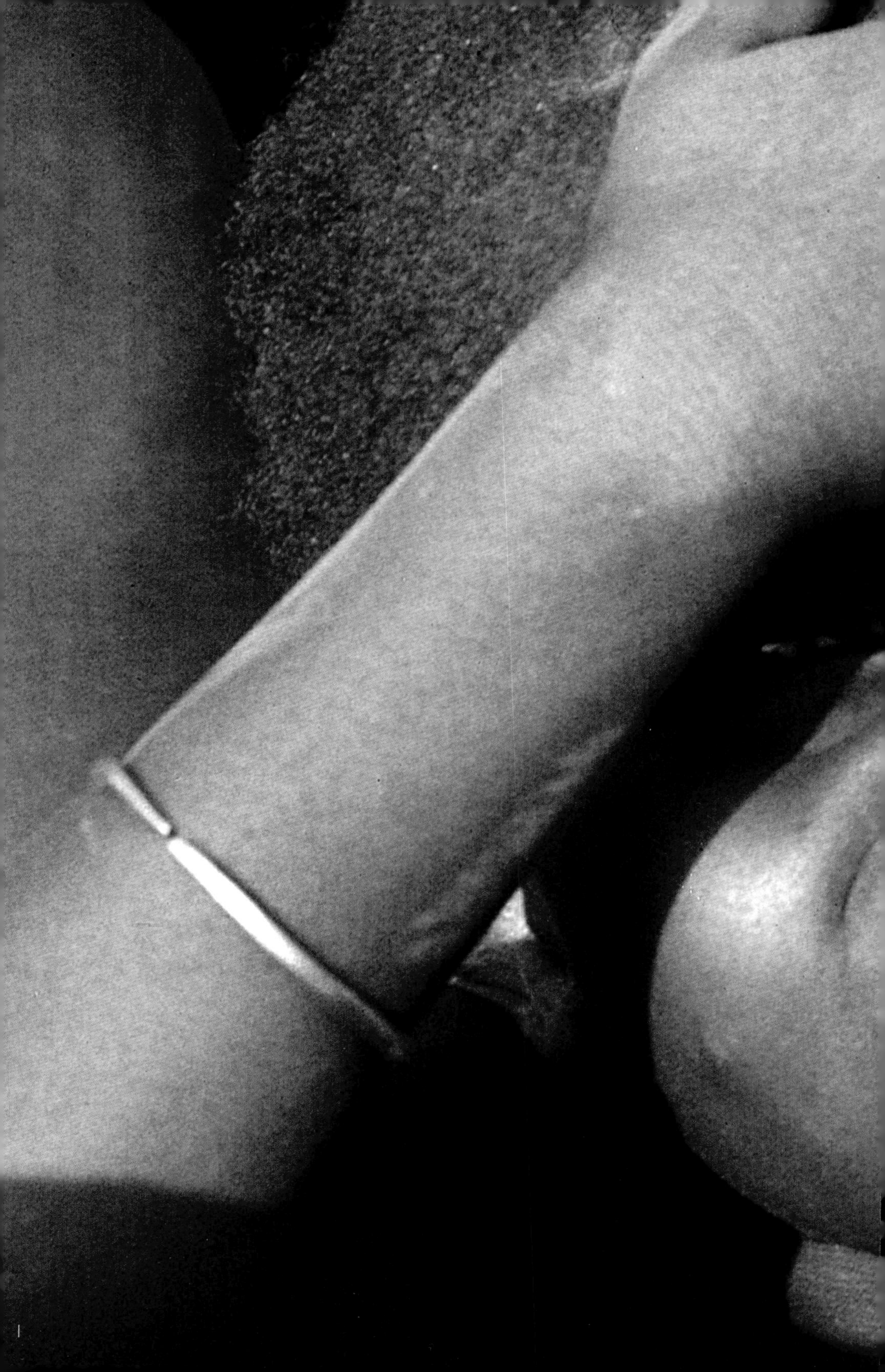

PART I
The Context

'I want to live a long life. Even if you are poor, it's still nice to live'.

Ciano, age 10 - The Philippines

Chapter 1

Introduction

Ten years on - a time to take stock

After many years of debate, the notion that children have independent human rights - and that those rights should be at the heart of all political, economic and social decision-making - was finally given form in the UN Convention on the Rights of the Child (CRC). This was adopted unanimously by the UN General Assembly on 20 November 1989. Since then, the CRC has been ratified by all but two of the world's governments, making it the most widely ratified human rights treaty in history. Over the past ten years it has helped establish an internationally accepted framework for the treatment of all children, encouraged a positive and optimistic image of children as active holders of rights, and stimulated a greater global commitment to safeguarding these rights.

But, ten years on, how far have we really come in realising the vision of the Convention? How much actual progress has been brought about for the benefit of children? What real action - rather than eloquent statements of well-meant ideals has been taken? These questions now need to be asked, to see whether the promises of governments around the world have meant anything at all for their children.

This is the purpose of this report. *Children's Rights - Reality or Rhetoric?* discusses the progress that has been made since the signing of the Convention to ensure that rights have real meaning for children. It calls governments to account, and, in doing so, aims to separate practical action from simple rhetoric.

In particular, it examines the degree to which the CRC has been implemented in the 26 member nations of the International Save the Children Alliance. This is not necessarily the most obvious starting point. Given that Save the Children works in more than 100 countries, with some of the world's most disadvantaged children, it is arguable that such an assessment should focus, in particular, on what has been happening in the developing world. It is, after all, in these countries that governments are having the greatest difficulty in finding the resources to implement the Convention. Weighed down by debt and struggling to cope with the impact of the AIDS epidemic and globalisation, such countries face an uphill battle to make good on their promises to children.

Ten years on, how far have we really come in realising the vision of the Convention?

However, the International Save the Children Alliance believes that more can be gained by beginning this review on their own doorsteps, in the countries where they have their head offices. After all, the CRC provides for every child and has equal relevance in all countries. One of the key lessons from the past ten years has been that no country in the world has yet fulfilled the rights of the child set out in the CRC and that all countries - rich or poor, east or west - have much more to do. This is confirmed by the evidence in this study from those Save the Children members in the north, representing some of the wealthiest countries in the world. Their findings provide a valuable and informative contrast with those of Save the Children members in a number of developing countries.

Howard Davies / Save The Children

The idea of individual country evaluations is not new. Each country is obliged to submit periodic reports to the UN Committee on the Rights of the Child. However, this is the first time that a comprehensive review of implementation across such a diverse group of countries has been attempted. This offers the opportunity to compare and contrast the situation for children in a range of different countries, providing an original perspective and allowing a unique analysis of the challenges that implementation of the CRC poses.

The report opens with an overview of the Convention. This first section (Chapter Two) examines the development of children's rights, setting them into context and looking at the vision contained in the CRC. It discusses the success of the last ten years, exploring the landmarks that have been achieved and the positive advances that have been made. Chapter Two also considers the failings of the last ten years and the obstacles which prevent effective realisation of the vision set out by the Convention.

Comparing the reality of life for children to the rhetoric of the Convention, identifies the role and responsibility of governments, calling on them to create the necessary conditions for positive change.

Against this background, Chapters Three and Four look at two key issues, child soldiers and child labour. These are global problems and, by considering them in greater depth, it is possible to understand why governments and the international community are still struggling to address them satisfactorily. They also highlight a number of the practical difficulties in implementing the Convention.

Chapter Five brings together a series of country reports, which outline the domestic situation for children and implementation of the CRC in individual member countries of the International Save the Children Alliance. These reports examine the reality of children's rights by focusing on a number of key issues. Children's rights and the issues surrounding them are broad-ranging, complex and often controversial. Given the comprehensive nature of the CRC it would be impossible to include every provision here. Four issues have therefore been selected as indicative of the wider situation:

- sexual exploitation - including sexual abuse and all forms of commercial exploitation;
- juvenile justice;
- displacement;
- education.

In each country report the situation on the ground is set against the provisions of the CRC. Both the successes and the failures in implementing the CRC are analysed in a candid critique of the performance of the governments of Save the Children's member countries in advancing children's rights. In comparing the reality of life for children to the rhetoric of the Convention, the reports identify the role and responsibility of governments and make recommendations for action, calling on them to create, as a matter of urgency, the necessary conditions for positive change.

The final chapter draws together common threads. It does not suggest that there are any simple solutions to the current difficulties in implementing the Convention. Rather, it suggests that the most important single factor in the process is political will and the strength of commitment of individual governments, non-governmental organisations financial institutions, corporations and the wider civil society. It highlights general trends, which should form a basis for action and provide a framework through which strategies of implementation must be developed.

It is a sad fact that, despite the strengths of the CRC as an international instrument, the denial of too many children's rights is commonplace.

In this way, *Children's Rights - Reality or Rhetoric?* reveals the situation for today's children and calls on governments to act where all but one (Sweden) have so far failed: to develop an explicit and coherent strategy to implement the CRC. It also challenges the wider international community to take heed of their collective responsibility in safeguarding the well-being and interests of all children and promoting their individual rights.

It is a sad fact that, despite the strengths of the CRC as an international instrument, the denial of too many children's rights is commonplace. It is clear that if children's best interests are to be upheld, the provisions of the Convention will have to be promoted and defended continually. Action needs to be monitored to ensure that, in a rapidly changing world, children's rights are being safeguarded in the most effective way and have a place on all political agendas.

Save The Children

Save the Children & Children's Rights

'I believe we should claim rights for children and labour for their universal recognition'
Eglantyne Jebb (1923), Founder of Save the Children

Since Eglantyne Jebb started her pioneering work with children immediately after the end of the First World War, the members of the Save the Children movement have dedicated themselves to making children's rights a reality. This fundamental goal now underpins everything that Save the Children does.

Over time, the Save the Children movement has grown as organisations from different countries of the world have joined forces to protect and promote children's rights. Together these organisations now form the International Save the Children Alliance, a global movement for children, which currently comprises 26 Member organisations, spanning the five major continents. Bound by a common vision and a joint mission, Save the Children remains committed to advancing children's rights and to bringing positive change in order to safeguard every child's right to a happy, healthy and secure childhood.

SAVE THE CHILDREN WORKS FOR

- **a world which respects and values each child**
- **a world which listens to children and learns**
- **a world where all children have hope and opportunity**

Save the Children now works in over 100 countries. Through long-term development initiatives and emergency relief programmes, Save the Children tackles key children's rights issues - health, education, nutrition and food, security, gender discrimination, disability and early childhood development. It also possesses considerable expertise in more specialised fields such as family tracing and reunification (for children separated by war or natural disaster), the rehabilitation of ex-child combatants, alternatives to institutional care and support for working children. In all this work it strives to implement a rights-based approach in its programmes, ensuring that all activities seek to integrate the key principles of the CRC.

In addition, Save the Children builds local, regional and global partnerships to establish a broader movement to support and implement children's rights. This involves working with international organisations and UN agencies and includes support to organisations run by children and young people to enable them to champion their own rights. In many countries Save the Children works with coalitions of children's rights organisations to develop awareness of children's rights. It is also piloting a variety of methods of enabling children to participate more actively in decisions that affect them.

To complement this work, Save the Children has provided training in children's rights for a wide range of key actors, such as governments, community organisations and partner organisations, to ensure a stronger awareness of children's rights and their realisation in policies and programmes.

In parallel with all of their activities, Save the Children plays a critical advocacy role. It lobbies governments, the international community and members of civil society, highlighting failures in public policy and private practice which represent violations of children's rights. In today's complex international environment, and for agencies such as Save the Children whose purpose is deeply rooted in children's rights, this role is crucial. Save the Children and other children's agencies must act as the custodians of children's rights, sharing the responsibility to fight for their recognition and defence.

'Kids opinions aren't taken notice of, yet they can have **important** *things to say - not just in things that* **affect** *them, but on other things as well. They are a lot* **smarter** *than most adults give them* **credit** *for'.*

Immanuel Heywood, age 17 - Sheffield, UK

Chapter 2

Children's Rights

Ten years of the UN Convention on the Rights of the Child

The first ten years in the life of the UN Convention on the Rights of the Child have been much like the first ten years in the life of a child. At the birth there was much good will and sentimental rhetoric. Adults - in the shape of national governments - queued up to welcome the new arrival. Those close to it placed their hopes for a better future in its potential to grow and change the world around it.

After the enthusiasm and novelty of the early years, a great deal of learning went on, with as many mistakes and wrong turnings as successes. As with all children, the Convention surprised, pleased and occasionally disappointed those around it, with its unexpected possibilities and unforeseen limitations.

Ten years on, the Convention looks well established. It continues to challenge those working with it, encouraging them to think afresh about the work they do and stimulating them to greater efforts. What has been the effect of the Convention on the lives of children? This is the inevitable question by which the long-term impact of the Convention will rightly be judged. Given both the nature of the Convention and the scale of the problems affecting children across the world, it is too soon to be able to make anything other than a preliminary assessment. This chapter therefore looks at the experience of the first ten years, identifies early trends and highlights the key difficulties that stand in the way of the full realisation of children's rights.

The UN Convention on the Rights of the Child

THE DEVELOPMENT OF A CONVENTION ON CHILDREN'S RIGHTS

The idea of a formal expression of children's rights which could be used to harness political and public commitment to improving the lives of children goes back much further than the post-war UN human rights system. The founder of the Save the Children movement, Eglantyne Jebb, believed that the obligation to protect and nurture children was not only the responsibility of parents but also of the wider community. She drafted the five points of the first Declaration of the Rights of the Child in

1923, and the League of Nations, the inter-war predecessor to the UN, adopted this the following year.

Jenny Matthews / save The Children

The gross abuse and violation of human rights during the Second World War led to efforts to establish an agreed international framework of human rights law that would set out clear standards and expectations for the behaviour of governments and others. However, there continued to be concern that children needed a specific expression of their rights that reflected their special needs and situation. In 1959, the UN went part of the way towards this by agreeing a revised version of Eglantyne Jebb's original Declaration of the Rights of the Child. However, the new Declaration was a statement of principles rather than a document to which governments could be held accountable for their actions. In 1978, a new and binding Convention on the Rights of the Child was called for, in advance of the following year's International Year of the Child.

The drafting of the Convention took a further ten years, during which Cold War rivalries played an important role in determining the wide-ranging nature of the new Convention. Non-governmental organisations (NGOs), including members of the International Save the Children Alliance, played an unusually significant part in the drafting of the Convention. The involvement of civil society at this early stage not only improved the content of the Convention but also generated an unprecedented level of commitment to making it work. By the end of the drafting period the Convention had become:

The Convention incorporates the whole spectrum of human rights - civil, political, economic, social and cultural - and sets out the specific ways in which these should be made available to children.

"a landmark at the end of the Cold War - the first international legal instrument adopted by consensus, bridging two political blocs, bridging the North and the South, bridging civil rights and freedoms with economic, social and cultural rights, bridging state accountability with the active involvement of civil society."

Marta Santos Pais, 'Children's Rights and Wrongs'. Paper given at the Conference on Children's Rights and Wrongs, Nicosia, November 1998

The text of the UN Convention on the Rights of the Child was adopted without modifications by the General Assembly of the United Nations on 20 November 1989. It entered into force as international law on 2 September 1990 after its ratification by the required 20 states.

What does the Convention say?

The 54 articles of the Convention can be divided into three main parts: key principles, specific rights and ways in which the Convention will be monitored. The key principles of the Convention are:

- the right to survival and development;
- respect for the best interests of the child as a primary consideration;
- the right of the child to express their views freely on all matters affecting them;
- the right of all children to enjoy all the rights of the Convention without discrimination of any kind.

The Convention incorporates the whole spectrum of human rights - civil, political, economic, social and cultural - and sets out the specific ways in which these should be made available to children:

- the definition of children as all persons less than 18 years of age, unless the legal age of majority in a country is lower;
- civil rights and freedoms, including the right to a name and nationality, to freedom of expression, thought and association, to access to information and to the right not to be subjected to torture;
- family environment and alternative care, including the right to live with parents, to be reunited with parents if separated from them and to the provision of appropriate alternative care where necessary;
- basic heath and welfare, including the rights of disabled children, the right to

health and health care, social security, child-care services and an adequate standard of living.

- Education, leisure and cultural activities, including the right to education, the aims of education and the rights to play, leisure and participation in cultural life and the arts.
- Special protection measures covering the rights of refugee children, those caught up in armed conflicts, children in the juvenile justice system, children deprived of their liberty and children suffering economic, sexual or other exploitation.

The last 13 articles of the Convention establish the ways in which implementation of the Convention will be monitored. These include the setting up of a Committee of the Rights of the Child which receives initial reports from governments two years after they have ratified the Convention and every five years thereafter. UN agencies and NGOs are invited to submit relevant information to the Committee in order to support its work.

Children are seen as full human beings, rights-holders who can play an active part in the enjoyment of their rights. They are not - as they have often been presented in the past - mere dependants, the property of their parents.

Every child is seen as important, no matter what its abilities, origins or gender. Their views and opinions are significant.

THE VISION OF THE CONVENTION

Legislation must offer an inspiring vision of the future to have real impact. This is particularly important for pieces of 'soft law' like the Convention, which rely on moral pressure, dialogue and co-operation rather than strong enforcement mechanisms.

At first glance, the Convention is noticeable for the 41 individual articles that contain a great deal of detail on a variety of specific children's rights. But the Convention does have a broader vision.

- Children are seen as full human beings, rights-holders who can play an active part in the enjoyment of their rights. They are not - as they have often been presented in the past - mere dependants, the property of their parents. They are not people who only become fully human when they become adults. They are in need of protection but also have strengths. Every child is seen as important, no matter what its abilities, origins or gender. Their views and opinions are significant. They are not to be seen merely as victims, workers, young offenders, pupils or consumers, but as complex and fully rounded individuals.

No child should live in poverty.

Children should be allowed to develop in an atmosphere of freedom, dignity and justice.

- Children are seen as active members of their local communities and national societies. They contribute their labour to a variety of work and care responsibilities inside and outside the home. They play an important part in cultural and leisure activities in and out of school. They are interested in what is going on around them, especially that which affects them directly. If encouraged, they become active and involved citizens.
- In the Convention parents and the family are seen as the primary carers and protectors of children and should be given every possible support in doing their best for their children. They are key partners in realising the rights of their children. They should provide guidance and direction for their children in exercising their rights - but in a way that reflects their children's own developing capacities, maturity and competence. Where children become separated from their parents, every effort should be made to reunite them. However, the Convention recognises that there are occasions when parents are unable or fail to act in the best interests of their children. Where these occur, there should be systems in place to protect the child and provide the best standard of alternative care.
- Society has obligations towards the children within it. The standards set out in the Convention for the treatment of children are those that any decent society concerned for the well-being and happiness of its children might want to attain. These standards correspond to fundamental values, such as a belief in human dignity, tolerance, equality, solidarity, peace and freedom. There is no place for discrimination against children nor for their exploitation and abuse. No child should live in poverty. A child's development should be nurtured and encouraged through education, health and other services to give it the best possible start in life. In times of war or civil unrest, children should be given special protection. They should be allowed to develop in an atmosphere of freedom, dignity and justice.

This vision has yet to be realised in any country in the world, rich or poor. It challenges all societies to make greater efforts on behalf of - but also, increasingly, with - their children. It expects greater achievement from richer societies with their greater resources but it also expects them to support, through their aid and development policies, poorer countries less able or struggling to achieve full respect for children's rights.

IMPLEMENTING THE CONVENTION

If the main strength of the Convention is its vision, its chief weakness lies in the mechanisms for its implementation. The Convention has no formal complaint mechanism and no effective sanctions it can impose on under-performing governments. It can make little real difference in the short term to the resources available to children and can be accused of 'failing' when economic growth falters or goes into reverse. Its implementation is in the hands of individual governments whose attitudes towards it vary from real enthusiasm to total indifference. The five year gaps between the progress reports made by governments mean that the state of children's rights is seen only in snapshot, rather than in the ongoing flux of progress and setbacks.

Sarah Muscroft / Save The Children

The UN Committee on the Rights of the Child, which has the responsibility to scrutinise governmental action to implement the Convention, has found it increasingly difficult to manage its workload. Even with the assistance of civil society organisations, it faces a major challenge in effectively scrutinising and challenging the actions and behaviour of all the world's governments. As delays build up in the examination of the reports made by governments and NGOs, the credibility of the monitoring process may begin to be challenged. Furthermore appointments to the Committee are subject to political considerations which have weakened its authority and effectiveness.

None of these limitations is a fundamental obstacle to the Convention's implementation. As discussed below, they can all be addressed provided that the political will to do so is there.

Assessing the impact of the Convention

This section considers the impact of the Convention during the 1990s. It begins by looking at the external environment in which the Convention has had to work. It then turns to the changes that can reasonably be seen as resulting from the

Convention's existence. The following section then considers the main challenges that hold back implementation of the Convention and threaten to limit its impact on children's lives.

KEY ISSUES IN CHILDREN'S RIGHTS IN THE 1990s

During the 1990s, the Convention operated in an environment that was extraordinarily hostile to its vision for children. The end of the Cold War was followed by a series of extremely bloody and prolonged conflicts in, for example, Colombia, Sri Lanka, Sudan, Liberia, Sierra Leone and Angola, which displaced millions of people, including large numbers of children. Fierce genocidal wars broke out in Africa and Europe, killing or traumatising children who witnessed unspeakable acts on their parents and relatives.

Nearly 600,000 children worldwide were infected with HIV by 1998. In some countries, AIDS reversed recent progress in improving child health.

The 1990s also saw a remorseless increase in the number of AIDS deaths and HIV infections, especially in sub-Saharan Africa.[1] More than eight million children lost their mothers or both parents as a result of the AIDS epidemic, leaving them vulnerable to discrimination and exploitation and at risk of losing out on education and health care. Nearly 600,000 children worldwide were infected with HIV by 1998. In some countries, AIDS reversed recent progress in improving child health, doubling or even tripling deaths among children under five in some countries in southern Africa, and diverting resources away from treating preventable diseases.

Sarah Muscroft / Save The Children

The end of the Cold War also saw the triumph of the free-market model of economic management. Many countries in central and eastern Europe, the former Soviet Union and East Asia embarked on a painful transition towards capitalism, reducing public child care and health and education services in the process. Other countries opened up their economies, willingly or unwillingly, in response to the 'Washington consensus' on the need to reduce the role of the state and encourage foreign investment

1 See UNICEF, 'The AIDS Emergency' in The Progress of Nations 1999, UNICEF, New York, 1999.

in order to survive the competitive pressures of globalisation. Despite increasing financial volatility and economic insecurity, structural adjustment and stabilisation programmes have encouraged greater private sector provision of basic social services and introduced fees and other charges into public sector schooling and health care.

Half the world's poor are now children and, as populations grow, there are more children living in poverty than ever before in history.

One hundred and thirty million children of primary school age are not in school.

An estimated 250 million children are now working worldwide, often in dangerous and exploitative conditions.

For some countries, this prescription led to economic growth, sometimes interrupted by dramatic recessions, as in the case of the late 1990s crises in the emerging markets of South East Asia. Other countries, notably in sub-Saharan Africa and most of the former Soviet Union, saw very little growth at all and growing destitution. Between a quarter and a third of national budgets in sub-Saharan Africa are now devoted to servicing these countries' debts. Expenditure on basic social services is often only a half or less of this. At the same time, aid flows have fallen by approximately one-third in real terms during the 1990s, with the Organisation for Economic Co-operation and Development/Development Assistance Committee member countries now contributing only 0.23 per cent of their combined gross national product as official development assistance (down from 0.33 per cent in 1992).[2]

Where growth occurred, even in the richer north, the benefits were unequally shared, with increasing polarisation of income. The richest fifth of the world's population now controls 86 per cent of the world's GDP, the poorest fifth just one per cent. Half the world's poor are now children and, as populations grow, there are more children living in poverty than ever before in history. These children fall sick, are underweight and are robbed of any chance of fulfilling their physical or mental potential. Each year, 12 million children under five years of age die from easily preventable diseases, and millions of others are ill because of unsafe drinking water and poor sanitation. One hundred and thirty million children of primary school age are not in school, and those that do attend are often offered desperately poor quality education. Girls, children with disabilities, children from minority ethnic groups and other marginalised populations face enormous obstacles to their development because of discrimination.

Children have been increasingly caught up in the market for labour. An estimated 250 million children are now working worldwide, often in dangerous and exploitative conditions. As well as their traditional involvement in agriculture and

2 See the World Bank, Global Economic Prospects 1998/99, World Bank, Washington, 1988; and OECD News Release of 10 June 1999, 'Financial Flows to Developing Countries in 1998', OECD, Paris.

Jenny Matthews / Save The Children

domestic work, children are now employed in a whole range of extractive and manufacturing sectors. In the worst cases, their bodies are trafficked between countries as part of a growing trade in child sex workers.

All this has made the Convention even more relevant and its implementation more urgent. But it has also increased the size of the task involved and the range of issues that must be tackled. Furthermore, governments were charged to implement the Convention at precisely the moment when their ability to do so was being most rapidly eroded. The 1990s saw the capacity of governments to bring about change increasingly constrained by cut-backs in resources, the competitive pressures of globalisation and the growing power of giant corporations whose wealth far exceeds that of many small and medium-sized countries. The ability of governments at the national level to manage their own affairs is being increasingly challenged, while the mechanisms of global governance are as yet too weak to control market forces.

The Convention alone cannot reverse the trends identified. Its success or failure must be seen in the light of its ability to generate commitment and practical efforts to respect children's rights by those who have some responsibility towards them.

The Convention alone cannot reverse the trends identified above. Its success or failure must be seen in the light of its ability to generate commitment and practical efforts to respect children's rights by those who have some responsibility towards them. These changes in the environment around the child should lead, in time, to progressive improvements in their everyday lives and opportunities.

What are the main achievements then of the first decade of the Convention?

ALMOST UNIVERSAL RATIFICATION

A common legal framework

Only two states have not ratified the Convention: the USA and Somalia.
The speed with which ratification occurred was impressive - a third of countries ratified in 1990, over a fifth the following year and nearly nine-tenths had been achieved within five years of its adoption by the General Assembly. Compared with other human rights treaties, this is a remarkable feat and reflects a profound common desire to achieve a better world for children. For many countries, the Convention was the first international human rights treaty that they had signed.

It is now possible to talk of a common ethical and legal framework relating to children that is virtually universally accepted. It cannot easily be argued that the Convention is a 'Western' view of the human rights of children, incompatible with, say, Asian or African views.

It is now possible to talk of a common ethical and legal framework relating to children that is virtually universally accepted.

Increased accountability

Ratification is a key step forward, whatever the motivation. It creates a real opportunity for public scrutiny of government performance and for a deliberate effort to work towards the fulfilment of children's rights. In ratifying, governments voluntarily accept the obligations set out in the Convention and hold themselves accountable for their success or failure in performing them. The fulfilment of children's rights passes from being an act of charity, an option or a favour, and becomes a responsibility of government.

The process of monitoring implementation has created the opportunity for much more public debate about the performance of governments in implementing the Convention and addressing children's issues. In many countries, civil society organisations have used it to increase the transparency of policy-making and to focus their advocacy towards government. Although by no means a perfect process, it has significantly improved the accountability of many governments and has the potential to be developed much further.

LEGAL AND INSTITUTIONAL REFORM

However much they may be committed to the Convention, governments are unlikely to have the structures, laws and activities in place to meet the challenges the Convention poses. Domestic legislation is likely to contradict the provisions of the Convention and administrative arrangements are unlikely to have been designed with the protection and promotion of children's rights as an aim.

The diversity of legislative and administrative systems across the world, combined with the unprecedented demands of the Convention, have meant that governments have had few examples of good practice from which to learn. The result has been slow but definite progress in adjusting legislative and administrative structures that would almost certainly never have occurred without the existence of the Convention.[3] In some countries, reform has been much faster and has shown what can be achieved with firm political leadership.

3 See, for example, S. Ruxton, Implementing Children's Rights, Save the Children UK, London, 1998.

Constitutional reform is a means by which countries can entrench children's rights into the foundations of their own legal system.

Constitutional reform

Constitutional reform is a means by which countries can entrench children's rights into the foundations of their own legal system. Nepal, Poland, Slovenia, Finland and South Africa, for example, have taken the initiative since 1989 to establish new constitutional rights for children that reflect the provisions of the Convention.

Reviews of domestic legislation

A number of countries, for example Ethiopia, Cambodia and Sweden, have undertaken comprehensive reviews of domestic legislation to ensure conformity with the Convention. In the case of Sweden, this has led to detailed work to change legislation on the treatment of refugees and asylum-seekers and to a comprehensive strategy to implement the Convention throughout Swedish public policy.

Other countries, among them Zimbabwe, Chile and the Netherlands, have undertaken partial reviews, concentrating on legislation that has direct relevance to children. The result has been the consolidation of statutes or codes relating to children, and the bringing together of previously disparate pieces of legislation. Examples include Brazil's Children and Adolescents' Act, Ghana's Children's Act, the Nicaraguan Children's Legal Code and Uganda's Children's Statute. Sri Lanka introduced a Children's Charter in 1992 which, although not enforceable law, establishes guidelines for the development of policy concerning children's rights. Other countries have revised particular pieces of legislation relating to, for example, the treatment of young offenders or asylum-seekers, inter-country adoption, children's rights under inheritance law and the physical punishment of children, to make them compatible with the Convention.

Dario Mitidieri / Save The Children

Independent children's rights watchdogs

A number of governments have established independent bodies as watchdogs of children's rights, with the aim of promoting respect for children's rights within government (for example, by monitoring legislative proposals or reviewing the impact of government initiatives), to increase public and official awareness of children's rights and to provide a means for children's voices to be heard on issues that affect them. In some countries, these institutions take the form of a specific post, such as a children's ombudsman or commissioner, while in others, they take the form of a national committee or commission for children. At present, such independent offices exist, or are being established, in over 20 countries. In countries such as Brazil and Uganda, sub-national institutions have also been established to watch over children's rights within provincial or municipal bodies.

The way in which children are seen has begun to undergo a significant change in the last ten years.

Co-ordinating mechanisms in government

The other main kind of institutional change has been the development of central co-ordinating mechanisms or bodies within government to maintain an overview of policy towards children. Inevitably, these bodies are dependent for their effectiveness on their composition, their access to real political power and the resources they can draw on. Although some have done important work, others have had only an advisory role or have been unwilling to monitor or intervene directly in violations of children's rights. Good examples of such bodies include the National Commission on Children in Ghana, which reports directly to the Office of the President, and the Danish Ministerial Committee for Children. In a number of other countries however, such as Bangladesh, Peru, India and Nepal, the responsibility to monitor policy towards children has been located alongside a similar responsibility to monitor women's rights, diluting the attention paid to children's issues.

THE CHANGING IMAGE OF CHILDREN

The way in which children are seen has begun to undergo a significant change in the last ten years. The Convention has not been solely responsible for this but it has played a major role in encouraging a re-evaluation of the ways in which adults see children. It has done this by making children more 'visible' to policy-makers and politicians and by beginning to reverse some of the traditional stereotypes of children.

Penny Tweedie / Save the Children

Making children visible

In the past, children were often 'invisible' inside families and communities, within which their specific interests were obscured. Governments introduced 'family policies' rather than 'children's policies' on the assumption that what was good for families would be good for children. Development projects were introduced that targeted families or women, in the hope that the benefits would 'trickle down' to children. Investment in children was seen as an investment in human capital: for tomorrow's adults rather than for today's children. Information specifically about children was rarely collected so that surprisingly little was known about their lives. Despite making up large percentages of the populations of most countries, children were rarely consulted about their views or wishes. Instead, other adults were asked to 'interpret' for them. In the 1990s this situation began to change.[4]

The Convention, by directing attention to the specific rights of children, has challenged governments and others to question their assumptions and value children for what they are today, not what they will become tomorrow.

The Convention, by directing attention to the specific rights of children, has challenged governments and others to question their assumptions and value children for what they are today, not what they will become tomorrow. As a result, children's issues have become a more explicit interest of governments and the international community. The second half of the 1990s saw a series of international conferences addressing issues such as the commercial sexual exploitation of children (Stockholm 1996) and child labour (Amsterdam 1997, Oslo 1998 and Geneva 1999). Regional preparatory conferences have enabled a wide variety of agencies and NGOs to involve themselves in these issues.

The World Summit for Children in 1990 began this process by calling for the development of National Plans of Action in every country, directed at implementation of the Convention and the achievement of 27 specific targets in health, basic education, water and sanitation, nutrition and child protection. One of the best-known examples of such a plan is the South African National Programme of Action that was introduced in 1996, and was designed specifically within the framework of the Convention. The World Summit goals have also been monitored at a regional level as a means of sharing experience and encouraging progress. In Latin America and East Asia, for example, there have been regular regional ministerial meetings to monitor progress towards the World Summit goals and implementation of the Convention.

Mani Lama

4 For more detail on the case of Latin America see E. Garcia Mendez, Child Rights in Latin America: 'irregular situation' to full protection,UNICEF, ICDC, Florence, 1998 and Save the Children UK, Servicios de Proteccion a la Ninez: analisis exploratorio a cuatro paises de America de Sur, Save the Children UK, Bogota.

Some governments have begun to move away from family policy towards more explicit children's or 'childhood' policies. In Europe, the Council of Europe's three-year Childhood Policies Project encouraged the collection of child-specific data to provide baseline information for monitoring the impact of the Convention. Norway, Finland, Greece, Italy and the UK have all taken initiatives to develop the methods required to carry out such work. Other initiatives are also being taken to develop ways of using this new data to carry out 'child-impact assessments' of government policy decisions and legislation, for example, in the analysis of national budgets and the design of overseas aid and development policies.

The Convention has challenged these views by emphasising children's dignity, competence, resilience and the right to have their views heard.

Perceptions of children

Traditional perceptions of children have often characterised then as incompetent, dependent, powerless and politically silent - too often the victims of circumstance. Adult interventions in children's lives were often based on concepts of charity, confused ideas of protection (of adults from children as well as the protection of children themselves), the need to isolate children from the adult world and the view that children should be 'seen but not heard'. The Convention has challenged these views by emphasising children's dignity, competence, resilience and the right to have their views heard. This has encouraged, for example, the formation of organisations of working children at national and regional levels across the developing world to fight abuse and exploitation. Tens of thousands of working children are now organised in movements to protect themselves against the dangers of work and to argue for the social change that would make it unnecessary for them to work. They have challenged the motivation and the effectiveness of government action to help them and demanded the right to be heard at international conferences.

PhotoDisc

THE CREATION OF A GLOBAL CHILDREN'S RIGHT'S COMMUNITY

The Convention has been a major catalyst to the development of a children's rights movement across the world. It has provided a shared vision of the fulfilment of children's rights that has found acceptance in both the developed and less developed worlds, in regions with very different historical and cultural traditions, and among groups of people who have thought of themselves as having little in common. By stressing that no society has fulfilled its aims, the Convention has developed a global sense of responsibility and commitment that transcends many of the traditional barriers to dialogue and joint working.

Human rights organisations are beginning to work more closely with children's organisations and development NGOs to support implementation of the Convention.

When the Convention was established, there was a sense in which it represented a new start, with everyone in the same position of needing to rethink how they worked and what they could contribute. At the same time, a common language and framework were being created for all those working for the fulfilment of children's rights. The monitoring and reporting process provided a common focus for attention and helped bring together a wide range of people who had rarely met together before.

Becoming a children's rights organisation

Like governments, non-governmental entities have been forced to re-evaluate their responsibilities and programmes in the light of the Convention. Many have adopted a more explicit orientation towards children's rights. The International Save the Children Alliance, UNICEF and many smaller organisations have adopted the Convention as a central part of their mission.[5]

In the early 1990s, this was often interpreted as participating in, or supporting, monitoring and reporting on, the Convention, or running training courses on the Convention and children's rights for other agencies. However, the danger with this approach was that children's rights were seen as an alternative or 'add-on' to other ways of working. More recently, efforts have been made to mainstream children's rights approaches to ensure that all work has a clear relationship with the overall goal of fulfilling children's rights. This has helped overcome the apparent divide between 'needs-based' and 'rights-based' approaches to work with children, by stressing the importance to the fulfilment of children's rights of projects developed to meet basic needs.

New networks and partnerships

In many countries, new national coalitions of NGOs have emerged to combine efforts in supporting the implementation of the Convention and holding governments to account for their obligations. Many of them have submitted 'alternative' NGO reports to the UN Committee on the Rights of the Child to supplement or challenge the official government reports.

Traditional development organisations have found themselves working with a wide range of new partners, such as the police, judges, teacher training establishments, private sector companies and trade federations. Human rights

5 For a discussion of this and the impact of the Convention on the work of UNICEF see K. E. Knutsson, Children: noble causes or worthy citizens? Unicef/Arena, Aldgate Publishing, Aldershot, 1997.

organisations are beginning to work more closely with children's organisations and development NGOs to support implementation of the Convention. Professional groups, such as health-care workers, teachers and social workers, have considered how they can integrate the principles and standards of the Convention into their work.

The belief that children have the right to express their views on decisions that affect them is one of the more radical thrusts of the Convention.

At the global level, there is increasing interest in bringing together the wide range of organisations now working with the Convention. The creation of the Children's Rights Information Network (CRIN) in 1995 provided a central focus and mechanism for sharing information on children's rights through a newsletter, website and email list. Over 900 organisations worldwide are now members of CRIN. Developments in communications technology have created easier access to databases on children's rights issues. For example, the Office of the High Commissioner for Human Rights hosts a website that brings together government reports to the UN Committee on the Rights of the Child and the Committee's concluding observations on these.

GROWING AWARENESS OF CHILDREN'S RIGHTS

The Convention has led to a surge of interest in children's rights by those directly involved in working with or for children. Many international organisations, including members of the International Save the Children Alliance and UNICEF, have fed this interest by developing training materials and activities for target groups such as government officials, politicians, NGOs, teachers, nurses, the media and, of course, parents and children. The aim of this training has been to heighten awareness of the Convention and to encourage groups to reflect on their own responsibilities for its implementation.

Jenny Matthews / Save The Children

ENCOURAGING CHILDREN'S PARTICIPATION

The belief that children have the right to express their views on decisions that affect them is one of the more radical thrusts of the Convention. When the Convention was introduced, there was great scepticism in many quarters about the value or practicality of encouraging children's involvement in decision-making, and little experience of how to go about achieving it. Some professionals saw it as a passing, politically correct fashion or as an unnecessary responsibility to impose

Governments, child-care professionals, NGOs and other civil society organisations, business, the media and international organisations - will need to play a much more active role in helping to fulfil children's rights if the Convention's vision is to be realised.

upon children. Others felt it questioned their own ability to do their jobs. In many societies in which there is no tradition of listening to children or valuing their views, it was a difficult goal to take on. It has sometimes proved hard to avoid tokenism, with groups of children paraded in front of adult audiences, or individuals asked to represent the views of whole groups of children.

However, at the local, national and international level, there has been a proliferation of experiments and initiatives that have demonstrated not only that children can be offered meaningful opportunities to participate, but that everyone gains as a result. Experience has been gained of the kinds of support and preparation children - and the adults working with them - need in order to make the best use of the opportunity.

Challenges for the future

A great deal of learning has taken place in the first ten years of the Convention and this has only just begun to be evaluated, codified and made available to wider audiences. The first significant assessment of the impact of the Convention on institutional change was only recently completed,[6] and it was 1998 before the first detailed reference handbook was published on the way the UN Committee has interpreted legislation, policy and practice related to the Convention.[7]

From this learning it is becoming clearer where the main challenges for the future lie. Unless these are overcome, full implementation of the Convention will be blocked or set back for a considerable period. Most of these challenges relate ultimately to the commitment and will of political and other actors who have some responsibility for implementation of the Convention. As discussed below, all these actors - including governments, child-care professionals, NGOs and other civil society organisations, business, the media and international organisations - will need to play a much more active role in helping to fulfil children's rights if the Convention's vision is to be realised.

RATIFICATION

Two governments have yet to ratify the Convention. One of these is the most powerful and richest nation on earth - the United States of America. It is imperative

6 L. Woll, The Convention on the Rights of the Child Impact Study, Save The Children (Rädda Barnen), Stockholm, 1999.
7 UNICEF, Implementation Handbook for the Convention on the Rights of the Child, UNICEF, New York, 1998.

that the USA commits itself as soon as possible to the defence of the human rights of its children and submits itself to international scrutiny of its efforts.

Governments and civil society organisations need to play a more active role in promoting children's rights and finding indigenous and local equivalents for the values and ideas of children's rights that will ease their acceptance into the general population.

RESERVATIONS

At ratification, a government may enter a 'reservation' to its commitment to the Convention, either limiting the application of certain rights or excluding them altogether. Governments may also enter general reservations relating to the entire Convention. For example, a number of Muslim governments entered general reservations by which the Convention is deemed to be subject to their constitutional law or to Islamic law. The only condition put on reservations is that they do not undermine the overall object and purpose of the Convention.

Where reservations restrict the application of the Convention, governments need to be encouraged to withdraw them. The UN Committee challenges governments on their reservations during the examination of their reports, but NGOs and other parts of civil society can also play a role in encouraging governments to withdraw restrictive reservations.

AWARENESS OF CHILDREN'S RIGHTS

There has been some success in increasing awareness of children's rights among key groups with a direct involvement in policy-making or running programmes for children. However, there has been much less success in raising awareness among the general adult and child populations of most countries. The reasons for this include: unfamiliarity with the concepts of human rights and children's rights; concerns that children's rights are in conflict with the rights of parents and adults in general; and the practical and resource constraints on running an awareness campaign across society as a whole.

However, unless adults are fully persuaded of the case for children's rights, difficulties in broadening the base of popular support for the Convention will continue. Governments and civil society organisations need to play a more active role in promoting children's rights and finding indigenous and local equivalents for the values and ideas of children's rights that will ease their acceptance into the general population.

Tim Malyon

DEEPENING COMMITMENT TO THE CONVENTION

Governments, inter-governmental organisations and NGOs have all been affected, to varying degrees, by the introduction of the Convention. All now need to go beyond the formal incorporation of the principles of the Convention into their mission statement or organisational goals. They need to see how far they can integrate the vision and practice of the Convention into their work in a real sense.

The next ten years should see greater efforts being made to tackle some of the areas of child rights seen as politically sensitive or contentious, such as the rights to freedom of information, association and religion.

Training on children's rights also needs more critical examination. Although there has been a great deal of training, there have been far fewer attempts to evaluate its success. One-off training, although helpful, often does not build the depth of understanding that enables policy-makers and other staff to maximise their role in the implementation of the Convention.

DIFFICULT AND POLITICALLY SENSITIVE ISSUES

In the early years of the Convention, there was a reluctance among many agencies to confront the more challenging implications of the Convention. Many continued to focus on their traditional areas of expertise - service provision addressed to basic needs, which was seen as an important contribution to fulfilling many of the provision rights of the Convention, such as education, health, social welfare and nutrition.

By the mid-1990s, more attention began to be placed on children's protection rights and raising the profile of issues such as abuse in the family, child labour and the trafficking of children. Greater efforts were also being made to enhance children's involvement in community and national decision-making. Children's forums, councils and parliaments began to be seen as means by which children could feed their views into decisions on issues like urban planning, the environment and the improvement of services.

The next ten years should see greater efforts being made to tackle some of the areas of child rights seen as politically sensitive or contentious, such as the rights to freedom of information, association and religion. At present, many governments concern themselves with the protection of children in these areas but do little to develop the positive, enabling aspects of these provisions. There is also growing interest in the question of individual violations of children's rights and how these should be reported and dealt with. A key area being examined is the torture of children (usually to intimidate or force an adult to come forward), which has been neglected by traditional human rights organisations more used to dealing with political dissidents and activists.

Penny Tweedie / Save The Children

Another challenge is to encourage the democratisation of schooling, to give children more influence on school management and a real opportunity to have their views heard. Also, ways need to be found of protecting children's rights within the family while, at the same time, respecting their dignity, privacy and integrity.

Another priority is to make much more effective the principle of non-discrimination, to ensure that girls, ethnic minorities, the disabled, children experiencing extreme poverty, and those on the streets and inside institutions are given the chance to enjoy the rights to which they are entitled.

Another challenge is to encourage the democratisation of schooling, to give children more influence on school management and a real opportunity to have their views heard.

IMPROVED INFORMATION AND RESEARCH

Good policy choices and effective programming are dependent on the quality of information available to the policy-maker and planner. Information is often still lacking in relation to key data and statistics. Governments and NGOs need to encourage census and other government agencies, academics and other researchers to dis-aggregate data to show what is really happening to children (and, within the overall population of children, to girls and boys; babies, younger children, middle-years children and adolescents; the majority and minorities).

Monitoring implementation of the Convention is a key step in holding governments to account for the fulfilment of their obligations.

REPORTING

Monitoring implementation of the Convention is a key step in holding governments to account for the fulfilment of their obligations. Yet the first ten years have highlighted wide differences in quality in the reports prepared by governments and in their attitude towards the reporting process. It is important to begin by highlighting that the majority of governments have managed to fulfil the minimum requirements of the reporting process. Many, though, have struggled to understand their responsibilities and have found the guidelines issued by the UN Committee to represent a challenge to their organisational resources and analytical capacity. Others have given the process a relatively low priority and have missed the deadlines for submission. Few have taken the opportunity to make the reporting process a vehicle for involving the rest of society in considering the state of children's rights. Even fewer - but important for the example they have given - have tried to reach out to their child populations and involved them in drawing up the government's report or providing supplementary information.

Some governments have used the preparation of their report as an opportunity to undertake a real audit of their successes and failures in promoting and defending children's rights. Others, though, have regarded the process as purely a formality and have used it as an opportunity to parade their achievements and downplay their failings. It will be important that all governments in the future use the reporting process as an opportunity to make a balanced assessment of their progress in implementing the Convention.

Peter Fryer / Save The Children

Governments could also do much more to publicise and encourage debate on the UN Committee's concluding observations on their report. In most cases, public awareness of these depends on the effectiveness of NGOs and others in disseminating them and the readiness of the media to promote them. There is also a need for much prompter and more substantive action to follow up these observations and ensure that remedies are put in place as soon as possible.

RESOURCES FOR CHILDREN AND 'CHILD-FRIENDLY' ECONOMICS

The Convention requires governments to allocate the 'maximum extent of available resources' towards the fulfilment of children's economic, social and cultural rights (Article 4). This may involve the provision of services (such as education, health and social welfare) or the transfer of various kinds of payments. Such expenditure already forms a significant element of much government activity and is under increasing strain as a result of declining government revenues, debt servicing, reductions in official development assistance, military expenditure and political pressures to cut back on public expenditure.

Careful thought must be given to maximising the use of currently available resources and to increasing the overall total available. The 1990s have seen increasing interest in exploring the links between the fulfilment of children's rights and economic policies and decisions. Tools such as those used to develop the South African 'Children's Budget' analysis have begun to be used to identify the amounts and purposes of government spending on children.[8] It may soon be possible not only to identify the proportion of national budgets devoted to fulfilling children's rights but also to see whether current expenditure is appropriate and cost-effective. A number of governments and research institutes are already using this approach to produce annual 'children's budget' analyses to make this information available to decision-makers and child rights advocates. It will also be possible to examine why countries with the same level of per capita income have very different outcomes in terms of the fulfilment of children's rights, such as access to basic social services. Over time, this work should improve the transparency of government decision-making under Article 4 of the Convention and enable better targeting and efficiency in the use of available resources.

Governments should be challenged on choices and priorities that place the purchase of weapons ahead of the education and health of their most vulnerable citizens.

For many countries in the less developed world, as discussed above, a major constraint on the availability of resources is the high level of debt repayments they are making. Urgent action is required to cancel all unpayable debt and to manage debt servicing in ways that release resources for urgently required basic services. Defence spending is another budget category that competes directly with children's services and is a major limitation on the ability of governments to meet their obligations under the Convention. Governments should be challenged on choices and priorities that place the purchase of weapons ahead of the education and health of their most vulnerable citizens.

The role of the international community is also critical. Donor countries and multilateral agencies need to re-assess their aid policies to increase the volume of aid and ensure that their activities contribute to national government action to implement the Convention. One way of achieving this is to become part of the 20/20 Initiative that aims to ensure that an average of 20 per cent of official development assistance is allocated to expenditure on basic social services.[9] Donors and agencies should also make an explicit commitment to assist governments to implement and report on the Convention, and achieve agreed children's rights outcomes. Aid programmes should be assessed for their focus on children, their role in encouraging the participation of children and their overall contribution to the fulfilment of the rights of children.

Sarah Muscroft / Save The Children

8 S. Robinson and L. Bierstecker (eds) First Call: the South African Children's Budget, IDASA, Cape Town, 1997.
9 UNDP et al., Implementing the 20/20 Initiative: achieving universal access to basic social services UNDP/UNESCO/UNFPA/UNICEF/WHO/World Bank, New York, 1998.

MAINSTREAMING CHILDREN'S RIGHTS

As we enter the second decade of the Convention, there is a growing awareness of the need to ensure that children's rights are mainstreamed throughout the rest of the human rights system.

For ten years NGOs and other civil society organisations working on children's rights have focused almost entirely on the meaning and significance of the Convention. For many of these organisations it was their first contact with human rights work and they had little understanding of the broader international human rights system. As we enter the second decade of the Convention, there is a growing awareness of the need to ensure that children's rights are mainstreamed throughout the rest of the human rights system. The first step in this direction has been to develop resource materials on the linkages between the Convention and the other parts of the human rights system.[10] Other work now needs to follow to ensure that the rest of the human rights system is fully utilised to defend and promote children's rights. This might involve, for example, presenting evidence on the situation of children's rights to other treaty bodies, and special rapporteurs who have responsibilities for children rights in their mandates. It also involves a more sustained effort to raise children's rights violations at the annual Commission and Sub-Commission on Human Rights, as well as at the Economic and Social Committee and the General Assembly of the UN.

CHILDREN IN CONFLICT

Although the Convention has proved to be a surprisingly comprehensive and coherent document, there remain significant gaps in the protection which it offers to children. The majority of these gaps exist in the protection offered to children caught up in armed conflict. There are two main weaknesses. Firstly, in the overall level of protection and respect for children during armed conflict, where the Convention fails to improve upon the already inadequate provisions of existing international humanitarian law. Article 38(4) of the Convention, for example, simply requires States Parties to take 'all feasible measures to ensure the protection and care of children who are affected by armed conflict'. Until this situation can be remedied, children will continue to be exposed to the suffering and long-term damage caused by exposure to the violence and brutality of war. The second key area is in the treatment of child soldiers. As discussed in more detail in Chapter Three the Convention currently permits the recruitment and use of child soldiers aged 16 and 17 years in armed conflicts.

10 e.g. Rädda Barnen , Advocating Children's Rights in the Human Rights System of the United Nations, Rädda Barnen, Stockholm, 1999, and Save the Children UK, Child Rights Advocacy Project at http:\193.129.255.93/whatnew/index.html, 1998.

THE POLITICAL WILL FOR COMPREHENSIVE IMPLEMENTATION

The most important factor affecting the present and future impact of the Convention is without doubt the commitment and resolve of all those who have the potential to play a role in realising children's rights. The vision of the Convention can only be achieved with the wholehearted commitment of every part of society - government, business and civil society.

The vision of the Convention can only be achieved with the wholehearted commitment of every part of society - government, business and civil society.

Governments have to offer leadership in this process, creating a framework that enables the rest of society to play their part. They need to establish a positive environment for change through encouraging debate, creating awareness, reforming legislation and structures, committing more resources and highlighting steps forward. Public opinion needs to be won over to the view that children's rights are not a threat to a society but one of the highest expressions of a country's belief in human dignity and its concern for its most vulnerable citizens.

As it becomes an ever more important partner in social development, the private sector should play a growing role in working with government to share the overall task of fulfilling children's rights.

A key objective of the next ten years should be the strengthening of the bodies, structures and mechanisms established by governments to assist them in delivering their obligations. Where governments lack these bodies, sustained pressure to introduce them must be applied. Where bodies already exist, greater commitment and support from political leaders are required to make them more effective. But national bodies are not enough. Implementation also needs to be decentralised to lower administrative levels, without sacrificing strong central leadership to the process. Decentralisation is key to ensuring that grassroots service providers and protection agencies are sensitive to children's rights and that efforts are made to reach populations in marginal or remote areas.

The private sector has to commit itself to achieving children's rights standards as a part of socially responsible business behaviour, and to stamping out the abuse and exploitation of children in its operations. Furthermore, as it becomes an ever more important partner in social development, the private sector should play a growing role in working with government to share the overall task of fulfilling children's rights. This is, in any case, in their own long-term interests. Children who are healthy

Hei Han Khiang

and well educated, and have been encouraged to get involved in the societies around them, will make a better and more skilful workforce for the future than those who are not.

Compared with many other parts of the international human rights system, the Convention on the Rights of the Child has made a profound difference in the first ten years of its existence.

More resources can and must be found to enable children in the poorest countries to enjoy at least minimum standards of health, education and social welfare.

Civil society, too, will have to increase its efforts to persuade, urge and insist that government and business meet their obligations. Civil society organisations need to improve their research, policy analysis and advocacy skills to enable them to engage more seriously with government on the design and implementation of children's policy. A key step is raising awareness of children's rights beyond the narrow confines of children's NGOs. Churches, community groups, women's and disability rights movements, environmental groups, trade unions, etc. all need to share the commitment to making a reality of the Convention's vision. The media should be targeted for briefing on children's rights issues and monitored for its reporting on children's rights news items. Children's groups and organisations need to be supported to become vehicles for children's participation and the expression of children's views. Civil society organisations in the richer countries need to put more pressure on their governments to support less developed countries in implementing the Convention through resource transfers and technical support, as they agreed when ratifying the Convention.

Conclusion

Compared with many other parts of the international human rights system, the Convention on the Rights of the Child has made a profound difference in the first ten years of its existence. It has established a new framework for looking at children which has been welcomed in every region of the world by a range of key decision-makers and bodies. It has stimulated new ways of working, encouraging the direct involvement of children in decisions that affect them and dialogue between sectors and groups who have often seemed to have little in common. It has thrown light on issues rarely looked at before and harnessed the energies of many organisations and individuals that identify with the vision of the Convention and wish to contribute to its fulfilment.

Even after ten years, much of this work is at an early stage. Awareness of the Convention and of children's rights is still extremely limited and there are major barriers to be overcome if its vision is to be achieved. Too many countries have entered reservations that hamper the full implementation of the Convention. The reporting process needs to made more timely and more transparent, with governments seeing it as an opportunity rather than a burden. A focus on the activities of central government needs to be complemented by examination of what is happening at the interface between children and government at the local level. Too little legal and administrative reform is translated into change for the better at lower levels of government. More resources can and must be found to enable children in the poorest countries to enjoy at least minimum standards of health, education and social welfare.

Civil society and the media must play their role in urging on the less committed and holding them to their obligations. Children themselves will surely become ever more powerful advocates for their own rights.

Nevertheless, although it is impossible to quantify, significant numbers of children have already benefited from the existence of the Convention. Many children now know that they have human rights and will carry that forward into their adult lives. The exploitation and abuse of children is now a subject discussed at the highest levels. Children caught up in wars as refugees are offered better - if far from perfect or universal - protection as a result of the integration of the Convention into the work of the UN and other agencies. Young offenders in many parts of the world are better treated and better protected than before and, in much traditional service provision for children, there is a new focus on the most excluded and discriminated against.

Neil Cooper

The balance sheet at the end of ten years of the Convention appears positive. What is required now is a sustained commitment by governments and civil society to build on the foundations of these first years. Even the governments most active in implementing the Convention will have to show that their commitment goes beyond the superficial. Civil society and the media must play their role in urging on the less committed and holding them to their obligations. Children themselves will surely become ever more powerful advocates for their own rights. All these will be vital contributions to the realisation of the vision contained in the Convention.

PART II
Global Issues

*'They **forced** me to learn how to **fight** the enemy in a war I didn't understand. We were **constantly beaten**, just to keep us in a state of **terror**'.*

Emilio, age 14 - Guatemala

Chapter 3

Child Soldiers

Behind the lines - children in combat

The idea that children should be engaged as soldiers - killing and injuring others and being liable to death and injury themselves - is morally repugnant to most people. Yet, at least 300,000 children are currently participating in armed conflicts around the world, and tens of thousands more are legally recruited members of armed forces and could be sent into combat at any time. It is surely paradoxical that any society can fully advocate the need to protect children and yet at the same time effectively endorse the involvement of children in armed conflict. There appear to be two fundamental reasons for this: the current international standards and the lack of commitment to stop such practices.

The 1989 UN Convention on the Rights of the Child (CRC) defines a child as being anyone up to the age of 18, unless, under the law applicable to the child in a country, majority is attained earlier.[1] One of the underlying principles of the CRC is the promotion of the best interests of the child, and in general it enhances the protection of children - in terms of the rights to both survival and development and protection from abuse and exploitation - in almost all respects over previous international law. In addition, it specifically prohibits the death penalty or life imprisonment for under-18s.[2] There is only one area where the previous standards for protection has not been improved: the CRC sets 15 years as the minimum age for participation in hostilities as well as for recruitment into armed forces. It does not even require that participants should have obtained majority under domestic law before being sent into combat. This anomaly appears to be a contradiction to the principles set out in the CRC. What possible justification could there be for such a lapse in the protective regime of the Convention? At the time of drafting, such justifications ranged from the difficulty of altering existing state practice through to legal wrangles about re-writing international humanitarian law by means of a human rights treaty.[3] However, some leading governments also argue strongly in favour of the recruitment of young people.

1 CRC Article 1.
2 CRC Article 38.
3 The 1997 Additional Protocols to the Geneva Convention set 15 as the minimum age for recruitment into the armed forces or armed groups and the participation in hostilities.

Save The Children Sweden (Rädda Barnen)

They suggest, for example, that once teenagers have left formal education, they have the right to choose their career and that, for many, the armed forces offer a secure and attractive profession providing what is often high-quality technical training. Under recruitment practices in the developed world, for example, teenagers are often recruited into the armed forces and then undergo three years of intensive training before being sent into active duty. Some advocates of the benefits of this for young people even deny that there is anything wrong with teenagers being sent into combat if they volunteer (and have parental consent if they are minors).[4]

Although such arguments are still heard, the position has begun to change in the years since the adoption of the CRC, and there are now few governments who defend their right to send under-18s into combat. However, the recent NATO action over Kosovo serves as a reminder that the UK and the USA are among those countries who routinely deploy under-18s and maintain that there is nothing wrong in doing so.

At least 300,000 children are currently participating in armed conflicts around the world.

It is surely paradoxical that any society can fully advocate the need to protect children and yet at the same time effectively endorse the involvement of children in armed conflict.

4 See the various reports of the UN Commission on Human Rights Working Group on a draft optional protocol to the Convention on the Rights of the Child on the involvement of children in armed conflict (E/CN.4/ WG.13/...) and the reports of the sessions produced by the Quaker UN Office, Geneva.

The global situation

Global child recruitment and participation in armed conflicts

Children under 18 years of age have been reported to participate in either government or opposition forces, or both, in armed conflicts which were in ongoing or which ceased during 1996 or 1997. The information is believed to be correct as of end 1997. Source: Save the Children Sweden (Rädda Barnen)

Of the 33 armed conflicts in which children were involved up to November 1998, 15 were in Asia, 11 in Africa and four in Europe.

In general, the distribution of child soldiers reflects the global distribution of conflicts.[5] No region of the world is exempt. Of the 33 armed conflicts in which children were involved up to November 1998, 15 were in Asia, 11 in Africa and four in Europe, with Asia and Africa between them accounting for about two-thirds of the 300,000 estimated total of child combatants worldwide. This is a salutary reminder that this is not 'an African problem', contrary to the image portrayed in the media.

However, there are large numbers of child combatants in Africa. It is estimated that between 8,000 and 10,000 children (teenagers and younger children) have been abducted from Northern Uganda by the Lord's Resistance Army since 1995. This includes teenage girls to serve as 'wives' as well as fighters. Thousands of children and adolescents have been fighting and committing atrocities in Sierra Leone, both for the rebel RUF and AFRC and for the government-aligned Kamajor militia, as well as in the Democratic Republic of Congo, both before

5 Coalition to Stop the Use of Child Soldiers, Stop Using Child Soldiers, 2nd edition, 1998.

and after Laurent Kabila came to power. In Asia, one of the best-documented examples is Myanmar, with recruitment of teenagers into the government armed forces as well as child and adolescent participation in the ranks of various armed opposition groups. The reduction in the numbers of armed conflicts in Latin America has considerably reduced the incidence of child combatants. However, a recent report from Colombia stated that 'most of the rebels killed in the (government) counter-attack were aged between nine and 14 years' and many teenagers are involved despite the fact that 16 to 18 year olds in the government armed forces are not meant to be sent to combat zones or used in armed confrontations.

In essence, the categories of children most likely to be child labourers in peacetime are also those most likely to become child combatants in time of war.

Child recruitment increases as conflict continues and the supply of adults diminishes through death, injury or evasion.

Child soldiers are rarely evident in the early stages of a conflict, or when the conflict is short-lived, except where recruitment of children into government armed forces is routine. In some long-term armed conflicts (e.g. Casamance in Senegal, West Africa[6]) there is no evidence of under 18s fighting on either side. It would be useful to ascertain why children have not become involved in these situations and what lessons can be learned from them.

Where child participation is common, it is important to recognise that not all children are involved. Indeed, research has identified the categories of children usually engaged as soldiers, regardless of country, continent or region, whether forced or voluntary, and whether fighting on behalf of a government or an armed opposition group.[7] These categories are:

- children separated from their families (orphans, unaccompanied refugee and displaced minors, street children);
- children with a disrupted family background (divorced or separated parents, single parents, step-parents);
- children with little or no education (those who never had access to school, who dropped out, or who failed to make educational progress);
- children from poor and marginalised sectors of society (rural and urban);
- children from the conflict zones themselves.

Children most vulnerable to being engaged as soldiers may come from one or several of these categories. The similarity of these categories to those of the child labour population is notable. In essence, the categories of children most likely to

6 Coalition to Stop the Use of Child Soldiers, The Use of Child Soldiers in Africa, March 1999.
7 Rachel Brett and Margaret McCallin, Children: The Invisible Soldiers, Rädda Barnen, Stockholm, 2nd edition 1998. In the absence of other references, this book forms the basis for this chapter.

be child labourers in peacetime are also those most likely to become child combatants in time of war. This fact has been acknowledged officially (albeit in a limited way) by the inclusion of child soldiering within the scope of the new International Labour Organization (ILO) Worst Forms of Child Labour Convention.[8]

Children, and particularly those without adult protection, are vulnerable to recruitment.

Why these children?

The main reason for child recruitment is the need for large numbers of soldiers, combined with circumstances in which it is easier to recruit children than adults. Child recruitment is rare at the beginning of conflicts but increases as the conflict continues and the supply of adults diminishes through death, injury or evasion. The legal conscription age may be reduced to meet this need and both armed opposition groups and governments may resort to forced recruitment, irrespective of the law.

Children, and particularly those without adult protection, are more vulnerable to forced recruitment (round-ups and press-gangs) than are adults. Not only is it harder for children to resist physically but they are also less likely to know about and be able to assert their rights. They may not know the legal recruitment age or, if they do, they may not be able to prove their own age, particularly if they are educationally, economically and socially marginalised children.[9] Such children and their families are unlikely to be able to buy or bribe their way out or to bring political influence to bear. Knowing this, recruiters target areas where these children abound (e.g. townships, shantytowns, rural buses and market-places) rather than wealthier suburbs.

Rich or middle-class families may take action to protect their children, sending them to another part of the country, or abroad, for education or relocating the entire family. This enables children to avoid conscription or forced recruitment, and also discourages them from volunteering as a result of peer-group pressure or ideology. Even so, the increasing evidence of recruitment of ethnic minority children from third countries (e.g. refugee children from Sweden[10]) demonstrates the continued pressure to join up that may be exerted even in these circumstances.

8 The Convention concerning the prohibition and immediate action for the elimination of the worst forms of child labour (June 1999), defines a child as 'all persons under the age of 18' (Article 2), and requires states parties to 'take immediate and effective measures to secure the prohibition and elimination of the worst forms of child labour as a matter of urgency' (Article 1), and includes in the worst forms of child labour 'forced or compulsory recruitment of children for use in armed conflict' (Article 3(a)).
9 Report of the UN Working Group on Arbitrary Detention, Report on the Mission to Peru (E/CN.4/1996/63/Add.2).
10 See entry in Brett and McCallin 1998, op.cit. note 7 above.

Jenny Matthews / Save The Children

Children who volunteer, or 'are volunteered' by their parents, tend to come from the same sectors of society. The inducements offered - pay, food, education or training (whether or not these are actually forthcoming) - are more attractive to those who have the fewest other options.

When an armed opposition group is recruiting, ideology may play a significant role if the group has a social or ethnic programme. The major reason for children volunteering to join an armed opposition group is their personal experience of ill-treatment by government armed forces, including harassment, torture, killing of family members and destruction of homes. The motivation is usually less a quest for revenge than a response to feelings of vulnerability and not knowing where else to turn.

Although at first glance the distinction between forced and voluntary recruitment may seem clear cut, in practice there are considerable elements of ambiguity. The child abducted in Northern Uganda by the Lord's Resistance Army is clearly forcibly recruited.[11] But what about a child who fails to return from a summer camp in Sweden organised by a Kurdish cultural organisation, who is eventually traced serving in the ranks of the PKK (Kurdistan Workers Party).[12] Or the child who enlists after a call for volunteers from an armed recruiting party? Or the child who is induced to join either side by a subsequently unfulfilled promise of money or education?

Even when the decision to enlist appears to have been based on free will, young persons cannot be expected to fully appreciate the implications of their decisions and actions or the dangers they may face.

Even when the decision to enlist appears to have been based on free will, it should be noted that young persons, who have not reached the age of majority, cannot be expected to fully appreciate the implications of their decisions and actions or the dangers they may face.[13]

Traditionally, a distinction is made between government armed forces and armed opposition groups, but there is an increasing tendency for a proliferation of armed groups. Some of these are surrogate government armed forces under various names - paramilitaries, militias, civil defence committees, youth groups - set up or authorised by the government (or the armed forces), or armed or permitted to carry arms by it. Other groups may be genuinely autonomous or aligned with

11 Amnesty International, Breaking God's Commands (AI Index: AFR59/01/97), London, 1997; Human Rights Watch, The Scars of Death, New York, 1997; Report to the UN Working Group on Enforced and Involuntary Disapperances (E/CN.4/1996/6, para. 307); Report to the UN Secretary-General on Abduction of Children from Northern Uganda (E/CN.4/1996/69).

12 Save the Children Sweden, Children of War, No. 3/98, Rädda Barnen, Stockholm, September 1998

13 Report of the UN Special Rapporteur on Extrajudicial, Summary or Arbitrary Executions (E/CN.4/1999/39), para. 73.

particular political or military leaders. Such diversification increases the general confusion and lack of accountability and, therefore, increases the likely involvement of children as a result of direct recruitment and the general breakdown of society.

New child recruits may be required to kill other children or family or community members known to them as a form of initiation.

Children are more vulnerable than adults not only at the point of recruitment but also after they have been recruited. It is harder for them to escape. Those without families or without strong emotional ties have less incentive to do so. Also, they are more willing to take risks as soldiers because they are not worrying about spouses, children and other dependants of their own. Military commanders seem increasingly aware of these factors, and there is a consequent tendency towards the deliberate recruitment of children.

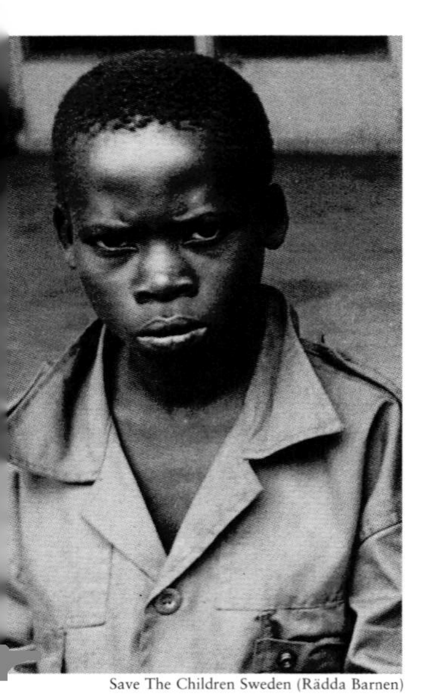

Save The Children Sweden (Rädda Barnen)

"Kadogos [kids] make very good soldiers because they think of nothing else. They obey without worrying about getting back to their wife or family. And they are not afraid."[14]

Treatment of child soldiers

In government armed forces, recruits are usually treated alike, irrespective of age. Such treatment is often brutal. This brutality may be a matter of policy, with initiation and toughening-up exercises designed to break the will of the recruits and make them obedient to their superiors in all circumstances, as well as physically fit. Or it may be the result of a culture of violence or a lack of sufficient supervision. The physical and emotional impact of such treatment on adolescents may be considerably greater than it is on adults, and more lasting. Deaths (including suicides), permanent disability and mental illness are frequently reported. In armed opposition groups, new child recruits may be required to kill other children or family or community members known to them as a form of initiation.[15] This not only serves the goal of brutalisation, breaking a child's taboo on killing, but also makes it harder for them to leave the group because they are afraid to return to a community that knows what they have done. This said, it should be emphasised that some armed forces and armed groups do seek to take a responsible attitude to the age and particular needs of young recruits.

14 Rebel officer in the Democratic Republic of the Congo (AFP, 8 October 1998).
15 Report of the UN Secretary-General on Abduction of Children from Northern Uganda (E/CN.4/1999/69), para. 5, 22.

Much of the treatment child soldiers experience pertains directly to their military service, such as the general beatings and punishments, the forced marches carrying heavy loads, exposure to malnutrition and disease, and the separation from family. Child soldiers may suffer additional incidental or deliberately exploitative abuse, such as sexual exploitation (of both girls and boys) and the provision of drugs and alcohol.

The risk of death and injury is greater for child soldiers. Children may be regarded as expendable, and natural teenage recklessness is often deliberately reinforced by the provision of drugs or alcohol.

Impact of child soldiering

The most immediate impact of the use of child soldiers is direct violation of the rights of the individual child. Some of this is inherent; some owes more to the way in which child soldiers are used. Most blatant is the likelihood of death or injury as a result of participation in combat. However, the ramifications are much broader, and include both direct and indirect effects on the individual child, the knock-on effects on other children, the ways in which conflicts are fought, and the long-term impact on society.

The risk of death and injury is clearly shared with adult soldiers, but the evidence points to its being greater for child soldiers. Children may be regarded as expendable, being used in 'human wave' attacks, including through minefields. They can also be perceived as having special attributes suiting them to high-risk functions. Natural teenage recklessness is often deliberately reinforced by the provision of drugs or alcohol, and may be exploited for suicide missions. Younger children may also be tricked into considering themselves invulnerable, despite all evidence to the contrary. Their size, weight and nimble fingers are well suited to the task of laying and detecting landmines. The large number of instances of loss of limbs among child soldiers reflects this propensity. Also common are loss of hearing and loss of sight, partly reflecting immature and more sensitive organs. Such forms of disablement at the beginning of adult life will not only have a permanent effect on the victims but, in an actuarial sense, will affect the victims for longer, and are likely to have a catastrophic impact on life prospects, particularly when suffered by children who have not acquired civilian vocational skills.

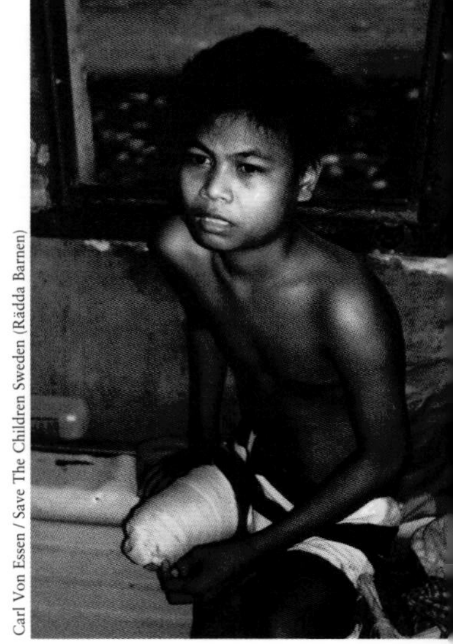
Carl Von Essen / Save The Children Sweden (Rädda Barnen)

Those enrolled as child soldiers are deprived of education, including vocational training, apprenticeships and simple learning in the home, as well as formal schooling.

Many child soldiers die without ever reaching the front line. This may be as a result of resisting initial recruitment, trying to escape punishment or simple elimination for physical inability to perform the tasks laid upon them or to keep up on forced marches. Alternatively, they may succumb to the rigours, privations, malnutrition and health hazards associated with military campaigns, such as skin and respiratory diseases and malaria. Other non-combat related injuries, which may leave permanent damage, range from beatings, through sexual abuse (and the consequent likelihood of sexually transmitted diseases and HIV/AIDS) and the effects of drug and alcohol abuse, to bone deformation through being forced to carry heavy loads. There are also all the possible risks for girls of pregnancy and its consequences. In addition, there are the mental, emotional and psychological effects of their experiences, which may include having witnessed or perpetrated atrocities.

Save The Children Sweden (Rädda Barnen)

Child soldiers are usually separated from their families, with consequent emotional and psychological dangers.[16] The UN Working Group on Arbitrary Detention has stated that forced recruitment ('levies') by government recruiters in Peru constituted arbitrary detention.[17] This practice has subsequently been declared illegal in Peru, but the destruction of records (making it hard for recruits to prove their age) and the refusal of judges to accept any alternative proof of age have led to much under-age conscription of both under-18s and under-15s. Those enrolled as child soldiers are also deprived of education, including vocational training, apprenticeships and simple learning in the home, as well as formal schooling.[18]

The violation of children's rights does not end with their active careers as soldiers. If captured, they may be executed,[19] or subjected to torture and other ill-treatment, including sexual assault in the case of girl soldiers.[20] Faced with child participation in armed opposition groups, governments tend to react by lowering the age of criminal responsibility in general or for 'terrorist' offences. In such circumstances, the legal safeguards normally available for

16 CRC Article 9.
17 Report of the UN Working Group on Arbitrary Detention, Report on the Mission to Peru (E/CN.4/1999/63/Add.2), para. 119-20.
18 CRC Article 28.
19 Human Rights Watch, Getting Away with Murder, Mutilation and Rape: New Testimony from Sierra Leone, June 1999.
20 Report of the UN Working Group on Arbitrary Detention, Report on the Mission to Peru (E/CN.4/1999/63/Add.2).

children and juveniles are often omitted. Thus, at the time when they need the greatest protection under the criminal law, their protection is the weakest.[21] This may lead to other violations of the rights of the child, such as the passing of life sentences or the death penalty.[22] At its most extreme, children originally abducted or recruited forcibly may find themselves charged with criminal offences and even with treason.[23] Furthermore, once children are known to be involved in combat, the rights of other children are put at risk; cases have been recorded of the arbitrary arrest, torture and beating of those merely suspected of having been, or likely to become, child soldiers.[24] Inevitably, those who suffer most from such abuses will come from the same disadvantaged groups already most at risk of being enrolled as child soldiers. In addition, once the use of child soldiers by one side in a civil war becomes widespread, there is a strong incentive for the other side to resort to pre-emptive recruitment of the groups at risk; thus, the more child soldiers there are, the less chance other children in the society will have of avoiding the same fate.

Gross violations of international humanitarian law, with children forced or induced by drugs or alcohol to commit atrocities - killings, mutilations, rapes - not only affect the children themselves but also undermine the whole notion that warfare should have rules and limitations imposed on it.[25] At the same time, to be faced with child fighters is a threat not only to the safety of the community - and of any outside peacekeeping forces - but also to its system of values; the normal protective attitude towards children in general is undermined as they are redefined as a potential threat. This may make it harder to end the conflict, especially in those cases in which large numbers of children have been involved effectively for the whole of their lives. Not only does soldiering become normality for them, but its end may lead of loss of prestige, power and livelihood. They may also have to live in fear of repercussions from an abused population. These factors come into play when demobilising and re-integrating into society children who have been engaged as soldiers. Long-term socialisation at a young age into a military environment, which is often extreme and cruel, has serious and pervasive effects on the normal social development of children and poses one of the greatest challenges when it comes to rehabilitation.

21 See, for example, Report of the UN Working Group on Arbitrary Detention: Report on the Mission to Peru (E/CN.4/1999/63/Add.2). The Working Group stated that in its opinion 15 is 'too young' for the beginning of criminal responsibility and is inconsistent with Principle 4.1 of the Beijing Rules (para.147).

22 CRC Article 37.

23 Coalition to Stop the Use of Child Soldiers, The Use of Child Soldiers in Africa, March 1999, p. 7; Report of the UN Working Group on Arbitrary Detention: Report on the Mission to Peru (E/CN.4/1999/63/Add.2), para. 148.

24 Human Rights Watch, Getting Away with Murder, Mutilation and Rape: New Testimony from Sierra Leone, June 1999; Report of the UN Working Group on Enforced or Involuntary Disappearances (E/CN.4/1999/6), para. 153.

25 Report to the UN Special Rapporteur on Exrajudicial, Summary or Arbitrary Executions (E/CN.4/1999/39), para. 73.

The numbers game

It is impossible to produce an accurate global figure of the numbers of children currently engaged as soldiers. The phrase 'at least 300,000 currently engaged in armed conflict' used by the Coalition to Stop the Use of Child Soldiers is deliberately vague and conservative. Since no one keeps real statistics, all figures will be guesses. Numbers fluctuate, as conflicts begin or end, or as offensives wax or wane. Child recruitment is often informal and, therefore, the number of children in any armed group can change radically. Furthermore, today's children are tomorrow's adults and, as far as statistics are concerned, each day a proportion of young soldiers cross whatever age threshold has been chosen. Therefore, any snapshot of numbers is not only inaccurate but also misleading, since the 12 year-old recruit who continues to fight will suffer the effects of his or her experience, whether he or she is demobilised at 17, 18 or 25. That there are thousands more child soldiers in armed forces or armed groups not currently engaged in combat who could be deployed at any time, and who are, in any case, at risk from many of the abuses outlined above, should not be overlooked.

Save The Children Sweden (Rädda Barnen)

Gender

There are fewer girls than boys engaged as soldiers but, in most situations, the popular designation 'boy soldiers' does a gross injustice to the many girl soldiers who share the same plight. The extremely limited information so far obtained indicates that, where girls are recruited, they constitute about one-third of the total number of child soldiers. All that has been said about child soldiers relates, without differentiation, to the experiences of both boys and girls. Over and above this, girls are exposed to the human rights abuses specific to women. In particular, the sexual exploitation of girls is frequently more systematic. Girls may be abducted specifically as 'wives' or concubines, but even girls who join voluntarily may be expected to provide 'comfort' to their male colleagues,

Where girls are recruited, they constitute about one-third of the total number of child soldiers.

in addition to bearing a full burden of the fighting. This sexual exploitation also carries with it the risk of pregnancy, with its additional physical and emotional burdens. Also, the girl may lack control over the outcome; she may be forced to abort or obliged to hand the child over for fostering. This said, there are societies in which girls have been keen to take an active role in armed struggle as a means of escaping from traditional constraints on the freedoms and status of women. Teenage girls contribute their share of suicide bombers; not only are they as vulnerable as adolescent boys to ideological pressure but also it is particularly easy for them to conceal explosives around the waist.

Save The Children Sweden (Rädda Barnen)

Age

The prohibition of the CRC on the recruitment and participation in hostilities of under 15s is being flouted routinely in many armed conflicts. The development and ready availability of cheap, lightweight, automatic weapons, such as the AK-47, make it possible for children as young as 10 to be effective killers. Although the use of even younger children has been reported they are not usually involved as front-line troops. The problem is that once the distinction between adults and children is breached there is no logical 'bottom line' except that of physical capability. In most situations in which under 18s are involved in combat under 15s are involved as well. In part, this reflects the fact that, in the absence of universal birth registration (itself a requirement of the CRC[26]), age in calendar years is often a question of guesswork. Whereas the physical distinction between an 18 and a 13 or 14 year old is usually easy to see, the distinction between a 13 year old and a 15 year old is not so readily apparent.

The ready availability of cheap, lightweight, automatic weapons, makes it possible for children as young as 10 to be effective killers, once the distinction between adults and children is breached, there is no logical 'bottom line' except that of physical capability.

26 CRC Article 7. August 1996; Brett and McCallin 1998 (op.cit. note 7); the Cape Town Principles and Best Practice on the Prevention of Recruitment into the Armed Forces and on Demobilisation and Social Re-integration of Child Soldiers in Africa (UNICEF, New York, February 1999); the Maputo Declaration to Stop the Use of Children as Soldiers and the Working Group recommendations from the African Conference to Stop the Use of Child Soldiers (Maputo, Mozambique, 19-22 April 1999); and the ARC (Action for the Rights of Children) Training Module on Child Soldiers (UNHCR and International Save the Children Alliance, 1999).

Liba Taylor

Demobilisation, reintegration and the post-conflict situation

Demobilisation of child soldiers raises many delicate issues. First, how it is done will depend on how the conflict has ended, how many children are still soldiers at the end, their ages, and whether the parties to the conflict acknowledge the use of child soldiers. Many of the adult soldiers, particularly if the conflict has been protracted, may be former child soldiers. They will face the same problems of health, lack of the education and skills needed to earn a living (without a gun) and loss of contact with family. They may have some difficulty readjusting to peacetime society and values and handling the loss of status that ceasing to be a soldier may entail. Also, the need to recognise the role the children have played must be balanced against the need not to encourage or reward child participation. If demobilised child soldiers are given advantages over those who have resisted or avoided recruitment, this sends out the wrong message. However, children who have fought, even if forcibly recruited, may feel discriminated against if adult soldiers receive a demobilisation package but they do not. A balance needs to be struck that addresses the particular needs of child soldiers while taking account of the needs of the child population as a whole.

If demobilised child soldiers are given advantages over those who have resisted or avoided recruitment, this sends out the wrong message.

However, children may feel discrim-inated against if adult soldiers receive a demobil-isation package but they do not.

Catching Up on Education in Liberia

Since June 1996 Save the Children UK has been working with ex-child combatants and children affected by the former civil war in Liberia. All have missed vital years of schooling and suffered severe trauma as a result of the war. The project initially began by working with a small group of former child soldiers in Virginia Town near Liberia's capital Monrovia. The aim was to put some structure in these childrens lives offering them a safe and secure environment while they were reintegrated into their communities. Play and sport formed a large basis of rehabilitation work, which focused on instilling a sense of self-worth coupled with individual responsibility. This project evolved into four more transit centres in central and northern Liberia, which provided basic education and literacy classes and skills training. A critical off-shoot of the catch-up education was the participation of children from the community forging peace and reconciliation and forgiveness amongst the communities at large.

)ne requirement specific to child soldiers that is rarely considered is that they hould be exempted from any future obligation to undertake compulsory military ervice. The problems of demobilised girl soldiers, with or without children, equire particular attention. Their particular health and economic needs must be ddressed, as must the question of their role in society and their prospects of narriage or family reunification.[27]

ddressing health problems (including substance dependency and sexually ransmitted diseases) is a priority, and must include checks for less obvious npairments, such as those to sight and hearing. Otherwise, the emphasis should e on normalising the children's situation and reintegrating them into the family r substitute family and the community. For some children, giving up their arms nd returning to their family may be their greatest wish, and the family may velcome them back. For others, the atrocities they have committed may make amilies and communities reluctant to accept their return.

Family Reintegration

In Uganda, Save the Children Denmark (Red Barnet) has been working with the local community in Gulu providing a programme of support to abducted children and ex-child soldiers. The project seeks to address the pyscho-social well being of children through community based activities aimed at promoting normal family and everyday life easing reintegration back into the community. Children are provided with material and emotional support, which once they have been reunited with their families is extended to embrace the whole family. Basic education and vocational training is also provided. Running parallel to this is a Children's Rights Awareness Campaign, which provides training for the range of professionals who have a responsibility for children.

7 Report to the UN Secretary-General on Abduction of Children from Northern Uganda (E/CN.4/1999/69), para. 23

Demobilised child combatants require exceptional support and assistance in order to give them even a chance of effective re-integration back into their own communities.

The children themselves may hesitate to give up their guns without compensating assurances about their economic future and other status. Older children. who have missed out on education. are unlikely to look kindly on returning to the classroom beside much younger children, highlighting the need for creative thinking about other forms of education, including vocational training, apprenticeships and the means of self-support while learning. This is not only an issue of how to address the needs of individual children, but will also 'require an "economic compact" that will give thousands of militia members and marginalised youth conditioned to surviving by force, an alternative to the AK-47.'[28] The growth of violent crime in many post-conflict societies is evidence of the problems likely to arise without careful policy-planning and implementation.

Careful attention then urgently needs to be given by all policy-makers, the international community, UN agencies, non-governmental organisations (NGOs) and governments to the pressing question of rehabilitation. Demobilised child combatants require a complex range of support and assistance in order to give them even a chance of effective reintegration back into their own communities. At the time of demobilisation the provisions of the CRC should constitute the guiding principles in all actions to protect their rights and welfare. The international community must ensure that the participation of children in conflict is recognised in all peace agreements so that their needs are not neglected but are incorporated as a matter of principle in plans for demobilisation, rehabilitation, and social reintegration.

Simon Wood

Once it is known that children are to be demobilised, international organisations (UNHCR and UNICEF in particular) and international and local NGOs should implement family tracing and reunification programmes as a matter of urgency so that children can return to their communities of origin. Communities should be given appropriate support in the rehabilitation process. NGOs have a crucial role

28 Report to the UN Commission on Human Rights by the independent expert on effects of structural adjustment policies on the full enjoyment of human rights (E/CN.4/1999/50).

› play in this. Programmes should be developed which involve the participation f the children, their families and communities, to enable them to normalise ıeir daily lives and prevent further recruitment. Attention to their immediate ealth and nutrition needs will be essential to ensure that they are not lured ack into armed groups who may be able to guarantee at least a degree of ability and security. Crucial assistance will be needed to help the children to e-learn' ways of relating to people in normal contexts, and in particular they ill require counselling to help reintegration back into a family situation. ducation and vocational training will be a priority, as will assistance to chart ıd develop their training in an appropriate and realistic manner to compensate ›r lost time. For older children, the creation of employment opportunities and nall business enterprises will be essential to offer a viable alternative to fighting. his process of rehabilitation is one of the most challenging difficulties and arrants a deep commitment of resources, personnel and time to ensure that is addressed effectively.

Crucial assistance will be needed to help the children to 're-learn' ways of relating to people in normal contexts, and in particular they will require counselling to help re-integration back into a family situation.

The needs of child soldiers must be addressed within overall planning and service provision for all children affected by armed conflict.

Resettlement in Colombia

Save the Children UK works with the Colombian Government and the Colombian Child Welfare Institute to address the problems of resettlement for former child fighters of the ongoing civil war. Save the Children has established an inter-agency working group to develop and implement a resettlement programme at the same time as establishing a country wide advocacy programme to prevent the recruitment of children into armed groups and encourage the various factions to release their child soldiers. Save the Children is seeking to develop ways to give these children a voice in their own future so that they can become active and productive members of their society. Often such children are not welcomed back by their family so emotional support and counselling is an important part of this work. The provision of basic education and vocational training opportunities is a central feature of Save the Children's programme.

'he needs of child soldiers must be addressed within overall planning and service rovision for all children affected by armed conflict, to ensure that they are not ıarginalised within their communities. Governments must ensure that there is ffective follow-up of demobilised child soldiers and take note of community ttitudes towards the culpability of children who were actively involved in conflict and ensure that they are awarded due protection. International and local NGOs should assist in these procedures and intervene where necessary to protect the rights and well-being of the children and to promote reconciliation and understanding of the causes and consequences of children's participation in conflict.

When we consider the full range of violations of the rights of the child that child participation in combat generates, it is remarkable how little unanimity there is about the need both to prohibit it by law and to act to prohibit it in practice.

Current and future challenges

When we consider the full range of violations of the rights of the child that child participation in combat generates, it is remarkable how little unanimity there is about both the need to prohibit it by law and to act to prohibit it in practice.

There are many tools to hand. The legal ones include: the Statute of the International Criminal Court, which makes it an international crime to conscript or enlist under-15s or use them in hostilities in either international or internal armed conflict; the new ILO Worst Forms of Child Labour Convention; the African Charter on the Rights and Welfare of the Child, as well as the Additional Protocols to the Geneva Conventions and the CRC itself. If all states were to become parties to these treaties and work seriously for their effective implementation, it would make a significant difference to the problem. If states were also to take measures consistently and seriously as part of their foreign, development and military policy, and complete the legislative framework by adopting an international ban on the participation and recruitment (the most effective means of preventing participation) of under-18s then the problem could be reduced from the current routine and systematic practices to isolated and sporadic incidents.

Simon Wood

To achieve this end, protective and preventive mechanisms must be developed. To ensure that they become a reality for children around the world, and not simply another rhetorical commitment to a worthy cause, a number of critical steps need to be taken. These are all aimed at one basic thing - to protect children most and risk - and they require the active commitment of the whole international community.

- **International ban on recruitment and participation under the age of 18**
  The only sure way of protecting children from the violence and barbarity of war is to establish international mechanisms which prevent any formal involvement of children in a conflict. Recruitment of children under 18, and their participation in hostilities, should be prohibited in all circumstances, including by regular governmental armed forces, irregular forces, or any other armed groups, such as militias, civil defence forces, opposition forces and private groups. This standard should be adopted internationally in the CRC Optional Protocol to Article 38 that is currently being negotiated. In civil wars all parties should be encouraged to make local agreements to this effect. The mutual nature of these agreements will go some way to encouraging parties to keep to them. All governments, relevant international and regional organisations, specialist agencies and international and national NGOs can assist in advocating such agreements. Proper safeguards, including proof of age, and military disciplinary or criminal penalties for infringements, should be available and enforced to ensure that under-age recruitment does not take place.

Recruitment of children under 18, and their participation in hostilities, should be prohibited in all circumstances, including by regular governmental armed forces, irregular forces, or any other armed groups.

International ban on recruitment and participation under the age of 18.

- **International commitment and diplomatic representation**
  Diplomatic representations and pressure should be placed by all members of the international community on those who use child combatants. This can be done using a variety of mechanisms. The international community must support the Optional Protocol and, in addition to this, commit itself to putting in place the necessary safeguards to protect children and prevent continued recruitment of child combatants. It is only through consistent international pressure that any change in established practices can be achieved.

Diplomatic representations and pressure should be placed by all members of the international community on those who use child combatants.

- **International arms embargo on armed groups using child combatants**
  International embargoes should be placed on the supply of arms or other military equipment and training to any armed forces or groups using children.

- **A universal birth registration system**
  The routine provision of birth records is essential for the prevention of under-age recruitment into government armed forces. Governments, as a matter of priority, should establish effective and universal birth registration systems and provide the necessary documentation. UNICEF and other international and national NGOs have a role in assisting governments to establish such systems.

As long as some governments continue to defend the use of under-18s in combat there will be resistance to the creation of international standards with effective prohibitions

- **Provision and maintenance of effective education facilities during armed conflict**
  Maximum access to education, including secondary education and vocational training, should be provided and maintained, as a priority, even during displacement and armed conflicts. This will offer a viable alternative to joining armed groups. The major international agencies and NGOs will have a considerable role in achieving this.

- **Protecting the family**
  Keeping families together and family reunification should be a priority. These are essential for protecting children at risk of joining armed forces. Supporting families and communities who resist child recruitment will be vital to ensure that they can provide their children an alternative to fighting.

- **Alternative means of support for children at risk**
  Alternative means of economic and social support for those children most at risk (and their families)must be provided. This may include small business enterprise schemes if conditions allow, or seeds and tools programmes for displaced or refugee families.[29]

However, as long as some governments continue to defend the use of under-18s in combat (and only a handful of the 191 states party to the CRC still do so), there will be resistance to the creation of international standards with effective prohibitions of such conduct, and to effective political and programmatic responses to such abuse. An example of this can be seen in the case of the limits placed by the UK on its assistance with child demobilisation in Sierra Leone. The African Charter on the Rights and Welfare of the Child prohibits the recruitment and in addition, the Government of Sierra Leone has promised the Special Representative of the UN Secretary-General for Children and Armed Conflict, Olara Otunnu, that it would demobilise all soldiers aged under-18 and make 18 the minimum age for entry into the new government armed forces. However, the UK has limited assistance in child demobilisation in Sierra Leone to children under the age of 16, undermining these higher regional and national standards, apparently on the sole basis of the donor country's own national recruitment practices.

29 For further recommendations, see the UN Study of the Impact of Armed Conflict on Children (A/51/306) of 26 August 1996; Brett and McCallin 1998 (op.cit. note 7); the Cape Town Principles and Best Practice on the Prevention of Recruitment into the Armed Forces and on Demobilisation and Social Re-integration of Child Soldiers in Africa (UNICEF, New York, February 1999); the Maputo Declaration to Stop the Use of Children as Soldiers and the Working Group recommendations from the African Conference to Stop the Use of Child Soldiers (Maputo, Mozambique, 19-22 April 1999); and the ARC (Action for the Rights of Children) Training Module on Child Soldiers (UNHCR and International Save the Children Alliance, 1999).

Save The Children Sweden (Rädda Barnen)

'My dream is that our parents can find it in their hearts to forgive us'

Stephen, age 17, former boy soldier, Liberia

'Everybody must get ***together*** *to fight the real problem -* ***poverty*** *-* ***not against*** *working children'.*

Ros Mery, age 15 - Peru

Chapter 4

Child Labour

Today's working children.

Child labour is now higher on the international policy agenda than ever before. In June 1999, the International Labour Organization (ILO) adopted a new convention on the worst forms of child labour. Many companies based in the West are taking steps to ensure that children are not involved in the manufacture of the products they sell. Major donors, recognising that hazardous or full-time work can jeopardise the development prospects of both individual children and society are funding child-labour programmes in a way that would have been unthinkable five years ago. This growing commitment to tackling child labour is both timely and welcome.

The issue of child labour[1] evokes strong passions and has generated much heated debate in recent years. Underlying this debate are differences in visions of the future and analysis of the causes of child labour. One side of the debate sees child labour as a major obstacle to social and economic progress, and looks forward to a world where all children are in school and not in the workforce. Others argue that children's work is a vital household response to poverty, and that work can be beneficial as well as harmful. The issue of harmful child labour - work that jeopardises the health, education or development of children - brings both sides of the debate together. Everyone agrees that eliminating this should be the priority for action.

Ensuring that children are not involved in harmful work presents a major challenge. Children work in a vast range of situations, for a variety of reasons, and 'solutions' will only succeed if they take this diversity and complexity into account. This chapter illustrates the range of work that children do and the ways it can affect them. It then examines some of the main reasons why children work and discusses approaches to the issue from a child-rights perspective. The focus of this article is child labour in the South, but there is some discussion of the situation in the North.

1 In this article 'child labour' refers to any work that children do, not exclusively to harmful work.

Liba Taylor / Save The Children

A child-rights approach to child labour

One side of the debate sees child labour as a major obstacle to social and economic progress and looks forward to a world where all children are in school and not in the workforce. Others argue that children's work is a vital household response to poverty, and that work can be beneficial as well as harmful.

The UN Convention on the Rights of the Child (CRC) states that children have the right to be protected from economic exploitation and from performing any work that is likely to be hazardous or to interfere with the child's education or to be harmful to the child's health or physical, mental, spiritual, moral or social development. (Article 32)

Notably the CRC does not prohibit children from working entirely, nor does it set minimum ages for work; these are covered by national laws, and the ILO Convention on Minimum Ages (138), in countries that have ratified it. Its focus on protecting children from harmful work implicitly recognises that not all work is harmful to children.

The areas of concern outlined in the CRC - work that exploits or harms children - are seen increasingly as the main areas that child-labour policies and programmes should tackle. Although what exactly constitutes harmful child labour is disputed, the growing consensus exemplified in the recently adopted ILO Worst Forms of Child Labour Convention is encouraging. Groups who historically have opposed one another now have a common focus for action.

Children have the right to be protected from economic exploitation and from performing any work that is likely to be hazardous or to interfere with the child's education or to be harmful to the child's health or physical, mental, spiritual, moral or social development. (Article 32).

Several other CRC articles also have a bearing on child-labour issues. These include: children's right to an education, to an adequate livelihood and to be consulted on decisions that affect them. At times, these principles may conflict with one another. For example, where children are working for their own survival, many would argue that this has to take precedence over their right to protection from harmful work. However, the fundamental principle of the CRC - that the best interests of the child should be paramount at all times - is a tool for helping decide what the most appropriate course of action should be. This principle underlines the importance of basing action on the realities of individual children, and ensuring that all action improves their welfare, principles which sometimes takes second place to the desire to show that no children are working.

ILO estimates from 1996 indicate that 120 million children under 15 work full time and another 130 million work part time.

These principles are revisited later in the chapter when effective and child-centred ways of tackling child labour are examined.

Who are today's working children and what kinds of work do they do?

Reliable statistics on child labour are difficult to obtain, partly because of differing views of what constitutes work, and partly because much child labour is illegal and there are strong pressures on governments, employers and children who want to retain their jobs to conceal the fact that they are working. Therefore, global estimates of the numbers of working children should be seen as 'best guesses' rather than definitive figures. Nonetheless, these estimates are widely quoted and serve a useful purpose in drawing world attention to the scale of child labour. ILO estimates from 1996 indicate that 120 million children under 15 work full time and another 130 million work part time. Approximately 61 per cent of the world's child workers live in Asia, 32 per cent in Africa and seven per cent in Latin America. However, a higher proportion of children in Africa work than in any other region. While many children start work below the age of 10, particularly those doing domestic chores or helping with family farms or businesses, the majority of working children are aged 10 to 14.[2]

Dario Mitidieri / Save The Children

Although child labour is widely seen as a thing of the past in industrialised countries, a high proportion of children and young people in the North do work. For example, research in the UK shows that two-thirds of children have worked by the time they are 16. Around 30 per cent work (illegally) at age 12.[3] Almost all working children in the North work part time, a small proportion to the detriment of their education. More children in the North are at risk of injury at work than is often assumed.

Worldwide, more boys than girls are in 'formal' paid employment. However, most statistics do not count unpaid domestic work, in which girls predominate. If domestic work is taken into account, then probably more girls work than boys.

Worldwide, more boys than girls are in 'formal' paid employment. However, most statistics do not count unpaid domestic work, in which girls predominate. If domestic work is taken into account, then probably more girls work than boys.

Children are involved in a huge range of work, including agriculture, street-vending, care of animals, domestic work (for their families or for others), deep-sea fishing, working in shops, as porters, in the manufacture of carpets or garments, and as sex workers. The vast majority of children worldwide work for their families on the family farm or, to a lesser extent, in other family-run businesses. An estimated 70 per cent of working children are involved in agriculture. Only about five per cent work in the production of internationally traded goods, such as the trainers and footballs that have attracted so much attention in the West in recent years.

TRENDS IN CHILD LABOUR

Is child labour increasing? Is hazardous and exploitative child labour increasing? In global terms, we don't know. Studies indicate a decrease in child labour in East Asia before the recent economic crisis but an increase in most other regions.[4] Certainly, the visibility of child labour is increasing and the forms of work in

2 International Labour Organization, Child Labour Surveys: Results of Methodological Experiments in Four Countries 1992-3, ILO, Geneva, 1995.
3 S. Hobbs and J. McKechnie, 'Children and Work in the UK: the Evidence' in B. Pettitt (ed), Children and Work in the UK: Reassessing the Issues, Save the Children/ Child Poverty Action Group, London, 1998.
4 R. Ebdon, Working Children's Futures, unpublished, Save the Children, London, 1999.

which children are involved are changing and becoming more diverse. Many observers in the South note an increase in the numbers of children begging, living on the streets and working in a variety of occupations, which indicates a general increase in child labour.

Working conditions and the risks they present vary considerably.

Taking this diversity into account is essential for effective action on harmful child labour.

The overall picture is less clear. The ILO has recently developed a statistical information and monitoring programme on child labour (SIMPOC), which aims to assist governments to track changes in child labour more accurately and rapidly. This should help clarify trends in child labour and contribute to better-informed policy formulation.

Effects of work on children

The effects on children of working depend on a range of factors, including the nature of the work, working conditions, the hours worked and the child's age. Working conditions and the risks they present vary considerably. Children working in agriculture may be in danger of inhaling toxic pesticides, while for others, accidents with machinery present a greater risk. While some child domestics are treated with kindness, others receive constant abuse. The stage reached in a child's physical and emotional development is also important. For example, carrying loads that would harm a 12-year-old might have no adverse effects on a 15-year-old. Taking this diversity into account is essential for effective action on harmful child labour.

Mani Lama / Save The Children

Some forms of work are obviously harmful to children. These include activities that jeopardise their health or development, either immediately or in the long term, and in some cases, their survival. For example, situations in which children are exposed to toxic substances, work underground or underwater, where they are abused by employers or customers, or are required to do work beyond their physical or emotional capacity are undoubtedly hazardous to children and are a priority for action. Similarly, work that prevents children from obtaining an education, or makes them too tired to study is clearly harmful. Some detailed examples are discussed in the boxes below.

Bangle-making

Ferozabad in India is the main centre for the manufacture of glass bangles. Thousands of children work with their families in a range of operations, including joining the two ends of the bangles, and cutting and painting designs. Many work in dark, poorly ventilated conditions, breathe kerosene fumes all day, and risk burns and other injuries. The payment children and their families receive is low, as there are often several middlemen involved.

Thousands of children work with their families in a range of operations

Miners

Children, particularly boys, work underground as miners throughout the world. Such children risk their health - underground miners everywhere are prone to respiratory diseases - and may even risk their lives if tunnels or shafts collapse.

Scavengers

Throughout the world, children work as scavengers, in the streets and on rubbish dumps, sorting out materials that can be resold. Rubbish dumps can be extremely dangerous for children's health since toxic chemicals are released as materials decompose. Children also risk acid burns, injuries from scrap metals and infections through cuts. In some cities, the rubbish trade is controlled by muscle men on highly exploitative terms, and children and families risk violence if they try to organise to improve their conditions.

Penny Tweedie / Save The Children

Domestic workers

Millions of children, particularly girls, work as domestic servants in other people's homes. In some places, this is light work for fixed hours but, all too often, child domestics live with their employers and are on call night and day. Such domestics are frequently not seen as children but as workers, and their needs and rights to affection, education and contact with their families are often denied. Their status as a servant is constantly reinforced. For example, in Bangladesh, child domestics are often expected to accompany their employers' children to school, but are rarely allowed to attend themselves. They may also be vulnerable to physical or sexual abuse. Non-governmental organisations, such as Shoishob in Bangladesh, and working children's organisations, such as the African Movement of Working Children and Youth, are working to persuade employers to treat their young domestics fairly and allow them time off to attend school.

Millions of children, particularly girls, work as domestic servants in other people's homes.

Often the damaging effects of work on children are not clear. Work can have positive as well as negative effects. Through working, children can learn useful skills for the future, they are socialised into the life of their community and gain approval through being seen to contribute to their family and community. Working can also increase self-esteem and enhance a child's standing within the family:

For very poor families, the immediate benefits of work are critical. Children's work can make the difference between two or three meals a day.

> *"I started selling papers and cleaning car windows at the street corner. I earned good money and took it to my mother; that's why, when they wanted to hit me, she would defend me. She used to tell my stepfather that I wasn't lazy or bad, that he shouldn't hit me because I was bringing a few pennies into the house".* (nine year old Mexican street vendor)[5]

For very poor families, the immediate benefits of work are critical. Children's work can make the difference between two or three meals a day. Also, working provides the funds that enable some children or their siblings to attend school.

At least 120 million children do work full time, and do not obtain a basic education. This and the fact that millions of other children are unable to learn because they are too tired from working is a serious cause for concern.

WORKING CHILDREN'S ACCESS TO EDUCATION

Most people think of school and work as mutually exclusive: children either work or attend school. This preconception is based on images from European history of children working in full-time industrial or agricultural jobs. However, many children work part time and attend school, particularly in Latin America, where schools often operate a double-shift system. Indeed, many children work for money in order to pay school fees or buy books, uniforms or other necessities.

This said, at least 120 million children do work full time, and do not obtain a basic education. This and the fact that millions of other children are unable to learn because they are too tired from working is a serious cause for concern. Rather than work preventing children obtaining an education in any simple sense, it is usually the child's poverty and the poor quality of schooling on offer that cause them to take up work. Compulsory education alone is unlikely to be the simple solution to child labour.

Many, though certainly not all, working children see combining school with work as the best way of preparing for the future.[6] As a declaration developed by working children and young people from 33 countries in Asia, Africa and Latin America states:

5 S. Arenal, cited in D. Green, Hidden Lives, Voices of Children in Latin America and the Caribbean, Latin America Bureau/ Cassell in conjunction with Save the Children (UK) and Rädda Barnen, 1998.

6 see, for example, M. Woodhead, Children's Perspectives on their Working Lives, Rädda Barnen, Stockholm, 1998; A. Swift, Working Children Get Organised, International Save the Children Alliance, London, 1999. However, many of the children and young people involved in the Global March believe that no child should work.

"We are against exploitation at work but we are for work with dignity with hours adapted so that we have time for education and leisure."[7]

Poverty creates a pool of children and families sufficiently desperate to be willing to take up hazardous or exploitative work.

EFFECTS ON SOCIETY

The effects on society of children working depend on the impacts on individual children. These vary according to the extent to which children suffer from immediate or long-term work-related health problems and the extent to which they miss out on education. The long-term costs to society of child labour have attracted little research. However, recent studies indicate that the costs of child labour-related injury in India are between 101 million and 2.43 billion US dollars per year (0.19 to 0.75 per cent of its gross domestic product) and, in the South African agricultural sector alone, 10 million US dollars.[8]

The costs of missed education (or limited learning) due to children's work have not been calculated. However, given the vital role of education in social and economic development, these costs are likely to be equally high.

Kerstin Hacker / Save The Children

Why do children work?

The reasons children work are often complex and context-specific. In this section, five major factors that lead to children working are considered: poverty; poor quality education; cultural and personal attitudes to children and work; willingness of some adults to exploit children; and limited enforcement of legislation.

POVERTY

Broadly speaking, poverty is the fundamental cause of child labour in the South.[9] Poverty creates a pool of children and families sufficiently desperate to be willing to take up hazardous or exploitative work. It also means that many families rely on their children's labour, rather than on hiring adult help. Poverty also puts education out of the reach of families who cannot afford the sometimes substantial costs of schooling.

7 This statement was developed at the First International Meeting of Working Children in Kundapur, India, 24 November to 8 December 1996.
8 P. Graitcer and L. Lerer, Child Labor and Health: Quantifying the Global Health Impacts of Child Labor, World Bank, cited in Ebdon (1999), see note 4.
9 In the North, a desire to earn money or learn skills is usually more significant.

Almost invariably, structural adjustment or other economic liberalisation programmes have increased inequality and have meant that the poorest families, particularly in urban areas, have become poorer still and increasingly reliant on their children to survive.

Children have always worked but the Structural Adjustment Programme has aggravated the necessity of work for all members of the family for collective survival.

The causes of poverty are numerous and often relate to long-standing inequalities in access to resources. In this section, three sets of factors that have exacerbated poverty and increased the need for children to work are discussed: contemporary macro-economic trends and policies; conflict; and the HIV/AIDS pandemic.

The dominant economic model of market liberalisation and reducing public expenditure has, in many countries, contributed to an increase in children working. Almost invariably, structural adjustment or other economic liberalisation programmes have increased inequality and have meant that the poorest families, particularly in urban areas, have become poorer still and increasingly reliant on their children to survive. These trends are visible in a variety of contexts, for example, African countries with heavy debt burdens and adjustment programmes, such as Tanzania, countries in transition from centrally planned to market economies, such as Mongolia, and countries that have pursued capital-intensive economic growth with relatively little attention to inequality, such as Brazil or Mexico. As one Nigerian observer puts it:

> *"Children have always worked but the Structural Adjustment Programme has aggravated the necessity of work for all members of the family for collective survival."*[10]

Although recent adjustment programmes seek to protect health and education budgets, social expenditure was often severely cut or capped during the 1980s and early 1990s. Many countries continue to cut social sector budgets, or to fund them at a level that cannot keep pace with population growth. This has led both to a decline in the quality of primary education - the only education most poor children receive - and to an increase in the costs to families of schooling. In numerous countries, school fees and other 'user charges', introduced in many countries on World Bank advice in the late 1980s and early 1990s, have put secondary and increasingly even primary education out of the reach of poor children. Families are often also expected to contribute to teachers' salaries, the upkeep of school buildings and teaching materials. On top of this, children may have to wear uniforms, provide all their books and, in some cases, even school furniture. The worldwide trend towards privatisation of education is thus a major cause for concern, and is likely to increase the numbers of children working full time.

10 S. Oloko, In-depth Country Report: Nigeria, International Working Group on Child Labour, Amsterdam, 1996.

Conflict and HIV/AIDS are having similar effects on child labour. Wherever adults die, are injured or are too sick to work, children have to work to survive. In many African countries, in particular, there has been a notable increase in the number of children being orphaned or living in child-headed households. Even with support from extended families, such children have to work to survive. A recent study in Rwanda showed that almost 20 per cent of children working on the streets of Kigali had lost one or both parents to conflict or HIV/AIDS.[11]

Jenny Matthews / Save The Children

A recent study in Rwanda showed that almost 20 per cent of children working on the streets of Kigali had lost one or both parents to conflict or HIV/AIDS.

POOR QUALITY EDUCATION

The quality of education has declined in many areas in recent years, as countries struggle to cope with increasing numbers of children and education budgets that are either in decline or cannot keep pace with population growth or high inflation. As a result, many schools are poorly equipped, class sizes are large (reaching 60-80 in many African countries), and teachers are often underpaid and unmotivated. Children in contexts as diverse as the Philippines, Bangladesh, Pakistan, Guatemala, Namibia and Ethiopia complain that teachers spend little time actually teaching but instead chat to colleagues, are drunk during school hours, sleep or simply do not come to class.[12] Furthermore, many children are dissuaded from school attendance by frequent use of corporal punishment.

Where rates of unemployment are high, many children and families are increasingly sceptical of the value of formal education in preparing for the future. As a result, families may choose to send some children to school and others to work, ensuring that children learn survival skills through working as well as, or instead of, attending school. In the words of a ten-year-old Senegalese shoe-shiner,

> *"I don't need to go to school. What can I learn there? I know children who went to school. Their family paid for the fees and uniforms and now they are educated. But you see them sitting around. Now they are useless to their families. They don't know anything about farming or trading or making money."*[13]

11 D. Sezikeye, Child Poverty: Street Children and Child Labour in Rwanda, Save the Children UK, Kigali, 1999.
12 Woodhead (1998), see note 7; Save the Children, Stitching Footballs: Voices of Children from Sialkot, Pakistan, Save the Children (UK), London/Islamabad, 1997; author observations, Namibia.
13 Cited in UNICEF, State of the World's Children, UNICEF, New York, 1998, p. 9.

Where formal education is widely seen to offer a way out of poverty, many families make enormous sacrifices to ensure their children attend school.

This said, it is important not to over-generalise. Many countries have seen rising school enrolments in recent years. Where formal education is widely seen to offer a way out of poverty, many families make enormous sacrifices to ensure their children attend school.

CULTURAL AND PERSONAL ATTITUDES

In all societies, learning how to undertake different kinds of work is an integral part of growing up. Domestic, agricultural or craft skills complement, and may be seen as more important than, those acquired through formal schooling. This is particularly the case with girls for whom domestic skills are essential for marriage, and in areas where crafts are passed down from generation to generation, or where there is one major source of livelihood, such as pastoralism. In most societies, all but elite children are expected to contribute economically to their families; thus, work is the norm, rather than the exception. In cultures in which it is shameful for women to work outside the home, and families cannot survive on one income, children are often expected to go out and work instead of their mothers.

Liba Taylor / Save The Children

Although many children are forced to work, many others want to work, for a variety of reasons. Some see it as the best option open to them. For others, working allows them to escape a difficult or violent home. For girls, paid work may free them from the drudgery of housework. For example, some Nepali girls view working in a carpet factory as preferable to the agricultural and domestic work they would have to do in their villages.[14] Other children value the chance to develop skills and experience of the world of work, or they want to earn money to support their families, and for their own use. For example, a recent study in the UK found that having their own money and developing skills for the future were important reasons why children work.[15] Throughout the world, children are increasingly exposed to advertising, and want their own money to spend on items that are seen as essential among their peer group.[16]

WILLINGNESS TO EXPLOIT CHEAP, DOCILE LABOUR

North and South, children are generally paid less than adult workers simply because they are young, whether or not they are equally productive. Children, who are socialised to respect and obey adults, are also less likely to demand higher wages or better working conditions. As a result,

14 V. Johnson, J. Hill and E. Ivan-Smith, Listening to Smaller Voices: Children in an Environment of Change, Action Aid, London, 1995.
15 Save the Children, 'Children's Perspectives on Work' in Pettitt (1998), see note 3.
16 B. White, 1996, 'Globalisation and the Child Labour Problem', Journal of International Development, Vol. 8.

mployers are often keen to take on child workers. In some cases, such as factory vork and prostitution in South-East Asia, and domestic work in West Africa, hildren are actively recruited, and often engaged with false promises of education nd light work. In certain industries involving very fine work, such as carpet nanufacture or ceramic painting, it is often argued that only children's 'nimble ingers' are small enough to do the work. However, this argument is false and dults have been shown to be equally able to undertake very fine work.

Employers often hold the key to ensuring that work is beneficial to children, rather than harmful, and should be seen as important stakeholders and partners in action on child labour.

Vhile many employers wilfully exploit children, not all do. Some ensure that hildren work in safe conditions or are able to attend school. Many employers vould argue that they are helping children by giving them a job. Nevertheless, nany child workers, like their adult counterparts, receive very low pay and work n dangerous conditions. Employers often hold the key to ensuring that work is eneficial to children, rather than harmful, and should be seen as important takeholders and partners in action on child labour.

IMITED LAW ENFORCEMENT

ll countries have legislation that sets minimum ages for work and outlaws certain orms of child labour. Many are signatories to international conventions with dditional provisions. However, legislation is frequently not enforced, because there s little local acceptance of its provisions and labour inspectorates are often over-tretched. Also, where rates of pay for labour inspectors are low, some are tempted o supplement their salaries through bribes to ignore breaches of the law. Even vhere employers are prosecuted, low fines or corruption within the judicial system an mean that legislation is ineffective as a deterrent to the abuse of child workers.

Tackling child labour - effective and child centred approaches

'he previous section outlined the main principles of a child-rights approach to hild labour. In this section, we examine the kinds of action that are necessary to radicate harmful child labour, to ensure that all children have access to a elevant education, and that any work they do contributes to their development nd well-being. Where possible, these are illustrated with examples from Save the Children's experience, or that of our partner organisations.

Regulation of the international economic system to promote stability and to underpin equitable and inclusive economic development is rarely discussed in relation to child labour, but is fundamental.

POVERTY REDUCTION

While poverty reduction alone will not eliminate harmful child labour, it is essential to eradicate the pool of children and families desperate enough to take up hazardous or exploitative work. It will require action at local, national and international levels. Strengthening livelihoods by increasing the access of the poor to resources is vital. Effective measures include: redistribution of land; improved access to credit and savings facilities; and job-creation programmes, so that poor people benefit from economic growth.

Strong safety nets and welfare measures that support rather than bypass the poorest families and children are also critical. Regulation of the international economic system to promote stability and to underpin equitable and inclusive economic development is rarely discussed in relation to child labour, but is fundamental.

Working to reduce poverty

Save the Children works to reduce poverty at local, national and international levels. Projects at local level include credit and savings programmes which in Bangladesh and Vietnam have reduced the numbers of children entering hazardous work and have increased children's school attendance.[17] Save the Children works with national anti-poverty programmes in various countries including Mongolia and Mali to ensure that poor and marginalised children benefit. Save the Children staff in countries as diverse as Ethiopia, Vietnam and El Salvador meet regularly with representatives of government, the World Bank, the United Nations Development Programme and other key donors to discuss key issues affecting children, including mainstream economic and social policies, and to promote approaches that enhance the well-being of poor children, including child workers.

EDUCATI ON

Ensuring that all children have access to free, good quality and relevant education would reduce children's involvement in harmful work, and contribute to social and economic development. Changes to some education systems so that children can combine safe work with education (for example by changing school schedules so they accommodate working patterns) may be necessary. One example is

17 R.Marcus, with B. Porter and C. Harper 'Money Matters: understanding microfinance', Working Paper 19, Save the Children UK, London, 1999.

:scuela Nueva, a government programme in Colombia, discussed in the box ›elow. In the meantime, formal or non-formal education programmes which nable working children (or formerly working children) to catch up on missed ducation and to enter or re-enter the formal system have an important role o play.

For many African and Latin American countries, in particular, debt relief linked to poverty reduction and investment in social services is vital.

Escuela Nueva

The Escuela Nueva (new school) programme in rural Colombia has adapted government schools in several ways so they both meet rural children's needs more effectively and offer them a better quality education. Children study in multi-grade classes at their own pace, enabling them to combine education and seasonal agricultural work that involves their entire families, and to progress to higher grades as they are ready to do so. Escuela Nueva has been successful in keeping 80 per cent of children in coffee-growing areas in school, and has been extended to secondary schools. Evaluations show that school drop-out and grade repetition have been much reduced, that teachers' job satisfaction has improved and that the quality of education in isolated rural areas has improved.[18]

undamentally, transforming education requires substantial financial investment. Vhile the primary responsibility lies with Southern governments, donors and nternational financial institutions such as the World Bank, the International Monetary Fund and regional development banks have an important role to play. or many African and Latin American countries, in particular, debt relief linked › poverty reduction and investment in social services is vital. For example:

"In Tanzania, households currently finance almost one-third of recurrent spending on education. This represents an enormous drain on household budgets ... but is equivalent to only 3 per cent of the resources currently spent on debt servicing."[19]

:HANGING ATTITUDES AND RAISING AWARENESS

ocal and national campaigns to change attitudes to working children, and ommunity mobilisation against the exploitation of children also play an nportant role in reducing harmful child labour. For example, in Cambodia,

M.C. Salazar and W.A. Glasinovich, Better Schools, Less Child Work: child work and education in Brazil, Colombia, Ecuador, Guatemala and Peru, UNICEF, ICDC, Florence, 1996.
Oxfam International, Education Now: Breaking the Cycle of Poverty, Oxfam UK, Oxford, 1999, p. 159.

many children and young people are promised good jobs and education by labou[r] recruiters who then sell them into prostitution. Save the Children is working with the Ministry of Labour and Social Welfare to raise awareness in communities about the realities of children's lives once they leave their villages. In combinatio[n] with skills training, this programme has helped over 300 children avoid recruitment into prostitution.

Without viable economic alternatives, there is a risk that former child workers will turn to other, potentially worse, forms of work. The most appropriate measures to prevent this will depend on the situation.

PHASING OUT CHILD LABOUR RESPONSIBLY

Many multinational companies are now taking steps to ensure that no children are involved in the production of the goods they trade. The new ILO Convention will give a fresh impetus for removing children from harmful work. Without viable economic alternatives, there is a risk that former child workers will turn to other, potentially worse, forms of work. The most appropriate measures to prevent this will depend on the situation but include:

- offering children's jobs to unemployed family members;
- skills training for adults and older children;
- credit and savings programmes;
- reducing hazards;
- ensuring children are only involved in light, safe work and are able to attend school.

Work with the football industry in Pakistan

Save the Children has been working with the football industry in Pakistan for several years to phase out child labour responsibly. In response to consumer pressure, many international companies wanted their Pakistani suppliers to stop children stitching footballs immediately. Save the Children warned that because most children stitch because their families need the money, there was a serious risk that children would take up more dangerous work, such as making bricks or surgical instruments. We therefore played a key role in developing a programme that safeguards family incomes through credit and savings schemes and improves the quality of schools so they are more relevant and attractive to children.

SUPPORTING WORKING CHILDREN'S OWN INITIATIVES

Working children's and youth organisations have grown up over the last 20 years in various African, Asian and Latin American countries. These provide a forum for working children to share experiences and support one another. Most are linked to non-governmental organisations that help children and young people access literacy classes or savings schemes. Some working children's organisations have also pressured employers for better conditions. As a young Senegalese housemaid explains:

Working children's and youth organisations provide a forum for working children to share experiences and support one another.

"*We have many problems with our employers, especially in my work as a housemaid. Sometimes they don't pay us for two or three months. If we protest, sometimes they beat us. Also if you accidentally break something they want you to pay for it. If you are sick, there is no health insurance ... It was because of these types of problems that we decided to [get] organised ... For example, we have set up our own health care fund. We have also arranged for schooling in the evening when we are not working ... There are certain things our employers wouldn't dare to do now.*"[20]

Although such organisations tend to recruit children working in the urban informal sector, the hours and conditions of which are the most flexible, this is not always so. Bhima Sangha, a movement of working children in southern India, has managed to organise children working in rural areas and those working in very difficult conditions in urban areas (for example, in hotels and restaurants where they are constantly on call). Both rural and urban child workers have been helped to reduce their hours and to join night classes.

Sarah Muscroft / Save The Children

Supporting these organisations is a practical way to help reduce children's involvement in hazardous and exploitative work, and to increase their access to relevant education. Save the Children is supporting working

20 Dibou Faye, cited in Save the Children,, Save the Children Communications Toolkit, Briefing on Child Labour, Save the Children, London, 1997.

children's organisations in Latin America, India, West Africa, and Mongolia, among other countries, all of which help children negotiate better working conditions or time off to study. They have also helped sensitise the authorities to the problems faced by working children.

Child labour policy has tended to be more concerned with a grand vision of a child labour-free world than with the realities of particular societies, cultures and local labour markets.

ENSURING THAT CHILD LABOUR POLICY AND PROGRAMMES ARE GROUNDED IN REALITY

Child labour policy has tended to be more concerned with a grand vision of a child labour-free world than with the realities of particular societies, cultures and local labour markets. To translate this vision into practice, policies and programmes must be based on thorough understanding of specific local conditions. This requires rigorous research and the greatly enhanced involvement of key stakeholders in developing programmes and policies. There is growing acceptance of the principle that working children and their families are stakeholders with important contributions to make. However, it is still rare that programme designers seek their participation.

Jenny Matthews / Save The Children

At policy level, the active involvement of working children and their families lags behind recognition of their insights. The various ways of promoting their participation include local, national and international consultations, and direct involvement in national planning. For example, in Senegal, the national working children's movement is part of a joint government and ILO initiative which has developed, and is now implementing, a national child labour strategy.

Given the diversity of children's work, it is important that policy draws on insights from a range of child workers, not simply those who are the best organised or most accessible to policy-makers. Non-governmental organisations, trade unions and other organisations that work with working children can play an important role in creating opportunities for dialogue with policy-makers.

Conclusions

The current international focus on child labour presents an important opportunity to mobilise resources, political will and action on child labour. Ensuring that no child's future is jeopardised by missing out on education or by exposure to hazards through work is undoubtedly a daunting task. It can, however, be achieved through a combination of the measures outlined above. The precise combination of measures will depend on local circumstances, and as far as possible, policies and programmes should be tailored accordingly.

Like other complex social problems, tackling child labour is often difficult. Its causes are often interlinked and require action at local, national and international levels.

Political will, and financial commitment in both the South and North are essential if harmful child labour is to be eliminated. Like other complex social problems, tackling child labour is often difficult. Its causes are often interlinked and require action at local, national and international levels. This will not be cheap. However, the costs of not eliminating harmful child labour both to individual children and to society - a continued cycle of poverty, ill-health, exploitation and social exclusion - are unacceptable. Ending harmful child labour, and ensuring that all children, whether or not they work, receive a good quality, relevant education, are important ways of reducing the poverty cycle and ultimately of creating a fairer world. Are we ready to take up the challenge?

PART III
Country Analysis

'People paint **young people** *as being a bad lot, but we've got* **so** *much to* **give**. *There'll be a lot more* **co-operation** *if the authorities give young people responsibility and* **listen** *to them. After all we are the* **next generation**'.

Joanne, age 14 - Newcastle, UK

Chapter 5

Country Reports

The reality against the rhetoric

This section contains country reports from 25 of the 26 members of the International Save the Children Alliance.

(The Faroe Islands, a protectorate of Denmark, is covered by the report prepared by Save the Children Denmark.)

Together, these reports comprise a wide-ranging assessment of the actuality of children's rights and welfare in a diverse range of countries, including industrialised, transitional and developing economies.

Approaches to children's rights, to the work of non-governmental organisations (NGOs) and to reporting, differ widely among the member countries of the International Save the Children Alliance. Equally, there are variations in the quantity and quality of detailed information readily available in each country. This has determined, to a certain extent, the nature and focus of each report. However, they all follow the same broad outline:

- a brief overview of the status of the CRC and government action in each country, noting general achievements;
- an assessment of the reality for children in each country by looking at four key issues:
    - sexual exploitation;
    - juvenile justice;
    - displacement;
    - education.

(Many of the original reports have had to be condensed for the purposes of this publication. Full versions are available upon request from individual members together with details of bibliographies and collaborating agencies. Contact details for each member can be found in Annex Two.)

In each of the reports the aim is the same - to set the situation on the ground in each country against the provisions of the Convention. They highlight the key points in relation to the CRC in general and to each of the four specific issues. They are necessarily subjective and Save the Children member organisations have sought to identify the key issues and areas of concern that they consider demand attention. Similarly, in making recommendations, they do not aim to provide a blueprint for policy but to provide starting points for action in future policy and practice. It should also be noted that some of the information contained in the country reports regarding government legislation may have changed since the time of going to print.

Four key issues

One of the strengths of the Convention is that it is so comprehensive and covers the full range of an individual's rights. However, it is not possible here to cover the concerns of each of the articles for each country. For the purpose of the country reports, four issues have been selected for reasons of expediency alone and not because these issues are seen as more or less important than any of the other areas the Convention covers.

A summary of the Convention's principal provisions relevant to each of the issues being considered is provided below. A full copy of the UN Convention on the Rights of the Child can be found in Annex One.

SEXUAL EXPLOITATION

Article 34

The child's right to protection from sexual exploitation and abuse, including prostitution and involvement in pornography.

Article 35 Sale, trafficking and abduction

The State's obligation to make every effort to prevent the sale, trafficking and abduction of children.

JUVENILE JUSTICE

Article 40 Administration of juvenile justice

The right of children alleged or recognised as having committed an offence to respect for their human rights and, in particular, to benefit from all aspects of the due process of the law, including legal or other assistance in preparing and presenting their defence. The principle that recourse to judicial proceedings and institutional placements should be avoided wherever possible and appropriate.

Article 41 Respect for existing standards

The principle that if any standards set in national law or other applicable international instruments are higher than those of this Convention, it is the higher standard that applies.

DISPLACEMENT

Article 2 - Non-discrimination

The principle that all rights apply to all children without exception, and the State's obligation to protect children from any form of discrimination. The State must not violate any right, and must take positive action to promote them all.

Article 9 - Separation from parents

The child's right to live with his or her parents unless this is deemed incompatible with his or her best interests; the right to maintain contact with both parents if separated from one or both; the duties of States in cases where such separation results from the State action.

Article 10 - Family reunification

The right of children and their parents to leave any country and to enter their own in order to be reunited or to maintain the child-parent relationship.

Article 20 - Protection of children without families

The State's obligation to provide special protection for children deprived of their family environment and to ensure that appropriate alternative family care or institutional placement is made available to them, taking into account the child's cultural background.

Article 22 - Refugee children

Special protection to be granted to children who are refugees or seeking refugee status and the State's obligation to co-operate with competent organisations providing such protection and assistance.

EDUCATION

Article 28 - Education

The child's right to education and the State's duty to ensure that primary education at least is made free and compulsory. Administration of school discipline is to reflect the child's human dignity. Emphasis is laid on the need for international co-operation to ensure this right.

Article 29 Aims of education
The State's recognition that education should be directed at developing the child's personality and talents, preparing the child for active life as an adult, fostering respect for the child's own cultural and national identity and those of others.

Save The Children

*'It's my **right** to live in **safety**'.*

Milad Abou Kharroub, age 17 - Lebanon

Australia

THE AUSTRALIAN GOVERNMENT AND THE CRC

The Australian Government ratified the Convention on the Rights of the Child in December 1990, just over a year after it was adopted by the General Assembly of the United Nations.

The Convention, however, is not automatically part of Australian law. For Australian courts and other decision-makers, the Convention will not be legally binding, in the strict sense, until an Act of the Australian Parliament enacts the Convention into law. The Government has so far chosen to ignore the obvious need for national legislation and national mechanisms to make the Convention effective in Australia. The failure to do this represents a broken promise by the Government to ensure Australia's compliance with the Convention.

Australia's federal structure, with eight state and territory governments and a national government, is a major factor affecting Australia's approach to implementation of the Convention. While the national government should be leading the way and ensuring uniform standards, state governments also have a major role to play in protecting and promoting children's rights. The provision of most children's services is the responsibility of States and Territories. However, no agencies in Australia have been given the authority, explicit role or resources to monitor Australia's compliance with the Convention in any effective way. There is no Minister for Children, or parliamentary committee focused on children.

The Australian Government was extremely late in submitting its report to the UN Committee on the Rights of the Child and, more importantly, failed to conduct a proper process of community consultation. This provoked an alternative report involving 200 individuals representing over 100 Australian non-governmental organisations.

Although deciding not to incorporate the Convention on the Rights of the Child formally into national law, Australia has already established a system of universal education that goes well beyond the minimum set by the Convention. In addition to this, a social security system exists that has long recognised the cost of child-rearing and the desirability of protecting families with children. Australia has developed an advanced health system and provides basic guarantees of access through Medicare.
The universal health system has helped Australia to reduce child mortality rates and hospitals recognise the child's right not to be separated from parents.

Australia has established a Children's Court and juvenile justice system, which deals with children's offences in markedly different ways from those of adults. More recently, Australia has taken steps to protect children from genital mutilation, and children of other countries from sexual exploitation by Australians travelling overseas. These measures have been undertaken as part of Australia's effort to implement the CRC.

Australia's long history of displacement, murder, exploitation, discrimination and the forced separation of indigenous children from their families has placed indigenous children in the most disadvantaged position. The legacy of these practices continues to impact today on many Aboriginal and Torres Strait Islanders.

Australian governments have made little effort to publicise the Convention or to promote its aims and objectives. The Federal Government has established no mechanism to implement the Convention or monitor its observance. There is no national agenda or plan of action for children and no strategy to ensure that children can exercise and enjoy the rights enshrined in the Convention. Young people and their advocates are largely excluded from policy planning, service delivery and monitoring of relevant areas of government.

There is mounting concern about:

- abuses in the care system and the failure of authorities to exercise their duty of care;
- paedophilia and the operation of paedophile rings;
- denial of the rights of indigenous young people in the legal and welfare systems;
- mandatory sentencing of children in the Northern Territory and Western Australia;
- lack of services for particular groups of children and denial of rights to children of asylum-seekers;
- youth homelessness and a rise in youth suicides;
- youth unemployment;
- declining standards in education;
- child poverty and homelessness.

Action is required to enact specific legislation to implement the Convention, create a Federal Commissioner for Children and develop and adopt a National Agenda for children.

The reality *against* the rhetoric

Sexual exploitation

The latest figures as identified by ECPAT (the international body combating child prostitution and trafficking) determined that 3,733 children are engaged in commercial sexual activities. The highest number of reported cases comes from Victoria, followed by New South Wales then South Australia. The majority of cases involved young persons aged 16 to 17 years, but a disturbing finding was the number of 10 to 12 year olds and some under the age of 10 who were reported as participants in commercial sex work. Children were found to engage in commercial sex activities to meet their basic life needs, such as accommodation, food, drugs, clothing and money to purchase goods and services.

It has been difficult to determine whether the number is increasing or decreasing, although anecdotal reports from sex worker organisations suggest that the numbers are increasing. The risk factors that have been identified include homelessness, poverty, unemployment, histories of abuse, dysfunctional family backgrounds, drug use, lack of self-esteem, isolation and marginalisation.

The dangers that young people face in commercial sex work are extreme and include drug use, threat of physical violence, sexual health risks, lack of respect for others and a lack of confidence in authority. To address the issue of sexual exploitation it is necessary to focus on the risk factors that lead children to engage in commercial sex work.

GOVERNMENT ACTION AND POLICY

Child pornography appears to be widespread. Developments in technology, such as the Internet, have made the distribution and dissemination of child pornography much easier and less detectable than in the past. The vast majority of material does not seem to be professionally produced. The Federal Government has made a strong commitment to the policing of the Internet and has proposed legislation to further that aim (Australian Broadcasting Services Amendment Bill to come into effect on 1 January 2000).

Evidence of Australians engaging in child sex tourism resulted in the Crimes (Child Sex Tourism) Amendment Act 1994. This has lead to six convictions. In New South Wales, the Wood Royal Commission focused the nation on the significant problem of paedophilia. The Commission's report saw significant developments in New South Wales with the establishment of a Child Commissioner. The Federal Government, in compliance with the Declaration and Agenda for Action developed at the World Congress Against Commercial Sexual Exploitation of Children, held in Stockholm in 1996, commissioned the Australian Institute of Criminology to conduct a review of laws, programmes and policies relating to the commercial sexual exploitation of children in Australia and to develop a national plan.

There is little evidence to suggest that children are trafficked to Australia for the purposes of commercial sexual exploitation, although this is very difficult to measure. However, anecdotal evidence suggests that children are being sponsored from the Pacific, Asia and Africa. The transactions can include bribery and abduction, false identification and documentation, sham marriages and adoptions, illegal immigration, violence and bonded labour.

The laws relating to sexual exploitation are complicated by the Australian federal structure. In some states, there is a mixture of new and old laws with some dating back to nineteenth-century imperial law. The Model Criminal Code Officers' Committee, convened by the Attorney-Generals in each state, has acknowledged the need for uniform law in relation to the protection of children from sexual abuse and exploitation. There is no uniformity in relation to age of consent law in Australia and there is differential treatment between girls and boys.

Currently, in the Northern Territory, it is an offence for a person under the age of 18 years to offer or provide sexual services for payment or reward. This is in clear contravention of Article 34 of the CRC. Having signed the Declaration and Agenda for Action, the Australian Government has an obligation to develop or strengthen and implement national laws, policies and programmes that protect victims of commercial sexual exploitation from being penalised as criminals.

A holistic response to sexual exploitation must include increased services for at-risk children, including street work programmes targeted at children involved in, or at risk of, commercial sexual activity, the provision of secure, accessible and appropriate accommodation, adequate and accessible income support and increased community awareness.

RECOMMENDATIONS

- **Uniform age of consent** - Uniform laws on age of consent for males and females across all Australian jurisdictions.
- **Decriminalise prostitution** - Uniform decriminalisation of prostitution across all Australian jurisdictions.
- **Decriminalisation of loitering** - Decriminalisation of the loitering laws to prevent the criminalisation of children on the street.
- **Protection of child witnesses** - The protection of child witnesses from being questioned about their sexual reputation in child sex tourism proceedings.
- **Research and programme development** - A research agenda to identify and prioritise topics such an effective programme provision.

Juvenile justice

Despite the public's perception that youth crime is increasing, the level of children's appearance before a court has remained stable for the last 15 years. At most, 2 per cent of young people aged between 10 and 17 encounter the juvenile justice system. Community concerns have led to the Government becoming more punitive with children. In all jurisdictions, children tend to commit non-violent offences such as breaking and entering, motor vehicle theft and offences against public order. Further, contrary to public opinion, seven out of ten offenders do not reappear before the court. A recent survey of young people found that a significant proportion of juvenile crime was committed to supplement income or obtain money.

GOVERNMENT ACTION AND POLICY

Pursuant to international law, the Federal Government has set down principles for the treatment of young suspects and offenders and to develop a separate juvenile justice system.

Article 40.3(a) - the age of criminal responsibility

The age of criminal responsibility is ten under federal law and in all other jurisdictions except Tasmania and the Australian Capital Territory (ACT) where the threshold is seven and eight respectively. There is a conclusive presumption that a child under the age of ten cannot be found guilty of an offence. In addition to the statutory minimum age there is a legal presumption known as doli incapax. This common-law principle presumes that a child under the age of 14 does not know that his or her conduct was wrong unless the contrary is proved.

In Victoria, Northern Territory, Tasmania and Queensland, children are dealt with in the adult criminal system once they turn 17. In all other states, in the ACT and under federal law, all children are juveniles for the purposes of criminal law until they reach the age of 18.

The Australian juvenile justice system draws upon the welfare model, seeking rehabilitation of the offender, and the justice model, which seeks due process and accountability. More recently, young people suspected of offences are increasingly being diverted from formal court adjudication to alternative programmes.
In addition, cautioning a minor or a first-time offender is now an important feature of most Australian juvenile justice systems. In Queensland, Western Australia, South Australia and New South Wales legislation regulates cautioning. However, it has been discovered that some children do not receive the benefit of cautioning at the same rate as the general population. For example, in 1994-95 only 11.3 per cent of Aboriginal juvenile alleged offenders in Victoria received formal cautions compared with 35.65 per cent of non-Aboriginal juveniles.

Another development in the juvenile justice system is family conferencing, which has the great advantage of allowing the child to participate. However, there have been concerns raised about conferencing, including the extent of police involvement, the child's lack of access to legal advice and the severity of penalties. Furthermore, a conference where large numbers are involved is as intimidating as a courtroom.

Article 37 (b) - detention must be used only as a measure of last resort and for the shortest appropriate period of time

Rates of juvenile justice detention are above the level that could be justified as a measure of last resort. There are reported cases of children being held in detention with adults and many cells lack privacy, natural light and proper ventilation. In remote areas, children can be detained for long periods in places which are not easily accessible to family members.

A serious problem is the high proportion of Aboriginal children in custody, which suggests problems within the police forces and the justice system in relation to racism against the Aboriginal community.

One of the greatest concerns in relation to breaches of the Convention is the mandatory detention provisions in Western Australia and Northern Territory, introduced in 1996. In the Northern Territory, if a child is found guilty of more than one property offence he or she receives mandatory imprisonment. One of the most serious aspects of these provisions is that they apply regardless of how minor the second property offence may be. At the end of 1996, the rate of persons aged 10 to 17 in juvenile corrective institutions was 68.8 per 100,000 in the Northern Territory compared with 14.9 in Victoria.

In Western Australia, legislation provides that when convicted for a third time, children must be sentenced to a minimum of 12 months' imprisonment or detention. The 'three strikes and you're in' legislation has attracted adverse comment from the President of the Western Australian Children's Court.

The Northern Territory and Western Australian laws breach a number of international human rights standards, including Articles 40 and 37 of the Convention on the Rights of the Child. Further, the Convention requires that sentences be reviewable by a higher or appellate court.

Article 37 (c) - the right of children deprived of liberty to be treated with humanity and to respect their dignity

Children who are refused bail are remanded in custody until their case comes before a court. The states and territories differ in their treatment of children on remand. In Victoria, children remanded in custody must be placed in a remand centre unless specified otherwise in regulations. Therefore children living in country or remote areas are held in police cells, although a child has a statutory right to be detained separately from adults. In Western Australia, police must take into consideration the distance travelled, conditions at the lock-up, the availability of escort staff and the need for family support before sending a child to a detention centre.

Children living in remote and rural areas are often remanded in detention centres hundreds of kilometres from their homes, disrupting schooling and family relations. These problems affect indigenous children in particular.

Article 15 and 16 - the right to freedom of association, to privacy and respect for family life

It has been reported that young people are regularly harassed by police when associating in public spaces. The harassment was reported to be verbal and physical. These problems have been exacerbated in more recent times when private security guards were given legislative authority to issue notices excluding people causing a public nuisance from retail centres for up to ten days. Thus, if a young person enters the area in breach of the notice, he or she commits an offence.

In a number of jurisdictions, police have the power to remove children from public spaces if they are considered at risk of offending although they are not suspected of illegal activity.

RECOMMENDATIONS

- **National standards for juvenile justice** - Development of national standards for juvenile justice to reflect Australia's international commitments and ensure a proper balance between rehabilitation, deterrence and due process.
- **Uniform age of criminal responsibility** - For the Federal Government to continue their work in creating a uniform age of criminal responsibility across all Australian jurisdictions.
- **Established age of majority under criminal law** - The age at which a child reaches adulthood for the purposes of criminal law should be 18 years.
- **Uniform legislation on cautioning** - Uniform rules regarding cautioning across all Australian jurisdictions.
- **Abolition of mandatory imprisonment** - Mandatory imprisonment rules, as they apply in the Northern Territory and Western Australia, should be abolished.
- **Improved custodial facilities** - Children being held in custody should be held in juvenile facilities within close proximity to their families.
- **Uniform powers of the police** - Uniform laws regarding police powers in relation to children and consideration of the degree of police harassment of juveniles.

Displacement

The number of people applying for protection visas or refugee status in Australia is currently around 10,000. In relation to children who are asylum-seekers and refugees, the Australian Government is falling short of meeting its obligations as articulated in the Convention on the Rights of the Child and, it could be argued, is in breach of the Convention.

GOVERNMENT ACTION AND POLICY

During the determination process, applicants are referred to as asylum-seekers. Once status is conferred, they can be legally referred to as refugees. The majority of people seeking asylum enter with a valid visa. They are permitted to remain in the country while their applications are being considered. Others arrive without adequate documents and are likely to be detained for the duration of the determination process. The rights of asylum-seekers differ for these two groups.

Those living in the community are able to seek employment only if they apply for refugee status within 45 days of their arrival. Similarly they can only receive medical benefits if they apply for refugee status within 45 days. They are then only able to seek assistance under the Asylum Seekers Assistance Scheme (ASAS) after a six month wait. If a person appeals against a negative decision they are ineligible for ASAS, however, they have the right to appeal to a negative decision at the Refugee Review Tribunal (RRT). Those people who fall into the higher needs/vulnerable groups, may also receive ASAS, while their cases are being assessed by the RRT.

At the present time the majority of asylum-seekers are ineligible for any financial services, either because they have been in the country for less than six months or because their cases are before the RRT. The children may also be traumatised by living with parents who are unable to provide support for them and they are often living without adequate care. The current system does not comply with the obligations as set out in the Convention of the Rights of the Child. This includes contravention of Articles 2, 3, 6, 2, 24 and 26.

Those in detention fare even worse. Although measures have been introduced to speed up determination of cases, asylum-seekers are being held in detention for periods of over one year. Although the Australian Government altered legislation to allow for the release of children and victims of torture, this does not extend to the parents or caregivers of these children. Some children in Australia have been detained for up to six months and there have been cases in the last ten years where children were detained for up to four years.

Opportunities for children to be taken outside the detention centres for education or recreation have varied. There have been extensive periods in all centres where children have not been offered any recreational activities and were not taken outside the centre.

The majority of children who are asylum-seekers are accompanied by a parent or caregiver but there is a significant number of unaccompanied minors. Although the Minister for Immigration is the legal guardian for all unaccompanied minors, it is rare for this responsibility to be approached in a proactive manner. The issue of guardianship of unaccompanied minors is usually only addressed after another agency has identified a child as being at risk of neglect or abuse. This has led to instances of children under the age of 14 being detained.

Individual claims of a child, as part of a family application for refugee status, will rarely be considered within a claim for refugee status. In some cases this would lead to the child fitting within the definition of refugee, thus conferring refugee status on the entire family. The Department for Immigration and Multicultural Affairs is working on the development of guidelines to deal with instances of child claimants.

Whilst it is common in many Western countries to provide legal assistance to asylum-seekers as a matter of course, Australia does not provide adequate opportunity for representation. Although assistance is provided by Legal Aid and Community Legal Centres, their funding has been cut severely which limits access to representation in the determination process.

RECOMMENDATIONS

- **Welfare assistance** - Provision of means-tested welfare assistance to asylum-seeking families with children.
- **Medical care** - Access to medical care.
- **Release of children and their families in detention** - Release from detention centres for children and their caregivers and access to welfare.
- **Access to education in detention** - While in detention there must be access to education and leisure activities.
- **Legal representation for unaccompanied minors** - In cases of unaccompanied children, a suitable adult must be appointed to take responsibility for ensuring that the child's legal and welfare needs are met.

Education

Throughout Australia schooling is compulsory between the ages of six and 16 (up to 15 in Tasmania). On completion of compulsory schooling, students can elect to continue their secondary education, or undertake vocational training. In 1997, there were 3,171,624 full-time students attending Australian schools.

There has been a reduction in spending on schools in Australia relative to other comparative countries. This has lead to an increase in class size and produced greater inequities between schools. Although education in Australia is notionally free and universal, there are charges for books and school activities. Due to the remote location of many Aboriginal children, their educational opportunities can be limited.

GOVERNMENT ACTION AND POLICY

Article 12- the right to be listened to and taken seriously

The principle that children are entitled to express their views on all matters of concern to them has not been incorporated into the educational system. Children should be encouraged to participate in school decision-making processes and in school dispute resolution.

A national survey of young people suspended or expelled suggested that many students are not told of their rights during disciplinary processes. They are also not informed about the ways to challenge certain decisions.

Article 28 -the right of all children to education on the basis of equality of opportunity

A range of inequalities exist within the Australian education system. Principally these inequalities are experienced by Aboriginal and Torres Strait Islander children, children from a non-English speaking background, disabled children, those from rural and remote areas and those living in poverty. Aboriginal children, in particular, do not always have access to education beyond primary school and finish primary school with only year three achievement levels. The education outcomes for girls in these groups are unacceptably lower than the outcomes for the total student population. Although there have been improvements in access to education for Aboriginal children, there remains gaps in the educational outcomes for the indigenous population of Australia. Children living in remote areas experience a lack of opportunities, such as limited subject choice, non-availability of the final years of secondary school and a high staff turnover.

In 1997, the Federal Minster for Schools stated that 30 per cent of young Australian teenagers cannot read properly and that there has been no improvement in literacy standards in the past twenty years. In March it was agreed that a national literacy and numeracy plan be instituted to ensure that children can read, write and spell adequately by their fourth year of school.

Financial constraints within the family often hinder children from receiving education. The Government instituted a programme to identify and support children at risk of dropping out of education. Unfortunately, this programme was wound up in December 1996. There are, however, a number of programmes in schools throughout Australia designed to address some of the health and nutritional needs of children from poor families.

Article 23(3) of the Convention on the Rights of the Child states that children with a disability must be provided with effective access to education to achieve the fullest social integration and individual development. In 1995 there were 74,315 children with disabilities in Australian schools. Families attempting to enrol disabled children in mainstream education, however, face significant barriers in addition to a lack of resources to accommodate the special needs of these children. This is highlighted by the fact that the third most common complaint to the Disability Discrimination Commissioner is access to education, which raises questions of Australia's compliance with Article 23(3).

Truancy has been considered a serious problem in Australian schools; however, there is no aggregate Australian data on school attendance. Recent state and national reports highlight the fact that truancy is widespread and is not well documented. In 1996, analysis of Tasmanian schools reveal that 19.25 per cent students were absent from school. There is substantial evidence to suggest that programmes to deal with truancy are under-resourced. Some states have acted to reduce truancy. In Western Australia, for example, the Government has considered introducing a system whereby parents can be fined if they do not ensure that their children attend school.

RECOMMENDATIONS

- **Training in the CRC** - The Government should encourage the inclusion of the CRC in training programmes for teachers and other professionals working with children.
- **Child participation in the decision-making** - Children should be encouraged to participate in school decision-making processes and dispute resolution.
- **Programmes for children at risk and drop-outs** - Programmes to identify and support at-risk and disadvantaged students and encourage their continued participation in education should be developed. Additional funding needs to be put into truancy programmes. Teachers and school counsellors should receive training in identifying children at risk of dropping out of school and referring them to appropriate government and non-government support services.
- **Disability training** - Each state and territory education department should ensure that all teaching staff and school administrators are trained in disability education, disability discrimination laws and obligations, and how to meet the educational and social development needs of students with disabilities. In addition, programmes designed to assist disabled children to enter mainstream schooling need to be sufficiently funded.
- **Culturally relevant curricula for Aboriginal children** - The education of Aboriginal children must be formally addressed by Government and culturally relevant programmes introduced.
- **Rural Children** - Improvements in access to education and increases in choices for children living in rural and remote areas.

*'Children have the **right** to go to school, and no one is **allowed** to lift a finger **against** other people'.*

Shane, age 13 - Kwazulu-Natal, South Africa

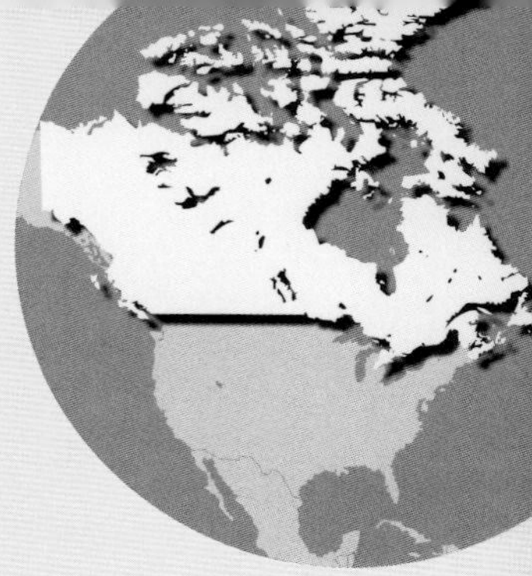

Canada

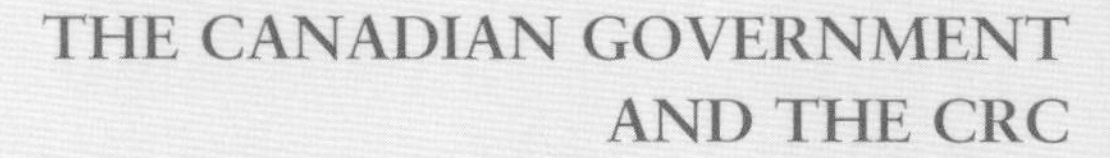

THE CANADIAN GOVERNMENT AND THE CRC

Canada ratified the CRC in December 1991 with two reservations to Articles 21 and 37. Reservations refer to two areas: 1) to ensure that, in determining the custodial arrangements for a young offender, the well-being of other young offenders and the safety of the public may be taken into account and 2) to ensure that the rights of Aboriginal children (under Articles 4 and 30) are not infringed upon circumstances.

The Government of Canada established the Children's Bureau under the Ministry of Health and Welfare Canada to ensure consistency and provide co-ordination for federal, provincial and territorial programmes and policies concerning children. The Bureau initiated two major programmes. In 1992 'Brighter Futures: Canada's Action Plan for Children' was published, listing over 30 steps and programmes to address the well-being of children. In 1993 the second major initiative, Child Tax Benefit, consolidated three existing programmes and represented an increase of $2.1 billion in federal government support for children and families.

The Human Rights Directorate of Multiculturalism and Citizenship Canada were funded to disseminate information about the CRC. The Directorate worked with schools, health-care and youth programmes, human rights commissions, non-governmental organisations (NGOs) and other federal departments to implement a national strategy. The Directorate also provided funding for NGOs, including Save the Children, to develop educational initiatives related to the Convention.

Canada's first report, which was submitted to the UN Committee on the Rights of the Child in May 1994, consisted of both federal government and individual provincial components.
In response the UN Committee has raised a principal concern that insufficient attention has been paid to the establishment of a permanent monitoring mechanism allowing effective implementation of the Convention in all parts of the country.

Other concerns included:

- that Canada reconsider its reservations to Articles 21 and 37;
- Canada's federal legislation relating to the basic provisions of the CRC, non-discrimination, the best interests of the child, and the respect of the views of the child;
- Child poverty in Canada;
- Canada's immigration practices;
- Canada's legislative measures to combat corporal punishment;

- the increasing incidence of suicide among young people;
- Canada's approach to vulnerable and disadvantaged children, such as Aboriginal children, and their fundamental right to education and housing;

Many of these same concerns still resonate in Canada today. While Canada has addressed the Committee's response in some areas, it has failed in others. The principles of non-discrimination and best interests of the child have been incorporated into legislation and policy. However, the CRC is not fully embedded in ongoing legislation and judicial developments relating to the Canadian Charter of Rights and Freedoms.

In general, the Government still faces three areas of primary concern:

- the co-ordination and dissemination of information and programmes protecting children's rights across provincial, regional, and local jurisdictions;
- strengthening the commitment to children's rights by devoting resources to long-term programmes addressing barriers such as economic disparity, child and family poverty, gender, racial, social, and cultural discrimination, and relations with First Nations Peoples;
- creating legislation and programmes that inject children's and young people's voices and participation, into the systems of justice, policy-making, and family and community life.

To address these issues, the Canadian Government has created new structures both at the federal and provincial level. The Children's Bureau has been replaced, in part, by the Citizen Participation Directorate who are responsible human rights issues, including those of children. The Ministry of Health and Welfare has become Health Canada and the Ministry of Multiculturalism and Citizenship's responsibilities now lie with either the Ministry of Canadian Heritage or Citizenship and Immigration Canada. The original programme 'Brighter Futures: Canada's Action Plan for Children' (CAPC) still exists under Health Canada. Provincial changes have been made with improvements to co-ordination and communication between federal, provincial and territorial legislatures. In the Canadian Parliament, there is also an advisor on children's rights to the Minister of Foreign Affairs.

The reality *against* the rhetoric

Sexual exploitation

The commercial sexual exploitation of children in Canada is generally linked to other social problems such as physical and/or sexual abuse in the home and poverty. Children from poor households are more likely to become involved in child prostitution as are children of Aboriginal families. The lack of data concerning sexual exploitation impedes Canada's ability to address these issues.

There has been a fall in the numbers of children arrested for acts of prostitution a reflection of a growing awareness that the commercial sexual exploitation of children is child abuse; the child is now seen more as a victim than a perpetrator. However there is no evidence to suggest that the number of children involved in commercial sexual exploitation has decreased.

In terms of sexual exploitation as a whole, there are relatively more First Nations People acting as prostitutes, with nearly 20 per cent of the total being Native Indian. It is uncertain if the figures are the same for children, but as young, sexually exploited youth often continue as sex workers as adults, it is thought likely. The average age of children entering the sex trade is 13, with reports of some as young as eight or nine. Very few complete grade 8 schooling and most lack the skills necessary for employment. Some engage in 'survival sex' for clothes, food or shelter and some work to feed drug and/or alcohol addictions.

There has been a reduction, or rather a displacement, of street child prostitution. Recent police efforts have concentrated on this visible aspect of the problem but the street trade only represents approximately 20 per cent of the total commercial sex trade. It is important that these crack-downs do not divert attention away from the real problem.

GOVERNMENT POLICY AND ACTION

Under the criminal legal code there are three key legal provisions concerning child sexual exploitation. The first addresses sexual activity with children outlawing touching children under the age of 14 with 'sexual purpose' and provides for penalties of up to ten years' imprisonment. Inciting another to touch a child under the age of 14 in a sexual manner is also illegal. The second provision details which activities associated with prostitution are illegal. Prostitution is not in itself illegal, but brothel-keeping, working in a brothel and procuring and/or living off the proceeds of prostitution are. It is also illegal for the customer, as well as the prostitute, to communicate in public for the purpose of engaging in prostitution. The third section concerns child pornography, which is pornography featuring those under the age of 18. It is illegal to make, distribute and/or possess child pornography in Canada.

Canada attended the 1996 World Congress Against Commerical Sexual Exploitation of Children in Stockholm. The Congress called for more research into the vulnerability of children to exploitation which Canada's representatives agreed with. However, the Congress did not include the views of many youths, this was seen as a serious failing. Out From the Shadows: International Summit of Sexually Exploited Youth was therefore held in March 1998 which allowed many youths from the Americas to speak of their experiences. Based on this Save the Children Canada has initiated a national project, "Out from the Shadows and Into the Light", aimed at preventing the commercial sexual exploitation of children and youth in Canada.

The Government's key failings with regard to Article 34 of the CRC concern both policy and practice. There is a lack of substantive research in the field making progress and measurement difficult and efforts to protect children lack co-ordination. There is a need for a holistic approach to connect causal factors with resultant behaviour. As poverty is a key factor increasing a child's vulnerability to sexual exploitation, the Government needs to address these underlying factors.

RECOMMENDATIONS

- **Government intervention in at-risk families** - Government and local community groups should continue to intervene in family life where children are known to be at risk of sexual exploitation. This intervention, however, should not come at the sacrifice of other fundamental human rights with respect to the accused.
- **Listen to the experience of young people** - Young people who have experienced sexual exploitation must be given a voice in national strategies to combat the problem.
- **Research** must be commissioned to enable the whole issue to be assessed and addressed with greater certainty.
- **Better professional education** - Professionals and workers who intersect with the sex trade should be better educated on children's rights and the overall abuse involved in child prostitution.

- **The Criminal Code should be clearer that prostitution in Canada is legal.**
- **Address the underlying social conditions -** Government sexual exploitation programmes should address the social factors placing children at risk.
- **Legal clarity** - Any contradiction regarding rights within Canadian legislation must be addressed to provide legal clarity. This is especially important with regard to the possession of child pornography.
- **Detoxification and substance abuse programmes** are essential to helping youths exit the sex trade.
- **Support for families** - Better networks of support should be provided for the families of children in the sex trade.

Juvenile justice

In Canada, serious violent crime involving youths has been declining since 1995 and property crime has fallen since 1990. Debate about youth crime, however, has become distorted and public concern regarding the problem has driven politicians to act in a tough manner, providing greater penalties for offences.

Young people in conflict with the law are dealt with in two categories. Children aged 0-11 become subject to provisions, which ensure their social and educational development. Young persons aged 12-17 are dealt with primarily through the Young Offenders Act (YOA), which includes punitive measures such as detention and alternative measures such as community service and suspended sentences.

GOVERNMENT POLICY AND ACTION

The YOA, initially struck a balance between the need to protect society and the need to rehabilitate young offenders. An amendment made in 1995 tipped the balance in favour of protecting society. The key new provisions lengthened the maximum sentence the youth court could give from five to ten years, and ruled that serious violent offenders could be transferred to the adult court at age 16. In 1997 the Standing Committee on Justice and Legal Affairs reduced the minimum age at which the YOA becomes applicable to ten, and devolved many responsibilities for youth justice to the provincial and territorial authorities.

In May 1998 the federal government introduced a new youth justice strategy which became the Youth Criminal Justice Act (YCJA) the key elements of which are:

- that the protection of society will outweigh the protection of the special needs of youth;
- the youth court can impose adult sentences and the age limit will be lowered to 14 for presumption of adult sentences;
- public identification of the youth will be permitted if an adult sentence is imposed or if the youth is dangerous and at large;
- victims will have the right to access youth records;
- voluntary statements to police can be admitted into evidence, despite technical violations of the statutory protections for young people;
- custody and re-integration decisions will be handed down to provincial and territorial governments.

There are a number of key areas where the new legislation may infringe the rights outlined in Article 40 of the CRC:

- the creation of new exceptions to the general principle of privacy for young offenders;
- the almost automatic transference of serious violent crime to the adult court signals guilt before a verdict has been given;
- the provision of translation and essential interpretation services for linguistic minorities are inadequate or unavailable often prolonging detention.

There are a number of alternatives to custody available for juveniles including community service, financial restitution and suspended sentences. However the picture is not the same throughout Canada. The YOA is federal legislation with countrywide jurisdiction, but it is up to the provincial and territorial governments to implement it and local authorities to enforce it. This can lead to very different approaches to youth justice. For instance, Quebec provides alternatives to detention which empahsise rehabilitation, whereas Ontario, Manitoba and Alberta have developed youth detention centres modelled on military boot camps.

Some of the Government's failings are specific, such as the infringements of Article 40 mentioned above, whilst others are more general, such as the regional variation in treatment of offenders and the tendency to make policy to gain political advantage. There is a real need to look soberly at what is effective not simply what plays well in the media.

RECOMMENDATIONS

- **Mutual principles** - The declaration principle of the YCJA should emphasise the mutuality of 'protecting society' at the same time as 'protecting the special needs of youth'.
- **Funding** - Formulas for funding the youth justice system should emphasise the need for preventive, restorative, and rehabilitative programmes.
- **Assessment of alternatives to detention** - There should be increased focus on creating long-term measures for preventive, community-based and non-custodial programmes
- **Public perceptions of crime rates** - There should be increased spending on public awareness relating to the reality of violent youth crime rates.
- **Safeguarding the rights of young offenders in custody** - Provincial and territorial governments should be made accountable, via an external non-partisan body, to safeguard the fundamental rights of young offenders while in custody.
- **YCJA** - ensure that:
  a) the minimum age of children falling under youth court jurisdiction is not changed;
  b) no presumption is made that those committing violent crime at age 14 or over be given adult sentences;
  c) the ban on public identification is not lifted in cases where adult sentencing is presumed.

Displacement

Canada resettles approximately 10,000 refugees a year and has one of the highest rates of acceptance of refugee claims at over 50 per cent per year. In 1997, 24,000 claims were processed. However, the rate of acceptance at different immigration offices is a cause for concern varying between 4 per cent and 82 per cent for refugees from the same country. In 1994, 700 unaccompanied children applied for refugee status.

GOVERNMENT ACTION AND POLICY

Although the provisions of the CRC have not been directly placed within Canadian immigration legislation, in practice children are generally afforded the rights as prescribed by the CRC. As Canada is a signatory to the 1951 Geneva Convention Relating to the Status of Refugees all refugee children and adults are guaranteed the full rights laid down in the Canadian Charter of Rights and Freedoms.

Historically Canada's courts have made some decisions which may be interpreted as against the spirit, of the CRC particularly in respect to the deportation of parents claiming refugee status whose child has become a Canadian citizen.
In 1996 Canada passed amendments to its immigration legislation incorporating the 'best interests of the child' edict and now parents may be permitted to remain in Canada.

There are a range of government policies providing for refugees, however, a number give rise to concern. Since 1996, child refugee claimants are provided with a representative to guide them through the claims process. They can resettle in Canada where support is provided. The province of Quebec, however, will not sponsor an unaccompanied child illustrating how provision can vary at the provincial and territorial level even when federal legislation is clear. Refugee selection processes also vary from one immigration office to another.

During the refugee claims process, claimants have a right to legal representation and an interpreter, however access to legal assistance at the initial interview can vary. The Immigration Legislative Review Advisory Board (IRB) has suggested that a protection agency be set up to ensure that unaccompanied children are represented and provided with guardianship. The legal process is lengthy and can take two and a half to three years to complete which is a cause for concern. There has been a recent proposal to collapse the three-tiered claims review process (status determination, post-determination risk review, risk-related humanitarian review) into one and to make eligibility criteria more rigorous. This is neither necessary nor desirable.

Citizenship and Immigration Canada have made proposals to change the legislation regarding family reunification. They maintain that the needs of common-law partners among others should be addressed and argue for bringing spouses and children to Canada on humanitarian grounds. They also propose that the age at which dependent children can apply for permanent residency should be raised from under 19 to under 22 and advise that legislation be re-examined to better incorporate the CRC. Increasingly rigid proof of family relationship are now required, including DNA testing for family reunification. The definition of family also remains very narrow and the charging of Right of Landing fees can pose an obstacle for families with insufficient funds.

There are a range of government policies providing for refugees, however, a number give rise to concern. Since 1996, child refugee claimants are provided with a representative to guide them through the claims process. They can resettle in Canada where support is provided. The province of Quebec, however, will not sponsor an unaccompanied child illustrating how provision can vary at the provincial and territorial level even when federal legislation is clear. Refugee selection processes also vary from one immigration office to another.

During the refugee claims process, claimants have a right to legal representation and an interpreter, however access to legal assistance at the initial interview can vary. The Immigration Legislative Review Advisory Board (IRB) has suggested that a protection agency be set up to ensure that unaccompanied children are represented and provided with guardianship. The legal process is lengthy and can take two and a half to three years to complete which is a cause for concern. There has been a recent proposal to collapse the three-tiered claims review process (status determination, post-determination risk review, risk-related humanitarian review) into one and to make eligibility criteria more rigorous. This is neither necessary nor desirable.

Citizenship and Immigration Canada have made proposals to change the legislation regarding family reunification. They maintain that the needs of common-law partners among others should be addressed and argue for bringing spouses and children to Canada on humanitarian grounds. They also propose that the age at which dependent children can apply for permanent residency should be raised from under 19 to under 22 and advise that legislation be re-examined to better incorporate the CRC. Increasingly rigid proof of family relationship are now required, including DNA testing for family reunification. The definition of family also remains very narrow and the charging of Right of Landing fees can pose an obstacle for families with insufficient means.

RECOMMENDATIONS

- **The benefit of the doubt for child refugees** - In the refugee determination process, guidelines should go further than considering the 'best interests of the child' and they should give children the 'benefit of the doubt' in legal terms.
- **Persecution** - In establishing 'fear of persecution', the IRB should consider the types of persecution that are unique to children and its decisions should reflect this.
- **Possible discrimination against those who might make high demands on health services** - Legislation should be changed so that persons in need of protection should not have to meet the requirements regarding excessive costs for health services.
- **Individuals should be able to claim refugee status from their home country** - When individuals facing persecution are not able to acquire visas (and their requisite identity papers) from their home country, they should still be able to make a claim from their country.
- **Protection agency for child refugees** - Citizenship and Immigration Canada should establish the refugee child 'protection agency' which can ensure that children in the system are guaranteed representation at all stages.
- **Reduce time taken to process claims** - Changes in legislation should be made to reduce claim processing time, but not at the expense of the legal process.
- **Income support and health care for claimants** - Legislation should require the federal government to assume all income assistance and health-care costs for claimants in the country, until the final determination of their cases is made.
- **Protect the current system of review** - New legislation should not collapse the current three-tiered system of refugee review into one, nor make eligibility more rigorous.
- **Facilitate family reunification** - In instances of family reunification DNA testing should not become the norm for proof of family relations.

Education

In Canada, education is a provincial concern except in the case of the three territories. Provincial and territorial legislation dictates the ages of 'compulsory' and 'entitled' education. For all children, including those with refugee status or who have parents with refugee status, education is compulsory from age 5, 6 or 7 years (depending on the province) to 16 years. It is entitled to children 5 or 6 years old (in provinces where it is not already compulsory) until they reach 18 to 21 years. According to Canada's first report to the Committee on the Rights of the Child, enrolment for children aged 4 to 17 is generally 90 per cent nation-wide.

There is little statistical analysis regarding many aspects of primary and secondary schooling and this is particularly important with regard to ethnicity. First Nations Peoples confront a number of social and cultural factors, which work against them. Statistics Canada maintains that the rate of improvement for these peoples is 'significantly behind all other groups in the country'. For Inuit communities, the rate of high-school graduation has been as low as 30 per cent. On a positive note, figures from 1996 indicate that 73 per cent of Aboriginal youth aged 15-19 were in school, so high-school graduation rates are likely to rise. Secondary school attendance and achievement vary greatly from province to province, as do funding levels.

According to Canada's first report (1991), 91 per cent of children with disabilities attend school in Canada and complete secondary and post-secondary education in the same proportion as non-disabled persons. However, at young ages, children with disabilities do not achieve comparable results and they are more likely to drop out of elementary education.

It is observed that children with the highest socio-economic status are two to three times more likely to be in the top percentage of their class in reading and maths. Children who have a low socio-economic status are three times more likely to be in a remedial education programme. The gap between the poorest and the richest has grown and this has particular effect on access to higher education, as tuition fees in the tertiary sector have increased faster than family incomes. Many provincial governments have changed budgetary priorities in the face of the economic orthodoxy of globalisation, and education has been a target. The curriculum is undergoing change and there is a tendency to develop subjects directly addressing the needs of industry rather than the developmental needs of the child work rather than life.

GOVERNMENT ACTION AND POLICY

The federal government has established the Canadian Millennium Foundation to offer scholarships for students demonstrating need and merit. Many provincial school boards have implemented programmes and other activities to reduce the gaps in development between children in various circumstances. In some areas, special provisions are made for resources and special curriculum needs for First Nations Peoples.

The curriculum aims 'to develop citizens with healthy personalities, informed on scientific, ethical, cultural, geographical, political and social matters and on the arts'. While evidence suggests this is being achieved, there are significant failings. Human rights in general, and children's rights in particular, are not widely taught although some regions are piloting projects. The lack of rights awareness, allied to the tendency of the curriculum becoming more training-orientated, has implications for the holistic development of the child.

Funding disparities are a growing concern. In recent years education at all levels, has been affected by funding cuts. According to the Western Report Vol 8 (41), funding in Ontario in 1996, was cut by $400 million by making junior kindergarten an optional requirement for schools. In 1995 Alberta cut its education budget by $239 million. There is a danger that provision may become markedly different from province to province, making the quality of a child's educational experience partially determined by place of birth.

Non-discrimination is an underlying principle of education in Canada and policies are in place to prevent racial, ethnic, cultural, gender or socio-economic bias in the curriculum or in schools. However, some biases remain entrenched, such as the gender bias towards males in science and engineering subjects. The social studies curriculum throughout Canada seeks to cultivate tolerance, caring and respect for others. Some of these initiatives are facing curtailment. These programmes are essential in developing children's awareness of, and respect for, cultures and societies other than their own.

RECOMMENDATIONS

There are three general areas of concern that emerge from this analysis. The first is that, as there is no federal/national ministry or department to set standards on behalf of the CRC and the availability of information about children's rights is insufficient. The second relates to funding cuts and impact of government fiscal policy, which affect the quality of education and the rights of children - especially with regard to Article 29. The third area is that successful spending initiatives, such as SchoolNet, tend to emphasise training skills geared toward the marketplace, at the expense of a curriculum aimed at developing the 'whole child' and its cultural identity.

With these areas of concern in mind, the following are recommendations that address Canada's situation and Articles 28 and 29 of the CRC:

- **Better co-operation and data collection** - Federal government should take more responsibility for establishing a forum for increased inter-provincial/territorial dialogue and data collection on education issues. The body would produce a report that would highlight aspects of the system in relation to equity, multiculturalism, and Articles 28 and 29 of the CRC.
- **Research** - The federal government should spend more resources on research such as the National Longitudinal Survey of Children and Youth. The public discourse surrounding such projects would re-instil positive attitudes regarding both the social realities and theinvestment potential of providing solid pre-school and school programmes.
- **Pre-school and child-care programmes** - The federal government should reinstate pre-school programmes and child care as measures to improve the level of education in Canada.
- **Reduce child poverty.**
- **Technology-based learning should not be at the expense of the wider curriculum** - The federal government should not promote high levels of spending on access to technology at the expense of promoting the development of the 'whole child.'

'I wish that everybody could live in their homes and never have to leave them'.

Jadranka, age 13 - Bosnia

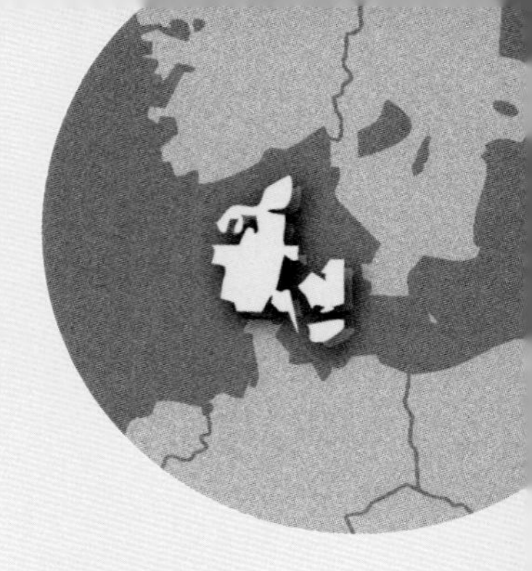

Denmark

THE DANISH GOVERNMENT AND THE CRC

The Danish Government ratified the CRC on 19 July 1991. A Ministerial Commission was established, together with a parallel civil servants' body, the Interministerial Children's Committee. These bodies are responsible for the co-ordination of the Danish Government's policy on children. In addition, the Interministerial Youth Committee was established in 1997 specifically to co-ordinate the Government's youth policy.

Unlike other Nordic countries, Denmark has not set up a Children's Ombudsman; instead the National Council for Children (NCC) was established in 1994, initially as a pilot scheme, but as of 1 July 1998 as a permanent institution. The NCC is set up in a similar way to a Children's Ombudsman, and in essence the principal aim is the same - to enhance the rights and interests of children in society. The NCC is increasingly used as an advisory body on various issues regarding the status of children and youth.

The principal tasks of the NCC include:

- securing children's rights, as well as focusing public attention on them;
- advising the authorities on questions about the status of children;
- integrating children's views and assessing the conditions under which Danish children live, regarding the regulations and intentions of the CRC.

On 1 July 1998 a new Social Assistance Act (SAA) came into force, which provides special support for children and youth. This new legislation is far more child-focused than previous legislation. However, in practice, children's voices are rarely heard in cases concerning them and their families.

The Danish Government submitted their first report on the implementation of the CRC to the UN Committee on the Rights of the Child in 1993. Save the Children Denmark (Red Barnet) submitted an alternative report to the UN Committee at the same time. The main comments of this report were generally incorporated into the UN Committee's recommendations to the Danish Government which were published in 1995. The UN Committee's comments to the Danish Government both praised and criticised Denmark's efforts in implementing the Convention.

Significant steps have been made in promoting and safeguarding the interests of children; the outlawing of the possession of pornographic material featuring children, the new regulations on shared parenthood, the founding of the National Council for Children and the establishment of a committee on ethnic rights were all identified as positive moves forward.

However, a number of general concerns were expressed. Several provisions of the CRC are not yet sufficiently reflected in Danish legislation. The Committee emphasised the priority that must always be given to the best interests of the child and stated that all children should be given the opportunity to express their own concerns. The Committee also recommended:

- establishing measures to fight discrimination against refugees, HIV-positive children and children with AIDS;
- emphasising the joint responsibility of parents for their children;
- taking further preventive measures against the sexual abuse of children.

There are no areas where the Government can be said to be simply failing to implement the CRC but, as the above suggests, there are some unresolved issues concerning the Convention. There is a strong need to integrate children's own opinions of events in their lives in a systematic and pragmatic fashion. For instance, during divorces or cases of forcible removal, the authorities need to listen to the children who are affected by such decisions. Greater awareness of the Convention is a must, as societal and legislative changes often go hand-in-hand. There is a need for a better balance between professional and family life; families are sometimes under strain because both parents need to work to contribute to the family budget. More work often means less time with the children. Single-parent families face difficulties that should not be underestimated.

For the Government to implement the CRC fully and effectively in Denmark it is important that legislation is followed up and reviewed in the light of experience and any necessary changes are made.

The reality *against* the rhetoric

Sexual exploitation

It is difficult to know the extent and nature of this problem in Denmark because there has not been enough research to examine it thoroughly. Such work as has been done suggests that a minimum of 1 per cent of boys and 2 per cent of girls have been seriously sexually abused. There may well be under-reporting of cases as the subject is generally taboo and victims can feel a sense of shame and responsibility. Boys seem to be more likely than girls to leave the exploitation unreported which may be related to a perceived loss of masculinity as a result of their complaint. As awareness of the problem grows, there appears to be an increase in sexual exploitation but it is likely that the reporting of offences is increasing faster than any rise in offending. Research concerning the social and cultural nature of child sexual exploitation has not been carried out and likewise research concerning the factors, which lead to abuse is still to be done.

GOVERNMENT POLICY AND ACTION

In 1994 the Government passed legislation making the possession of pornographic images involving children illegal. The aim of this law is to try to prevent the creation of child pornography. There is no coherent plan of action for the prevention of sexual exploitation. However in 1999 an expert panel under the auspices of the National Council for Children was established. The objective of the panel is to analyse the extent and nature of the problem of sexual exploitation and to put forward suggestions for preventing sexual abuse in all its forms.

RECOMMENDATIONS

Growing awareness of this problem has led to increased debate and there is now a need for the Government to take several steps to address the issues raised above.

- **Improved research and data collection including a central database of information and statistics.**
- **A specialist investigation unit** - Establish a national team to investigate cases of sexual abuse.
- **Monitoring areas where children are at risk** - The environments in which pederasts may abuse need very careful monitoring and regulation. This is true at local, national and international levels (i.e. communication networks, especially the Internet).
- **Police vetting of all professionals working with children** - All volunteers and paid staff who will be working with children should be subject to police certification and examination of their work history.
- **Awareness training for professionals working with children** - Issues concerning sexual exploitation must be on the curricula of teacher-training colleges. In addition, all people who work with children should have access to courses and information to help them identify and care for the victims.
- **Specialist treatment for victims and perpetrators of sexual abuse** - Establish treatment facilities for those that have suffered abuse and offer treatment to abusers with a view to prevention.
- **Legislative change allowing a longer period in which to report crimes of a sexual nature** - At the moment an offence of sexual abuse must come to the authorities' attention within ten years of its being committed. This law should change so that the ten-year period starts after the abused reaches the age of 18.
- **Awareness campaigns for children** - Educate all children so they know that they have a right to their own body.

Juvenile justice

Children under the age of 15 cannot be prosecuted under Danish law. There are approximately one million children in Denmark and of those 7,740 were charged with an offence in 1998 - 215 less than in 1997. In June of 1999 only ten young people were held in custody - half the number of previous years.

Political concern and debate might lead an observer to think that crime committed by juveniles (age 15-17) is on the increase when in fact the opposite is true. Over the last ten years the number of crimes committed by this age group has fallen by 20 per cent. This should be judged against a background of a sharp increase in the number of crimes committed by all age groups. Increased preventive measures have played their part. The last ten years have seen the implementation of the SSP facility which fosters co-operation between schools, social authorities and the police. Despite the overall fall in crime for juveniles, it is noted with alarm that the number of offences involving severe violence has increased over the ten-year period.

Juveniles involved in violent crime usually come from threatened or marginalised groups. During the 1980s, ten per cent of the youths leaving education ended up as long-term unemployed, i.e. marginalised on the job market. A youth might suffer from another form of marginalisation, such as being a member of an ethnic group which has not yet fully integrated into Danish society. Other forms of marginalisation include, for instance, a severe lack of love and care. There are many factors which make youths turn to crime and often they act in concert with each other, and in the particular life circumstances of the offender. It is felt that, as the nature and extent of these factors grow, the more susceptible a young person may become to the temptations of a criminal career.

Boys commit more crimes than girls. In the 15-17 age group girls were responsible for 13 per cent of the offences committed during 1993. Of this percentage half were involved in cases of shoplifting. Most of the boys (40 per cent) are involved in cases of infringement of traffic regulations. Violent crime has risen and the number of girls involved in these crimes has risen relative to the number of boys.

There is no death penalty or corporal punishment for anyone in Denmark. The sanctions available for judges are the same for youths as they are for adults. The judges may choose to use the sanctions in different ways when considering someone's youth.

GOVERNMENT POLICY AND ACTION

The Government has put aside DKK 40 million annually for the period 1997-2000. Communities and/or provinces can receive co-funding for initiatives aimed at preventing youths offending or re-offending. The 'violence treaty' has been adopted by the Government. This is targeted specifically at those who have been involved in violent crime and aims to reduce recidivism.

Youth contracts have been introduced for those aged 15-17. A contract is made between the social authorities, the police and the offender with the consent of his or her parent/guardian. The youth may avoid a custodial sentence by undertaking to follow educational opportunities or attend courses at certain times for a certain period. These contracts are generally made available to first, second and third-time offenders whose crimes are not so serious.

Juvenile offenders are, in general, accorded all the rights laid down in Article 40 of the CRC. The Government is currently debating its reservations towards Article 40. 2(b)(v) concerning the need for a any sentence to be able to be reviewed by a higher authority. The Government does not provide separate facilities for youth offenders in custody even though there are only a small number to cater for.

RECOMMENDATIONS

- **Legislative change** - Denmark should withdraw its reservations to Article 40.2(b)(v) and ensure that any sentence given, or provision made, can subsequently be tried before a higher body.
- **Separate detention facilities for children** - Separate facilities should be made available so that young offenders do not mix with adults.
- **Abolition of isolation imprisonment for juveniles** - Although rare, isolation imprisonment is known to have been used on offenders as young as 15; this must be outlawed.

Displacement

Refugee children who arrive in Denmark unaccompanied by their families are cared for by the Danish Red Cross (DRC). In 1997 there were 184 unaccompanied refugee children in Denmark and in 1998 there were 229. They are split between approximately one-third girls and two-thirds boys. The refugees come from a number of nations; the largest single group in 1998 numbered 42 and was from Iraq; 39 children came from Sri Lanka and 20 from Afghanistan in the same period. The largest number of unaccompanied refugees occurred in 1993 when 350 children arrived. Since then the trend has been mainly downward.

GOVERNMENT ACTION AND POLICY

Public welfare provision falls into two phases; the pre-asylum phase - the period from the child's arrival but before an asylum/residence permit is obtained - and the integration phase - the period after asylum/residence has been granted until the child is independent, economically and socially.

During the pre-asylum phase, the Danish Foreign Authorities and The Danish Immigration Service (DIS) are responsible for all refugees. The actual care of these people is, to a large extent, delegated to the DRC, with the DIS providing funding. All the asylum centres are run by the DRC and besides food and lodging they administer many other welfare tasks such as providing access to health care and education.

For unaccompanied refugee children, dedicated asylum centres have been established as this vulnerable group demands special care. These centres have far more staff and better resources than the ordinary centres; these children may well have enhanced educational and leisure opportunities. Apart from the daily necessities, each child receives pocket money according to his/her age.

During the Integration phase, children are often adopted by Danish families; some of the older ones might share a flat and some may live in Save The Children's children's houses. Refugee children have the same rights to education, health care, protection, etc. as those children who are born in Denmark.

The Government is under no legal obligation to look for the parents of children who arrive unaccompanied. Sometimes the policy of the DIS works against the interests of children. For instance, if a child has arrived and been granted asylum status because they were unaccompanied, this status may be revoked if the child's parents find the child. However, some children do have contact with their parents and if this contact is facilitated by the DRC they are under no compulsion to tell the authorities. Where children do not know the whereabouts of their parents, the DRC and the Danish Refugee Council will conduct a search if the child so wishes. Any search is curtailed if it threatens the well-being of the child's family.

In the light of the conflict in Kosovo, the Government has made special provision for those children who have been granted temporary residence. The effect of this is to enable refugees to partake fully in schooling, although the exact nature of this education is, as yet, unclear.

RECOMMENDATIONS

Save the Children, the Danish Red Cross and The Danish Refugee Council make the following recommendations:

- **Personal counsellors for refugee children** - Every child should have a guardian or counsellor who follows the child's progress from arrival until the age of 18 (the age of majority in Denmark). This person will be committed to administer the interests of the child during both the pre-asylum phase and the following stay in Denmark. (In 1993 it was decided that children have the right to an assessor during all meetings with public authorities. The assessors are employed by DRC who administer the scheme.)
- **Legal representation for refugee children** - Every child should be granted a lawyer during the asylum phase. At present, a lawyer will only be assigned when the application for asylum has been rejected and the decision is being appealed.
- **Greater efforts to trace and reunite unaccompanied children with their families** - In the case of unaccompanied children all relevant authorities should actively co-operate in tracing a child's family after his/her arrival. This may help reunite families and could help to address the trauma of separation.
- **Enforcement of the principle of best interests of the child** - A child's residency entitlement should not be endangered because the parents become known. The authorities tend to repatriate children whose family's whereabouts become known. Every single case should be carefully evaluated with the interests of the child uppermost - is it best for the child to stay and for his/her parents to join him/her, or is it best for the child to return to the nation where they originated.

Education

In Denmark education is free for all. In 1972 so-called 'compulsory basic education' was extended from seven to nine years. Denmark differs from most other countries by imposing an obligation to be educated, as opposed to an obligation to go to school. It also has liberal rules for supplying public funds to private schools. According to current figures, approximately 89 per cent of children attend state schools and 11 per cent attend private institutions.

GOVERNMENT ACTION AND POLICY

Basic education is offered in what are referred to as primary schools, which offer education for children from 6 to 15 years of age (grades 1 - 9). Pre-school facilities are offered for five and six year olds on a voluntary basis and have increased considerably over the last 30 years and now 97.9 per cent of children attend Pre-school. A tenth grade is also offered for 15-16 year olds, again this is voluntary. Three out of every four young people go on to some form of continuing study (including both academic and vocational training). There is a range of different types of high school in Denmark, all of which give access to university, and 46 per cent of students go on to one of these. These offer a variety of different types of technical and academic courses. At high school, girls tend to outnumber boys by six to four and gender differences are marked in relation to the selected fields of study. An alternative to high school, and a growing area of the education system, are basic training institutions which provide opportunities for apprenticeships and prepare young people for the labour market by equipping them with useful productive skills. The technical schools have almost exclusively male students, while schools which provide commerce or social and health education courses are generally attended mainly by females.

The Social Commission has realised that there is still a significant group of youth who fail to graduate from the basic education system. An estimated 11.6 per cent each year drop out of school with no recognised qualification. Approximately 13 per cent of pupils leave basic education before reaching the ninth grade. After-school courses or youth schools offer alternative education, equivalent to that of the basic education system. Attendance is much higher (about 80 per cent) for children whose parents are professionals. Research has shown that children whose parents are unemployed stand a greater risk of dropping out of school before completing their final exams.

The state schools in Denmark are based on a differentiated mode of education to be able to care for the individual child's need. Nevertheless, increasing numbers of parents are choosing private schools (11.4 per cent annually). In higher grades the percentage is above 14 per cent (1994). The share of the children being educated by private schools has been steadily growing since the 1970s when only 6 per cent were enrolled in private schools.

All children in Denmark have equal rights to education. However, there still exists a significant social bias regarding the completion rate of higher education.

RECOMMENDATIONS

- **Alternative provisions for young people not continuing in formal education after the age of 16** - There is a need to be aware of the needs of young people who do not continue in high schools or at technical training institutes after completion of their basic primary education and to create alternative provisions for them. Young people without formal qualifications are at risk of being margi nalised in the labour market.
- **Increased vocational opportunities for non-academic children** - For young people without academic skills, vocational training should be given greater priority.

Dominican Republic

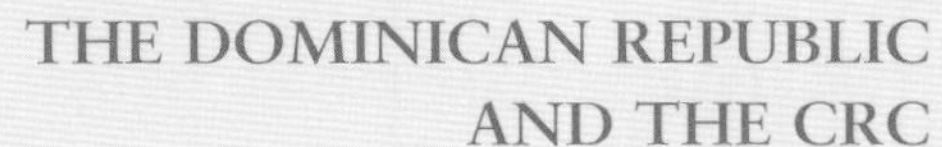

The Dominican Republic ratified the United Nations Convention on the Rights of the Child on 8 August 1990 and it came into effect on 11 July 1991.

The Government and a number of non-governmental organisations (NGOs) have made efforts to incorporate the CRC into domestic policy and practice. The World Declaration on the Survival, Protection and Development of the Child in the 1990s prompted the Government to develop a National Plan of Action which cited 27 major goals. The following broad areas were addressed: health and nutrition; education; children and adolescents in especial difficulty; women; water and sanitation; politics and social promotion.

The National Plan was followed up by a national commission consisting of 37 governmental institutions and 128 NGOs. A strategy has been developed which involves community groups, NGOs, religious organisations, town halls and provincial authorities. Running alongside the National Plan is the National Social Development Plan, which has the rights and needs of women and children as one of its priorities. Its three main goals are: the eradication of poverty; the creation of productive employment and social integration.

Following ratification of the CRC, the Government began a process to review national legislation with regard to children and young people. The result of this process is the Code for the Protection of Children and Young People (CPCYP) which came into force on 1 January 1995. The Code is an improvement on previous legislation and was given force of law by the National Congress. This is important because it means its provisions can be directly invoked before any judicial or administrative authority. The Code creates a system of protection for children and adolescents within a judicial institutional framework and it foresees three key bodies within the system: the ruling body; provincial and regional branches and national and regional councils.

The Government has been working with UNICEF and other international aid organisations to disseminate information about the content of CRC. Written materials have been produced, conferences organised and workshops arranged for both professionals and the general public. UNICEF, the Catholic church and several other public and private institutions have developed a project called, 'The country that we want: the children have a voice'. This project both allows children to participate in education projects regarding their rights and gives them a voice in how policy and practice should be developed. A National Day of the Rights of the Child has been established on 29 September which involves special as well as general educational activities.

The reality *against* the rhetoric

Sexual exploitation

Although statistical knowledge is somewhat scarce, the information available suggests that sexual exploitation in the Dominican Republic is a serious and growing problem. A survey carried out by UNICEF in 1992 reported that the estimated number of victims of commercial sexual exploitation was 25,455. The main age group was between 12 and 17, of which 64 per cent were girls and 36 per cent boys.

The frequency of sexual exploitation is rapidly increasing in tourist areas. Several tourist locations have become associated with child prostitution, causing local, national and international concern. The main factors for the rise in this trade are the strategies for survival that some families are forced to adopt. Poverty, unemployment, poor housing and education and inadequate nutrition and sanitation lead to a situation where prostitution has become one of the most important forms of income generation for adults, adolescents and children.

GOVERNMENT ACTION AND POLICY

The Government has established the National Inter-institutional Commission for the Prevention and Eradication of Child Prostitution (NICPECP) and the focus of its work concerns the tourist areas. The Commission has drawn up a strategy for the protection and care of children and adolescents who have been sexually exploited.

NICPECP held a workshop on 28 September 1997 in Bocachica (one of the country's main tourist centres) to address this problem. There are plans to organise further workshops on a nationwide basis, particularly in areas with a high incidence of child prostitution. Activities focused on prevention are carried out in schools and the beach areas of tourist resorts, which are often the market-place for this form of sexual exploitation.

RECOMMENDATIONS

- **Holistic approach** - A holistic approach is necessary in this area. The Government must address the underlying socio-economic factors related to the growth of sexual exploitation.
- **Increased co-odination** - Greater co-ordination is necessary in the adoption and implementation of policy and practice. There is a need for greater consultation with the victims of sexual exploitation and with local authorities and communities.

Juvenile justice

Children under the age of 12 are not considered legally responsible. Young people aged 13-18 are described by the law as adolescents and are subject to the same laws as adults, but some aspects of their treatment are different.

In the last two years for which figures are available, 1996 and 1997, the number of young people who came into conflict with the law remained fairly stable. In 1996, 1,479 juveniles were convicted, of whom approximately 83 per cent were male and 17 per cent female. The majority of offences were ones of robbery - about 75 per cent of the total. The other major categories of crime were: fighting (12 per cent), drugs (5 per cent) and assault (4 per cent).

The death penalty and life imprisonment are outlawed for all citizens including children. The CPCYP prohibits the use of torture and ill-treatment. Cases have been successfully brought against officials for negligence and the national police for ill treatment.

GOVERNMENT ACTION AND POLICY

To incorporate the CRC into domestic law, the Government created a different structure for the administration of juvenile justice. The CPCYP created 17 special courts in each municipality within the country. The Government also created the Commission for the Support of Reform and the Modernisation of Justice which has facilitated the training and development of professional, technical and auxiliary staff working with children who have come into conflict with the law. The Commission, in co-operation with other bodies, has also started a public defence programme which aims to provide a legal defence paid for by the state for those who cannot afford one for themselves. Children must also be taken to the relevant judicial authority within 24 hours of his/her arrest.

These provisions represent progress towards the goal of ensuring that children enjoy all the rights in Article 40 of the CRC. However, there is a great need for a continuing programme of education and a culture change for the judiciary. At the moment the doctrine of an 'irregular situation' (where the police can detain on suspicion and the judiciary act in a summary manner) is sometimes incorrectly invoked. This bypasses all the rights laid out in the CPCYP and many of those in Article 40.

There have been some attempts at providing alternatives to detention. These should be to the advantage of the young person involved, although careful monitoring is necessary to ensure that this is so. For example, if a court cautions a minor with 'serious behavioural problems', the court may order the internment of the child for observation and diagnosis. This involves an investigation into personality, the young person's family background, social factors and the circumstances under which the offence occurred. The Minors' Preparatory Institute is run by a Catholic order and provides a technical, artistic or vocational education. The young people sent to this institution may be said to be at 'semi-liberty', and whilst seen as a generally beneficial experience their legal status is somewhat vague. Overall, there are a lack of systematic alternatives to detention for young people.

In rural areas young people are often detained with adults. There are only two internment centres for the whole country. There is a particular problem in the city of Santo Domingo, which has the highest number of juvenile offenders and some of the poorest provision for them.

RECOMMENDATIONS

- **Specialist training for the judiciary** - Further training and education is needed for all members of the judiciary, especially with regard to the legal importance of the Code for the Protection of Children and Young People. This is particularly important for those who believe that invoking the doctrine of an 'irregular situation' overrides all other rights.
- **Alternatives to detention** - Establish systematic and wide-ranging alternatives to detention for juvenile offenders. Monitor their impact with regard to recidivism.
- **Improved detention facilities** - Improvements to the infrastructure of detention must be carried out in order to provide sentencing alternatives and to ensure young offenders are not detained with adult criminals.

Displacement

There was no reliable data or information regarding the presence and/or status of refugees in the Dominican Republic available at the time of going to print.

Education

The Education Reform Law of April 1997 made basic (primary) education mandatory and free for all. Education in the Dominican Republic has four levels. Initial - up to the age of 6, basic from 6 to 14 years of age, medium (secondary) from 14 to 18, and higher from 18 upwards.

Data from 1996/97 shows enrolment in primary school at 91 per cent. In 1995 the figure was 97 per cent and secondary enrolment was 37 per cent. Eighty-eight per cent of the population was considered literate. However, these figures can only be seen against the background and recent history of education in the Dominican Republic.

The 1980s saw a very marked deterioration in the public education system. Successive governments, having already under-funded education, made further cuts in the light of structural adjustment programmes implemented as a condition of the World Bank and International Monetary Fund. Spending dropped to below 1 per cent of GDP and teachers salaries were lower than those of domestic servants. Teacher-training programmes were nearly non-existent, virtually no textbooks were available and the infrastructure of schools was left to decay. Compounding this resourcing problem education was generally not valued as an investment in the future of the nation.

Faced with crumbling public provision some communities decided to form their own schools, with varying degrees of funding and success. The Government took no part in overseeing the performance of these schools.

GOVERNMENT ACTION AND POLICY

The Ministry of Education, the Dominican Teachers' Union, some NGOs and the United Nations Development Programme carried out a nationwide review of education in the Dominican Republic. In late 1992 this led to a ten-year plan, the Plan Decenal, which recommended far-reaching changes to the whole of the education system. The key points were:

- significant decentralisation of services and decision-making;
- a more active, learner-focused form of teaching;
- a dramatic increase in funding for education;
- comprehensive training of personnel;
- the provision of relevant, high-quality texts for all students.

The provisions were enacted by the Education Reform Law, approved by the Dominican Congress on 15 April 1997.
The major sources of funding for the reforms were the World Bank, the Inter American Development Bank and the European Union.

The ten-year education plan has resulted in the retraining of many teachers bringing their knowledge and skills up to date. Some of the physical infrastructure of schools has been repaired and replaced, although there is much work still to done. In 1996/97 one million textbooks were printed, with the goal of providing free textbooks to all children in public education.

RECOMMENDATIONS

- **Equal access to education** - Full access for all children from all geographical areas and social classes is still not a complete reality and the Government must strive to make this so.
- **Community involvement in education** - Community and parental involvement should continue to increase the growing awareness of the importance of education so as to make sure it remains high on the Government's agenda.
- **Increased levels of funding** - Although funding has increased, it is insufficient to fulfil the potential of the children of the Dominican Republic.

Egypt

THE EGYPTIAN GOVERNMENT AND THE CRC

Egypt ratified the United Nations Convention on the Rights of the Child on 5 February 1990. The CRC came into effect on 2 September 1990.

In order to further Egypt's compliance with the children's rights laid down in the CRC, the Government established the National Council for Childhood and Motherhood (NCCM) in January 1998. The NCCM has a very wide-ranging mandate. Its main tasks are:

- to produce policy with regard to mothers and children;
- to formulate a national plan covering areas such social and family care, health, education, culture, information and social protection;
- to monitor and review policy from ministerial sources and comment with regards to the interests of mothers and children;
- to gather and compile research and data concerning childhood and motherhood.

The NCCM is conceived as a body that oversees the work of national and local government and that of other public bodies. Its key goal is to ensure the interests of mothers and children are paramount.

The NCCM has established a working group of representatives from the Ministry of Justice, the consultative council, the popular assembly and judicial academics in order to review all legislation that affects children and mothers, in the light of Egypt's new commitments following the ratification of the CRC. Some revision of existing legislation was necessary and the Supreme Constitutional Court made a decree forbidding the passage of any draft bill that does not fully take into account the provisions of the CRC.

The NCCM is responsible for the dissemination and promotion of the CRC and has used print media, broadcast media, audio-visual materials and seminars.

Despite all these attempts at informing people of their rights as guaranteed by the CRC, some groups remain unaware of the freedom and protection afforded by it. Equality between the sexes is formally assured by Egyptian law but in reality girls have fewer rights than boys in many areas, especially in access to education.

The reality *against* the rhetoric

Sexual exploitation

Public belief is that the sexual exploitation of children in Egypt is very rare. Both in terms of abuse and in terms of prostitution. The Government and the wider community believe this is due to the religious education of Egyptians who show a deep respect for the teachings of Islamic Law.

GOVERNMENT ACTION AND POLICY

Several laws provide for different punishments aimed at protecting minors against corruption or perversion. Article 23 of the Law on Minors No. 31/74 establishes sanctions of three months' to five years' imprisonment for anybody who exposes a minor to delinquency. Delinquency, in this case, includes sexual perversion and the consumption and/or trafficking of drugs. In cases of prostitution it is the man seeking to buy sexual favours who is considered the criminal. Legislation provides punishment of one to three years' imprisonment, whatever the age of the victim. Sentences can be increased to a maximum of five years if the victim was younger than 21 years old.

There is no data or research concerning the use of children in the production of pornography in Egypt, and its incidence is thought to be very low or non-existent. There is provision to punish anyone who publishes pornography, with sentences of up to two years. Law no 430/55 regulates government censorship of the arts and media and forbids anything that offends public morality and good manners.

The NCCM has asked the National Council for Social Research to study the circumstances in which children live. Part of its remit is to examine the phenomenon of sexual exploitation. Depending on its findings, the NCCM will develop strategies to deal with the situation.

RECOMMENDATIONS

- **Improved levels of research** - Although the Government seeks information regarding this matter, data collection should be more focused. If there is a problem, no matter its size, it must be addressed with the utmost urgency.

Juvenile justice

In Egypt, a person is unable to give evidence in court until he/she is 21. At the age of 18 a person becomes an adult in the eyes of the law and can become subject to sanctions as dictated by the criminal law. From birth to the age of 18 a person is treated as a child and can become the subject of a case in the civil courts where matters of family and child protection are determined. He/she can also be brought before the juvenile court. Juvenile courts are required to take the age of the offender into account as well as the circumstances which led to the offence. There is no minimum age of legal responsibility.

Little reliable data concerning the total number of young offenders in Egypt is available. Figures from 1989 indicate that the number of minors held in detention was 226. The number of convicted but not interned juveniles is not recorded. Data regarding socio-economic background, gender, ethnic origin, geographic area or any other field which might reveal more significant analysis is not readily accessible.

GOVERNMENT ACTION AND POLICY

Young offenders are tried before juvenile courts and, if sentenced to detention, they should be sent to special institutions. The institutions aim to provide training and care aimed at rehabilitation. The Ministry of Social Affairs has the power to decree a young person as potentially delinquent in which case protective, curative and developmental measures can be taken to prevent the young offender 'impeding community progress' as defined by the state.

The two main types of institutions for the detention and correction of young offenders are:

- **closed penitentiaries.** These are for those convicted of delinquency and those thought to be potentially delinquent. Social, psychological, health, educational and vocational services are available.
- **comprehensive juvenile care institutions.** These provide integrated care for those children who have come before the civil courts.

The Egyptian Government clearly fails to uphold the standard of rights as detailed in Articles 37 and 40 of the CRC. The key failings are detention without trial and no minimum age of legal responsibility. The debate concerning children's rights in Egypt needs to be carried out in the wider context of human rights in the country.

RECOMMENDATIONS

- **Legislative change** - The Juveniles Act of 1974 needs to be revised to incorporate the rights detailed in the CRC as well as other international standards in this field, such as the Beijing Rules, the Riyadh Guidelines and the Rules for the Protection of Juveniles Deprived of their Liberty.
- **Alternatives to detention** - Detention should be made the last possible option to be considered when dealing with a young offender. Detention in social care institutions needs independent monitoring.

Displacement

There was insufficient reliable data or information regarding the presence and/or status of refugees in Egypt at the time of going to print.

Education

Primary education is obligatory and free in Egypt. It comprises two phases, primary and preparatory, and is known as basic education. It lasts for a total of eight years from the age of six to the age of 14. Access to the primary stage (ages 6-11) is free. Continuing attendance during all phases of education is dependent upon success in exams, which leads to a high drop-out rate. Attendance at the primary level appears high in statistical terms at 96 per cent for the year 1987/1988. However this only includes children who have progressed successfully; 25 per cent of children of school age have failed exams or are not attending school for other reasons but they are not included in the attendance statistics.

The number of pupils per class during basic education is approximately 43. Just over half of those who have attended and succeeded at primary level proceed to preparatory level. At primary level the division between gender is roughly equal, but as age increases the number of boys in education increases relative to the number of girls.

Secondary education is not free and attendance is voluntary. Secondary education includes general and technical education and lasts from 14 to 18 years of age. General education is academic and technical education is vocational in nature. Technical education includes commercial, agricultural and industrial skills training.

The official drop-out rate does not include those children who fail at exams; in the year 1984/85 it was 2.5 per cent. There are internal and external factors which affect the incidence of drop-out. Internal factors include the distances some students may have to travel to school, a didactic rote-learning approach that does not suit all children, and the density of population in poor areas leading to under-provision. External factors include low family incomes; children are often required to work to supplement the family budget. This problem is getting worse in agricultural areas as many adults have left to seek a living in the towns. Some drop-out is due to an attitude in society which sees education as less important for women. Families with little or no history of formal education often do not see the point in their children acquiring 'outside' skills and knowledge.

GOVERNMENT ACTION AND POLICY

The Ministry of Education approved a plan to provide greater amounts of teacher training in 1990, However, this plan was principally aimed at prospective teachers who were still in secondary education. Only 16 per cent of existing teachers benefited from any in-service training. Primary school teachers are not required to have a university education and often enter teaching with little or no knowledge beyond the secondary level. The NCCM has proposed a five-year plan to bring all teachers up to graduate level but so far no action has been taken in advancing this goal.

The Technical Committee of the Consultative Council (TCCC) has proposed a wide range review of technical education. Technical education has a very low status and prevents good students from progressing to higher education and there is a very bad fit between the needs of industry and commerce and skills taught in the technical schools. The TCCC has therefore proposed to revise all study plans in the technical sector; improve buildings and equipment to better suit the needs of industry; increase the technology aspect of the curriculum; and make sure that graduates with good marks are able to progress to higher education. Access to some professions should be limited to those who are suitably qualified.

Education in Egypt is seriously underfunded. The lack of premises and equipment means that even with ideal social conditions the state would still be unable to make free access to education for all a reality. Class sizes remain very high at all ages and materials and text books are invariably insufficient. Research is currently underway to assess the level of resources required to fulfil existing commitments and to highlight future needs.

The exam process is under review by the Ministry of Education. Its major failing is an over-reliance on the regurgitation of facts without demonstrating an understanding of them. It is suggested that exams should be changed to measure the pupils' knowledge of the fundamental aspects of a particular subject, their ability to adopt a scientific approach in its use and the application and their ability to solve problems in a creative way.

RECOMMENDATIONS

- **Improved access to education** - Access must be increased to facilitate the whole population, regardless of geographic location or socio-economic background.
- **Better resources** - Resources must be made available to build and equip new schools and repair and re-equip old ones.
- **Improved teacher training:** Teacher training needs significant investment and the curriculum should be revised to suit the needs of society.
- **Better examination methods** - Exams need to provide a test of a candidate's understanding of a subject - they should not just be tests of memory.

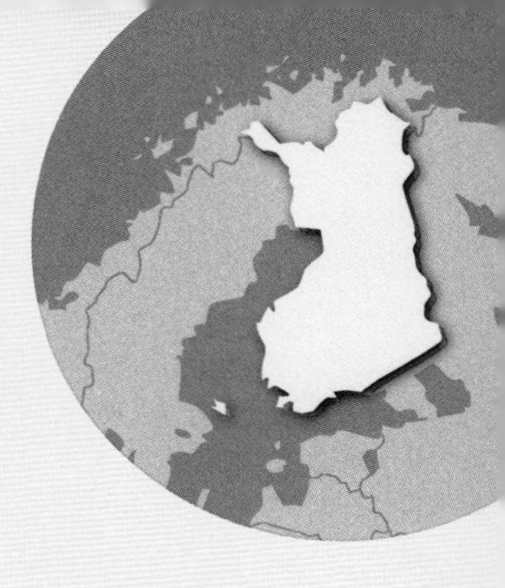

Finland

THE FINNISH GOVERNMENT AND THE CRC

Finland ratified the United Nations Convention on the Rights of the Child on January 1990 and it came into force in June 1991.

The most important legislative change was the 1995 Constitution Act which modernised and refined the Finnish system of fundamental rights, extending its scope to a wider range of persons and extending constitutional protection to new fundamental rights.

The principles of the Convention have been incorporated in the 1995 Constitution, stating that 'children shall be treated equally as individuals and shall be permitted to influence matters affecting them according to their degree of maturity'. Public authorities are charged to support the family (or other persons responsible for the child's care) to ensure the well-being and individual development of the child.

However, there are still some shortcomings in the protection of children's rights. One such gap, identified in a government report of 1995, points out that there is a need for a children's ombudsman to monitor and promote the rights and interests of children throughout the counrty at the administrative, socio-political and legislative level. He or she would also supervise implementation of children's rights and provide information on the progress of the Convention. A parliamentary committee has requested that the Government take measures to establish this office and the Ministry of Social Affairs and Health has been examining the possibility of doing so.

The Government has suggested reform of the Parliamentary Ombudsman and the creation of two Assistant Parliamentary Ombudsmen. The reform would place supervision of the implementation of Convention in the remit of one of the Assistant Parliamentary Ombudsmen.

The Ministry of Social Affairs and Health has also set up a working group to investigate any deficiency or conflict in the legislation relating to the protection of immigrant children. This group will propose measures to protect these children in accordance both with the provisions of the Convention and with Finnish legislation.

In the field of education, Finland has participated fully in the activities of the European Union, including the promotion of children's rights. The Ministers of Education meeting within the Council of the European Union issued a Declaration in December 1996 on protecting children and countering paedophilia. The Council's conclusions on safety at school were adopted on 22 September 1997. These conclusions aim to foster safety at school by supporting an information exchange and pilot projects across the nation to protect children from abuse.

There is a need for a general public awareness programme concerning the CRC to ensure it is built into all parts of society's decision-making processes. Children are still overlooked in these processes and the views on children put forward by various authorities differ considerably.

The compilation of child-oriented statistics has increased as data and analyses are included in published population and family statistics. Particular focus has been placed upon the economic and social conditions of families with children. Local and international projects have been undertaken, but the lack of statistical information is still a problem.

Regrettably, in the recent past, the situation of young people in Finland has deteriorated considerably due to the economic recession. The most urgent problem is youth unemployment, which is the highest in Europe as a percentage of the working population. Concern has been voiced at the danger of social exclusion which threatens some young people who are not in training or employment.

The participation of non-governmental organisations (NGOs) in child policy in Finland is active and well developed. NGOs are using their influence, for example, on the drafting of legislation and on the work of public authorities.

Among Finnish NGOs, the Mannerheim League for Child Welfare (MLCW) has had an Ombudsman for children since 1981.
UNICEF invited the Ombudsman for Children to become a member of the European Network of Ombudsmen for Children (ENOC). The Ombudsman for Children is assisted by a team of seven lawyers. They undertake legal work both with the implementation of children's rights as a whole, and with individual children.
The team runs a telephone helpline for children and young persons which is, at present, the most extensive in Europe (more than 40,000 contacts per year).

Despite the efforts by the Government in the field of law reform, several areas should be the focus of further governmental attention.
Some of these areas are:

- ***Statistics*** - The production of statistics should be further developed in order to clarify the circumstances of children.
- ***Governmental policies*** - Further steps should be taken to strengthen co-ordination between all governmental departments working with children's rights, at both central and local levels, and to establish a co-ordinating body to harmonise sectoral activities and policies. A national delegate for children should also be established.
- ***Dissemination of the CRC*** - Greater efforts are required to make the provisions and principles of the CRC more widely known and understood by adults and children alike.

The reality *against* the rhetoric

Sexual exploitation

The commercial sexual exploitation of children has been increasing in Finland in the 1990s but active attempts are being made to prevent this phenomenon. Unfortunately there is a lack of comprehensive and reliable data on the prevalence of commercial and/or other forms of sexual exploitation. It is therefore difficult to assess accurately the real nature of problem.

GOVERNMENT ACTION AND POLICY

The Finnish Government is committed to the prevention of sexual exploitation. For example, the Social Affairs and Health Committee of Parliament consults experts and has held seminars to examine the matter. Working groups and committees have also worked on the problem and proposed recommendations. In 1998 the Ministry of Social Affairs and Health also initiated a plan for the prevention of child prostitution within a wider project on the prevention of violence against women.

Parliamentary negotiations are under way to amend the Penal Code so that a Finnish citizen, or a foreign citizen residing permanently in Finland, could be convicted of an offence of the sexual abuse of children whilst abroad. Furthermore, child welfare organisations have repeatedly demanded that the possession of child pornography, at present permitted, be made a criminal offence. Such legal provision entered into force on 1 January 1991.

In the past few years, there has been a huge growth in a new form of sexual exploitation - the telephone service. There is alarm at these services as it is suspected that children (rather than the intended adults) may use them and obtain inappropriate material. It has been suggested that telephone services providing sexual entertainment, as well as conversation lines, should be made subject to an agreement between the telephone subscribers and the telephone company, rather than simply being available to anyone who calls.

RECOMMENDATIONS

- **Greater protection of children** - Children should be protected from accessing telephone sex services and the potential risk of being sexually exploited by paedophiles through these services.

Juvenile Justice

There are only a small number of persons under 18 years old imprisoned or in pre-trial detention in Finland. Fifty to 80 young people under the age of 18 are sent to prison each year and most of those are in pre-trial detention. In 1997 there were four prisoners under 18 serving a sentence, and 48 young people were in pre-trial detention. On 1 January 1998, there were eight minors in prison (less than 1 per cent of all prisoners), all of whom were in pre-trial detention.
The small number of prisoners under 18 results partly from the fact that, since the amendment to the Conditional Sentence Act, it is no longer possible to issue unconditional sentences for offences committed by a person under 18, unless considered necessary because of the serious nature of the offence.

The minimum age for criminal liability is 15 - anyone younger cannot be arrested or imprisoned. A child who has reached the age of 15 may be arrested and imprisoned on such grounds as are provided by the law, but only if it is reasonable given their age. If an offence was committed by a person between the ages of 15 and 20, he or she is regarded as a young offender to whom a number of special provisions apply.

GOVERNMENT ACTION AND POLICY

Finland is, at present, introducing major reforms to its criminal legislation.

In Finland, a child or young person may be subject to deprivation of liberty only on certain grounds provided by law and detainees are entitled to fair treatment and respect for their dignity. When a sentence imposed on a young offender is enforced, attention is paid to the special needs caused by the age and maturity of the prisoner. Every effort is made to keep young offenders separate from adult prisoners and this is generally possible. Prisoners under 18 have a named support person to arrange activities and take care of their prison conditions.

Periodically there are debates on raising the age ofcriminal liability, but this has never resulted in action. This age limit does not apply to liability for damages imposed on a minor, even if he or she is not sentenced to prison on grounds of age.

Capital punishment for crimes committed in peacetime was abolished in Finland in 1949, and for all crimes in 1972. The prohibition of torture and degrading treatment was also included in the Constitution Act in accordance with the provisions of international human rights conventions.

RECOMMENDATIONS

There are no specific recommendations with regard to juvenile justice.

Displacement

Approximately two per cent of the population are foreign citizens. Most foreigners are of working age - between 15 and 64 years old - but some 20 per cent are children. The proportion of children is highest in those groups that have arrived in Finland as refugees from Bosnia and Somalia. Of the asylum-seekers who have arrived in Finland in the 1990s, less than 10 per cent are unaccompanied minors.

Approximately half the minors are 14 to 17 years old. According to 1997 estimates, Finland has received some 14,000 refugees. Refugees have arrived as quota refugees, as asylum-seekers and through family reunification. There are also some 20,000 returnees from the former Soviet Union.

GOVERNMENT ACTION AND POLICY

On 16 October 1997 the Government adopted the Programme on Immigration and Refugee Policy, and this will be implemented in stages in accordance with economic resources.

The objectives of the Finnish immigration policy are to integrate immigrants, including refugees, into society. Immigrants should be able to participate in the economic, political and social life of society. The Government is ensuring that all the fundamental rights enshrined in the Constitution are available to refugees. The integration of immigrants will be implemented in the form of a three-level policy: national integration, a municipal programme for immigration policy and an integration plan for individuals and families.

A Bill on the integration of immigrants and the reception of refugees was introduced to Parliament in May 1998. It proposed that a representative (probably found with the help of NGOs) would be designated for each unaccompanied child who is applying for asylum to assure the legal rights of the child.
The representative would use custodian rights in matters concerning the person and property of the child but would not take care of the upbringing of the child. The Commission of the European Communities has financed a project to develop this system of representatives.
The custody of a child who has been granted a residence permit will be ensured in the same way as the custody of a Finnish child, by naming a custodian or a trustee for the child.

The Government provides various arrangements for child asylum-seekers. Unaccompanied minors are placed in special child units at reception centres. Each unit is responsible for the care, upbringing and education of the child, and initiates a search for the parents and arranges contact if possible. The reception centre employs youth workers of the same ethnic group of the majority of children; others receive lessons and contact with persons speaking their home language.

Some children may be placed in the homes of relatives, providing the social welfare authorities approve. Minors who have been granted a residence permit are transferred from the reception units for children to reception units for families maintained by municipalities. These are home-like units where the number of children and personnel, as well as the qualifications of personnel, correspond to the requirements set by the Child Welfare Decree. When a person has reached 18 years of age, he or she may live in a flat arranged by the municipality.

A combined reception unit for children and families has been established which makes it possible to avoid the transfer from one place to another. The combined unit is small but it has adequate resources and works flexibly.

The Government has responsibility for satisfying the basic needs of asylum-seekers arriving in Finland. If possible, asylum-seeking families with children are accommodated in reception centres where the environment and services correspond to the needs of the children. The reception centre takes care of the subsistence of the asylum-seekers and arranges for social welfare and health-care services when necessary.

Immigrant children of school age are entitled to the same free comprehensive school education as Finnish children. Special services are provided for these children to ease their integration into society, including preservation of their own language and culture. Preparatory education at comprehensive schools may be arranged in a separate group for all immigrant children. Immigrant pupils may also get remedial education at comprehensive schools and upper secondary schools. They can also study Finnish or Swedish as a foreign language. Children and young persons speaking a foreign language may have their own language taught as their mother tongue.

RECOMMENDATIONS

- **Unaccompanied children** - Upon arrival in Finland, all unaccompanied children seeking refugee status should be informed promptly of their rights in their own language.

Education

Education in Finland is not split into primary and secondary phases as it is in many other countries. This is because formal instruction does not begin until children are seven. Before this they are engaged in guided play aimed at developing a wide range of skills.

Children have the right to receive comprehensive school education free of charge. This education must be arranged so that the child's age and preparedness for learning are taken into account. This means that even severely disabled children are taught at comprehensive schools. Children start school at seven and compulsory education continues for ten years, or until the completion of the nine-year comprehensive school curriculum. There are also supervised private institutions in nearly all fields of education, having the same minimum standards of education as state schools.

Only 0.03 per cent of all pupils did not receive the prescribed education in 1996-97. These pupils had either completely dropped out of school or had attained the age at which compulsory education terminates. As regards professional education and upper secondary schools, the proportion of drop-outs increased during the economic boom at the end of the 1980s when the rate of unemployment was low. The subsequent economic recession reduced the proportion of drop-outs - in 1995 the proportion of students dropping out of upper secondary schools was four per cent.

A Bill to amend school legislation has been submitted to Parliament. One purpose of the amendment is to reduce the number of existing Acts to fewer, more consistent entities.

GOVERNMENT ACTION AND POLICY

As the average level of education has increased in the general population, those who remain without adequate education are finding it harder to obtain work. Unemployment, especially long-term unemployment among the young, is still a serious problem in Finland. Despite the overall positive picture of the Finnish education system, some concerns remain.

At the local level, the Child Welfare Act requires municipalities to provide adequate support for educational guidance, to promote measures to remove social and psychological difficulties of pupils, and to enhance co-operation between the school and the home. Psychosocial support in schools is undertaken by municipal school psychologists and school welfare officers. The purpose of their work is to minimise problems in learning and to take the maturity of pupils into account. However, the offices of school psychologists and school welfare officers are not evenly distributed across the country, as nearly 90 per cent of school psychologists and 80 per cent of school welfare officers work in southern Finland.

There is now vigorous public debate concerning the increasing instances of bullying in schools and the need to understand what causes it.

The education of children of Roma parentage needs to be addressed. Due to their cultural background Roma children have, even in the past few years, often failed to complete their schooling. Although school attendance and post-school education has clearly improved, drop-out rates among Roma children are disproportionately high. The Comprehensive Schools Act and the Upper Secondary Schools Act made it possible to teach the Romani language (as well as the Sami language and an additional foreign language) in which case the second national language taught is either Finnish or Swedish.

Requirements concerning the size of groups have made it slow to extend the teaching of the Roma language as the mother tongue to children living in sparsely populated areas. The Advisory Board for Roma Affairs believes that the economic problems of municipalities make it difficult for schools to adequately teach the mother tongues of ethnic minorities. The Sami language is taught, and teaching is given in the Sami language, mainly at primary schools in the municipalities of the Sami area. The greatest problem at secondary schools and upper secondary schools is the lack of both materials and qualified teachers.

New workshop schools have been developed for those who have not received post-school education or who have dropped out of school. Practical and vocational work constitutes a significant part of the their curricula.

The Finnish school system does not include preparatory (primary) schools in the proper sense of the word but pre-school education given by comprehensive schools and day-care centres. Municipalities are not under a statutory duty to organise pre-school education. Pre-school education provided by day-care centres, is sometimes subject to fees with fees depending on the size and income of the family and on the number of children in the family participating in day care. In 1996 the National Board of Education, together with the National Research and Development Centre for Welfare and Health drafted a curriculum for pre-school education aimed at creating a stimulating learning environment where the child has an opportunity to learn multiple skills together with other children. Individuality, active learning and growing as a member of a group are all emphasised.

The curricula of all schools emphasise the importance of personal guidance for each pupil. The need for guidance has increased due to the wider freedom schools have to decide on the number of hours spent on each subject. The ability of schools to provide study guidance has become limited, certain municipalities provide study guidance but others have had to lay off their entire guidance personnel in order to save money. In 1997, 47 municipalities lost teachers; or made other arrangements interrupting teaching. In total, the measures affected 1,500 teachers approximately 4 per cent of all teachers in comprehensive schools.

The curricula provided by schools are fairly comprehensive. The national framework for the curricula was reformed between 1994 and 1996 with the aim of changing both the contents of education and, above all, teaching methods. Using common guidelines, municipalities have been able to establish a curriculum for schools and, if necessary, individual curricula for pupils. The guidelines emphasise the active role of the pupil and the importance of taking his or her talent, interests and learning difficulties into account.

Sustainable development is emphasised across the curriculum and the guidelines promote awareness of environmental issues, ecological processes and biodiversity. Multiculturalism is another new and important topic - with an emphasis on cultural identity and international communication.

Tolerance and openness to different cultural backgrounds, opinions and languages create a basis for mutual interaction between pupils and for international co-operation. Knowledge of other cultures is allied to human rights teaching. Individual school legislation and the Act on Equality requires that the promotion of equality between women and men is one of the aims of education as a whole. The objective is that boys and girls will have equal rights and obligations in family life, work and society.

RECOMMENDATIONS

- **Address school drop-out levels** - All necessary measures should be taken to reduce number of pupils dropping out of school.
- **Increased provision for children from ethnic minorities** - Sufficient teachers and appropriate resources for minority children should be available in all areas of the country.

'I want my family out of the life we have now. Education is the only thing that can make something of you'.

Edgar, age 15 - Honduras

France

THE FRENCH GOVERNMENT AND THE CRC

France signed the United Nations Convention on the Rights of the Child on 26 January 1990 and ratified it on 7 August. It came into effect on 6 September 1990. France entered one reservation and two interpretative declarations. The reservation concerns Article 30, which is in conflict with Article 2 of the Constitution of the French Republic. Article 2 upholds the principles of equality and non-discrimination, and so the existence of minorities, in the sense of groups enjoying a special status, cannot be recognised in France.

French civil law contains a definition of the child, which corresponds with that given in Article 1 of the Convention, 'a minor (child) is an individual of either sex who has not yet reached 18 years of age'.

France's administrative machinery has been modified by decentralising legislation and this has given local authorities a sizeable proportion of the powers hitherto held by the state. This has affected who is responsible for implementing children's rights - for example, the responsibility for social and medical welfare now rests mainly with the Regional Council (although child welfare is not assured solely by government services but also by publicly-funded non-profit associations) - and this may cause problems. The decentralisation of power may generate a disparity in local policy and the state must ensure that the principle of equality of citizens before the law and the public services is respected.

The Act of 27 January 1993 commits the Government to submitting a report to Parliament every year on the implementation of the Convention and on its policies. The Childhood and Family Institute, a national public body, leads a working group which, at the end of 1991, included some 100 associations working actively for the promotion and defence of children's rights. This group has acquired independent status and, on 7 February 1992, formed the French Council of Associations for the Rights of the Child (COFRADE). These organisations have been extremely active in publicising the Convention.

As a result of decentralisation, and the new administrative measures, activities relating to children are undertaken in France by a very large number of public and private institutions. Co-ordinating these activities and assessing their impact on children's lives is, therefore, a constant and difficult challenge for the authorities. Care must be taken that the large number of institutions does not impair the overall coherence of policy relating to children.

One key concern is the phenomenon of social exclusion, which affects many young people. For many, entry into active life at the end of their schooling has become a time of uncertainty and destabilisation. For structural reasons related to inadequate links between training, qualifications and labour market requirements, young people are quickly affected by any slowdown in economic growth and the subsequent increase in unemployment. Moreover, some encounter specific problems, particularly those who live in the suburbs of large cities and those who belong to the second generation of immigrants.

The Government should address the following points:

- Co-ordination. A permanent mechanism of co-ordination and evaluation of the policies used to implement the Convention should be established. A comprehensive, holistic approach to legislation is necessary. The multi-agency approach means that a clear guide to their various responsibities is required so that problems, when identified, can be addressed to the correct authorities.
- Co-operation. The importance of close co-operation between the central Government and the local authorities should be stressed to minimise disparities between the regions as to the provision of services. This necessarily includes budgetary considerations.

The reality *against* the rhetoric

Sexual exploitation

In 1988 a campaign was launched to prevent sexual mistreatment. It was aimed primarily at pornography, prostitution, incest and paedophilia. The key finding of this campaign was how the sexual exploitation of children had been obscured by denial and incredulity. This situation has now changed and greater efforts are being made to address this serious, if relatively small-scale, problem. The prior lack of acknowledgement means that research and data are in short supply, therefore it is difficult to supply any meaningful figures regarding the scope and scale of the situation.

GOVERNMENT ACTION AND POLICY

Although the phenomenon of sexual exploitation is thought to be relatively rare in France the authorities have taken several initiatives to prevent it. The prevention of sexual violence forms part of the campaign for the prevention of mistreatment of children.

An inter-ministerial group was constituted in Sept 92 to study 'children used for the purposes of pornography or prostitution'. French criminal law has, for a long time, imposed stiff penalties against those whose victims are minors, especially where rape is concerned and where pimps use children as prostitutes. Other categories of offences are specifically designed to protect minors and these include: indecent acts with or without violence or constraint, inciting a minor to sexual activities and abduction of a minor. The new Penal Code, which came into effect on 1 Sept 93 refines and strengthens laws concerning dangerous and immoral behaviour, especially where minors are the victims.

Where the perpetrators of sexual abuse are the parents, the legal guardians of the victim, the Act of 10 July 1989 allows for an ad hoc administrator to represent the child in the proceedings. The beginning of the period during which a prosecution may be brought for offences committed against the child by parents may be postponed until he or she reaches the age of majority.

RECOMMENDATIONS

- **Information** - Efforts must focus on the technical improvement and development of information gathering facilities as part of continuing public awareness campaigns.
- **Training** - Professionals such as judges, teachers, doctors, social workers and police officers should have appropriate training in dealing with the victims of sexual exploitation.
- **Co-operation** - The Government should work more closely with relevant non-governmental organisations (NGOs) in order to improve policies and practices. Furthermore, the National Advisory Commission for Human Rights should establish a working group on ethical issues related to pornography and prostitution where children are involved.

Juvenile justice

Since the mid 1980s youth crime has been on the increase. Populist thought sees this largely as a result of family breakdown and lack of parental authority.

In France, although a very young child may be found criminally liable, only educational measures can be put in place and no criminal penalty can be imposed before the age of 13. Between the ages of 13 and 16, pre-trial detention is possible only in connection with criminal acts. However, there is concern that legislation and practice relating to arrest, detention, sentencing and imprisonment within the juvenile justice system might not be fully consistent with the provisions and principles of the Convention.

GOVERNMENT ACTION AND POLICY

Major legislative changes mean that the concept of physical custody has been replaced by that of parental authority and children have been allowed the right to voice their opinions in some matters that affect them.

In the legitimate family (i.e. where the parents are or have been married) each parent now has parental authority even if he or she does not live with the child and, in such circumstances, the parent maintains the right to supervise the upkeep and upbringing of the child. The law also simplifies the joint exercise of parental authority in the natural family (i.e. where the parents are not married) by allowing the parents to make a joint declaration of their mutual responsibilities for the child before a judge. Divorce proceedings take into consideration the sentiments of the child who, if he or she is over 13 years old, will, in principle, be heard.

Public opinion considers the right for children to be heard in certain circumstances as the major contribution of the CRC to life in France. However, recent decisions by the *Cour de Cassation* (highest criminal and civil court) with regard to this matter have questioned the status of the Convention in the national legal framework.

Legislation relating to the civil courts, the family and the rights of the child has established the post of judge for family affairs and incorporates into law the principle in Article 12 of the Convention concerning recognition of the right of minors to express themselves in court. A child who is capable of forming his or her own views is entitled to be heard in any proceedings affecting him or her. These provisions are not simply an extension of previously existing rules (ie designed to enlighten the judge and to assist in making decisions) they effectively establish a new right for the child, the right to speak in proceedings.

Since it is only a right of expression the new law does not confer upon a child the capacity to be party to all proceedings. When a minor requests a hearing, his or her right can only be denied by a specially reasoned decision except when the child's liberty is at stake when a hearing is always given. The child may be heard alone, with a person of his or her choice, or with a lawyer. If the interests of the child and his or her parents are divergent then an ad hoc administrator may be appointed.

Minors in conflict with the law are subject to special arrangements. These are applied by specialised juvenile magistrates and juvenile courts for minor offences and all offences committed by minors under 16 years. Juvenile assizes courts are used for serious offences committed by juveniles aged from 16 to 18. All courts have a duty to decide, as a matter of priority, measures for the protection, assistance, supervision and education of offenders.

Detention cannot be imposed on children under 13. For those between 13 and 16 detention is exceptional and must be for a short period only. For those above the age of 16 detention may be used, although a mitigating plea of diminished responsibility due to youth may be submitted. Pre-trial proceedings are obligatory in all cases relating to offences committed by minors.

Criminal cases concerning minors, or cases in which both minors and adults are involved, are investigated by examining magistrates specialised in juvenile cases. The simplest cases are heard in chambers by the juvenile magistrate. If the minor is found guilty, the juvenile magistrate may reprimand him or her or order various educational measures. The more complex cases are tried by juvenile courts.

There are a number of special guarantees for minors. Parents must be closely associated with all stages of the proceedings and the minor must have the benefit of counsel. In order to ensure better protection for the minor, hearings at the trial are not public and may not be reported by the media. Recent legislation now means pre-trial detention is a measure of last resort, restricted to the most serious cases.

On reaching the age of majority, or at the end of a sentence, a young offender's record is expunged. This promotes rehabilitation, as those with criminal records may encounter problems when seeking education or employment.

RECOMMENDATIONS

- **Legislative change** - Legislation and practice in the field of the administration of juvenile justice should be fully consistent with the provisions and principles of the Convention. In addition, the status of Article 14 of the Convention in the national legal framework should be clarified.
- **Monitoring and reporting** - Annual reports concerning policy should be adopted in order to ensure that the CRC is fully realised.

Displacement

Recent legislation in this field has mainly been concentrated on efforts to ensure the provisions of Article 10 of the CRC are incorporated into French law. This article concerns families that have been separated during the immigration process.

Unfortunately, the author was unable to access reliable official statistics on refugee figures in France at the time of going to print.

GOVERNMENT ACTION AND POLICY

The CRC affirms the child's right to preserve contact with both parents beyond national borders. Two multilateral conventions are in force in France: the European Convention on Recognition and Enforcement of Decisions concerning Custody of Children and on Restoration of Custody of Children (1980), and the Convention on the Civil Aspects of International Child Abduction (The Hague, 1980). Their purpose is to prevent child abduction and ensure the efficacy of court decisions establishing conditions for the exercise of parental authority. Unfortunately, the objective is to guarantee only legitimate children the right to maintain regular contact with their separated parents and, thus, dissuade the parents of natural families from illicitly transporting their children. This process clearly discriminates against a child whose parents were not married at the time of his or her birth - violating France's constitutional principles of equality and non-discrimination.

New legislation has been adopted concerning nationality, the entry and residence of foreigners, refugees and asylum-seekers and family reunification.

Under the so-called family regrouping procedure, the French Government authorises the entry into France of children of foreigners who regularly reside in the country. Children then have the right to residency and work permits similar to those issued to their parents. Only very serious reasons, described in law, can justify refusal of entry into France and of a residence permit. A child born in France to foreign parents will acquire French nationality only from the age of 16 as a result of the new legislative measure introduced in 1993.

NGOs and civil society are very concerned at the situation of unaccompanied children who arrive unexpectedly in France in order to obtain refugee status. It is alleged that state support is inadequate for this group. Most of the time these children rely on NGOs, churches, other organisations or individuals. NGOs are also concerned about the lack of a comprehensive system of protection for unaccompanied children involving the social and/or judicial authorities while they are subject to the jurisdiction of the state, as well as in the process of their possible return to their country of origin.

RECOMMENDATIONS

- **Legislative compliance with the CRC** - The constitutional principles of equality and non-discrimination should be applied when dealing with legitimate and illegitimate children. Furthermore, all the provisions of the CRC should be ensured for foreign children under Article 55 of the French Constitution.
- **Development of policy and provisions for all foreign children** - A comprehensive policy which more effectively promotes the integration of foreign children, including refugees, should be worked out by all stakeholders. Also, a realistic action plan with clearly identified targets should be put in place in order to deal with the phenomenon of exclusion which affects immigrants and refugees to a greater extent than those born in France.

Education

Education is compulsory for children aged from six to sixteen. At the age of three, every child should be able to attend a nursery school or kindergarten if his or her family wishes.

The right to education is guaranteed to everyone. The education system is centred on the needs of pupils and contributes to equality of opportunity. However, it must be pointed out that, despite these principles, a significant number of children from underprivileged groups cannot, for various reasons, make the best use of the French education system. As a result, schools and high schools are used increasingly by pupils as a place where they can express their frustration with society. This situation is now common across the country. Immigrant children are affected by the same degree of frustration as is expressed by French children. This phenomenon is spreading across the social structure of the country including the middle class.

GOVERNMENT POLICY AND ACTION

The acquisition of cultural capital and recognised qualifications is guaranteed to all young people, regardless of their geographical or social origin. Continuing education offers everyone an opportunity to raise their educational level to adjust to economic and social change and to obtain required knowledge.

As far as pre-school education is concerned, enrolment from two years is given priority in schools situated in socially under-privileged environments, as long as places are available. Pupils from under-privileged backgrounds may be provided with financial assistance. The right to educational and vocational information and guidance forms part of the right to education.

In order to provide a better response to its overall objectives, the Ministry of Education and Culture carries out a number of activities in partnership with different ministries, with local authorities, with major national bodies such as the French Committee for Health Education, and with international bodies such as UNICEF. A guide to schooling entitled The School Support Charter, published in 1992, meets two objectives: to publicise educational support measures in the most under-privileged districts and rural areas, and to monitor these.

To supplement the education system, an extensive vocational scheme has been established for the young people most in difficulty. Information and guidance offices provide support for every young person in building up his or her qualifications and preparing for vocational and social integration. Established on the initiative of the local authorities and presided over by an elected chairman. Local agencies bring together the state services and other economic and social partners.

The aims and objectives of the French education system closely match the provisions of the Convention. Promoting the development of the child's personality is an aim that was reaffirmed by legislation which states that 'education must develop in the young a taste for creation and for the practice of cultural and artistic activities and participation in community life. Furthermore, the education system must also provide for physical education and sports.'

Civic education is a compulsory subject throughout schooling. Education in human rights is given in primary, secondary and high schools. The education in human rights given in secondary schools comprises the study of the principles on which the Republic is founded, such as liberty, equality and tolerance, and an understanding of the rules of French democracy. The environment is also accorded a strong place in education.

Because of high levels of unemployment, some experts believe that the education system needs to be adapted to match more closely to the employment market. A recent report commissioned by the Government has endorsed this view. However it is most important that this training-based model of education does not inhibit the acquisition of a wider cultural capital.

RECOMMENDATIONS

- **Curriculum development** - Educational curricula should be reviewed to make them more interesting for the pupils. In addition, measures should be adopted to deal effectively with the causes of frustration expressed by pupils. Pupils should also be more widely consulted on what their needs are.
- **Training** - New working methods and better training for teachers should be initiated.

Greece

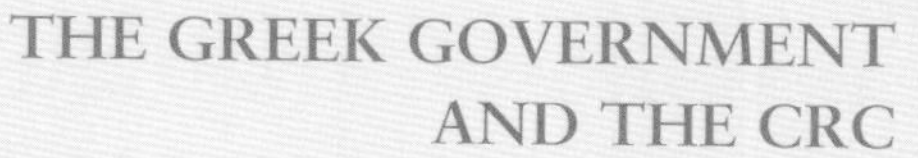

THE GREEK GOVERNMENT AND THE CRC

Greece became a signatory to the UN Convention of the Rights of the Child in 1992. Although the CRC has influenced some practices in Greece, its profile is virtually non-existent among most government bodies, other than those working directly with children's issues. More recently, some efforts have been made by non-governmental organisations (NGOs) and other agencies working with children to raise awareness both among policy-makers and the general public on the CRC. Although these efforts have been positive, a great deal still remains to be done.

Children's and youth issues fall under the remit of the General Secretariat for Youth of the Ministry of Education and Religions. In recent years a growing interest in children's rights has been demonstrated. For example;

- The development of a multifaceted plan of action for the promotion of children's issues and rights. This addresses issues including education, employment, youth enterprise, health, youth participation in society and actions against social exclusion. This is an encouraging start but the effects still remain to be seen.
- Some new institutions for the promotion of children's rights have been established in recent years.
  National Observatory for Children's and Youth Rights Founded under the auspices of the Ministry of Education, its primary goals include:
  - the promotion of research into children's issues, revealing the real situation for children in Greece;
  - the evaluation of Greek legislation in terms of its effects on children and youth;
  - annual reporting on the situation of children in the country and preparation of as well as an annual plan of action.

  Interministerial Committee on Youth
  This committee aims to co-ordinate the actions of the different ministries which share responsibility for the care and provision of services to children. It includes representatives from the Ministries of Education, Development, Agriculture, Work and Social Welfare, Health and Welfare, Culture and the General Secretariat of Youth. It seeks to address the needs of the whole child in a co-ordinated way.

A Citizens' Ombudsman
Although its mission does not specifically include the promotion of children's rights, it is hoped that this will be followed by the establishment of an ombudsman for children.

Despite these positive steps, no actual implementation of the CRC is evident in the actions of many ministries and governmental bodies (except the Ministry of Education).

Although Greece ratified the CRC in 1992, it is only now nearing completion of its first report to the UN. A positive sign in the preparation process was that NGO views and experience were requested, but in reality their involvement was limited and circumscribed. However this hopefully constitutes a timid but promising start for a more extensive collaboration between Government and NGOs in the preparation of future reports, as well as for the better promotion of children's rights in Greece.

The reality *against* the rhetoric

Sexual exploitation

In recent years Greece has seen a significant increase in the sexual trafficking and sexual exploitation of children and in the dissemination of child pornography, especially through the Internet. As in other countries, the existence of all forms of sexual abuse and sexual exploitation of children is acknowledged in Greece, yet little systematic data exists.

Sexual abuse
One study on the sexual abuse of children in Greece indicates that among a small sample of college students aged 18-20, 17 per cent of the girls and 7 per cent of the boys had experienced some form of sexual abuse before they reached the age of 18. Abuse was generally carried out by a family member, by someone the child was less closely acquainted with, or by a person unknown to the child.

The reported incidence of such crimes are relatively low, but has increased over recent years as the level of awareness of child sexual abuse increases. In 1997, 62 cases of sexual abuse were treated by the Children's Psychiatric Clinic of the St Sophia Children's Hospital in Athens. In several of these cases, sexual abuse was accompanied by physical abuse. In the same year, the police sub-directorate for Juvenile Protection reported only 11 cases of sexual abuse and 10 cases of exhibition. This clearly demonstrates the lack of accurate systematic data. More reliable data on the subject exists only for the cases reaching the judicial system.

Sexual exploitation - prostitution and trafficking of children
Interlaced with international organised crime in Greece, this phenomenon has shown an increase correlating with the increase of illegal migration into the country principally from Eastern Europe. Again limited official data exists.

A recent study indicated that approximately 5,500 children have been pushed into prostitution in Greece in the last three years. In the period over which the study was conducted, from September 1995 to March 1997, 2,990 children working in the Greek prostitution market were located.

Children deemed to be most at risk include children in social exclusion and in poverty, children from dysfunctional families, migrant children (especially illegal migrants), and street children

GOVERNMENT ACTION AND POLICY

Greek criminal law contains several articles that provide protection for victims (of any age) of sexual abuse and exploitation, by punishing the perpetrator. There are no special provisions for children.

Until recently the legal provisions for the protection of children from sexual exploitation have been based solely on a punitive approach, rather than a preventive and therapeutic one. However, the Ministry of Health and Welfare is now developing a more broad-reaching strategy based on primary prevention (early detection).

Currently, there is no blanket provision of alternative approaches (for example, therapy) for either victims or perpetrators. Therapeutic support for child victims and their families does exist, but is provided to only a small number, in the Athens area. The 1996 World Congress against Commercial Sexual Exploitation of Children in Stockholm has, as yet, not constituted an effective stimulus for the Greek Government to adopt an appropriate plan of action.

RECOMMENDATIONS

There are a number of key areas where the Greek Government could ensure better implementation of the CRC.

- **Amend the legal framework referring to sexual exploitation and abuse of children -**
a) Allow for therapeutic and preventive, rather than punitive, approaches to the problem/cases of child sexual exploitation and abuse.
b) Allow for the therapy and protection of illegal migrant children who are victims of sexual exploitation.
c) Include a provision dealing with the production, possession and distribution of pornographic materials involving children.
- **Establish a national prevention programme** This should be based on the promotion of the spirit of the CRC (best interests, protection and participation of children).
- **Improve the quality and quantity of data collected** - The collection of better data on the issue should be encouraged and better resourced.
- **Prioritise the continuing education and training of professionals** - The continuing education and training of the police, judicial, social and education professionals on the recognition of sexual exploitation and abuse should be promoted.
- **Strengthen existing therapeutic centres** - In order that they can better deal with child victims of sexual exploitation and abuse

Juvenile justice

The Penal Code of Justice in Greece determines a 'juvenile' to be a child between the ages of six years and one day and 17 years (until his or her 18th birthday). According to this law, 'children' are up to 12 years old and 'adolescents' are those of 13 to 17 years inclusive. Thus, only children above the age of six years and one day old can be treated by the juvenile justice system. Children are held criminally liable from the age of 12 years. In contrast, under the separate Civil Code of Justice, juveniles are individuals from birth to 18 years of age.

According to the official police statistics (Statistical Review, Subdirectorate for Juvenile Protection, Attica, Ministry of Public Order, 1997), 20,599 children committed criminal acts in 1997. This is an overall increase of 12.9 per cent since 1992. The majority of these crimes (96.9 per cent) are committed by adolescents (13-17 years). However it is also significant to note that the incidence of crimes committed by children (those between 7 and 12) over this same period more than doubled from 316 to 644.

The most frequent offence among the 7 to 12 year olds is begging, whilst among the 13 to 17 year olds the most frequent offences are against special provisions of the criminal law - for example, violence, the possession of guns and explosives, car-related crime, drugs-related offences and illegal migration. Overall, 91 per cent of juvenile criminal activity is carried out by boys.

Begging is considered a criminal offence in Greece rather than being seen as an indication of inadequate socio-economic conditions. Begging constitutes 35.2 per cent of all offences dealt with by the juvenile police services. It is not surprising that, due to their economic disadvantage, illegal migrants made up 51.7 per cent (513) of the youth offenders convicted of begging, and were deported.

Greece has abolished the death penalty for all offences. In addition, it does not allow corporal punishment for any offenders - youth or adult. There is no substantiated data suggesting that ill-treatment of young offenders occurs by the juvenile police services or by other services of the legal system.

GOVERNMENT ACTION AND POLICY

Juvenile young offenders do not go through the adult legal system. Instead, there are special juvenile courts where hearings are held in private. The Probation Service carries out the research for the case, proposes measures to the court and later, after the court decision, undertakes to support and monitor the child or youth's development.

For child offenders (six years and one day to 12 years old), the court can decide to apply either:

- reformative actions - reproach, placed under the care of the parents or of a probation officer, or placement in a reformatory or welfare institution; or
- therapeutic measures - such as psychological support in a psychiatric institution.

Adolescents (13-17 years old) can also be sent to a correctional facility for more serious or recurring offences. The minimum time a child may serve in a correctional facility is six months. Generally, the most commonly used measure for children is to be placed under the care of a probation officer. Unfortunately, the number of probation officers is small in comparison to the needs, limiting the effectiveness of this mechanism.

The law also provides for Societies for Juvenile Protection; these are institutions which operate special services/dormitories, where young offenders can be sent. These have been similarly under-resourced in recent years.

Young offenders are, on the whole, provided with adequate representation and can either be represented by probation officers or lawyers. Their views can be heard in the juvenile courts, although sufficient emphasis is not placed upon this. If interpretation services are needed, they are provided at all the stages of the case.

At present there is no promotion of alternative approaches to deal with juvenile crime. However, discussions have now begun to promote the welfare model which views juvenile offenders as children that need protection and support.

RECOMMENDATIONS

- **Increase the minimum age children can be held responsible for criminal action**
- **Provide alternatives to the deportation of migrant juvenile offenders** - especially when the offence is begging.
- **Improve the standard of existing institutions** - Update the centres and increase the expertise of staff.
- **Establish an independent service of juvenile judges** - This is essential to ensure that the judges have the right level of training and experience of juvenile cases. The same holds true for the police. There should be more police departments designated to deal with juvenile offences throughout Greece (currently there are just four). Police officers should have the choice

to specialise (through training and actual service) in the treatment of juvenile offenders and to remain in this department throughout their career.

- **Children's rights welfare service** - New institutions are needed which will promote children's rights and welfare. These institutions could also provide an alternative to the deportation of migrant young offenders
- **Children's ombudsman** - The establishment of an ombudsman for children as well as institutions for the protection and support of young offenders are just two examples of such institutions.

Displacement

During the last decade the influx of refugees and asylum-seekers in Greece has increased. The presence of an office for the United Nations High Commissioner for Refugees (UNHCR) in Athens and their co-operation with local and national authorities have undoubtedly led to an improvement in the situation for refugees and asylum-seekers in the country.

Refugees mainly come from near and neighbouring countries, including Iraq, Iran, Turkey, Afghanistan, the states of former Yugoslavia and West Bank and Gaza.
In 1998 Greece received 549 refugee children. The majority, over 65 per cent, came from Iran and Iraq.

GOVERNMENT ACTION AND POLICY

The provision for refugee children in Greece is not consistent. In some cases refugee children are not designated as 'vulnerable' and therefore receive no prioritised, specialised treatment. Alternative service provision is carried out by NGOs working in liaison with UNHCR to meet refugee children's needs. The state provides some basic services, but these focus on a limited number of children and only cover recognised refugees and asylum-seekers.

Reception and accommodation

Greece has only one reception facility, the Lavrion Reception Centre, for refugees and asylum-seekers. Unaccompanied children are always given preferential treatment here. However, service provision is not guaranteed and many families find themselves homeless, resorting to makeshift accommodation. Some shelter projects exist, set up by the Greek Council for Refugees and the Social Service for Refugees of the Social Work Foundation. Rent subsidies (UNHCR-funded) are also provided for recognised refugees and in exceptional cases for 'vulnerable' asylum-seekers. Families with children are not necessarily guaranteed special consideration. On the whole, most refugees and asylum-seekers with children live under very poor conditions.

Nutrition and provision of supplementary aid

Feeding programmes and other social services are provided by the Hellenic Red Cross at the Lavrion Reception Centre. However they meet the needs of only a few. Children's health and nutrition programmes are also run by the Social Service for Refugees of the Social Work Foundation along with the Greek Council for Refugees. In addition, NGOs (including Save the Children Greece) also offer a range of social services to help refugees and asylum-seekers in difficult situations.

Health facilities

Free medical care is available to all refugees and asylum-seekers in public hospitals. Care is not problematic as long as individuals have registered and carry the relevant identification card, issued by the Ministry of Public Order, and have been referred by social services. Children and pregnant women are normally prioritised with a simple referral.

The provision of medicine and drugs, however, is a problem. In some cases, medicines can be provided by the hospital pharmacies. In general, however, they have to be purchased. To address this, UNHCR has assisted by covering medical expenses after an assessment of the case.

Cases that cannot be assisted through these channels rely on the support of operational NGOs in the region, such as Medecins du Monde and Medecins Sans Frontières.

Education

All students, including children of refugees and asylum-seekers, by law have access to primary, secondary and tertiary education.

In practice, access for refugee children is hindered primarily by the lack of documentation (specifically birth certificates, which can create problems with registration) and the lack of a clear legal framework. Although the law provides integration classes for refugee children, they do not take place at the actual school or within the general school schedule. Furthermore, the lessons are limited to language courses and mathematics. As a result, children can be excluded from the everyday school procedures, and contact with their school-friends is limited.

Another problem is the ineffective (sometimes non-existent) training of educators on inter-cultural issues. Efforts are being made by NGOs, such as the International Social Service, to implement classes for children of refugees and asylum-seekers with teachers who are recognised refugees themselves and speak the children's mother tongue.

Child protection

Family tracing and family reunification are undertaken by NGOs such as the International Social Services in close co-operation with UNHCR and the Greek Council for Refugees. Public authorities provide the necessary documentation, after they are given written confirmation that the children are already accepted by a third country where parents or other family members are waiting. In cases where family reunification is not possible, there is no legal framework to protect the children who cannot be repatriated.

Child protection institutions (such as SOS Children's Villages) do not accept children of refugee or asylum-seeker status and provision of allowances by the state is possible only in cases of recognised refugees. Children of asylum-seekers are not entitled to allowances as other Greek children are.

RECOMMENDATIONS

During the last decade, Greece has introduced a range of legal measures to promote children's rights. However, in practice, implementation of these measures is difficult, as there are no governmental guidelines. The interpretation of the law can be so wide that agencies escape with barely meeting the minimum standards. In the absence of governmental direction, the only published guidelines which exist for the protection of refugee children, are those introduced by UNHCR.

The following recommendations are, therefore, made:

- **Produce guidelines for protecting refugee children's rights** - Greek refugee law must include special guidelines and measures for the protection and promotion of the rights of these vulnerable children.
- **Co-ordinate service provision** - A co-ordinating committee, to deal exclusively with the cases of refugee and asylum-seeking children should be created. This should co-ordinate the efforts of all organisations who are working to promote and protect children's rights and take action in cases where these rights are violated.
- **Offer protection for asylum-seekers** - Greek law must provide for the protection of those whose asylum application is rejected. Currently, this group is assisted by a limited number of NGOs or volunteer associations only.

- **Create a refugee children's register** - An advanced computerised network that will facilitate the collection and dissemination of information regarding refugee and asylum-seeking children in Greece.
- **Establish more reception centres** - Currently, the only centre is Lavrion, which is funded by the Ministry of Public Order and UNHCR, in co-operation with the International Social Service and the Hellenic Red Cross.

Education

Primary education (first to sixth grades) and secondary education (sixth to ninth grades) have been compulsory and free in Greece since 1976. It is estimated that a very high majority of pre-school children attend kindergarten and in general school attendance rates are high. Over 95 per cent of students attend and girls are well represented, making up 48.5 per cent of primary school students and 47.6 per cent of 'gymnasium' students (sixth to ninth grades).

In compulsory education, drop-out rates during 1994-95 reached 0.5 per cent of students in primary schools and 3.9 per cent at gymnasium level. An analysis of drop-out rates reveal a number of general trends:

- drop-out rates are higher among boys than girls;
- rates are higher in the islands (e.g. Crete, 7.5 per cent) than the mainland. This is attributed to the employment opportunities presented by the tourist industry;
- Thrace and East Macedonia have higher drop-out rates (4.5 per cent), a contributing factor being the lower socio-economic development of the area;
- studies based on data from 1991-92 indicate that gymnasium students in agricultural areas quit school much more frequently than the students from urban areas;
- children from large families are more likely to drop out from school.

Senior secondary education is offered in the 10th to 12th grade at the 'lyceum' level where general academic and vocational courses are offered. Vocational schools offer alternative training opportunities. In the final grades of lyceum, students are orientated towards university entrance exams and most also attend additional private educational institutions in preparation, at an additional (sometimes very high) cost to their families.

Emphasis is too often placed on instructional learning, rather than the development of each student's capabilities. Innovative programmes like health promotion in the schools have, however, introduced new teaching methodologies, to develop each student's skills. The school curriculum, in theory, strives to address social issues such as cultural diversity, environmental degradation, drugs awareness and HIV and Aids; the adoption of alternative teaching methodologies would help promote this aspect of the education system.

GOVERNMENT ACTION AND POLICY

While education is, in principle, free to all children, access to schools is not equal. Poverty, social exclusion, cultural differences, geographic isolation and the special needs of children with learning difficulties all bear negatively on school attendance.

The Ministry of Education has taken steps to combat these including:

- the introduction of additional educational help courses in 1982. The effectiveness of these, however, is limited as they are not favoured by students and are under-utilised.
- additional classes for students with special needs including ethnic and migrant students;
- the establishment of special schools for students with more serious learning problems;

- the introduction of some minority schools, and the provision of introductory courses for non-Greek speaking students to help them attain sufficient fluency in Greek to attend regular school classes.

Finally, accommodating Gypsy children, whose families are highly mobile, has proved difficult. An extremely positive move to encourage regular school attendance has been the introduction of a 'transcription card', which allows them to register in whichever school they happen to be close to at any time of the year.

RECOMMENDATIONS

- **Increase levels of funding** - In order to promote and realise children's rights fully in schools, legislation is not enough. Appropriate levels of resources and facilities need to be guaranteed and teachers must be well trained and well motivated. They should all be fully acquainted with children's rights and have full respect for different cultures and alternative teaching methodologies, which cultivate students' skills and develop the whole child.
- **Develop a more applied school curriculum** - Secondary education should not be totally orientated towards the university entrance exams. Instead, it should aim to cultivate students' individual potential. The health promotion programme and environmental education have provided some good examples.
- **Provide equal access to education** - Economic support to children and families in poverty and social exclusion must be considered, including to those with language barriers. Financial support schemes should be set up, and bilingual resources must be made available. Extension work with the whole community, which reinforce the benefits of education, also need to be undertaken.
- **Increase student participation** - Any positive changes in the educational system require the effective participation of the students and the teachers in the planning and implementation process.

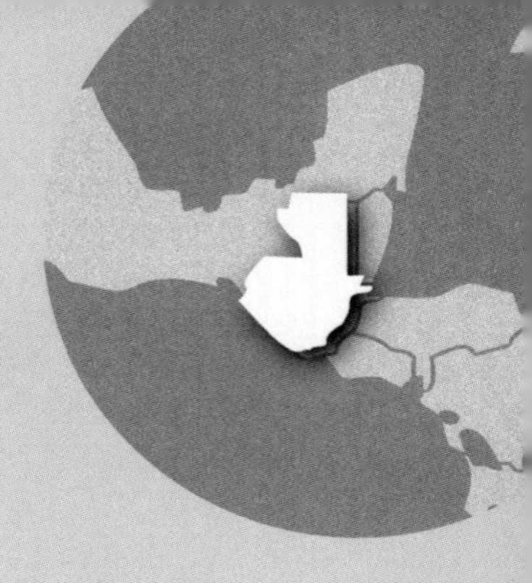

Guatemala

THE GUATEMALAN GOVERNMENT AND THE CRC

The Guatemalan government signed the Convention on the Rights of the Child on 26 January 1990. It was ratified on 10 May 1990. The Convention was incorporated into the country's legal system and is located between the Political Constitution and the Ordinary Laws, together with other international agreements.

Local government is autonomous and decentralised in Guatemala and in 1995 Save the Children saw a need for it to become involved in the process of implementing the CRC. Although only a small number of municipal governments have adopted the Convention so far, it is an important development especially for the more remote communities.

Awareness of the CRC has grown over the years, mainly through educational and promotional work undertaken by organisations such as UNICEF and The International Save the Children Alliance. The status of the CRC in political terms is fairly low and, overall, very little substantial progress has been made in the last nine years. However, some measures have been taken to enable Guatemala to adhere to the CRC more fully. The task of ensuring implementation was given to the recently created Commissioner for Human Rights who established the Council for the Defence of Children Committee and the Convention on the Rights of Child Committee (PRODEN) - made up of both non-governmental organisations (NGOs) and government agencies.

PRODEN gives leadership to participating NGOs and has also promoted the drawing up and submission of proposals for modifications to national legislation on childhood and youth. It also submitted an alternative report to the United Nations Committee for the Rights of the Child.

The Government's first report was met with a very clear and straightforward recommendation to implement fully the Childhood and Youth Code which had been approved by Congress in 1996. To date the implementation of the Code has been postponed three times and this has led directly to the second report being delayed, since it cannot yet report that the Council's recommendations have been implemented.

Generally speaking the Guatemalan Government has made some efforts to comply with the obligations entailed in being party to the Convention. However the philosophy, principles and spirit of the Convention have not been taken to heart, far less incorporated into the kind of legislation that would greatly improve the situation of children.

The reality *against* the rhetoric

Sexual exploitation

The sexual exploitation of girls and boys in Guatemala, according to studies by the sociologist Marìa Eugenia Villarreal, is a hidden phenomenon which has always existed but is now on the increase. Forms of sexual exploitation of children include; pornography, sexual tourism, prostitution and the trafficking of boys and girls from the age of 12. There is little research in the area most is qualitative, aimed mainly at facilitating understanding of the problem. Debate in this area focuses mainly on children involved in prostitution and the research and discussion below also concentrate on this area.

A high percentage of young girls and adolescents working as prostitutes were victims of childhood sexual abuse within their own family. Some testimonies also bear witness to sexual abuse and harassment committed by teachers in secondary schools. Research shows that the majority of girls lose their virginity long before the end of their childhood - some between the ages of 8 and 11, and the rest only shortly after they are into puberty. Approximately 20 per cent of prostitutes are under the age of 15 and 60 per cent are aged between 16 and 18. Prostitution mainly involves girls although some boys are involved, principally in the areas bordering Mexico.

Most of the children and young people involved in prostitution tend to be from the very poorest in society although this is not always so. The majority of prostituted girls are of Guatemalan origin, contrary to a widely held belief that the victims are immigrants. Those that come from other countries generally claim to have become prostitutes as a means of survival, having been abandoned by immigrant smugglers who promise illegal entry to the USA. There is also a perception that the problem is bar and brothel based, but the reality is that the streets are a more common location for the trade.

According to other research, carried out by PRONICE, the risk factors at the root of these problems are many and include: poverty; family breakdown; the absence of a father and/or mother due to death or abandonment; poor relations with a step-parent in the home; the sheer numbers of children in a family and overcrowding; expulsion of children from the family home; intra-family violence; discrimination (even within the family), and the low level of schooling especially for girls. These should be seen in the light of the fact that often recriminations are aimed at the child prostitute while the actions of the clients pass unnoticed. There exists a kind of legal and moral complicity where the prostitutes are seen as intolerable but the organisers of the trade are accepted.

GOVERNMENT ACTION AND POLICY

Government action and policy lack any new initiatives. The authorities focus on prosecuting and detaining the girls and young women involved in this trade. This method of law enforcement simply makes the trade more clandestine, and the prostitutes more at risk, as they find themselves totally dependent on the parasitic people surrounding the business.

Following the World Congress Against Commercial Sexual Exploitation of Children (Stockholm 1996), the Government undertook to develop a National Action Plan concerning all forms of sexual exploitation. To date no plan has been submitted and therefore there are no new resources and/or initiatives to deal with the problem. Recently, Dr Débora Cóbar, from the Office of the Chancellor of the Nation, publicly acknowledged the alarming growth in these problems. In response, joint measures with the national civil police have been developed to protect the victims of sexual exploitation.

RECOMMENDATIONS

- **Implementation of the Childhood and Youth Code** - The code, approved by Congress in 1996, must be brought into effect and the organisational structure envisaged within the Code implemented.
- **National support network** - A national network against the exploitation and sexual abuse of children and young people should be formed. This should comprise government organisations, NGOs, organisations representing the victims, the Council for the Defence of Children, Child and Youth Councils at a national, regional and municipal level, magistrates, churches and health-workers. This network could be linked to other Latin American and Caribbean initiatives tackling the same themes.
- **National Plan of Action** - A National Plan of Action against sexual abuse and exploitation within the framework of the principles and aims of the Stockholm Conference should be drawn up and implemented by the Government in collaboration with the national network. Action should be aimed at the protection and care of the victims as well as educational and preventative initiatives aimed at the whole community.

Juvenile justice

In Guatemala there is no minimum age below which a child cannot be prosecuted for a crime. The law states that a person reaches the age of majority when he or she is 18. The laws relating to childhood and youth are scattered among the different codes, but the conceptual framework which governs them is the so-called 'irregular situation doctrine' on which the current Minors' Code is based. The basic premise of this concept is that the police and the authorities can deem a certain social sector as 'marginal' and then they can arrest and detain children at their will. Children do not need to have broken any written law to be detained in this manner. The 'irregular situation doctrine' is a kind of martial law which can be instigated by the police when they feel it is necessary. Children detained in this way are denied most of the fundamental rights detailed in the CRC. Children who commit offences against a law that is on the statute books fare little better, becoming subject to 'discretionary measures' - most often detention for an indefinite time period. Should they come to trial there is guarantee of a legal defence.

GOVERNMENT ACTION AND POLICY

A great deal of effort has been made by NGOs and a wider social movement to get the Government to act on this. Lobbying eventually resulted in the Government approving the Childhood and Youth Code, which had been through a consultation process for two years and is designed to include the rights detailed in the CRC. However, the implementation of the Code has been postponed three times and the current date for its implementation is March 2000. It is likely that the Code will gradually come into effect following some revisions.

Whatever the outcome, lobbying for adoption of the Code has brought the situation of children and the law into close focus nationally. It is the most widely debated law in the history of Guatemala. These debates have been positive as they at least make decision-makers and opinion-formers aware of the plight of some of Guatemala's children.

While the Childhood and Youth Code remains unimplemented, none of the criteria and recommendations contained in Article 40 of the CRC are incorporated into Guatemalan legislation. The current law, the Minors' Code, was issued before the Convention on the Rights of the Child existed and therefore is based on totally unrelated concepts.

The Government is failing to meet its obligations to the CRC but is trying to address the matter. The key problem is that existing legislation and the proposed legislation are so different that it is difficult for many people to imagine how the new legislation will work.

RECOMMENDATIONS

- **Legislative changes** - All necessary amendments should be incorporated into the Childhood and Youth Code as soon as possible to ensure that the fundamental rights in Article 40 of the CRC are given to all children.
- **Resources and support for training** - Before, during and after the Code becomes law, there is a pressing need for the Government and wider society to make provisions regarding the funding of the law, staff training and public education. Without adequate funding the law might become a dead letter.
- **Legal status for the Council for the Defence of Children** - The Office of the Commissioner for Human Rights has created the Council for the Defence of Children and this must be given legal standing and a budget in order to carry out its work.
- **Creation of a Childhood and Youth Council** Childhood and Youth Councils need to be created within the municipal corporations so that local government can effectively monitor the implementation of the Code and CRC in their respective areas.

Displacement

The Historical Clarification Committee has noted with particular concern that a large number of girls and boys have been the direct victims of arbitrary executions, forced disappearances, torture and sexual assaults, among other actions in violation of their basic rights. In addition, the armed conflict left a significant number of children orphaned or abandoned, especially among the Mayan people, whose family environment was broken up.

This observation sums up the pathetic situation suffered by Guatemalan children during the armed conflict. It also illustrates some of the causes of the massive displacement which, according to estimates, varied from 500 thousand to a million and a half people in the period between 1981 and 1983 alone. Some left the country, mainly for Mexico, Honduras, Belize and the United States. Many of these refugees have returned to Guatemala in an organised manner to build new communities. The ones who were dispersed across the capital city and other cities on the south coast are known as displaced. Those who took refuge in the mountains, living a nomadic life, organised in self-defence to protect themselves from action by the army are known as Communities of Population in Resistance. The process of returning, reuniting and reconstructing communities for the refugees, the displaced and the populations in resistance is currently taking place.

According to a report by the Catholic Church, Recovery of Historical Memory, 18 per cent of the total number of registered refugees and displaced were less than 18 years of age. Of the total number of children and young people affected by the conflict, 49 per cent are orphans, 22 per cent have been witness to torture and 10 per cent have been the object of attacks and threats. According to the government committee for the refugees who were in Mexico, 30 per cent of the displaced people in the regions of Huehuetenango and El Quiché were children and adolescents. A high percentage of them were separated from their families; some were given away for adoption and many others simply do not know where their homes were.

Some of the consequences of displacement include: increase in poverty due to lack of land and employment, lack of freedom of expression and movement, vulnerability of certain communities, particularly the Mayan groups, the negative stigma applied by the army to refugees, identity loss, anonymity and the denial of, and lack of access to basic services.

GOVERNMENT ACTION AND POLICY

Following on from the recommendations by the Historical Clarification Committee and on the initiative of the Commissioner for Human Rights, a Multi-Institutional Agency has recently been set up, which includes a Child and Youth Committee. Among other things, the Child and Youth Committee will monitor the situation of children who were orphaned or who disappeared during the conflict.

There has been very little government action explicitly aimed at helping refugees and the displaced.

RECOMMENDATIONS

- **Support for rehabilitation programmes** - Support should be given to emergency programmes and projects aimed at the return and resettling of communities of the populations in resistance, the refugee population and the displaced people. Projects should be focused on promoting better nutrition, health, education, housing and recreation for children and adolescents with their families.
- **Support for the new youth structures** - Support should be given to the recommendations of the Historical Clarification Committee and particularly any actions and plans issued by the Child and Youth Committee of the Multi-Institutional Agency.
- **Local community counselling services** - Initiatives aimed at psychosocial recovery should be developed at the community level, allowing the recovery of identity and the rebuilding of the family and community fabric as an ideal environment for the full development of children and young people.

EDUCATION

The number of students enrolled in education in Guatemala has risen from 0.4 million in 1965 to 2.1 million in 1996. The greatest growth has been at primary-school level. However, there is a very significant short-fall in provision. Quality and quantity, in terms of human resources, are lacking. The options for young people to continue their basic studies are limited since there are far too few teachers and establishments. Members of communities outside the mainstream suffer particularly poor provision. The number of girls participating in the national education system is significantly smaller than the number of boys.

GOVERNMENT ACTION AND POLICY

The principal and most effective efforts to promote multilingual and multicultural education have come from civil organisations. However, there have been some very recent efforts by the Ministry of Education. These include the setting up of Mayan schools, Mayan educational centres for the middle levels in rural areas, Schools Without Frontiers, Talita Kumi and Don Bosco Centres, the Indigenous Institute of Santiago, Xch'ol Ixim, Majawil Q'ij, Unitary Schools for Bilingual and Intercultural Education, local Mayan Education Units and the Integral Rural Education High School. These continue to develop programmes which respond to the social and cultural needs of the indigenous population.

As a result of the Peace Agreements, the Government is undertaking a reform of education to increase access and improve quality and equality in education. However, this is not enough. Greater efforts are needed to provide an appropriate educational response to the needs and characteristics of the indigenous population.

RECOMMENDATIONS

The main failings of the education system in Guatemala centre around the simple problem that there is not enough provision, in terms of quality and quantity, for the children of the nation. This is true at both primary and secondary level.

- **Greater funding and resources** - More resources must be found both for capital investment and recurrent expenditure.
- **Support for national peace and development initiatives** - Support is needed for government and NGO initiatives aimed at fulfilling the goals set out in the Peace Agreements and the National Development Plan.
- **CRC teaching programmes** - Teaching programmes for the Convention on the Rights of the Child should be a mandatory part of study at all levels.
- **Student participation** - The organisation and participation of students in the different educational spheres, particularly as a central axis for the planned educational reform, should be promoted.

Honduras

THE HONDURAN GOVERNMENT AND THE CRC

The United Nations Convention on the Rights of the Child was ratified by Honduras on 24 July 1990. A participatory process ensued between governmental, non-governmental and international institutions and this resulted in The Children's and Adolescents' Code which is a distillation of the philosophy and core principles of the rights of children found in the CRC. By 1997, 272 out of 297 municipalities had a Municipal Ombudsman for Children's Rights.

Whilst it is true that the Government has, to some degree, provided a favourable legal and political framework for the CRC, it is felt that the political status of children's rights must be much higher before Honduras can claim to be fulfilling all its obligations under the Convention. There are also institutional and cultural limitations on the effective implementation of the CRC.

There is no countrywide strategy to address children's problems, with an evident lack of coordination between the Ombudsman, the District Attorney and the Institute for the Child and the Family (INHFA), or indeed between government, non-government and international agencies. An example of the Government's failure to provide a basic institutional necessity for the welfare of children is the continuing persistent difficulty in issuing birth certificates for some Honduran babies, resulting in lifelong problems concerning age and access, for example, to education, health care and justice. Another example of an area where much work is still to be done is with the municipal ombudsmen. The national Government set them up but they have not appeared on the agenda of local government. As a result, most mayors have paid little or no attention to them, other government institutions only work with them to a small degree and a legal framework to validate their actions is lacking.

There is a deep need to effectively disseminate the ideas and moral values that lie behind the CRC . Limiting factors in this endeavour are prevailing cultural norms that are strongly authoritarian and patriarchal. It is difficult for the voices of children and their rights to be heard against this noisy background of 'tradition'. This is of particular concern with regard to Article 2 of the CRC, which relates to non-discrimination due to gender and ethnic origin, and to Article 12 regarding the right of children to have their opinions respected. Certain cultural factors can limit efforts to prevent sexual aggression and exploitation.

Honduras' problems must be seen in the light of its economic condition and demographic reality. An estimated 60 per cent of the population is under the age of 18 and more than 60 per cent of the nation's people live in extreme poverty. Structural Adjustment Programmes (SAPs) have reduced the amount of resources available for social needs and focused on repaying foreign debt. The worsening social inequality that such a situation involves often impacts hardest on children and, by extension, the future prosperity of the country. However, even within the confines of the poor economic situation, it is felt that the Government must give a higher priority to the rights of the child. There is also a need for society as a whole to give voice to a social movement, which would enable the goals and values of the CRC to be society's own.

The reality *against* the rhetoric

Sexual exploitation

The United Nations Children's Fund (UNICEF) has recently carried out surveys which indicate a significant increase in the sexual exploitation of children and juveniles in Honduras. As in most countries, it is likely that this problem has existed for a very long time and the surveys probably indicate both a real rise in the phenomenon and a rise in awareness of the situation.

Some of the processes of globalisation have not only increased sexual exploitation in Honduras but also changed its nature. The increase in sex tourism from so-called developed countries and the publishing of pornographic images of boys and girls on the Internet are examples of this. Children have also been offered for sale via the Internet for a variety of sexual purposes.

Many children involved in pornography and prostitution are street children but this fact can conceal the circumstances which led them to abandon the family situation in the first place. Approximately 47 per cent of girls involved in prostitution suffered sexual and/or physical abuse when they lived at home. Half of these girls became prostitutes between the ages of 9 and 13. Some were commercially exploited by their own families and some left their families rather than suffer abuse and incest at home. Once in the street environment, children find themselves cared for by few in society and are therefore at risk of a type of exploitation often as concealed as it was within the family home.

There is widespread acceptance of the notion that what occurs inside the family home is private business and this, alongside a highly patriarchal society, creates a situation where both sexual and physical abuse can be regarded by some families as an acceptable norm. Children are not seen as individual owners of rights and, for some adults, this extends to the area of sexual exploitation.

Child trafficking and kidnapping has been detected as a growing problem in Honduras and the media covered 66 instances of this in 1997. The Office of Criminal Investigation and the Office of the District Attorney have also been collecting data and investigating this new and worrying development. The reasons for kidnapping are not clear - hypotheses include prostitution, sale of human organs, illegal adoption and others.

GOVERNMENT POLICY AND ACTION

Apart from the limited attempt to acquire data to estimate the scale of the problem, mentioned above, there is not much evidence of government action in either policy terms or on the ground. Indeed Honduran laws often contain provisions that wittingly or unwittingly support abusers. For instance, if a person abuses a 12 year old it is considered a public misdeed; it can be denounced by anyone and the authorities can prosecute. But if the victim is between 12 and 18 years, and neither the child nor her/his parents wish to make an accusation, no person or organisation can denounce the wrongdoing as it is considered a private misdemeanour. The Government is failing to uphold its obligations under the CRC in not protecting children from sexual exploitation of all kinds.

RECOMMENDATIONS

- **Legislative review** - There should be a complete legislative review to identify and change existing legislation that may promote sexual exploitation. New legislation is needed which will prevent the forms of abuse detailed in Article 34 of the CRC.
- **Public education programme** - A public education programme aimed at highlighting the emotional damage that sexual abuse creates and a discussion about the true nature of rights is required. Children's rights exist and are applicable both in public and private spaces.
- **International mechanism for combating Internet crime** - Appropriate and comprehensive international alliances against the growth of child Internet pornography and sexual tourism should be formed.
- **Facilities for victims of abuse and exploitation** - Establish new institutions with properly trained staff, which can cater for those children formerly involved in the sex trade and those that have suffered abuse at home.

Juvenile justice

The basic principles of juvenile justice in Honduras are enshrined in the Children's and Adolescents' Code (CAC). The principal point of the Code is that children are not subject to the provisions of the adult criminal law; they can only be charged under the provisions of the CAC. Children under the age of 12 are not considered legally responsible and special protection measures can be applied if they violate the law. Children and juveniles aged 12 -18 are charged under the provisions of the CAC. Children and juveniles are dealt with in 'infantile' courts.

There is a great lack of statistical evidence regarding the number of juvenile offenders and the nature of the crimes with they are charged and/or have committed.

GOVERNMENT ACTION AND POLICY

The CAC was intended to provide a system of justice separate from the provisions made for adults and to provide a system focused on rehabilitation and education. In practice, a very different and worrying set of circumstances has arisen, many of which lie in opposition to the rights of child offenders as laid down in the CRC.

The INHFA created Children's Development Centres in the light of the CAC. These had the dual purpose of assisting children in conflict with the law and of providing protection for those children identified as at risk. The Government became frustrated with the fact that only a judge could say whether or not there was a case to answer and commit the case to trial, and so the power to refer children to these centres was extended to the police, the Office of Criminal Investigation and the Public Security Force. This has meant that children can be detained on suspicion alone, with the result that these centres very quickly became full of 'presumed perpetrators' who entered and left the facilities without any due process before the law.
A system partially designed to treat children has resulted in many of them losing their most fundamental legal rights, which are enshrined in the CRC. If a juvenile can be detained without trial then it follows that all other rights, such as legal representation or to have an independent judge preside over the proceedings, cannot follow.

Another result of this policy and practice is that young adult offenders are often described as juveniles as a matter of expediency, thereby mixing much older people with very young children. Escapes from these centres are often led by the older detainees.

As well as denying the rights of those who have not committed a crime, the system does not serve society as a whole. About 50 per cent of children detained in the centres are in and out within a 60-day period. Children who have committed a serious crime sometimes do not spend long enough in detention for their case to come before the authorities. Records are kept of a child's entry to a centre but not whether or not he or she was actually the perpetrator of the crime, therefore some are inevitably seen as hopelessly recidivist without any real evidence.

The CAC was intended to signal a change of direction away from detention as the only cure for crime committed by children but this has not occurred and the situation can, in some ways, be seen as worse than before. It is not helped by a general belief that imprisonment is the only real way of dealing with offenders. Even when it is clear that the system cannot deal with the number of detainees it creates, and that some are unfairly detained, many people still see deprivation of freedom as the only solution.

RECOMMENDATIONS

- **Review of the Children's and Adolescents' Code** - The Children's and Adolescents' Code needs to be re-examined in the light of Articles 40 and 37 of the CRC.
- **Greater resources to develop alternative punishment systems** - More resources are needed to establish a working parole system, sufficient re-education centres, community service, etc. as an alternative to detention.
- **Separate detention for juveniles** - Boys and girls must be detained separately from adults.
- **Special detention facilities for those under 12** - Adolescent perpetrators must be detained separately from those under 12.
- **Special procedures for juveniles with no identity paper** -There is a need to identify and provide a system for dealing with minors without any documentation.

Displacement

It is estimated that at the end of the 1980s, Honduras provided refuge to approximately 240,000 people (37,000 recognised as refugees and the remainder as internally displaced), mainly from Nicaragua, El Salvador and Guatemala. According to the official census for 1988, this represents approximately 5 per cent of the total Honduran population. These refugees eventually returned to their countries. Refugees from Haiti arrived on the Atlantic coast where they settled and are now integrated. The children born in the country have been registered as Hondurans. The Commissioner for Human Rights is responsible for the care of refugee children.

Overall the situation of displaced people including children in Honduras is not easy. Their status is not fully realised and efforts to develop policy and practice regarding the displaced are in progress.

GOVERNMENT ACTION AND POLICY

The National Commission for Refugees was created on 15 January 1981 to confront the problems arising from the massive immigration of refugees. At present, it is also the liaison office between local and regional authorities, non-governmental organisations and the United Nations High Commissioner for Refugees (UNHCR).

On 23 January 1992 Honduras approved the bye-laws of the 1951 Convention on Refugees and the Additional Protocol of 1967. The national law determining the condition and applicable treatment and assistance of a refugee is presently under debate. An inter-governmental commission, together with non-governmental organisations (NGOs) and the UNHCR are presently responsible for this project. In this law they envisage the integration of an inter-governmental commission for the selection of cases and a chapter for the particular situation of women, disabled people, elders and children.

At present Honduras does not have a law clearly defining the status of refugee. The State of Honduras had its reservations with regard to the 1951 Convention, restraining and limiting the application of the rights granted therein. In practice, Honduras has provided to the UNHCR all the facilities necessary in terms of studies, mobilisation, medical and sanitary care, etc. By extension these provisions have also been given to refugees. The Government has respected the rights of refugees as being essentially the same as those of its own citizens.

Cases involving children, whether by themselves or with their family, are referred to the INHFA. A temporary home is provided, action taken concerning the child's origin and the whereabouts of his or her family are sought. The goal is to reunite families who have become separated.

Whilst it cannot be said that Honduras has a systematic, coherent policy concerning the plight of the displaced, realistic efforts are being made to develop one and, in practice, the displaced are accorded a degree of assistance and concern.

RECOMMENDATIONS

- **Inter-agency co-ordination** - Continue co-ordination of all relevant bodies in the development of policy and practice regarding the displaced.
- **Implementation of provisions for all children** - Children must be accorded special status under provision for refugees and the principal of non-discrimination must be fully adhered to.
- **Specialist training** - Training should be provided for all parties who come into contact with the displaced, especially immigration staff, the police and the army.
- **Refugee register** - Provision should be made for the recording of data and the tracking of the destinations of refugees in order to monitor the effectiveness of any eventual policy and practice changes.

Education

Education in Honduras consists of three main age groups: kindergarten from ages 4 to 7, elementary (primary) from 7 to 13 and secondary from 13 to 18. Elementary education is compulsory and free in Honduras. However, full access to education for children and young people is still to be achieved. Approximately 10 per cent of boys and girls (150,000) have been denied entry to elementary school; only 33 per cent make it to secondary school, and scarcely seven per cent into the university. Thirty-three per cent of young people are illiterate, meaning they lack the necessary education for the labour market. In general, the educational system offers few options for vocational education and therefore those children who, for whatever reason, fail in their academic studies find themselves ill-equipped for the world of work.

The priorities of the educational sector have changed after Hurricane Mitch. A growth in the demand for elementary education, allied to the hard fact that many schools and their materials were destroyed, means that the normal implementation of the educational system for 1999 is not expected. Given that unemployment and under-employment have dramatically increased, a best-case scenario would be that government assistance to schools will be maintained at the levels prior to the hurricane.

Pre-school education is of particular importance in Honduras as it is expected to prepare children for successful entry into the first grade of elementary education at age seven. Seventy-four per cent of children do not attend formal pre-school, mainly because these institutions are concentrated in the urban areas. However, there have been great efforts in recent years to facilitate preparation for primary school in non-formal pre-school education centres with both Government and NGOs playing their part - the Government providing some funding and local communities establishing educational facilities. Despite limitations in the formal sector, the task of preparing children to enter the first grade has, in large part, been achieved.

Approximately 90 per cent of children attend elementary school, with a drop-out rate of 3.5 per cent and a repetition incidence (i.e repeating one or more grades to progress to the next) of 12 per cent. Repetition and drop-out rates are mainly caused by socio-economic factors such as malnutrition and the use of child labour. The national picture somewhat clouds problems at the regional level; of particular concern is the western region where an estimated 47 per cent of schools have only one teacher for all six grades and 26 per cent have only two teachers covering the same age range. This teaching generally occurs in a single classroom.

At secondary level, the statistical picture is not at all clear. Some reports indicate that about 850,000 children were eligible to enter secondary education and only 33 per cent were given the opportunity. At the institutional level, it is estimated that only 55 per cent of demand is satisfied leading to overcrowding, a severe shortage of materials and a high pupil-teacher ratio. Thirty-five per cent of institutions are official state schools, ten per cent are semi-official schools attempting to achieve official status and the rest are private. The latter often provide an education which does not reflect the high level of fees they charge.

The quality of education at this level is affected by a number of factors. Firstly, only 11 per cent of secondary teachers have recognised teaching qualifications, the rest being graduates with no formal teacher training. Secondly, the curriculum has a rigid and uniform character which is unable to reflect local needs, paying little if any attention to cultural, economic or social features of a particular area or region. Thirdly, the Government's assessment of educational achievement is based on the number of schools built and not on the success of the students or the suitability and effectiveness of the curriculum.

GOVERNMENT POLICY AND ACTION

Recent government policy initiatives have focused on providing some form of vocational education and providing assistance to the poorest of families. As mentioned above, all initiatives and programmes have been affected by the results of Hurricane Mitch.

In December 1998 the Law Project for the Development of Non-Formal Alternative Education was instigated. This was aimed at helping the large number of children unable to take advantage of formal schooling and providing vocational skills alongside the formation of civil and moral values including instruction in democratic principles. The project has a large scope but at the moment there are only two secondary-level technical schools providing vocational education and these have been funded by foreign donations. It is unclear where continuing funding will come from.

The Family Assignation Programme (PRAF) is under discussion and is aimed to provide financial support to the poorest for education. It includes a subsidy for good attendance and some school materials. It also provides encouragement for the use of primary health services. A grant for travel to school is available to secondary school students. In 1999, a Scholarship Programme for academic excellence in elementary and secondary schools was initiated.

It is clear that these policies do not go far enough in addressing the basic educational needs of the children of Honduras. However it is felt that the existing structure and institutions could be improved to facilitate that goal. Current resources are inadequate and it is felt that this is the primary reason for the limited success of the elementary and secondary sectors.

Ten per cent of students proceed to higher education and during the period 1990-95 enrolment grew by 2.3 per cent. Women make up 39 per cent of students enrolled. There are 13 higher education centres, five public and eight private; these offer applied courses such as medicine, architecture and engineering. The National Autonomous University of Honduras and the Pedagogical University 'Francisco Morgan' provide education at no cost and constitute 94 per cent of university enrolment. In recent years, distance learning programmes have been developed by both private and state institutions.

RECOMMENDATIONS

Despite the resource constraints, we believe it is possible to undertake, or at least plan to undertake, the following steps to improve children's access to education in Honduras.

- **Improved pre-school facilities** - Although this age group has seen significant recent improvement it is necessary to complete its coverage. Of particular importance is learning of socialisation skills which enable the child to adapt easily to the learning environments.
- **Focus on basic skills** - Devote more time in the first grade to reading, writing and elementary maths. Without this a child cannot pass to the next grade or indeed make sense of it.
- **Greater access to basic educational materials** - Find some means of providing greater access to books and learning materials for all children. There may be scope for community involvement here.
- **Flexible school terms to accommodate community needs** - Increase sensitivity to local needs so that, for instance, children who cannot attend a full school year for agricultural reasons are not penalised for this, as is often currently the case.
- **In-service teacher training** - Greater teacher knowledge of pedagogy, including the management of multi-grade classrooms, co-operative learning, small group work, etc. Topic knowledge is essential but many teachers come to the classroom ill-equipped to deal with the reality of so many hungry minds at different stages of development.
- **Additional language provision** - Develop ways to assist children for whom the language of instruction is different to that spoken at home.
- **Nutritional support in schools for poorer families** - It is estimated that some 50 per cent of rural children are malnourished and nationally the figure is around 40 per cent. Hungry children do not learn well. Nutritional supplements at school could help address this.
- **Increased decentralisation and local responsibility for education** - Continue the process of the decentralisation of the education system as the most dramatic recent improvements have resulted from greater local input and involvement.

'...there'll **always** *be people who doubt me because of my disability ... It's all a question of* **never** *accepting the limits* **others would like** *to impose on me but* **choosing** *my own* **goals***...'*

Roz Davis, age 15 - "Me and my electric chair"

Iceland

THE ICELANDIC GOVERNMENT AND CRC

The Icelandic government became a signatory to the Convention on 26 January 1990 and it was ratified on 28 October 1992.

An Ombudsman for Children was established in 1994 and the Government Agency for Child Protection came into being in 1995. The latter supervises the work of the Child Welfare Committees and provides training for them with regard to the CRC, ensuring that the best interests of the child are uppermost in any programme designed for children.

The Convention has been published in three different editions for age groups 6-9, 9-12 and 12-15. Approximately 50,000 copies were produced and distributed to all compulsory (primary) schools. Manuals for teachers were produced to help them introduce the CRC into their teaching. Teachers could also attend courses concerning human rights and these were offered by Save the Children Iceland, by the Human Rights Centre and The University College of Teacher Training Continuing Education Programme.

In 1997, Parliament raised the age of majority from 16 to 18 years, in line with the Convention. Initially, parlimentary opposition to this provision was strong but lobbying by both non-governmental organisations (NGOs) and those government officials who work with children proved effective.

In the same year, Parliament also resolved that the Government should formalise a comprehensive policy on the family and plan actions to strengthen the status of the family. But this policy still remains to be published.

Political awareness of the CRC is extensive, although it cannot be said that its status is high or always apparent. It would be an improvement if the interests of children were placed on the everyday agenda of politics in Iceland to provide a holistic overview of legislation that both directly and indirectly affects children.

The Government gave its initial report to the UN Committee on the Rights of the Child in January 1995. There was no NGO involvement in the report process but Save the Children Iceland submitted a supplementary report. The Committee made eight suggestions, including the establishment of a means of enhancing coordination of government policy between central and local authorities concerning children's rights. It was noted that Iceland did not have a comprehensive and systematic set of training programmes for professionals working for and with children, such as policemen, lawyers, magistrates or doctors. In the light of Article 4, the state was urged make the maximum possible budgetary allocations for this. As Save the Children Iceland had pointed out to the Committee, Iceland lags behind other Nordic nations in this regard especially when the percentage of young people (26% under 16) in the population is taken into account. The Committee emphasised that the Convention provides for the protection and care of children, and in particular for the recognition of the child as the subject of his or her own rights. The Committee noted that this essential aspect of the Convention is not yet fully reflected in Icelandic law. This is still the case.

The Government has generally made good progress towards implementing the CRC although there is room for further improvement. One recurrent difficulty in compiling this report is the lack of comprehensive and reliable statistics on the situation of children in Iceland. There is an urgent need to address this, and the Government must establish mechanisms to undertake more systematic analysis of the real situation for children throughout the country.

The reality *against* the rhetoric

Sexual exploitation

Awareness of children's sexual exploitation is rather new to the Icelandic people. To date, very few formal studies have been published and therefore it is unclear how the problem is changing. The number of cases reported is growing, and the average age of the children involved is younger, but this does not necessarily mean that the problem is getting worse. It may be that, as awareness has grown, it has become easier for children to seek help.

This growth of awareness is a sign of change across the nation. A once-taboo topic, even in professional circles, is now discussed and acknowledged by the population as a whole. Since the signing of the CRC, great progress has been made regarding the status and treatment of children who have suffered sexual abuse.

In 1997, a report on the sexual exploitation of children was published by the Government Agency for Child Protection which detailed cases reported in the years 1992-96. It was met with shock as the number of cases was higher than expected - around 100 a year. In 1998, a Children's Assessment Centre was opened in Reykjavik and in its first six months was notified of 85 cases.

The most commonly reported form of exploitation concerns abuse of a child by a family member. According to information from Stígamót (which until recently was Iceland's only information and counselling centre for victims of sexual abuse), 60.6% of victims in the period 1992-97 were victims of incest. Commercial sexual exploitation of children is not seen as a big problem in Iceland. However, Internet use is very high in the country, and therefore the potential is there for a growth in child pornography through paedophiles making use of this technology to gain access to children.

It is difficult to identify the main factors that contribute to sexual exploitation in Iceland. Given the fact that unlawful sexual activity is the main type of abuse (as opposed to pornography or prostitution) and as the abuse is most often carried out by someone the child knows and trusts, it may be that the relatively weak and ambivalent status of the child within the domestic setting is a factor.

Girls were more at risk than boys during the period 1992-97; 93.6% children attending the counselling centre were female and 6.4% male. At the City Hospital in Reykjavik, 95% of adolescent victims (aged 12-18) were female during the period 1993-97. Although data is scarce, it is felt that the mentally and/or physically handicapped are particularly vulnerable to abuse.

GOVERNMENT POLICY AND ACTION

The Icelandic Government did not send a delegate to the World Congress against Commercial Sexual Exploitation of Children held in Stockholm in 1996. However, a delegate from Barnaheill, Save the Children Iceland, was funded to attend the conference representing both the Government and the NGO community. Unfortunately, to date, no National Plan of Action has been developed. The Government, however, has addressed the problem with a number of legislative measures and institutional initiatives. Amongst these are the Government Agency for Child Protection, the Ministry of Social Affairs and the Children's Ombudsman.

The Children's Ombudsman published a report in 1997 concerning the status of children within the justice system who have suffered sexual abuse. Following suggestions made in the report, the Government submitted legislation to the Parliament which became law in 1999. The new law protects the child whilst an investigation takes place. The child does not have to recount more than once the events that took place. Every child is appointed a legal guardian to assist in the protection of their rights in what can be a complex process.

The Children's Assessment Centre is a government initiative designed to protect children by intervening on their behalf. Its multi-disciplinary team means assessment, investigation, referral for prosecution and treatment of child sex abuse are organised at one location. Protection from post-episode trauma is minimised by making all the processes involved as co-ordinated and collaborative as possible.

The Act of Protection of Children and Youth is the principal legislative tool used to monitor the sexual exploitation of children. This obliges professionals and other citizens to report any suspicion of child maltreatment to the Child Welfare Committees. Anyone who does not do this could be prosectued.

In terms of prevention, this legislation has had a beneficial effect. The expansion of public discussion and education regarding this matter has also had a preventive effect. Save the Children Iceland produced materials for all parents of young children which presented three key preventive ideas: that a child has a right over her or his body, she or he has a right to say no and all children should be raised in awareness of these matters.

The Government has, to its credit, enacted legislation to comply more fully with Article 34 of the CRC but regrettably the penalties for these forms of sexual exploitation are too lenient. Society as a whole is appalled by the notion of child sexual exploitation but the sentences suggested by law do not reflect this feeling.

RECOMMENDATIONS

- **Systematic data collection** - Improve the systematic collection of data regarding the frequency and nature of child sexual abuse. This data could assist both protection and prevention.
- **Codes of good practice for all professionals working with children** - Examine and amend the curriculum and mandate all of those who will be working with children, such as teachers, doctors, nurses, the judiciary, etc.
- **Legislation for juvenile sexual offenders** - Introduce legislation for young people under the age of 18 who commit crimes of sexual abuse against children. There are currently no solutions for offenders of this age group. Many of those who offend whilst young go on to become serial offenders and therefore we feel it is vital to intervene whilst they are still young.

Juvenile justice

In Iceland a person between the ages of 15 and 18 is regarded as a youth. People of this age are subject to the same laws as adults. Children under the age of 15 cannot be charged under the criminal law.

It is difficult to access comprehensive data on juvenile crime in Iceland and statistics are only available for the city of Reykjavik. During the three-year period before signing the CRC, between 1986 and 1989, the number of juveniles dealt with by the judiciary on an annual basis never rose above 57. From 1989 to 1997 the number varied between 51 and 134. On average, girls represented around 20% of the total. Approximately 20% of the juveniles were unemployed at the time of their offence. There are no statistics kept regarding ethnic or socio-economic background.

The death penalty and corporal punishment have been abolished in Iceland. In 1993 a case of mistreatment of juveniles came to light, but in no way can the state be said to condone mistreatment of any detainees.

GOVERNMENT POLICY AND ACTION

Children under the age of 15 are not held to be legally responsible and cannot be charged with committing a crime. If they commit an offence the Child Protection Authorities deal with it.

Young offenders are dealt with by the same judicial system as adults but the Government has put in place several safeguards to ensure their fair treatment. When an allegation has been made against a child or a juvenile the police must notify the Government Agency for Child Protection who in turn notify the child's parents or guardians. A representative of the agency is permitted to be present during police questioning except in certain rare circumstances. Young offenders are provided with legal representation and interpreters (if required).

There are no special prisons for juvenile offenders but the law states that the age of the offender should be kept in mind when a place of detention is being selected. It is very rare for a person aged 15 to 21 to be given a custodial sentence; for a first offence a suspended sentence is generally the result. If a young person is sent to prison, the opportunity for parole is almost always available. In 1998 the Prison Administration and the Child Protection Agency agreed that offenders under the age of 18 should usually go to a treatment centre run according to the lines stated by the Act on Child Protection.

There are no specific programmes to deal with the problem of juvenile offending.

RECOMMENDATIONS

- **Development of specific juvenile legislation** - The Government is failing with reference to Article 40.3 in that they do not seek to promote the establishment of laws, procedures, authorities and institutions that are specifically applicable to children. However, in reality offenders are dealt with in a generally appropriate manner.
- **Strategies for the prevention of habitual crime and reoffending** - A comprehensive set of policies and strategies is needed to prevent offending and recidivism. The current practice of generally giving suspended sentences to juveniles means that many have a collection of suspended sentences by the time they reach the age of 18. It is important to intervene more proactively by addressing their behaviour at an earlier stage.

Displacement

There is no history of refugee children arriving in Iceland in unexpected circumstances. Those that have arrived have done so under the auspices of the Icelandic Red Cross. There are an established 300 refugees in Iceland, mainly from Eastern Europe and Asia. So far all the children who have arrived have been accompanied by their families.

GOVERNMENT POLICY AND ACTION

Iceland has acceded to the 1951 United Nations Convention on Refugees and the rights of children are granted in accordance with that provision. There is no comprehensive state legislation concerning the status of refugees.

Refugee children living in Iceland enjoy the same rights as local children with regard to access to education, health care and other social services.

It is not known how the authorities would react to a situation where a child had become separated from his or her parents or guardians. It is expected that every effort would be made to reunite the family.

RECOMMENDATIONS

State provision for refugees is adequate and there are no major failings in regard to the CRC. However there are some areas where improvement could be made.

- **Legal status of refugees** - Legislation is required to establish the legal status of refugees.
- **Racial tolerance** - Legislation is required to promote racial understanding and fight against discrimination of all forms.
- **Greater support for refugee children** - Children of refugees need greater support in the school environment. Language support is particularly important for both the children and their parents.

Education

Primary education - known as compulsory education in Iceland - has been provided for all and for free since 1907. Attendance at compulsory basic school (age 6-16) is 100%, and pupils have a right to attend a school in the area where they live. All pupils who have completed compulsory education have a right to attend secondary school, regardless of their results in the 10th grade. For some branches of study, access to upper secondary level is based on performance but everyone has a formal right to education at this level.

Attendance in upper secondary schools is quite high - approximately 89% of 16 year olds and 77% of 17 year olds were enrolled in upper secondary schools in 1997. In comparison with other Nordic countries, though, these figures are slightly lower, as the average figure for the same year was approximately 90%. It is difficult to quantify the drop-out rate. After the age of 16, the number of students at school drops by about 10% each year until the age of 18 when 66% are in attendance. As some upper secondary schools offer one and two-year courses, the figures do not tell us much about those that actually drop out. The real rate of drop-out is still very much a cause for concern.

Upper secondary school attendance is slightly lower in rural areas than in the capital city and its environs. Young women attend upper secondary school in larger numbers than young men and this seems to have been consistent since 1994. The gender difference diminishes from around 20 years of age and thereafter. Upper secondary level education is free to all. It is recognised that it is more expensive for rural residents to attend upper secondary school than for children from urban centres, and if the school is outside the students' municipality, the state provides some assistance.

The picture is, possibly, very different for those children whose ethnic origin is other than Icelandic. For example, only about 50% of children whose mother tongue is not Icelandic attend upper secondary school. Similarly, the drop-out rate for this group is higher; the Education Counsellor for Bilingual Children reports rates as high as 60% for some courses. However this statistic is somewhat misleading as it does not include children from this group who are not in need of language assistance. Bilingual children who have successfully integrated with Icelandic schooling are not recorded in this statistical process. The Ministry of Education has recently published a report with recommendations to address this issue.

The state education system, via its schools, does promote respect for children's fellow-citizens and respect for the cultures of other nations and peoples. There is perhaps not enough accent on teaching children to cooperate in democratic processes and there is a lack of systematic learning concerning human rights.

GOVERNMENT ACTION AND POLICY

People living in rural areas may have difficulty attending upper secondary school and the state provides a grant for travel, extra living costs and, if necessary, for rent. It is not a large sum but does at least acknowledge the difficulty that some of the rural population have in taking full advantage of educational opportunities.

The Government has recently taken steps to address the rather academic focus of both compulsory and secondary education. There have been recent attempts to offer more arts and vocational courses in the last year of compulsory schooling and it is no longer mandatory for pupils to take the academic national exams. Opinion is divided on how exactly this will affect the students. In upper secondary schools about one-third of students follow vocational programmes. This proportion should probably increase, but more research is needed before any dramatic changes are made.

As mentioned before, the drop-out rate for secondary schooling is somewhat clouded by a lack of statistical analysis. However the Ministry of Education has recently issued a report suggesting that the provision of counselling services in schools has had a beneficial effect on drop-out rates. Other services, such as extra-curricular activities and parent/student programmes, do exist but have not been analysed with regard to their affect on attendance and/or the drop-out rate.

Access to higher education in Iceland is based on ability and students who have successfully passed the Icelandic Matriculation Examination may enter university or any of the other higher education institutions. Provision is also made for those who have finished equivalent education or have, in the view of the university in question, acquired equivalent maturity and knowledge.

RECOMMENDATIONS

The key problems in Icelandic education lie more in the implementation of policy than in the policy itself. The issues of teacher recruitment, retention and reward are the most pressing.

- **Raise in teacher's salaries** - Teachers' salaries do not attract enough graduates to service the compulsory school sector. It is difficult to suggest one simple solution to this problem but it is clear that the salaries of teachers have fallen relative to other professions.
- **Strategies for attracting more students into the teaching profession** - The University College of Education is not able to meet the high demand from young people wishing to train as teachers. The Government needs to urgently address this.
- **Comprehensive statistical date collection** - A comprehensive set of data must be acquired concerning the drop-out rates for secondary education.
- **Assistance for non-native children** - Bilingual children need greater assistance both in the instruction of Icelandic and in the provision of materials in their mother tongue so as they do not get too far behind their peers.

Japan

THE JAPANESE GOVERNMENT AND THE CRC

Japan ratified the United Nations Convention on the Rights of the Child on 21 September 1990. The Japanese Government fulfilled their initial reporting requirements by submitting their first report to the Committee on the Rights of the Child in May 1996, which was supplemented by three alternative non-governmental organisation (NGO) reports. The Committee returned its concluding observations in May 1998.

Following ratification, Japan took some initial steps to ensure that Japanese legislation complied with the provisions of the CRC. However, as is highlighted by the alternative NGO reports to the UN Committee, these steps have been nominal and, in reality, insubstantial. Instead of establishing a child ombudsman system, for example, the Japanese Government set up a Civil Liberties Commission for children's rights to supervise the prevention of violation of the rights of the child. Although a positive action, as the UN Committee notes, the Commission lacks independence and is accorded insufficient authority to ensure the effective monitoring of children's rights. There is a clear lack of NGO involvement in the Civil Liberties Commission for the Rights of the Child and the Government has made little effort to disseminate information about the Convention to key public audiences.

A key criticism made by the UN Committee is that ratification has in essence changed little and the provisions of the CRC remain simple rhetoric. The committee's principal observation states that 'although the Convention on the Rights of the Child has precedence over domestic legislation and can be invoked before the domestic courts, in practice, courts usually do not directly apply in their rulings international human rights treaties in general and the CRC in particular'.

The NGO reports raise a host of concerns regarding failures of the Japanese legislative system to implement fully the provisions of the CRC and follow the spirit with which it was prepared. The principle of non-discrimination (Article 2), one of the fundamental underpinnings of the CRC, is, for example, flouted by the fact that children born out of wedlock do not have access to the same benefits as other children. Similarly, the safeguards to ensure the 'best interests of the child' in instances of inter-country adoption are not in place. The high incidence of school phobias, stress disorders, youth crime and youth suicide all indicate that there are fundamental flaws in the current education system. The provision of adequate leisure and recreational facilities for children has also been found wanting. These all raise concerns regarding the compatibility of Japan's provisions for children with those of the CRC.

The reality *against* the rhetoric

Sexual exploitation

According to the Government White Paper on Youth, the number of children involved in some form of sexual exploitation decreased over the decade from 1983-93. In 1997, however, there were 4,912 reported cases, 67.1 per cent of which involved junior or senior high-school students. It is unclear if the decline reported in the Government White Paper is an actual decline in the incidence of sexual abuse and exploitation or simply a change in the frequency and manner in which cases are being reported. The 1997 statistics, however, reveal that it remains a problem.

According to NGO reports to the UN Committee on the Rights of the Child, Japan is currently renowned as one of the worst countries worldwide for producing and propagating child pornography. Child pornography is widely available, found in magazines sold in convenience stores with little regulation. The proliferation of such materials is disturbing. There are other alarming practices which promote the sexual exploitation of children; one such example is that of young schoolgirls earning pocket money by selling their under-garments to stores where girls' used underwear and school uniforms are sold which are widely found in large cities. Another is an increase in the number of telephone clubs where, all too often, young girls are drawn into explicitly sexual conversations. This practice has been proved to be psychologically and emotionally damaging to these girls. The enforcement of existing provisions is clearly insufficient as videos featuring adolescent girls are freely available to rent at video shops and more explicit 'underground' videos, featuring girls in their low teens, are routinely sold through door-to-door services.

In recent years there have been an estimated 34 reported cases of Japanese citizens being arrested in other Asian countries for sexual violence against children. Bilateral investigations into these crimes have hardly been pursued and little effort has been made to combat the proliferation of these crimes.

GOVERNMENT ACTION AND POLICY

There are many weaknesses in the legislation which has been drafted to combat the problems of sexual exploitation of children in Japan. In reality, the level of protection which can be assured is critically low. Adolescents involved in prostitution are more likely to be treated as delinquents than victims of crime, and the police notoriously undertake adversarial interviews or interrogations that can infringe on the child's privacy. In addition to this, under the current legal infrastructure, there is no provision for punishing the offending 'client' in cases of child prostitution and the production, dissemination and possession of child pornography.

Fortunately, the Japanese Government has taken steps to address this situation and on 18 May 1999 the Diet passed the Prohibition Bill of Child Pornography and Child Prostitution. This will take effect within six months and it is hoped it will improve the protection of children and bring Japan more in line, specifically with the provisions of Article 34 and, more generally, with the underlying principles of the Convention.

RECOMMENDATIONS

- **Awareness raising** - A comprehensive awareness campaign should be launched for children in schools and promoted in the home as well as at all levels of the community, to enable children to protect themselves and to promote a balanced and healthy view of an individual's sexuality.
- **Rehabilitative care and counselling** - Counselling services and specialist

psychotherapeutic care must be made more widely available to help children cope mentally and physically with experiences of sexual abuse or exploitation.

Juvenile justice

All young people and children under the age of 20 are regarded as juveniles in Japan and fall under the auspices of the juvenile justice system. Children are not considered to be criminally responsible until they reach the age of 16 and thus cannot be subject to criminal procedure.

Over the last decade the number of crimes committed have fluctuated from year to year, with a minor reduction in the overall figures. In general, over 75 per cent of these crimes are committed by boys, with the highest levels being committed by youths aged between the ages of 14 and 16 who are predominantly high-school students, with a smaller number of non-school attenders.

GOVERNMENT ACTION AND POLICY

Juvenile crimes are normally dealt with by a family court, which plays not only a judicial but a welfare role to ensure the psychological and social needs of the child are also taken into account. The Government has sought to establish laws, procedures, authorities and institutions that specifically apply to children, and children are mostly accorded their full rights as prescribed under Article 40.2(a) and (b), ensuring correct levels of representation during the judicial process. However, as the alternative NGO report points out, the right of a child to appoint defence counsel tends to be no more than nominal.

In practice, little consideration is given to the special needs of juveniles. There is little guarantee of legal assistance before the prosecution, nor referral to the family court during or after the trial or hearing. This is largely because the importance of an attendant is not recognised and funding is not readily available to provide for this service. The NGO report to the UN Committee highlights this as a major failure in meeting the standards set out by the Convention. Consequently, the proportion of cases in which attorneys are appointed as an attendant remains as low as one per cent for general juvenile cases.

Similarly, although the current legal system ensures that children have the correct representation as outlined in Article 40.2 (b) ii, this right is not guaranteed in practice. Interpretation services are available, but the quality cannot be assured. Additionally, while the right of a juvenile to express his or her own views is legally guaranteed during legal proceedings, in practice, in Japan, a structured system for the child to exercise this right is not sufficient. Speaking up independently in court is both a daunting and onerous task and requires the appropriate environment and the correct level of support and advice for the child. As most cases are directed to the family court, it is felt that this is a sufficient measure to provide a child-focused environment and few alternative mechanisms for giving a deposition are available.

The death penalty is still enforced in Japan for serious crimes. For children, however, Article 51 of the Japanese Juvenile Legal Code provides that any person under the age of 18 who commits a crime punishable by the death penalty will have their sentence commuted to life imprisonment instead. Under the present juvenile justice system, no person under the age of 18 will receive a life sentence without the possibility of release. After 10 years, he or she will be eligible for parole and normally life sentences range from 10 up to 15 years.

RECOMMENDATIONS

- **Promotion of the best interests of the child** - The attendance of an attorney at all hearings with

with juveniles should be mandatory to prevent illegal interrogations and to ensure that the best interests of the child are protected.
- **Legal assistance** - A system of providing legal assistance funded by the state for all juveniles under detention should be established so that all juveniles have adequate and equal access to legal counsel.

Displacement

Compared with other developed nations Japan has a relatively low number of people seeking asylum each year. Over the period 1985 to 1995, only 1,151 people applied for asylum in Japan and of these only 208 were formally recognised as refugees. The Government has not issued information on the origin of these refugees, but unofficial reports from Amnesty International released in March 1993 indicate that over 70 per cent of these are Vietnamese, followed by a small number of Iranians, Afghans and Burmese. Information regarding the asylum application process is not easy to obtain and on the whole it is an unclear and complex process.

GOVERNMENT ACTION AND POLICY

Japan revised the Immigration Control Order to establish the system of refugee recognition, and enforced the new system in January 1982, when the 1951 Refugee Convention and its 1967 Protocol entered into force. Japan is making efforts to co-operate with the United Nations High Commissioner for Refugees (UNHCR) and provide them with information on all applications and decisions made.

Children applying for refugee status are given protection and humanitarian assistance. The Government, through the Refugee Resettlement Assistance Headquarters of the Foundation for the Welfare and Education of the Asian People, supplies funds for those applying, including children. In addition, the Child Welfare Law is applicable to children applying for refugee status. Children recognised as refugees are provided with access to a range of provisions including education, social security and housing.

However, applications for asylum are dealt with in a restrictive manner. The asylum procedures themselves have many problems, which include:
(a) the so-called '60-day rule' which requires all asylum applications to be submitted within 60 days from the date of arrival in Japan, or strict application of the rule regarding fear of return;
(b) a lack of sufficient explanation concerning the rights and the procedures provided by law;
(c) the absence of effective legal assistance, including legal counsel;
(d) the lack of independent bodies carrying out the assessment of appeals; and
(e) the usual detention of asylum-seekers and those who have not been recognised as refugees.

In addition there are no procedures which take into account the special needs of the child. Children who arrive in Japan either as refugees or immigrants are not registered from birth and are, as a result, not given automatic access to education facilities. Those who do often find that lessons are not provided in their own language. Children who only have asylum-seeker status are not given equal access to health care.

RECOMMENDATIONS

- **Comprehensive review of asylum** - The asylum procedures should be reviewed comprehensively in the context of the Convention on Refugee Status and the UNHCR guidelines.
- **Relaxation of application of the so-called '60-day rule'** and the dissemination of information regarding the rights and procedures prescribed by law.
- **Reconsideration of the process of application for asylum** - These should be reconsidered to safeguard individuals' rights
- **Institute special provisions for displaced**

children to ensure that they have access to the same education, health facilities and protection that national children benefit from.
- **Provide free, effective legal assistance and legal counsel to asylum-seekers.**
- **Appeals against asylum decisions must be carried out by independent bodies.**
- **Asylum-seekers not accorded refugee status should not automatically be detained** - Alternative systems must be made available.

Education

Article 1 of the Fundamental Law of Education states that 'education shall aim at the full development of personality, striving for the rearing of people sound in mind and body who shall love truth and justice, esteem individual value, respect labour and have a deep sense of responsibility, and be imbued with an independent spirit, as builders of the peaceful state and society'.

Following this principle, compulsory education is provided in Japan over a nine-year period (six years in primary school and three years in junior high school). Senior high school (three years) is not mandatory, although the percentage of children entering senior high school is as high as 97 per cent.

To ensure that every child receives compulsory education, the municipal board of education registers all school-age children in the student list and designates guardians in schools. The school's principal is required to keep precise records of the attendance of enrolled students and provide appropriate guidance. The School Education Law provides that those who graduated from a lower secondary school or its equivalent, or those who are considered to meet the required academic level are eligible to enter an upper secondary school, regardless of sex, race, nationality or any other factor. In reality, however, most upper secondary schools including government-run schools have entrance examinations to screen applicants.

Compulsory education offered by national and public schools is free of charge. Textbooks are supplied free by the Government, not only to pupils and students of national and public schools, but also to those in private schools. Financial assistance for those who are unable to enter school for economic reasons is also provided through scholarship funds and other bursary systems. Indeed, under current legislation, the National Treasury is obliged to encourage school attendance of pupils with financial difficulties and the Government has to subsidise municipalities to encourage education by offering school supplies to students who have difficulties attending school for financial reasons. These measures for free compulsory education apply to non-Japanese children as well.

In schools, guidance and counselling is given to students to help them have a clear idea of their direction and goals in life. In co-operation with schools, the Public Employment Security Office offers systematic vocational counselling so that new graduates can select occupations according to their aptitude and ability. The General Vocational Aptitude Test and the Occupation Readiness Test are conducted to determine aptitude and promote self-understanding.

While there is considerable provision in place to ensure an effective education system, in reality there is an increasing incidence of students suffering from so-called 'school phobia'. These students do not, or cannot, attend school, mainly due to psychological, emotional, physical or social factors. Recently, bullying has become a serious problem in Japan. There are more than 60,000 reported cases of bullying per year in schools (of these 34 per cent have occurred in elementary schools, and the remainder in lower and upper secondary schools). The gravity of the situation is reflected by an increasing number of suicides thought to be caused by bullying. The Ministry of Education has acknowledged more than ten cases of suicide induced by bullying in recent years. National campaigns aimed at curbing bullying have been run with the support of schools, families and local communities and the police are making efforts to identify bullying cases promptly and to prevent their recurrence.

In Japan, school rules must be deemed reasonable and necessary for achieving educational goals. The Government instructs educational institutions, when taking disciplinary actions, to consider carefully whether they are necessary from an educational viewpoint, and to pay full attention to the view of the student by listening to his/her explanation and opinions. Corporal punishment is prohibited under Article 11 of the School Education Law. However, there is considerable evidence which contradict the government directives and the Law.

Specific lessons are provided to non-Japanese students, outside their classes, and 'team-teaching' has been adopted to try and assist them in their acquisition of Japanese. The Government is also preparing and distributing textbooks for study of the Japanese language, and guidance materials for non-Japanese children. Additional training is provided for teachers, and extra teaching staff are posted to schools with high numbers of non-Japanese students. The Government has also designated some schools as 'pilot schools' to promote teaching methods for non-Japanese children.

Controversy is rife over the nature and focus of the curriculum. The standards for school curricula are set out in the 'Course of Study Programme', which all schools are legally obliged to follow. However, the problem with the Study Programme is that it comprises too many subjects and as a result, many children cannot keep up with lessons. There is little room for children and teachers to follow a more flexible course of study, allowing students to develop other essential life skills.

GOVERNMENT ACTION AND POLICY

Education is highly valued within Japanese society. However, a close look at the reality of the current education system highlights the fact that there are many issues which need to be addressed to realise the principles and provisions enshrined within the CRC.

In the realm of education, there is still a general tendency in Japanese society to consider children as objects of protection and control. It is, therefore, still widely believed that children should concentrate on schoolwork, and harsh discipline, including sanctions, tends to be prescribed. This form of 'control-oriented education' is implemented through rigid school rules and strict guidance.

As a result of the rigidity of the current system, the fixed range of subjects and the intensity of a competitive educational environment, children are deprived of leisure opportunities. Rule systems are harsh to the point of being considered excessive, prescribing even the close-cropped hair styles for all boys and detailed regulations on clothing. Little attention is paid to the notion that parents, children and representatives of the community should have any involvement in school management. Parents and pupils do not have automatic access to the detailed educational reports and 'naishin-sho' (confidential school reports to higher educational institutions) which are prepared by the school and educational board. These documents are only disclosed after an application process to the local government.

Under present legislation, all parents are obliged to send their children to school. Alternative forms of education, including home-based education, are not approved. Nearly 100,000 students drop out of secondary school every year. The drop-out rate amounts to 2.1 per cent. One of the main reasons is the prevalence of 'unwilling entrance' due to the so-called 'slicing' education system. In this system, students are screened out on the basis of their academic performance and are forced to enter upper secondary schools within reach of their abilities, not in accordance with their wish. Some schools force their students with behavioural problems into 'voluntary withdrawal' from school. Once a student has dropped out of school it is extremely difficult to return.

Contrary to the global trend, education programmes for disabled children segregate them into different schools and classes. There are schools for children with a range of disabilities including visual impairments, auditory and speech problems and other physical and mental disabilities. However, when disabled children are mainstreamed in an ordinary class, special provisions such as a support teacher or an additional helper cannot be assured.

RECOMMENDATIONS

- **Equal access for all children** - For example, children who graduate from Korean schools should be given unlimited access, like Japanese children, to higher education institutions.
- **No segregation of children with disabilities** - This practice of segregation should be abolished within the education system.
- **Carry out a comprehensive review of the education system** - Ensure that children's rights are fully guaranteed as provided for in the CRC.
- **Permit and develop alternative forms of education** including home-based education.
- **Provide counselling facilities for victims of bullying** - In order to make it easy to discover and resolve bullying, appropriate conditions should be created to enable children to consult somebody about it without anxiety.

*'My **dream** is that there will not be a war anywhere. I would **like** to **study** like girls... before the **war**, and to have enough food'.*

Gayurova, age 13 - Tajikistan

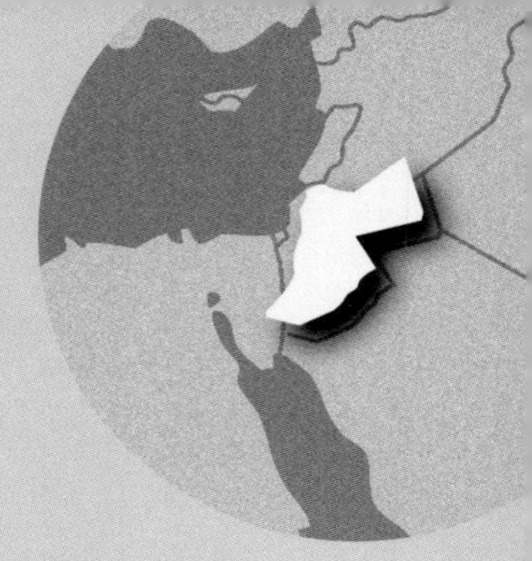

Jordan

THE JORDANIAN GOVERNMENT AND THE CRC

Jordan ratified the CRC on 29 August 1990 and it entered into force on 23 June 1991, albeit with some reservations to Articles 14, 20 and 21. Jordan's national legislation conforms with the text of Article 1 of the Convention, defining a child as all persons below the age of 18, unless majority is attained earlier.

Several steps have been taken to bring domestic law into line with the Convention through the enactment of new laws and the adoption of specific programmes aimed at promoting and protecting the rights of the child.

The fundamental principles of the CRC have been incorporated into domestic law. The texts of the Jordanian Constitution, the National Charter and Jordanian legislation apply to Jordanians in general, without any discrimination on grounds such as sex, language, religion, age or colour. Article 6 of the Constitution stipulates that Jordanians are equal before the law and the National Charter states that all male and female Jordanians are equal before the law, without discrimination. Under the Charter, children have the right to the highest possible standard of care and to protection from their parents and the state so that they can develop independent and co-operative personalities.

Despite the clear articulation of these principles and enshrining them in law, discriminatory attitudes and prejudices are still alive within society, and in practice disparities exist, in particular with regard to inheritance rights, the right to leave the country and the acquisition of Jordanian nationality. National legislation with respect to the minimum age for marriage may, in fact, not be fully compatible with the non-discrimination provisions of the Convention. Moreover, it seems that there is discrimination resulting from the coexistence of different personal status regulations according to a child's religion.

In many ways the Jordanian legislature appears to be diligent in safeguarding the interests of children, especially in matters of direct concern to them. Article 118 of the Civil Code, for example, protects children stating that: 'the acts of a child endowed with the power of discernment shall be valid if they are beneficial and invalid if they are purely detrimental'.

Jordanian law protects the right to life and punishes anyone who violates it. This principle safeguards the child in all phases of its development: while it is in its mother's womb, after birth and during the subsequent stages of his or her life. Jordanian law prohibits abortion; Article 150 of the Personal Status Act states that every mother is obliged to breastfeed her child and shall be forced to do so if there is insufficient money to hire a wet-nurse, if there is no other female volunteers to undertake that task, or if the child does not accept the breast of another woman.

All Jordanians, including children, are guaranteed freedom of opinion whether expressed orally, in writing, pictorially or through any other form of expression, under Article 15 of the Jordanian Convention.
In practice, the Government protects this freedom within specified limits, so that it can have no adverse effects on society by promoting inter-communal or racial hatred, disseminating propaganda for war or prejudicing national security.

Despite all this, insufficient steps have been taken to bring existing legislation into full conformity with the CRC. This includes overcoming discrepancies or gaps in national legislation, particularly in laws relating to marriage age and the administration of juvenile justice.

It is also necessary to recognise the economic and social difficulties which have been faced by Jordan in the aftermath of the Gulf crisis and which have, consequently, affected the situation of children.

Interesting initiatives have been undertaken in the field of child participation. The Jordanian Women's Union (JWU) organised a four-day Jordanian Children's Conference in 1996 in which 700 children participated representing the entire Kingdom. During that Conference, children discussed many issues, such as the CRC and the Jordanian Child Rights Act Draft prepared by the Ministry of Social Development. A follow-up committee has ensured the implementation of the 1996 Conference recommendations, including the preparation for a second conference in 1997. This involved 500 children between the ages 13 and 17, from public, private and United Nations Relief and Works Agency (UNRWA) schools, in addition to children with special needs. They emphasised their rights to participate in all areas pertaining to children and agreed that this could be achieved through a Child Parliament. The internal regulations of the Parliament were established and the children elected members of the Parliament on the basis of the population of each governorate.
The Parliament is now well established and comprises 120 children - 60 boys and 60 girls - who represent the entire Kingdom and are elected once every two years. The principal goals of the Children's Parliament are to:
- enforce and raise awareness of the CRC;
- consolidate equality between girls and boys and work towards fighting all aspects of discrimination;
- enforce democratic attitudes which should be based on respecting and believing in human rights;
- activate the child sector through development of their talents and abilities;
- organise and join children's efforts to get all possible support on both government and non-government levels.

The Government should still address important issues:
Reservations - First of all, the Government should withdraw its reservations to Articles 14, 20 and 21 of the Convention.
Monitoring/Co-ordination - A national mechanism should be established to co-ordinate the implementation of the CRC and the monitoring thereof. Co-ordination between the various government agencies and non-governmental organisations (NGOs) involved in the implementation and monitoring of the Convention should be strengthened.
Statistics - A mechanism should be developed for the determination of appropriate indicators and for the collection of statistical data on the status of children. These can be used as bases for designing programmes to implement the Convention.
Discrimination - Discriminatory attitudes and prejudices should be prevented and eliminated, and effective protection against discrimination should be ensured, particularly with regard to the girl-child and children born out of wedlock, as well as any differentiation resulting from the status of parents.

The reality *against* the rhetoric

Sexual exploitation

Little information is available on the incidence of sexual exploitation (abuse or commercial) in Jordan. However, there are some legal provisions which try to combat its occurrence.

Article 302 of the Penal Code lays down that anyone who, using deception or coercion, abducts a male or female person and absconds with him or her to another place shall be liable to the following penalties:

- two to three years' imprisonment if the person abducted was a male under 15 years;
- a term of hard labour if the person abducted was a female;
- a term of not less than 5 years' hard labour if the person abducted was a married female, regardless of whether she was under or over 15 years;
- a term of not less than 10 years' hard labour if the male or female person abducted was raped or sexually assaulted;
- a term of not less that 10 years' hard labour if the female person abducted, being married and under 15 years, was raped.

It is perplexing to find that the abductions of males and females carry penalties which differ in severity. A concern is that this does not offer adequate protection and that, in itself, encourages a form of discrimination by placing different values on individuals, male and female, married or single.

Juvenile justice

In 1992, the number of juveniles arrested amounted to 4,995, of whom 4,801 were males. There were 555 anti-begging campaigns and the number of juvenile beggars caught amounted to 187 males and 344 females.

GOVERNMENT ACTION AND POLICY

Jordanian legislation in this area appears to conform with international standards. Under the Jordanian Penal Code, a child under the age of seven is not regarded as criminally responsible. Article 92 of the Penal Code stipulates that full criminal proceedings in adult courts can be brought against a child once they have reached the age of 17. However, the law provides further protection for children, ruling that if it can be proved that, at the time of the crime, a person under the age of 18 was not capable of knowing that he or she should not have commited a crime, they cannot be held criminally responsible for that crime.

Jordan has specialised courts to hear juvenile cases which are governed by special legislation. This regulates all matters concerning the powers of these courts, the trial proceedings and the penalties that can be imposed.

Under Article 8 of the Constitution no one may be detained or imprisoned, except in accordance with the provisions of the law. It is also an offence to subject a person to any form of violence or coercion prohibited by law with a view to obtaining a confession to a crime. The Juvenile Act prohibits juveniles being sentenced to death.

The Juvenile Act No. 24 of 1968 stipulates that juveniles should be detained in a juvenile remand home or any national institution, approved by the Minister. They may also be detained in prisons, in a section set aside for juvenile detainees, if they are found to be of bad character or disruptive, so precluding their placement in a remand home. Authority to detain juveniles is vested solely in the courts. If the juvenile reaches the age of 18 before completing his or her sentence, he or she may be transferred to a prison to serve the remainder of the sentence by order of the court which passed the original sentence. On the basis of a written request from the Chief Probation Officer, the court may extend the period of a juvenile's detention in the reform institution until he or she reaches the age of 19 so that they can complete vocational training which they began in the institution.

The Juvenile Act makes provisions for the establishment of specialised institutions for juveniles. These institutions, which are designated as 'reformatories', are of two types which perform different functions: correctional, for the detention of offenders on whom final judgement has been passed by a court, and preventive, for the detention of juveniles who are exposed to the dangers of delinquency or vagrancy. These juvenile institutions are administered by specialised staff working for the Ministry of Social Development. The duration of these placements shall be specified but shall not be less than one nor more than five years and shall be ordered only by a court.

The director of the reformatory, acting with the approval of the Chief Probation Officer, may permit any juvenile placed in the institution to attend any public or private school in order to continue his or her academic or vocational education. The director may also permit juveniles of outstanding conduct to absent themselves from the institution for a period of up to one week in order to visit their families.

Despite the principles laid down in Jordanian legislation, there are serious concerns about the application of Article 92 of the Penal Code, and also about existing detention practices. Currently, children who are taken into custody before they are convicted of any criminal offence may be detained with convicted persons. This needs to be addressed.

The Government seems committed to the rehabilitation and treatment of juveniles in conflict with the law. The Ministry of Social Development has established a Directorate of Social Defence to supervise the treatment, rehabilitation, training and education of juveniles with a view to reform rather than punishment. There are additional programmes to curb begging and vagrancy through the provision of cash and assistance for needy persons.

RECOMMENDATIONS

Major areas for government intervention may be identified as follows:

- **Training** - Law enforcement officials, judges, other administration of justice officials and, more generally, members of professions concerned with the implementation of the Convention should be provided with adequate training on the basic principles and norms contained in the CRC.
- **Reform** - The state envisages undertaking a comprehensive reform of the system of juvenile justice. In this context, the Convention and other international standards in this field, such as the Beijing Rules, the Riyadh Guidelines and the UN Rules for the Protection of Juveniles Deprived of their Liberty, should be seen as guides for this revision. Furthermore, measures for rehabilitation and social reintegration should be adopted.

Displacement

Unfortunately, at the time of going to print, little substantial information regarding the number of refugees and government provisions was available. According to UN statistics for 1988, the number of registered Palestinian refugees living in the East Bank at that time amounted to 87,490 persons dispersed among a number of camps in various areas of the Kingdom.

GOVERNMENT ACTION AND POLICY

Since the unification of the two banks of the Jordan in 1950, Palestinian refugees have shared the same rights as Jordanians - enjoying political representation, exercising their rights and fulfilling their obligations on an equal platform with Jordanian nationals.

The Government has strived to ensure that they are treated equitably. It has provided them with financial and moral assistance and, in collaboration with UN agencies, is providing health and educational facilities. The Jordanian Government has not yet acceded to the Convention relating to the Status of Refugees or the Protocol, although this possibility is being considered. In the meantime, however, there is growing concern that refugee children may not be given full protection.

RECOMMENDATIONS

- **Ratification** - The most important step in this area would be that the Jordanian Government ratify the 1951 Convention relating to the Status of Refugees and its 1967 Protocol in order to ensure that all refugee children or children seeking refugee status enjoy their rights.

Education

Article 6 of the Constitution stipulates that the state shall do everything within its power to ensure the availability of work and education.

Primary education is compulsory for Jordanians and is provided free at government schools. The provisions of the Education Acts No. 16 of 1964 and No. 27 of 1988 conform with the general provisions of the CRC. In the academic year 1990/91 (the latest data available), 94.2 per cent of all persons aged 6-15 were enrolled in the basic education system and 65.8 per cent of all persons aged 16 and 17 were enrolled in the secondary education system.

GOVERNMENT ACTION AND POLICY

The main tasks of the Government in the area of education are:
- the establishment, under the control and direction of the Ministry, of various types and levels of government educational institutions which must be provided with the required qualified human resources and educational materials;
- the provision of suitable premises for schools and the supervision of all private educational institutions.

Article 4 of the Education Act encapsulates the underlying philosophy of education in Jordan. The aim is that all children, through their education, should become good citizens, imbued with belief in God, inspired by a feeling of belonging to their country and nation, and endowed with virtues and humanitarian sentiments, in such a way as to ensure their personal, physical, mental, spiritual, emotional and social development. These objectives are reaffirmed by the Jordanian National Charter. They form the basis of the school curricula and serve as the guiding philosophy for the overall development of education in Jordan.

Kindergarten education is seen as an important foundation for children inJordan. On reaching the age of three years and eight months, children can enroll at a kindergarten, for a maximum period of two years. The objectives of the Educational Development Plan for kindergartens includes the provision of more extensive technical supervision, further training of their supervisory and teaching staff and co-operation with the private sector in various fields relating to their development. To attain this, a National Committee of Kindergartens was established to formulate a draft development programme covering the curriculum, social and recreational activities and the training of teachers and supervisors.

Basic education is compulsory and free at government schools and students are obliged to attend school until they are 16 years of age. Secondary education consists of two main streams: the general secondary education stream, comprising common general education and specialised academic or vocational education, and the applied secondary education stream, comprising vocational training. Although school textbooks are distributed free to students in all government schools, some families cannot afford even the few dinars required to provide their children with basic school items, such as pencils, crayons, notebooks, maths sets and mandatory sports clothing and shoes. Teachers report a high incidence of drowsy and listless students who cannot concentrate and sometimes even faint because they do not get enough nutritious food at home. A particular concern is that children are dropping out of school as a result of economic difficulties in their family.

In order to promote and improve perceptions of vocational training, the Government has established a specialised institution - the Vocational Training Authority.
Non-governmental bodies are also helping to promote vocational training in Jordan through the provision of assistance in cash and in kind for the establishment of the centres and institutions in various parts of the Kingdom.

According to Jordanian legislation, communities have the right to establish and run their own schools for the education of their members. Such schools must comply with the general provisions of the law and be subject to government supervision of their curricula and education policy.

RECOMMENDATIONS

Further work should be carried out in the area of education:

- **Education policies** - Emphasis should be given in school education to the important values of peace, tolerance and respect for human rights. Furthermore, the active participation of children should be encouraged. Similarly, efforts should be undertaken to develop new channels, including membership of associations, through which children may make their views known and have them taken into account. Finally, school curricula should be adjusted to make room for education about the Convention.
- **Drop-out levels** - Steps should be taken to improve school attendance for children living in remote areas, to reduce school drop-out levels and to raise the standard of literacy, particularly among females.
- **Economic and social factors** - Over-crowded schools should be checked regularly to ensure there are essential supplies, and school health programmes expanded; the poorest families should be helped to obtain essential books and school uniforms.

Korea

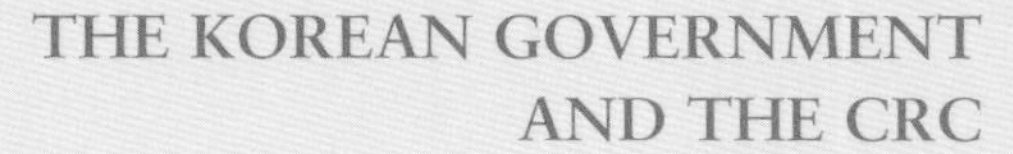

The Republic of Korea signed the UN Convention on the Rights of Child on 2 September 1990 and ratified it on 20 November 1991.

The Government has established some new laws and authorities in order to fulfil its obligations to the CRC. A Children's Ombudsman has been introduced and the Children's Welfare Law has been revised and improved. The task of disseminating information regarding children's rights was taken on by non-governmental organisations (NGOs) including the Korean Committee for UNICEF, Save the Children - Korea, the Korea Association for the Prevention of Child Abuse, Neglect and The Korean Council for Children's Rights. These organisations also organised workshops and training courses for professionals working with children.

Korea sent its first report on the CRC to the Committee on the Rights of the Child on 8 November 1994. The Committee's recommendations and suggestions have led to improvements and revisions to laws relating to welfare, labour, education, child abuse and neglect, juvenile justice and displacement. NGOs have played an important part in this process of revision and improvement as well as creating new initiatives.

The political status of the Convention is fairly low and there has not really been any change in this since ratification. A partial explanation for this may be Korea's cultural background. Korea is an Asian country strongly influenced by Confucius. Filial piety is one of the Moral Principles and Precious Virtues for Confucians. People in Korea tend to believe that the rights of children lie in opposition to those of adults and elders, with the concomitant belief that a strengthening of children's rights will weaken those of adults. Only a few politicians actively make children's rights part of their agenda in Korea. Clearly there is a need for education in this area but it will take a considerable period of time to address these issues.

On becoming a signatory to the Convention Korea reserved part of three Articles of the CRC: Separation from parents - Article 9.3, Adoption - Article 21(a) and Administration of Juvenile Justice - Article 40.2(b). The Government is obliged to submit its second report to the Committee by the end of 1999. The draft of the report is already available and the above issues remain outstanding. They are likely to do so for some time. The cultural reality of Korea means that some of the provisions of the CRC are difficult to implement.

The reality *against* the rhetoric

Sexual exploitation

Sexual exploitation of all kinds is, in all likelihood, a growing problem in Korea. The available statistics record the reporting of abuse and it is presumed that this provides only part of the picture. In 1998, the Violence Counselling Office found that 46 per cent of all offences in this area were committed against children and young people aged 0 to 19. Children under seven suffered 10 per cent of the offences, 7 to 13 year olds 14 per cent, and 14 to 19 year olds 22 per cent. The most commonly recorded form of abuse recorded is sexual harassment with 351 cases, followed by rape, and then attempted rape. Ninety-eight per cent of victims are female and 35 cases involved children under the age of seven. About 25 per cent of victims are under the age of 13 and around 70 per cent of these knew the person who abused them.

Child sexual abuse is still a partially taboo subject in Korea. More counselling centres are needed, counsellors, parents and children must be encouraged to report this kind of offence.

Another form of child sex abuse is the growing commercialisation of sex and the objectification of women which contributes to a climate of exploitation. More 'traditional' forms of pornography are now joined by the Internet, with its ability to evade national legislation and grant anonymity. Korea's society is very patriarchal and children and women are subservient to men. While this is not a direct cause of child sex abuse, the unequal power relationships involved in this cultural norm may lead to exploitation. A sense of all-powerfulness may come easily to an abuser, making any attempt to stop the abuse difficult. The social status of the victims is often low and this too may be a contributory factor in the exercise of power.

GOVERNMENT POLICY AND ACTION

The Government established a law in 1997 to try and address some of these problems. Teachers and counsellors are now obliged to report cases of suspected sexual exploitation. The new law made it possible for relatives such as uncles and aunts to be prosecuted for sexual harassment. There are now more sensitive provisions concerning the examination and questioning of victims and more counsellors are available, although there are still not enough.

RECOMMENDATIONS

- **Awareness campaigns** - Sex education could include informing children of their rights regarding their own bodies.
- **Counselling services** - Improved and more widely available counselling services for victims of sexual exploitation are required.
- **Change in regulations for child witnesses** - In Korean law the testimony of children and young people under the age of 16 can only be used as a 'reference' and not as a form of proof. In the light of child sexual exploitation this should be changed.

Juvenile justice

In Korea, a juvenile offender is aged between 12 and 19. The law defines two types of behaviour - criminal behaviour and law-violating behaviour. Criminal behaviour gives rise to penal-code violators and law-violating behaviour gives rise to special law-violators. Children aged 12-13 can only be prosecuted for law-violating behaviour and are exclusively dealt with by the juvenile court, whilst young people from 14 to 19 years of age can be prosecuted for criminal behaviour and may be tried by the criminal court. Two types of case can be brought against a young offender - protection cases and criminal cases. If an offender is under 14 years of age, a protection case is brought against them; this is also the case if the offender is aged 14-19 and considered prone to crime but has not actually committed a crime. A child under the age of 12 is not considered legally responsible.

In 1996 (the last year for which figures are available) there were 137,503 young offenders. They were responsible for approximately 7 per cent of all crime. The number of young offenders has decreased in some years but overall the trend is upward. However, as a proportion of all offenders, the number of juveniles has remained constant. About 30 per cent of the young offenders are penal-code violators and 70 per cent are special law-violators.

In gender terms, approximately 8 per cent of young offenders are female and this figure has shown a steady increase over recent years. The social class of offenders can be estimated (though social class can only be defined in very inexact terms) at around 71 per cent lower class, 28 per cent middle class and 1 per cent upper class. A recent trend has been an increase in the proportion of middle and upper-class offenders. For 1996, the age distribution of young offenders was as follows: 42 per cent aged 14-15; 35 per cent aged 16-17; 20 per cent aged 18-19; and three per cent below the age of 14. The trend over time has been for the number of offenders aged 14-15 to increase, whilst those aged 18-19 has decreased, suggesting that the average age of juvenile offenders is falling. The proportion of offenders with prior records is increasing. As Korea is almost exclusively ethnically Korean it follows that virtually all young offenders are from the same group.

For offenders under the age of 18, capital punishment, life imprisonment and torture are outlawed.

GOVERNMENT ACTION AND POLICY

In Korea emphasis is placed on aspects of treatment rather than those of punishment. In many respects, throughout the entire juvenile justice process, juvenile cases are treated and disposed of quite differently from adult cases.

The Juvenile Act of 1958 and its three revisions detail the way in which the government deals with juvenile cases. The Act creates the two categories of protection cases and criminal cases. In general, protection cases are adjudicated by the juvenile court, whereas criminal cases are tried in the criminal court and sentences are imposed according to the Criminal Act. The treatment of young offenders following sentencing is generally different from that for adults. They may be sent to Juvenile Training School or to Juvenile Prison. Some young offenders are detained in adult institutions.

The Government has reserved part of Article 40 (the Administration of Juvenile Justice - section 2 sub-section b). Criminal cases provide the rights detailed in Article 40. They are dealt with in the same way as adults and therefore a juvenile has access to legal representation provided free if they are unable to pay. Interpretation services are available if requested.

In protection cases, juveniles are not provided with all the rights detailed in Article 40.2(b). Protection cases are held in a closed setting presided over by the judge of the juvenile court. A young offender can make his or her own views known on any matter concerning the case, and the presence of parents and/or guardians is permitted. An offender is informed of his/her rights prior to commencement and is not compelled to give testimony and/or confess guilt.

The Government has provided a variety of alternatives to judicial proceedings concerning juveniles. Public prosecutors in Korea have a range of discretion and authority. For example, they are authorised to make decisions on whether to indict to criminal court, invoke the summary proceeding, transfer the case to juvenile court, suspend the prosecution or discharge the case. For juvenile cases, the prosecutors often suspend the prosecution on the condition that the young person shall be placed under care of guardians who are appointed from responsible people committed to the prevention of juvenile delinquency. This programme was first implemented as an experiment in 1978 in one district public prosecutor's office in a southern province. Since then, it has been implemented in all the prosecutors' offices across the nation.

There are a number of programmes designed to prevent and reduce juvenile offending. These include: education and counselling, monitoring of runaways, providing shelter and a mentor programme. In Sept 97 the 'Initiatives for Safe Schools' project began which takes a multi-disciplinary approach to the reduction of violence in schools, and juvenile crime and delinquency in general.

The Government provides a number of alternatives to detention in an institution. These include vocational training programmes, probation, rehabilitation programmes (i.e. expert counselling, foster care), attendance centre orders and community service orders. These last two have proved fairly successful in reducing the rate of recidivism, and probation has also had some success.

The Government is failing to meet the standards of justice as laid out in Article 40 with respect to protection cases and in the use of pre-trial detention. Although the right to due process is guaranteed to adult criminal offenders and to juvenile offenders handled through criminal cases, there is no explicit provision which mandates the application of the Code of Criminal Procedure in protection cases. A child can also become subject to a protection case if he or she is considered prone to crime but has not actually committed a crime. Pre-trial detention can be ordered under a number of circumstances and these are not clearly laid out in the Juvenile Act.

RECOMMENDATIONS

- **Amendment to judicial procedure** - The right to due process must be clearly stipulated in the Juvenile Act so that protection cases are treated in the same way as criminal cases.
- **Greater availability of resources** - More resources are needed in the examination and investigation of criminal cases to develop the competency and fairness of the judicial process.
- **Clear rules on pre-trial detention** - The clauses allowing for pre-trial detention of juveniles should be clearly stated in the Juvenile Act in order to prevent the abuse of pre-trial detention.
- **Separate juvenile detention** - Although there are Juvenile Prisons there should be further provision to make sure no juveniles are detained with adult prisoners.

Displacement

There are very few refugees or displaced persons in Korea. The refugees that have settled here are almost exclusively from North Korea - since 1994, 362 North Koreans have sought refugee status in the Republic of Korea. Thirty-nine of these people were under the age of 19.

GOVERNMENT ACTION AND POLICY

On arrival a child, whether accompanied or not, must apply for refugee status and his/her application is then considered by a committee. If the child qualifies as a refugee then legal status and financial support are available. North Korean refugees are provided with money to support their settlement, housing, medical and living costs. A child is provided with free access to education until the end of university or, if appropriate, is provided with vocational training.

In July 1994 the Korean government revised its law concerning immigration. The two key elements of this legislation in relation to refugees allowed for them to stay for 90 days (in accordance with the UN Convention on Refugees) and made it impossible for them to be unwillingly returned to their nation of origin. Children are given support to facilitate the reunification of their family.

RECOMMENDATIONS

There are currently no precise recommendations concerning refugees in Korea.

Education

In 1958 the Government acted to make primary school education free and available to all. Further work was necessary to ensure this was so, particularly on the islands and in other remote places, and further legislation was enacted in 1967. By 1997 it was possible to state that education was truly available to even the most isolated of children. Since 1975 attendance to the six-year primary education programme has been very high, with a figure between 99 and 100 per cent.

Secondary education began with a three-year middle-school programme for all children. By 1984 a six-year free secondary education was available to all children at schools in subdivisions smaller than a 'myeon' - a small township. Over the last 20 years there has been a very substantial increase in participation in secondary education, partly as a result of government initiatives but also because of economic improvement and a substantial rise in parental interest. In 1975 just 52 per cent of children attended secondary school; by 1998 virtually 100 per cent were able to take advantage of it.

Drop-out rates are extremely low and the only figures kept detail those who cannot attend for whatever reason, and not just those who 'dropped out'. In primary schools, 0.3 per cent of children fail to attend, at middle schools the figure is 1 per cent and at secondary schools it is 1.1 per cent. Vocational schools have a greater rate of non-attendance, at 3.9 per cent, although this compares well against institutions of a similar nature in other countries.

Extensive efforts have been made to make sure children from all geographic regions have access to education. There is no information regarding the ethnic origin or socio-economic status of students in Korea - it is unlikely that there are any issues of concern arising from these matters.

GOVERNMENT POLICY AND ACTION

All children have equal access to middle and secondary education. At secondary school, the curriculum is divided into general and vocational classes, providing a path to university or to a trade or skill. The vocational route has six different emphases to provide a thorough training for particular careers.

In 1998 there were 772 vocational high schools (447 state-run and 325 in private hands) and over 900,000 students attended these exclusively vocational establishments in areas such as agriculture, fisheries and the technical trades.

As the development of secondary education is a relatively recent phenomenon in Korea, efforts have been made to provide adult education to previous generations who may have missed out on formal schooling. In 1974 the Air and Correspondence High Schools initiative began, and after 1977 some industrial companies provided evening classes for employees to improve their general education.

RECOMMENDATIONS

There are at present no recommendations concerning education in Korea.

'First comes education. Then when I am big I can go and get a good job'.

Nealo, age 12 - South Africa

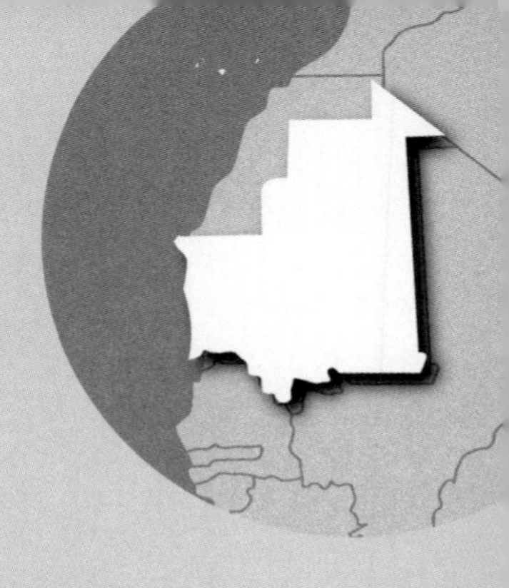

Macedonia

THE MACEDONIAN GOVERNMENT AND THE CRC

The Convention on the Rights of the Child was ratified by the former Socialist Federal Republic of Yugoslavia in November 1989. When the Republic of Macedonia gained independence on 17 November 1991, the CRC automatically entered into force as the Government took responsibility for its own international affairs. The Government of Macedonia then formally ratified the CRC in its own right in November 1993, submitting the first report to the UN Committee in February 1997.

In Macedonia, all international agreements ratified by the Government are a part of domestic law (Article 118 of the Macedonian constitution) and such is the case for the CRC. However, in spite of this legal commitment, in practice it has had very little impact. No governmental departments or programmes have been established to deal with children's rights issues, and repeated attempts by UNICEF, in co-operation with the Ministry of Education, to establish a child's ombudsman have failed. Dissemination initiatives, education programmes and children's rights projects, amongst others, have all been implemented by UNICEF, Save the Children Macedonia and other non-governmental organisations (NGOs) operating in the country. There has been no clear commitment on the part of the Government to improve the situation for children, nor is there an expressed desire to ensure effective implementation of the CRC itself. In reality, in recent years, a reduction in the social provisions for children has occurred, with free kindergartens being the most recent casualty of increasingly scarce resources and spending cuts.

In modern day Macedonia it is evident that children are marginalised within society. Despite ratification of the CRC, no child-focused policy-making has taken place within the Government. Children are viewed very traditionally - their needs, expectations and opinions are neither seen nor heard. They are far from being considered as individuals with rights. There is no special Children's Bureau or ombudsman to oversee general service provision to children or to ensure adequate implementation of the CRC. It is apparent, from the few agencies working in child protection within Macedonia, that the contents of the Convention and its general principles are poorly understood and little, if anything, is known about children's rights in general. Even amongst professionals working with children on a daily basis, there is insufficient knowledge of the CRC. Although family law and the law on social protection technically provide for children, under both of these, children are treated as objects rather than the subject of rights. Their rights are viewed as subordinate to, and derived from, those of their parents.

A great deal has to be done to raise the profile of the CRC in Macedonia, and far more resources need to be committed to children's issues. This is, of course, a difficult challenge given the current weak economic state of the country. Although a well established social protection, health and education system is in place, state funds are inadequate to maintain effective levels of operation, still less to develop them further to meet the increasing demands within the country.

The reality *against* the rhetoric

Sexual exploitation

There is little specific data available on the incidence of sexual abuse and exploitation of children in Macedonia. Independent researchers maintain that an average of 0.2 per cent of recorded criminal activity is related in some way to sexual abuse, with between 20 and 30 convictions a year. However, those organisations working closely with children and children's issues believe that this does not reflect adequately the reality of the problem.

Sexual abuse is a highly taboo subject and rarely acknowledged. A combination of shame, guilt and denial creates a complicity of silence. Cases of sexual abuse go unreported, making detection, prevention and protection very difficult tasks. Those who work directly with children who have been the victims of sexual abuse report that, since 1990, parents have been more encouraged to talk openly about this problem. It is therefore now becoming more widely acknowledged as an issue that needs to be addressed.

GOVERNMENT ACTION AND POLICY

Sexual crimes against children are covered by Article 188 of Macedonian criminal law and the production and propagation of pornographic material featuring children is outlawed under Article 191. However neither of these offer adequate protection for children. There is no formal body responsible for monitoring sexual crimes or for identifying and protecting children who are at risk. Despite the fact that the problem of sexual abuse is becoming more widely acknowledged and discussed, there appear to be no effective steps being taken to prevent the proliferation of these activities.

Currently the only recourse available to children who have been the subject of sexual abuse or suspected abuse is to report it to the police. Yet the police have no training in dealing with crimes of this nature and their inexperience and general lack of sensitivity prove to be damaging rather than protective. Psychologists and psychiatrists who are in contact with the problem agree that the investigation of reported abuse can be even more traumatic for the child than the crime itself. The child is invariably placed under severe scrutiny, questioned in a sterile and clinical manner by a number of professional strangers, with few allowances made for the sensitivity of the situation or the age of the child. Some experts from these fields believe that, in such circumstances, it might be better for the issue to be taken out of the criminal process altogether for the child's sake. Save the Children Macedonia has attempted several times to initiate the foundation of the Commission on

Mental Health, which would take over the responsibility of handling these cases. Before entering into any proceedings they would determine what is appropriate in the 'best interests of the child'. To date there have been no advances on this issue.

RECOMMENDATIONS

- **Impose stricter sanctions** - In the first instance criminal law should be amended to impose much tougher sanctions for any form of sexual abuse or exploitation involving children.
- **Promote sexual awareness** - Children should be provided with information and education through schools and other community structures to raise their awareness of the problem in order to help them better protect themselves against sexual abuse.
- **Identify children at risk** - Establish mechanisms for identifying children at risk (from violence in the home, teachers and other youth professionals) and put into place protection strategies.
- **Develop investigative guidelines** - Put in place better procedures for investigation and develop guidelines for good practice. Alongside this, police and social workers need to be given appropriate training to deal with children who have been traumatised.

Juvenile justice

Juveniles are technically defined as persons under 18. However, children are not regarded as criminally responsible until they reach the age of 14. Under Macedonian legislation, juvenile delinquency is regarded broadly as referring to difficult behaviour. It refers not only to those children who have committed a crime, but also those with anti-social behaviour (such as truants and runaways) and those who are educationally neglected and abused (beggars, street children, vagrants and children working in the sex trade). The juvenile justice system, therefore, seeks not only to provide services for children who have committed crimes, but also to be preventive in serving children who might be at risk of breaking the law.

On average between 1,300 and 1,500 juveniles are convicted of criminal acts in Macedonia each year. Of these, the vast majority are sentenced to corrective measures rather than detained in juvenile prisons. Most of the crimes committed tend to be theft and bodily harm. In recent years more organised crime has emerged, involving gangs of youths working together, committing crimes such as theft and burglary mainly, often under the direction of adults. Increasingly at risk of falling into criminal activity are children who abuse drugs. Under Macedonian law, encouraging others to take drugs is also a criminal offence. Over the last decade there has been a proliferation of drug-related crimes, with the involvement of drug-abusers in a variety of criminal behaviour including prostitution, burglary, armed attacks and even murder.

GOVERNMENT ACTION AND POLICY

In Macedonia, there is no special court through which the juvenile justice system is administered. The system states that legal proceedings can only be initiated against a juvenile upon the request of the District Attorney, which must be done within three months of the date of the offence. Special judges and juvenile councils then oversee all juvenile cases. Because of the age allocated for criminal responsibility, sanctions cannot be applied to juveniles who were younger than 14 at the time of the crime. In these instances the youths are placed under the responsibility of the Centre for Social Care, who are advised on what action and corrective measures to take.

Overall it is considered that juveniles are accorded their rights as outlined in Article 40.2 (a) of the Convention. For crimes punishable by imprisonment of over five years, a juvenile must have a defender from the beginning of the legal proceedings. Where detention of a juvenile is necessary, the parents or legal guardians are immediately informed and the young person is interviewed in the presence of the parents or guardians. Specially trained interviewers carry out all interviews and allowances are made for the child's age and gender. Where necessary, police will invite other specialist services such as social workers, health-care professionals and psychologists or psychiatrists to ensure that juveniles under investigation are dealt with in the most appropriate manner. During preliminary proceedings, a juvenile accused can only be detained for up to 30 days and they will normally be held in separate accommodation from adults. A relatively good system is in place and trained professionals are used in criminal proceedings. However there is still evidence of police using repressive techniques and flouting the system and standards which have nominally been established.

Criminal sanctions

A two-tiered system of sanctions has been established for juvenile offenders. The nature of the sanction is determined by the nature of the crime.

1. Educational measures

- Disciplinary measures - reprimand or referral to a juvenile centre.
- Enhanced supervision - by parents or legal guardians or the Centre for Social Work.

2. Institutional measures

- Referral to educational institution or correctional home.
- Juvenile prison (for 16- to 18-year-olds only)

The rationale for educational correction is to rehabilitate for juvenile offenders and strive towards the appropriate development of the juvenile through supervision and the provision of protection, support, vocational training and development of personal responsibility. Measures vary widely and can be as basic as an apology to the victim of their crime, through to attending school regularly, or receiving counselling and undertaking community service. If a juvenile fails to meet the obligations prescribed a stiffer sentence can be imposed.

Only criminally responsible juveniles can be jailed for a crime sanctioned with an imprisonment of more than five years. However, such sentences are only used in instances where the consequences of the crime are so severe, and the level of criminal responsibility so obvious, that an educational measure could not be justified. Wherever possible, juvenile councils seek to offer constructive sanctions, which are issued in the best interests of the child and which seek to prevent re-offending.

RECOMMENDATIONS

- **Develop a code of good practice for the police** - The police are notoriously repressive in their handling of juveniles. While there are clearly established principles for dealing with juvenile crimes, the practice is too often far from the ideal. The reality of the juvenile justice system in Macedonia often fails to meet the standards set out under Article 40.
- **Fully trained professionals** - All procedures involving juveniles must be undertaken by experienced and trained professionals.
- **Establish an official juvenile court** - A separate court and associated system for juvenile justice should be established.
- **Appoint a child rights ombudsman** - A deputy responsible for the administration of juvenile justice or preferably an Ombudsman for Child Rights should be appointed.

- **Provide alternative measures for first-time offenders** - Alternative measures, such as community work and educational alternatives, should be available for corrective first-time offenders.
- **Enhanced co-operation between social institutions** - Co-operation between the courts, the police, centres of social work and youth organisations needs to be improved and developed so to ensure that there is coherence in the way in which juvenile offenders are being treated.

Displacement

Since gaining independence in 1991 the Republic of Macedonia has received two significant influxes of refugees escaping from hostilities in the former Yugoslav territories. The first was from Bosnia and the most recent from Kosovo.

During the Bosnian conflict some 60,000 refugees sought safety in Macedonia. Provided with food and clothing, they were housed in youth recreation centres and other municipal buildings across the country. Children were absorbed into the normal education system and social workers (both governmental and non-governmental) worked with refugee community groups. Now most Bosnian refugees have either returned home or moved on to other countries. The few remaining are now benefiting from social provisions equal to those available to nationals.

According to UNHCR figures issued in June 1999 there were 277,153 Kosovars who sought refuge in Macedonia. However it is thought that these figure were not entirely accurate, as many refugees fled before the airstrikes and were not registered. It is estimated that around 40 per cent of these Kosovan refugees are under the age of 15 and, according to available statistics, around 176,000 of these have been placed with families. It is likely that many have now returned to Kosovo; however, no hard data was available to verify this at the time of going to print.

GOVERNMENT ACTION AND POLICY

The Macedonian Government has sought to place all refugee children in host families. The children have been absorbed into the existing educational structure, with UNICEF and other humanitarian organisations providing them with educational materials. Those not placed with a family have been housed in refugee camps, which have been constructed by the state with the assistance of international relief agencies. For these children the situation is a little different. UNICEF has been collaborating closely with the Macedonian Ministry of Education to set up the school programme in tented structures for over 30,000 children in six camps (at June 1999). Over 80 per cent of the registered refugee children were receiving some form of formal education.

Psychosocial care has been provided for children and their families by humanitarian agencies working in the region. Refugees who are professional teachers, psychologists and health-care specialists were provided with additional training, to help ensure adequate service provision for refugees in the camps.

Health care has been provided through the established Macedonian health-care service and temporary health-care centres were set up with ambulances available in the camps. UNHCR has met the additional health costs and widespread vaccination programmes were undertaken.

Family tracing and reunification has been addressed through inter-agency efforts, for example, making mobile phones available in all camps for family members to keep in touch with each other.

RECOMMENDATIONS

The Macedonian Government has, on the whole, been working hard to respond effectively to the needs of the refugee communities. Predictable and commonplace in any emergency situation, problems such as overcrowded camps existed for the duration of the most recent crisis, the blame for which cannot be placed on the Government, which worked closely with all the international humanitarian agencies to resolve the problems as they arose. It is felt, however, that greater attention should be given to the needs of refugee children.

- **Improve co-ordination and inter-agency planning** - The Government must work closely with all international humanitarian agencies, so that effective service provision can be assured. Adequate contingency planning and co-ordination are essential to mitigate the problems which always arise in such volatile refugee situations.
- **Develop greater focus on the child** - A stronger focus on the needs of refugee children must be adopted to ensure that Articles 22 and 10 of the Convention have full effect.

Education

The Constitution of Macedonia guarantees every child's right to equal access to education. Primary education is mandatory, with children enrolled at six and continuing for eight years until the age of fourteen. Attendance rates are high and in 1997/98 over 95 per cent of children of primary school age were attending school regularly.

Although primary schools are principally funded by the state, parents are obliged to provide books, stationery and other school materials. The state makes some attempt to ensure that all children complete at least four years of their primary education and strict penalties are in place for parents who fail to send their children to school.

Secondary schools offer a further four years of education. Upon completing primary education every child has the right to enrol but, it is not compulsory. Until very recently, students had to take an enrolment test before being admitted into secondary school, and this also took into account performance in primary schools .

In both primary and secondary education, children can exercise their right to study in their mother tongue. The ethnic mix is broad and therefore education is currently offered in Macedonian, Albanian, Turkish and Serbian schools. The largest majority of students attend Macedonian-speaking schools (68.48 per cent of primary students and 85.29 per cent of secondary-school students). Ethnic Albanian students account for the second largest group (29.04 per cent of primary-school students and 14.04 per cent of secondary pupils), their numbers having increased considerably in recent years. The remaining number of students is made up of ethnic Turks and Serbs. Every school also provides teaching on the relevant culture and history. It is positive that Macedonia is relatively forward-thinking in providing most students with the opportunity to study their own language, but it hinders the development of multi-culturalism throughout the school system and fails to address the issues of inter-ethnic tolerance.

School attendance is fairly high, overall, but it is apparent that, as children get older and school seems less relevant to them, the drop-out rate increases. It is encouraging to see that, in recent years, the number of children opting to continue in school is growing, perhaps a reflection of the increasingly difficult employment market.
In 1994/95, 0.94 per cent of students failed to complete primary school. This fell to 0.85 per cent in 1996/97. Non-attendance is highest amongst Albanian, Turkish and Roma children and particularly amongst girls. The trend is, not surprisingly, most apparent in rural areas, where girls continue to be locked into more traditional

lifestyles. Parents are invariably uneducated and expectations are that children will work on family farms and contribute to the family income as soon as possible.

GOVERNMENT ACTION AND POLICY

Although all children in theory have equal access to secondary school, the additional costs such as books and other school materials are often prohibitive for poorer families. The preference is, therefore, for their children to stay at home to help in the family business, to care for younger siblings or to enter the workforce to bring additional income into the family.

Over 80 per cent of primary schools are in rural areas and in recent years many schools have fallen into disrepair. With a declining economic situation, refurbishment is out of the question and it proves a struggle even to meet overheads. Many schools lack the most basic educational resources.

A major criticism of the current education system is that it remains somewhat conservative and antiquated in its outlook. A disproportionate focus is placed on knowledge acquisition rather than the development of the child as a whole. Insufficient attention is dedicated to social and communication skills, which are an integral part of a child's progression into adulthood.
In general, the vast education curriculum leaves little room for personal development and prohibits children from pursuing their own interests.

RECOMMENDATIONS

- **Streamline the educational curriculum** - The current curriculum is far too complicated and its constant state of flux makes it difficult for both teachers and children to follow. The old-fashioned emphasis placed on the acquisition of knowledge hampers progress for children and little attention is given to the development of other crucial skills. The curriculum, therefore, needs to become more simplified in its content and more applied in its focus.
- **Improve the quality and scope of personal development and vocational education** - The education system needs to address the full development of the child. Much more focus needs to be given to personal development, and vocational training should be made more widely available. Children's voices are not currently heard in schools and therefore forums need to be developed which ensure that children are able to express their own views. As part of this, the principles of the CRC and the rights it accords to children must be incorporated into all school curricula.
- **Increase the level of investment in education** - Greater investment is needed in schools. A focus must be placed on training teachers further, to ensure good quality and highly motivated staff who possess the capability and confidence to implement the restructuring which is so urgently required.
- **Enhance co-operation with other NGOs and international organisations** - The Government needs to co-operate more readily with agencies such as UNICEF and other NGOs committed to working with children.

*'...You are **treated** as if you are a completely different species ...You **feel** you are a terrorist applying for asylum you have **no identity**'.*

Meron Abebaw, age 19 - arrived in the UK as a refugee from Ethiopia when she was 14

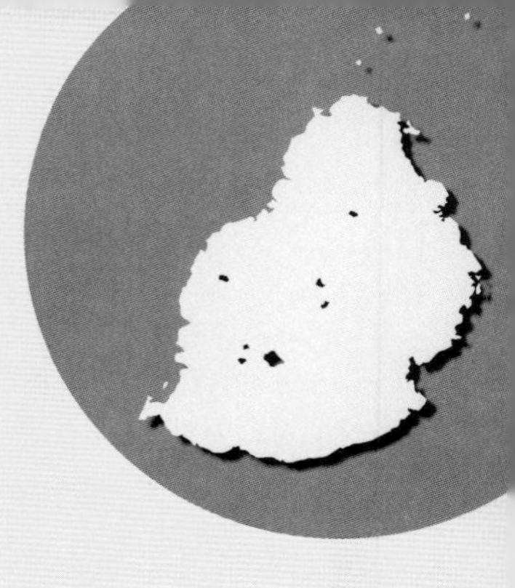

Mauritius

THE MAURITIAN GOVERNMENT AND THE CRC

The Government of Mauritius signed and ratified the United Nations Convention on the Rights of the Child on 26 July 1990, with one reservation (see section on displacement). The Government was due to submit its initial report to the UN Committee on the Rights of the Child in September 1992 but it did not complete it until July 1995. Non-governmental organisations (NGOs) were completely ignored when the report was being drafted. The major problem concerning the CRC is that the Convention has only been ratified by the Council of Ministers and not by the National Assembly itself. There is no constitutional provision to force the Government to go to the National Assembly before ratifying any convention. Thus the ratification of the Convention was made through the executive in Mauritius.

There has therefore been no debate in the National Assembly about the CRC, with the result that the Convention has been given a low profile by the Government. The majority of Members of the Assembly are unaware of the Convention and this is reflected in day-to-day political life. During debate on the Child Protection Act only four members out of 70 debated the motion. The Convention is not an integral part of the national legislation, and national laws and regulations are not fully consistent with the principles and provisions of the Convention.

The Government has, however, adopted some positive measures in order to comply with its obligations under the CRC. For example, the National Children's Council has been established, under the aegis of the Ministry of Women's Rights, Child Development and Family Welfare. An inter-ministerial committee on child prostitution has also been set up. The Child Protection Act was passed in November 1994 and the Government National Programme of Action for the Survival, Development and Protection of Children has been implemented. The latter was in response to the recommendations and goals stated in the Declaration and Plan of Action adopted by the World Summit for Children in September 1990.

The Government has set up a Law Commission to review Mauritian laws in general. Nothing has been mentioned in relation to the Convention and no related documents have been submitted by the Ministry of Women's Rights, Child Development and Family Welfare. Therefore the overall process of harmonising Mauritius' laws with the provisions of the Convention remains largely undone. The Government report to the UN Committee mentions only three major policy decisions: the right to a free education, the formation of an adoption council and the aforementioned child protection legislation.

The major concern regarding education is the inability to deliver sufficient quality - more children fail their exams than pass in Mauritius. For those that can afford it, the solution is private tuition, but many cannot. The Government is failing those children who cannot afford extra tuition. The drop-out rate is worryingly high.

The National Adoption Council Act (NACA) has been enacted without prior debate. NACA's priority is to regulate foreign parents who want to adopt Mauritian children. This Act does not standardise Mauritian laws on adoption nor does it legislate the need for follow-up in cases where Mauritian children have been adopted. The Child Protection Act 1994 has been ushered through the National Assembly after pressure and complaints from civil society. The Child Protection Act has many imperfections and limitations.

Insufficient attention is paid, at both national and local levels, to the need for an efficient monitoring mechanism. An effective system could provide systematic and comprehensive research and data concerning all the areas covered by the Convention. This is especially important with regard to child abuse, ill-treatment and exploitation. Mauritius has not yet fully taken into account the general principles of the Convention with regard to non-discrimination (Article 2), the best interests of the child (Article 3) and respect for the views of the child (Article 12). Neither has the Government taken sufficient measures to make the principles and provisions of the Convention widely known to adults and children alike, as stated in Article 42

With respect to the concerns expressed above, the following issues need to be addressed:

- Legislation - The Convention should be integrated into the national legislation, and national laws and regulations should be fully consistent with the principles and provisions of the Convention. Furthermore, the Government should pursue its efforts to strengthen the institutional framework designed to promote and protect human rights in general and children rights in particular.
- Dissemination of the CRC - The Government should work closely with NGOs to launch a permanent and visible campaign about the Convention for both children and adults.
- Monitoring mechanism - The establishment of an independent mechanism, such as an Ombudsman for children's rights, should be seriously considered.

The reality *against* the rhetoric

Sexual exploitation

Child prostitution is a visible and extensive problem in Mauritius. Prostitution is a taboo subject and this means little is done actively to control it in any way. Child prostitution is a particular problem in tourist areas. Sexual abuse is under-reported, as children often do not realise when they are abused or that they have a right not to be. A campaign of public awareness is required for both children and adults. The situation is summed up by the fact that no cases of sexual exploitation have yet been officially recorded.

GOVERNMENT ACTION AND POLICY

Section 14 of the Child Protection Act makes provision for a maximum fine of US$2,854 and imprisonment for a term not exceeding five years for any person who causes, incites or allows any child to be sexually abused by him/her or by another person, to have access to a brothel or to engage in prostitution. In the case of a victim who has learning difficulties, the fine is more severe - a maximum of US$4,281 and imprisonment for a term not exceeding eight years.

In addition, the Child Protection Act stipulates that: 'a child shall be deemed to be sexually abused where he or she has taken part as a willing or unwilling participant or observer in any act which is sexual in nature for the purposes of: (a) Another person's gratification, (b) Any activity of pornographic, obscene or indecent nature, (c) Any other kind of exploitation by any person.' The penalties are the same as those noted above.

Despite these efforts, the provisions of the Penal Code in relation to protection against sexual abuse (which provides no safeguards at all for male victims) look inconsistent with the principles of the CRC.

RECOMMENDATIONS

- **Dissemination** - A public information and awareness campaign on child prostitution and how it relates to the Convention should be launched. Children and the general public should be encouraged to report sexual abuse to the authorities.
- **Specialist training** - There should be a provision for comprehensive training on the Convention for all the agencies in the criminal justice system and for teachers and journalists.
- **Monitoring** - There is a need to monitor closely child prostitution, especially in tourist areas.

Juvenile justice

Eighty per cent of juvenile offenders are aged between 14 and 16; 95 per cent of offences committed by juveniles are related to theft. The ratio of male to female juvenile offenders is 11:1.

The Mauritian juvenile justice system deals with all young offenders under the age of 17 and distinguishes between children (persons under the age of 14) and juveniles (those aged 14 to 17).

Mauritian citizens have the right not to be subjected to torture or to inhuman or degrading punishment under Chapter 2 of the Constitution. Neither capital punishment nor life imprisonment is imposed for offences committed by persons below the age of 18. Moreover, the Child Protection Act provides for the protection of children with respect to physical, psychological, emotional or moral injury, as well as sexual offences and sexual exploitation.

GOVERNMENT ACTION AND POLICY

There are special judicial arrangements regarding offences committed by children under the age of 14. The court proceedings take place in chambers and in the presence of a responsible party.
A child under the age of nine is allowed to be a witness in court proceedings as long as, in the opinion of the court, they understand what it is to 'tell the truth'.

No child or young person is deprived of his or her liberty unlawfully or arbitrarily. A young offender is likely to be sent to a reform institution, rehabilitation centre or probation hostel, as decided by the magistrate. There are various forms of institutional placements: the Probation Hostels for Boys, the Probation Homes for Girls, the Rehabilitation Youth Centre and the Correctional Youth Centre. The prison authority runs these reform institutions. The fact that there is only one of each of these institutions covering the whole of Mauritius, and that none is stretched beyond capacity, is a positive feature.

There is concern about current legislation for young offenders as the Juvenile Offender Act is 60 years old and, according to NGOs, it has never been properly revised. The Government missed a chance to bring the Juvenile Offender Act in line with the Convention when they passed the Child Protection Act through the National Assembly.

No juvenile court, as such, exists in Mauritius. Instead, juveniles attend special hearings but these are held in the district courts with the same court structures and the same magistrate as adults. These magistrates do not have any specialist training in cases involving young offenders. No lay persons are involved in any capacity in the administration of 'juvenile justice'. The isolation experienced by a young offender in such a situation can be psychologically harmful. In addition to this, some offences, including all offences against the State, are excluded from the jurisdiction of juvenile provisions and are dealt with under the adult judicial system.

There are also major shortcomings in the arrest and investigation procedures for children and young people. For example, the same standard of suspicion is applied to both adults and children, causing great prejudice to children who have been arrested by the police. 'Reasonable suspicion' should not be enough to warrant an arrest. The arrest of children is often carried out in full public view and the child is often handcuffed. The escorting police officers are usually male, with no training whatsoever in dealing with children. The officer making the arrest is often the investigating officer and this leads to a lack of objectivity in the case. The arresting officer's testimony concerning the circumstances of the arrest is not tested until the psychologically daunting court environment. There are no provisions for facilities specifically for children, so they are kept in custody together with adults in cramped and filthy police cells

There is a great deal of work yet to be done by the Mauritian Government with regard to juvenile justice. For instance, children and young people should always be given bail, unless police officers can persuade the court beyond any reasonable doubt that the interests of justice will be hampered by bail being denied. If a child or juvenile is found guilty by the courts there should be an in-depth probation report on the child's family and surroundings. The report should be written in simple language and should be disclosed to the child's lawyer well in advance so that he or she may comment on, argue and amend any pleas of mitigation before the court sentences the child.

Sentencing which includes deprivation of liberty should be imposed only in exceptional cases. The Juvenile Offenders Act does not leave many sentencing options. A special education home for children deprived of liberty must be provided, as well as access to a social life. Every child suspected of an offence should be given legal assistance at the expense of the State.

RECOMMENDATIONS

- **Establishment of juvenile courts** - Juvenile courts should be set up as soon as possible and magistrates with specialist training should ensure that the rights within the Convention are upheld at all times when young offender has come into conflict with the law.
- **Review of juvenile arrest** - The powers and exercise of the law on arrest of young offenders should be reviewed.

- **Regulation of custody practices** - Measures should be taken to ensure that young offenders are not kept in custody with adults and that custody is the exception rather than the norm.
- **Juvenile police unit** - A specialised police section should be created in order to deal sensitively with children and young people in conflict with the law.

Displacement

When signing the Convention, Mauritius expressed a reservation concerning Article 22 as it was thought that granting refugee status might result in a large number of refugees. Subsequently, however, Mauritius adhered to the African Charter on the Rights and Welfare of the Child and made no reservations in regard to refugee children, and it withdrew the reservation made in respect of Article 22 of the Convention.

GOVERNMENT ACTION AND POLICY

According to NGOs, the state and civil society, there are no refugee children from other nations in Mauritius. However, there are some categories of Mauritian refugee:

- exiled families from Diego Garcia;
- economic refugees from Rodrigues;
- post-cyclone refugees living for a long period in refugee camps. These refugees cannot be compared with refugees from countries undergoing trauma from war or economic collapse. Nevertheless, many of the provisions needed for refugees from other nations are also necessary for this group.

RECOMMENDATIONS

- **Compliance of existing policy with the CRC** - Measures should be taken to ensure that current policy and practice reflects the withdrawal of the reservation made in respect of Article 22 of the Convention. Furthermore, a comprehensive integration policy should be provided for exiled and displaced children. Measures should be adopted in order to ensure compliance of national legislation by utilising the international treaties that define the status of refugees.
- **Public awareness of the needs of refugees** - Appropriate measures should be taken to make the public aware of issues affecting refugees and displaced children.

Education

In Mauritius, primary and secondary education is free and primary school has been compulsory since the 1991 Compulsory Education Act. Children start pre-primary school at the age of three; they join primary school at the age of five and stay for six years before joining a secondary school. Children can stay in secondary school until the age of 19, when they either progress to tertiary education or enter the world of work.

There are 35,000 children of pre-primary school age. Of these, the great majority attend school. There are about 1,400 pre-primary schools, most of which are privately run. The Government runs 119 pre-primary classes in primary schools.

There are 289 primary schools in Mauritius and most children have access to a primary school within two kilometres of their home. The primary cycle lasts six years, from standard I to standard VI. Until standard VI, progress to the next standard is automatic. At the end of standard VI, all children sit for the Certificate of Primary Education (CPE) set by the Mauritius Examinations Syndicate.

Generally the languages of instruction are English and French; in addition seven Asian languages are taught in primary schools: Hindi, Urdu, Arabic, Tamil, Telegu, Marathi and Mandarin.

GOVERNMENT ACTION AND POLICY

There is a clear commitment from the Government towards education. A Master Plan for Education has been drawn up with assistance from United Nations agencies and is being implemented.

The Government aims to have all children of pre-primary school age attending pre-primary schools in suitable buildings with trained teachers, adequate playing space and appropriate teaching materials. The Ministry of Education and Science has established a pre-primary unit in order to co-ordinate its policy and actions in this area. It has to be noted, however, that despite the Government's investment, pre-school education is very costly and a large number of children cannot attend simply because their parents cannot afford to pay.

Many children fail the exam at the end of the primary cycle in Standard VI. Forty per cent fail the CPE at their first attempt and 25 per cent fail after one year of repetition. Of the 13,000 or so who leave primary school without having obtained their CPE, only about 4,000 are admitted to vocational training. Six per cent of primary school children leave the education system virtually illiterate and 20 per cent functionally illiterate.

Schools, especially those which achieve good results, are excessively geared to success in the CPE. There is a tendency for non-examination subjects to be squeezed out of the curriculum. There is strong pressure on children - especially in Standards V and VI - to take private tuition. The Education Act was amended in April 1991 to ban private tuition for children in Standards I to III. There is a wide gap between the highest and lowest achieving schools in terms of success in the CPE. The curriculum is excessively rigid and makes insufficient allowance for children of different abilities. The combination of automatic promotion with a lack of remedial assistance for less able children means that those who fall behind are likely to remain behind.

There are deficiencies in the provision of support services, teaching aids and equipment. There is no programme for the regular maintenance and repair of school buildings, furniture and equipment so they are frequently delayed. There has, in the past, been insufficient provision for in-service training for teachers. In some schools, there is a high rate of absenteeism amongst pupils and teaching staff.

Cases of child abuse at school have been reported to the National Children's Council, though it is not clear how widespread the problem is. In each case, investigations are carried out and pupils now receive protection through section 13 of the Child Protection Act.

The secondary education cycle in Mauritius lasts seven years (from I to VI). The School Certificate Examination takes place after five years of schooling and the Higher School Certificate examination is at the end of the cycle. In this phase of education, the drop-out and repetition rates are high. Only 15 per cent of students in secondary schools reach the required academic level to proceed to further studies. Remedial teaching facilities are scarce and students receive inadequate information and guidance about their study choices and prospects. The long-term aim of the Government is that all children should receive a secondary education of high quality that is easily accessible, and be provided with courses that suit their aptitudes and abilities.

Since 1989, when the Industrial and Vocational Training Board (IVTB) was established, the vocational and training infrastructure of the country has undergone rapid development. The mission of the IVTB is to provide quality training at good value at all levels. The IVTB operates 11 pre-vocational training centres in various regions of the country, including Rodrigues. More than 3,000 pupils in the 12-15 age group are following courses in these schools. The IVTB also offers an apprenticeship scheme whereby 15-year-olds are posted in private firms under contractual agreements with employers.

Education fails many students in Mauritius. Despite the fact that about 13 per cent of total governmental recurrent expenditure is on education, the results are disappointing. It is also necessary to point out that the Mauritian education system is very elitist and cannot claim that equal opportunities are offered to children of different socio-economic backgrounds.

RECOMMENDATIONS

- **Tackling abuse** - There should be greater awareness and openness about child abuse and ill-treatment in schools, and opportunities for children to report it.
- **Raising the standard of attainment** - The percentage of passes at all levels (primary and secondary) should be improved through regular inspections and monitoring. Furthermore, measures should be adopted to ensure that privately run schools provide a high-quality service.
- **Focusing on primary education** - The educational objectives of primary schools, as outlined in the Master Plan, should be reviewed in a more realistic way. Also, the primary-school cycle should be extended to nine years, thereby eliminating the 'waiting period' from 12 to 15 years, during which those who leave the system cannot aspire to become apprentices.

'My ambition is to live in a house with my family members all together'.

Sugath, age 9 - Colombo, Sri Lanka

Mexico

Mexico signed the CRC in 1989. The Convention was then approved by the Chambers of Senators of the Congress of the Union on 19 June 1990. According to the 1990 cencus 38 per cent of the Mexican population was 15 years of age and younger and 50 per cent was 19 or younger. The circumstances under which Mexican children live and survive are gradually improving but the emergent political-economic model does not inspire confidence. It is very difficult to see how the current orthodoxy will overcome problems such as malnourishment, diseases, poor development and mistreatment.

Efforts have been made to bring domestic law into line with the Convention through new laws, the amendment of the Constitution and the adoption of programmes specifically aimed at promoting and protecting the rights of the child.

In 1991, a National Commission was set up, which drafted the 1991 National Programme of Action for Children (NPAC). The NPAC focuses on health, education, basic sanitation and assistance to minors in especially difficult circumstances. Most federal organisations now have their own action programmes for children. In addition, the Council of the National Human Rights Commission (CNDH) agreed to create a programme for children in order to address the violation of human rights concerning children and families. The Law on the Treatment of Juvenile Offenders was also adopted and the right of everyone to education was incorporated into the Constitution.

Current national legislation regarding children, however, is not yet in full agreement with the provisions of the CRC. There is no provision relating to the best interests of the child nor the prohibition of discrimination against children. Demands to update and harmonise federal and state laws and provisions to make them consistent with the Convention, are still on-going. There is also the need to standardise state laws, so that 18 is the minimum age for a person to be legally prosecuted as an adult. A monitoring mechanism should be established to follow the implementation of the Convention.

There have been some advances in relation to the welfare of children. For example, significant changes have taken place in regulating and standardising education. However, there are still unacceptable deficiencies concerning the situation of indigenous children, working children, street children and children with

HIV/AIDS. In addition, the federalisation of education and health has neither overcome centralism nor guaranteed a just distribution of resources. Indeed in some cases, it has increased inequity within the states.

Regrettably, the rights of children as with many Mexican laws exist on a formal level, but are not translated into practice. Indeed children's rights are still not a priority for many social organisations. Even groups which actively promote human rights do not pay particular attention to the needs of children. Within civil society itself, organisations have not assigned children roles that see them as protagonists in their own future rather than simply consumers of adults' ideas.

There are grassroots organisations which could make important contributions to analysing the situation of children, but they have neither the time nor the tools for collating and sharing their insights. Lack of co-ordination and information has caused a duplication of effort and a failure to address some issues. The absence of reliable data, difficulty in gaining access to existing sources and the lack of research in many areas act as obstacles to addressing these issues. Government institutions, for instance, do not readily grant access to their information sources and the results of their research and evaluations are considered confidential.

While some positive action has been taken, there remain a number of key concerns.

- Legislative steps should be taken to fully harmonise federal and state legislation with the provisions of the CRC.
- Principles relating to the best interests of the child and the prohibition of discrimination in relation to children should be incorporated into domestic law.
- Relevant mechanisms should also be set up to monitor the implementation of the Convention at all levels. All elements of civil society should be involved in the design, analysis and monitoring of policy and practice as it affects children.
- A single Code for Minors should be applicable throughout the country, giving legal status to minors so that they can challenge violations of their rights without needing an adult to validate their claim.
- The results of any research and evaluations of programmes for children should be widely distributed in a timely fashion.
- The recognition of children as subjects, and consideration of their social rights in new laws, should be promoted.

The reality *against* the rhetoric

Sexual exploitation

The problem of child prostitution is not well known or recognised in Mexico. It is a complex phenomenon involving clandestine groups, networks and activities. There are various forms of child exploitation, including child pornography, prostitution, sexual tourism and direct abuse. In most of these activities, some people in public authorities are involved as accomplices, either by obtaining economic rewards through extortion or by not preventing or prosecuting those who exploit minors.

Poverty and associated rural to urban migration are the general causal factors behind the increase in commercial sexual exploitation. This exploitation is concentrated in metropolitan, tourist and border areas. Poverty can work to fracture family structure and this may lead to a weakening of social and moral values as the natural protection of the family is weakened. On the other hand, sexual abuse within the family can be the beginning of a child's exploitation which then moves into the commercial sector.

The most visible form of sexual exploitation of children in Mexico is prostitution - and this includes employment as table dancers or strippers. The use of children in pornography is also reported anecdotally as quite common, but facts and data are much more difficult to establish due to the secrecy that typifies this kind of exploitation.

GOVERNMENT ACTION AND POLICY

In a federal government like Mexico, each state has its own legislation relating to the protection of children's rights. This has led to a great divergence of laws across the country. In many cases these laws are not in accordance with the relevant international standards. The Government of Mexico is aware of the need for urgent action with regard to the commercial sexual exploitation of children. However, while the political will to address the problem is quite perceptible, there are no systematic and concrete strategies in place to deal with it. The commitment of relevant authorities to address these problems is far too often dependent on the dedication of individuals in positions of responsibility.

One of the major concerns is the tacit participation of law enforcement authorities who help to maintain a climate of impunity in which the more organised networks for child prostitution and pornography can operate. In particular, tourism, immigration and customs officials still appear to deny the existence of the problem at all.

Whilst serious attention has to be given to sensitisation of the law enforcement authorities, the alleged involvement of some law enforcers in abuses against children, either by themselves or in collusion with others, deserves urgent investigation. The lack of reported cases specifically concerning commercial sexual exploitation of children might be attributable to the disinterest on the part of both the police and a large part of the general public.

There is also a need to maximise resources and information through better co-ordination and networking of Government and NGOs. Very often, what little co-ordination exists is merely sporadic and ad hoc. This creates duplication in some areas and leaves gaps in others.

RECOMMENDATIONS

- **Statistics** -The lack of statistics and data concerning the scope and scale of commercial sexual exploitation of children should not be an excuse for non-implementation of both preventive and protective measures.
- **Legislation** -The criminal justice system must be child-friendly particularly at the level of law enforcement. Training on children's rights for customs officials in the field of commercial sexual exploitation is required. It is necessary to review both federal and state legislation affecting children with a view to harmonising them with the provisions of the CRC.
- **Protection of children at risk** - Constant monitoring and supervision of places where children are at risk, and implementation of programmes for their protection, are necessary. The role of the national System for the Integral Development of the Family (DIF) should be enhanced through uniform programmes, addressing and eradicating the main causes of child abuse, especially intra-familial violence and sexual abuse.

Juvenile justice

In 1994, 3,794 alleged juvenile offenders were dealt with by the Procurator's Office of the

Federal District. The Office for Preventive Measures and Treatment of Juvenile Offenders dealt with 2,986 young people, and the Children's Council dealt with 1,695.

On the basis of legislation governing the treatment of juvenile offenders, the Ministry of the Interior created the Children's Council and the Office for the Preventive Measures and Treatment of Juvenile Offenders. This legislation aims to regulate state protection of children's rights and the social rehabilitation of those whose behaviour is characterised as criminal. It applies in the Federal Districts in common matters and throughout the Republic in federal matters.

The Children's Council is the body authorised to dispense justice for minors through the advisory boards (the bodies responsible for instituting the necessary investigations and legal proceedings in respect of children referred to them).

The Office for Preventive Measures and Treatment of Juvenile Offenders is the administrative unit. It operates through its juvenile commissioners who are legally responsible for investigating violations of the criminal law by minors, and for verifying the facts of such crimes, as well as investigating the situation of the children accused of committing them. The Office has two diagnostic centres - one for boys and one for girls - whose function is to produce a physical and psychological profile of the alleged juvenile offender.

Despite new legislation and these new institutions, the lack of implementation, in practice, of the provisions of the Convention and domestic law related to the administration of justice and the treatment of young offenders, is a considerable concern.

GOVERNMENT ACTION AND POLICY

The current legal framework protecting children has serious limitations in respect of the treatment of those boys and girls who have committed an illegal act. The accent is almost always on punitive measures and not rehabilitation. Furthermore, there are no established guidelines or procedures for the behaviour of the police and guards - 'normal' standards are imposed with no reference to those that are fair.

There are many complaints about the ill-treatment of children by the police and security and military personnel. This is combined with an all-too-common failure to take effective steps to punish those found guilty of such violations or, for those who are punished, to make public their punishment. This has led to the commonplace belief that officials can behave with impunity and that it is useless, or too dangerous, to bring complaints before the relevant authorities. In practice there is little real implementation of the CRC.

RECOMMENDATIONS

- **Action against ill-treatment of juveniles by state officials** - Determined and consistent action must be taken against all those who ill-treat children, especially where acts of violence are involved. The police, security services and the military should become the focus of this action.
- **Evaluation of the impact of legislation affecting juveniles** - Serious research is needed to evaluate the psychological consequences of the procedures established in the legislation for juvenile offender. Specialised education and training is essential for those responsible for the monitoring and the administration of justice for minors. The creation of an Institute for Research and Education about the problems and rights of minors and lawbreakers is highly recommended.
- **Involvement of civil society** - The professional participation of civil society in the design of policy and practice in relation to young offenders should be considered the norm and not the exception.

Displacement

Along the northern border of Mexico, there are approximately two million minors out of five million inhabitants. Of these children, 66 per cent were born in other states but migrated to the border zone; 25 per cent are exposed to poor nutrition, abandonment, drugs, anti-social activities and sexual exploitation.

In confinement centres for children without documents, 74 per cent of children are reported to be well cared for; 7.1 per cent reported racist harassment and insults; 4.3 per cent didn't receive any water or food during their seclusion and eight per cent had been psychologically or physically tortured. In some border states, deported children are sent to juvenile centres together with juvenile offenders, where they may be exposed to other vices and mistreatment.

Refugee children make up a large part of the Guatemalan population settled on Mexico's southern border (mainly in the states of Chiapas, Campeche and Quintana Roo). It is estimated that more than 50 per cent of the refugees are children born on Mexican territory. In 1995, the Mexican Commission for Aid to Refugees (COMAR) provided help for 33,862 Guatemalan refugees - more than 50 per cent of them were aged 14 and under. The main purpose of this assistance was to safeguard the children's physical and mental health by providing health and education services.

GOVERNMENT ACTION AND POLICY

One positive note is that children born to refugees in Mexico have been accorded the same legal status as all other Mexicans. A number of measures have been taken to expand community infrastructure and incorporate the refugee settlements into mainstream society. A 'regularisation programme' has been introduced with the aim of offering the parents of refugee children born in Mexico the possibility of remaining in the country with their children, if they so wish.

Children repatriated from the USA are left vulnerable to many kinds of abuse unless they are returned to their families or referred to a welfare agency. A major goal of the NPAC is to provide care and support for repatriated children in hostels and social welfare institutions.

RECOMMENDATIONS

- **Increased resources** - Greater federal financial support should be granted to border states' budgets for assisting the displaced and refugees. Lack of resources is one of the main reasons that deportations sometimes take place in too hasty a manner, with the result that children may become separated from their parents.
- **Support to NGOs supporting refugees and displaced people** - Support to NGOs and civil organisations working in this field should be strengthened.

Education

For many years, the Mexican Government has considered basic education (primary and secondary) of fundamental importance. Education lasts for nine years: six at primary and three at secondary. Recently, pre-school education has also become available, although it is not compulsory. The state is obliged to provide at least one year of pre-school education.

Access to basic education, and completion of primary education has improved, with at least 80 per cent of children of school age in school and non-school systems. Disparity in the levels of achievement between boys and girls has been reduced.

However, between 1.5 and 2 million minors still do not have access to primary education and among those who have the opportunity of studying there is a high percentage of truancy. The quality of education is, on the whole, poor.

GOVERNMENT ACTION AND POLICY

The Government's declared policy is that education is crucial to the future of Mexico and its people. Unfortunately, some of its efforts are insufficient and some unproductive.

The Government sets aside 5.4 per cent of the GDP for education but recognises that this is not enough to cover basic needs. According to the recommendations of the Organisation for Co-operation and Economic Development, 6.9 per cent is required in order to improve the current situation. It is important to emphasise that between 1990 and 1995, the budget intended for education increased by 100 per cent in real terms. This increase has been very important in quantitative terms but it has not been reflected in terms of quality.

A positive note is that the repetition rate (the numbers of children who have to repeat a year of study) for the first grade of primary school has dropped significantly. This reduction is due to a new measure which extends from one to two years the time allowed for a student to learn how to read and write. The Mexican Government has also put in place several programmes to decrease the level of truancy, and there are programmes and grants which offer special support to pupils living in extreme poverty, who are most likely to drop out of primary school. The Education Programme - Health and Nourishment has an element which specifically aims to helps girls who have abandoned their studies.

Secondary education in Mexico is free and obligatory but families must equip their children, and the relatively high cost of this means that many children are unable to attend. At this age, some children are simply put off by the authoritative and conservative nature of education in Mexico - discipline and order are always given preference over creativity and originality. As far as vocational training is concerned, the modernisation of the educational system is guided by the requirements of the North American Free Trade Agreement (NAFTA) whose aim is to double the enrolment in technical and technological education by the year 2000. Despite all the Government's efforts, it is unlikely that such an objective will be achieved by that time.

The National Commission on Human Rights and the Public Education Secretariat have reviewed textbooks with the goal of incorporating the values and provisions of the CRC into them. Textbooks are free at the beginning of each school year.

Another area of concern is the physical punishment of students, which is not outlawed by the General Law of Education. Currently, if children and their families wish to bring a complaint on an educational matter, they have to take it to the Local or National Human Rights Commission. Statistical data on indigenous or Amerindian populations is not accurate, since language is the predominant fact used by the census to register people as indigenous. Consequently, minors who no longer speak their group language, or who are bilingual, are not represented in the data. In areas where there are high concentrations of indigenous people, conditions are alarming: poorly trained teachers, severe shortages of books and resources, a rudimentary curriculum focused on teaching in Spanish, and multi-grade classrooms as the norm, are a few of the more significant failings. Budgets in these schools are much lower than for schools where the population is predominantly of Spanish heritage.

RECOMMENDATIONS

- **Development of pre-school and primary education** - Greater attention and more education should be given to children under four years old, especially children of working mothers.
- **Child-centred education** - The education of children should be adapted to the individual developmental stage of children and to their own needs. The quality of education should be improved and the participation of pupils in the decisions of the school should be encouraged.
- **Greater participation of the family** - The participation of the family in scholastic decisions should be encouraged. There should be support and education for parents so that they can provide better attention to, and improve interaction with, their children.
- **Government policies to address inequalities** - The Government should adopt a policy for education, which explicitly addresses the problems related to socio-economic inequalities.
- **Education subsidies for disadvantaged areas** - A clear policy for compensation is required in order to support those Mexican states with the greatest economic and social difficulties.
- **Continuing teacher training** - The Government should adopt a policy which supports the continuing education of teachers and provides up-to-date training and information.
- **Increased funding for the education of indigenous peoples** - Schools in areas where the Amerindian population is predominant need at least equitable, and preferably, greater funding. The treatment of children in these areas is a clear breach of the principle of non-discrimination, which underpins the CRC and indeed all human rights.

'I'd like people to be ***friends*** *and* ***not argue*** *all the time'.*

Jessica, age 10 - UK

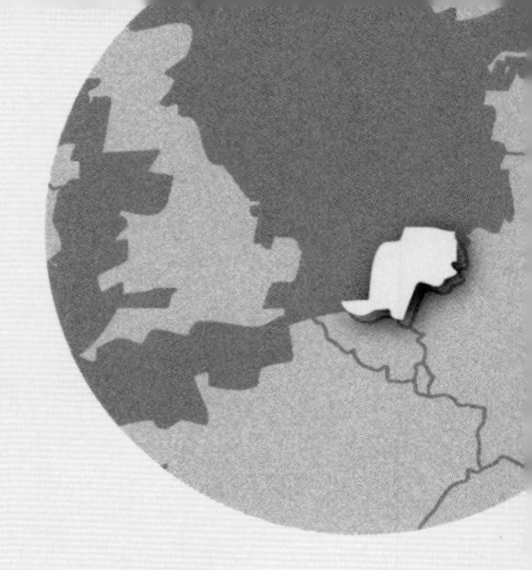

Netherlands

THE NETHERLANDS GOVERNMENT AND THE CRC

The Netherlands ratified the CRC on 7 March 1995 with one reservation in relation to juvenile justice.

To mark the ratification of the Convention, the First National Youth Debate was held in the Lower House of the States General on 20 November 1995 which is Universal Children's Day. A non-governmental organisation called Codename: Future held a Youth Referendum in October of the same year and followed this with second one in 1996. At this event 200,000 young people made known their views on a wide variety of topics.

Youth participation in decision-making is an area where many local authorities are seeking an effective format. The central Government provides for political participation via youth community councils made up of secondary school students.

The Government has no plans to appoint a children's ombudsman but it does provide co-financing on a temporary basis for pilot projects involving regional ombudsmen. The work of these ombudsmen is varied and, at the moment, the boundaries of their concerns and responsibilities are unclear. A general aim is to create the conditions in which it is possible for children to stand up for themselves. Several organisations are involved in this work, providing information, advice and legal assistance. The Ministry of Justice has been funding children's legal centres since 1999.

Children remain dependent on legal representatives to take any kind of legal action in the Netherlands because they have no capacity to act in a legal manner themselves if their rights are violated.

The Government has made an effort to disseminate information regarding the CRC. A campaign called 'By Talking You can do Yourself Justice' operates at both national and local levels. At the national level, TV and radio commercials are broadcast and printed information is made available at libraries, post offices and town halls. Advertisements are placed in youth magazines and school diaries and children's TV programmes carry free publicity. Dutch Education Television has made a series of programmes concerning children's rights. At the local level, local authorities, schools and other organisations which come into contact with children are urged to promote the campaign. The campaign is the only source of information regarding the CRC and it is not known what kind of reach it has achieved.

The Government delivered its first report concerning the Convention to the UN Committee for the Rights of the Child in May 1997. It was only published in English and was not made accessible to children.

The Government's failings with regard to the CRC are by no means fundamental but they are significant. The key issues which need attention are:

- that the Government's reservations concerning juvenile justice remain unresolved;
- that research into existing and new forms of participation is required and that children's views and ideas are central to this work and any resultant legislation;
- that a national office for a children's ombudsman should be created and the existing regional arrangements be reviewed, strengthened and funded on a permanent basis;
- that children be allowed to bring legal proceedings before an independent third party; that all preceding and subsequent communication with the UN Committee for the Rights of the Child be published in Dutch and that children have access to this material.

The reality *against* the rhetoric

Sexual exploitation

It is believed that the sexual exploitation of children is on the increase in the Netherlands. It is difficult to be sure as there is a lack of reliable data and the known recorded incidences of abuse do not convey the whole picture. Society has a growing awareness of this problem and it is hoped that this will result in a greater reporting of abuse, improvements in the care of victims, better strategies for prevention and protection and research into the whole area.

GOVERNMENT ACTION AND POLICY

New legislation concerning sexual exploitation took effect on 1 December 1991. It covers three major areas: trafficking, the time-limit on prosecutions for sexual offences committed against minors and child pornography.

The trafficking of human beings, including children, has been addressed with three strategies and clear guidelines to ensure effective enforcement. The authorities are determined to close the organisations responsible for the trade, to protect the victims and to confiscate any profits made from the activity.

Research has demonstrated that children may well take a long time to come to terms with any abuse they have suffered and to be able to tell anyone of their experiences so as to facilitate prosecution. With this in mind the Government has decreed that the statute of limitations for sexual offences against minors should begin when the victim has reached 18 years of age and not at the time when the abuse occurred.

With regard to child pornography, it has been made a criminal offence for anyone to produce, import, distribute, publicly exhibit, convey in transit, export or stock any pictorial (or other storage medium) representation of a sexual act involving a person who has not clearly reached the age of 16. The new act on child pornography, which came into effect in February 1998, is being interpreted so that the mere possession of such materials is also covered by the scope of the legislation. Prosecutions focus on commercial production, distribution and large-scale bartering of such material and the police have been issued with guidelines to aid their investigations and the chances of successful prosecution.

The nature of the Internet means it is very difficult to police, its supra-national characteristic making national legislation difficult to enforce. However, since 1996, the Ministry of Justice, at the suggestion of Internet service providers, has set up the Internet Contact Point on Child Pornography where people can report sites which feature such material. In reality very little action is taken against those who produce child pornography for cyberspace. The police need additional funding and greater expertise to fight this form of exploitation in an effective manner. Despite the difficulties, research has to be carried out to find ways of addressing this global problem.

Video recordings featuring naked children have been discovered which have been made without the consent of the children or their parents. These recordings are the subject of both formal and informal trade, again without consent. The legal representatives of children or their parents can apply to the civil courts for an injunction preventing publication and ordering the destruction of this material. However, there is often a long passage of time before the injured party knows about the existence of the material; indeed she or he may never know about it. Matters could be improved by allowing the public prosecution service to institute civil proceedings on behalf of the injured parties, even in their absence.

Sex tourism involving under-age children has become a recent source of great concern and new legislation is proposed. The major goal of a new law is to make sure that any Dutch national committing such an offence can be tried when they return to the Netherlands.

The duties of the police in relation to the treatment and care of children who have become victims of sexual exploitation have received considerable attention. Training both at a basic level and through the provision of specialist courses has been vastly improved.

In 1995 the responsibility for co-ordinating information on child pornography moved to the National Criminal Intelligence Service (CRI), in order to create a database concerning all related matters and to centralise investigative efforts. The same body has begun a register of all known sex-offenders, in an effort to protect children from abuse by repeat offenders. Although progress has been made in this field, there is still insufficient information and greater efforts need to be made by both the police and the CRI.

Despite these initiatives, the Government is only now in the process of developing a National Plan of Action as called for by the 1996 Conference on Sexual Exploitation in Stockholm. Overall the Netherlands would benefit from a holistic and wide-ranging set of policies to combat and prevent child sex abuse and exploitation.

RECOMMENDATIONS

- **Research and planning for social provision** - Research needs to be undertaken concerning child prostitution; out-reach programmes are needed. Alternatives to forced institutionalisation must be found.
- **Greater penalties** - Greater penalties must be paid by those who use child prostitutes.
- **Expertise within the police and mechanisms to police the Internet** -The police need more expertise and resources to fight child pornography on the Internet and legal research, possibly at a supra-national level, should be undertaken to find effective ways of policing cyberspace in this regard.
- **Reform of court proceedings** - With reference to the unauthorised trade in video recordings, the public prosecution service should be able to act on a victim's behalf in the civil court.
- **The National Plan of Action** - The National Plan of Action to combat all forms of sexual exploitation should be finalised and implemented as soon as possible.

Juvenile Justice

The number of crimes committed by young people is on the increase and the nature of these crimes grows more serious. The Government responded by introducing legislation on 1 September 1995 which allows for harsher sentencing and a tightening of the law with regard to young people.

The key controversial issue arising from the new law is the one that resulted in the Government issuing its single reservation to the CRC. Young people aged 16 and 17 can now be tried in an adult court. The criteria for re-direction concern the gravity of the offence, the personality of the offender and the circumstances in which the offence was committed. The result of this policy is that young offenders can be detained with adults and may be sentenced to life - options not open to the youth courts.

Children under the age of 12 are not criminally responsible and cannot be prosecuted but they can be arrested and taken to a police station for questioning if they have been involved in some form of criminal activity. The juvenile criminal law applies to young people aged 12 to 18 except in the circumstances mentioned above.

GOVERNMENT ACTION AND POLICY

Wherever possible, criminal cases involving young people are disposed of without a criminal conviction being made. There are a number of strategies for this. The police can choose not to proceed with a case if the offender has no prior record, the offence is minor in its nature and the offender is willing to pay for any damage caused. The police can choose to dispose of a case by means of an out-of-court settlement leading to a fine. Prosecution may also be avoided if the offender is willing to take part in community work or make repairs to any damage inflicted. Public prosecutors as well as the police can arrange these alternatives to a full judicial process. A public prosecutor must inform a young offender whether charges will be brought or dropped within two months of any offence being committed. A young offender can choose to challenge these decisions in the district court.

Cases involving minors are tried by a special judge in private. If the case is heard by a multi-judge chamber, the juvenile court judge sits as a member of the chamber. A minor is entitled to be assisted by a counsel under the legal aid scheme and the parents or guardians can also attend the trial. They are given the opportunity to put forward a defence on behalf of their child against certain statements.

The main sentences handed down by courts in the Netherlands are youth detention, fines and community service or training. A young offender whose behaviour is seen as disturbed may be admitted to an institution for young people. A young offender in such an institution may be put in an isolation cell for up to four days for the purposes of order and security.

A young offender who has committed, or is suspected of committing, a crime for which custody on remand is allowed may be detained for up to three days if this serves the investigation of the crime. A further three day period may be granted if the circumstances warrant it. Remand usually takes place in a youth custodial institution. Youth detention generally takes place in institutions, where education and/or employment opportunities are available. Detainees can receive visitors and write and receive letters from other persons, which may in special instances be censored by the authorities. Communication between an offender's legal counsel and his or her parents is always in confidence and cannot be accessed by the authorities.

The Government has two central strategies in the field of juvenile crime, prevention and/or punishment. There are signs that it is becoming more inclined to use punishment as deterrence; the recent increase in cell capacity is a sign of this. Once young offenders are detained, too little attention is paid to them; greater emphasis should be put on their re-integration into society.

RECOMMENDATIONS

- **Withdrawal of reservations** - The Government should withdraw its reservation to the CRC and if necessary provide greater resources to meet its obligations under it.
- **Monitor re-integration of offenders** - The Government should invest in strategies to monitor and effect the re-integration of offenders into society.
- **Support to the families of young offenders** - Where offenders are under the age of 12, greater assistance should be provided to them and their parents when they are convicted of a crime.

Displacement

A child of any age from any country can apply for asylum in the Netherlands. The Geneva Convention of 1951 and its 1967 Protocol are used to determine whether any asylum-seeker is a genuine refugee. There is only one category of refugee and therefore children are treated in the same manner as adults.

GOVERNMENT ACTION AND POLICY

If a child seeks asylum and is accompanied by his or her parents, they will generally apply for asylum on the child's behalf. This is done at an application centre, where an initial decision is made as to whether the application has a reasonable chance of success. If the decision is positive, the family is moved to a reception centre where they will be interviewed at greater length. Young people over the age of 15 are always interviewed, and those aged 12 to 15 are upon request. Families are assessed collectively, therefore if parents are given refugee status, or other reasons to stay, their children are automatically given the same rights and status. If the parents are not eligible for admission then the children must return to the country of origin.

If a child seeks asylum and is not accompanied by either parent, nor by a blood relative or relative by marriage, the admission policy for unaccompanied children comes into effect. Those over the age of 12 may apply by themselves while those under 12 can only do so when custody has been arranged. After reporting to an application centre, registration takes place and the child is then transferred to a reception centre. Children over the age of 12 are interviewed concerning their reasons for application. This takes place over a four week period to afford a degree of acclimatisation to the new surroundings of the asylum-seeker. Children under the age of 12 are not interviewed.

Generally children are sent to reception centres with special facilities for minors, although some find themselves in adult facilities which is undesirable. After custody arrangements have been made, the person awarded custody becomes responsible for reception. Young children are usually placed in foster families. Young people may be placed in separate homes where the amount of adult supervision varies according to need. At the moment there is a drive to increase communication between the authorities responsible for initial reception and the guardians who provide subsequent reception. There is very little continuity of care in the treatment of refugee children and they often find themselves transferred from various institutions and local authorities during the first two years of their time in the Netherlands. Care is not given as high a priority as logistical and supervisory matters.

Access to education for all asylum-seekers of school age is provided although there are problems with the provision of secondary care and education for unaccompanied minors - mainly a delay in access to it. All asylum-seekers are automatically insured against medical expenses and virtually all medical facilities are available to them. There are often substantial delays in moving asylum-seekers from reception centres and other institutions to small housing units - a wait of a few months is typical for young people.

Over the years a large backlog of cases has built up and the Government is showing no signs of committing extra resources to deal with it. Long delays are the norm and these create long periods of uncertainty for asylum-seekers. Further complexity and delay is caused because the division of responsibilities between national and local government is unclear. The National Ombudsman has commented that the standards of second hearings are well below average.

In March 1996 the Government introduced age screening in cases where there is serious doubt concerning the age of an asylum-seeker. The asylum-seeker must give consent to participate in an enquiry regarding his or her age, but obviously failure to co-operate is not seen in a good light. There are ethical, medical and legal objections to age tests and there are no measurable criteria as to their accuracy. The age tests have created an air of arbitrariness which has no place in a fair and equitable process.

RECOMMENDATIONS

- **Improved reception of unaccompanied minors** - The reception of unaccompanied minors needs to be reviewed in order to ensure that they are not housed in adult reception centres.
- **Improved care for all refugee children** - The care and welfare of child refugees should be given the highest priority and its continuity must be ensured.
- **Equal access to education** - Access to education must be made available to all as soon as possible after arrival and the existing delays must be reduced.
- **Review of age tests for refugee children** - Age tests should be reviewed and alternatives sought to remove the arbitrariness that has arisen from their introduction.
- **Provision of counselling services** - Counselling care for young asylum-seekers should be made in accordance with the Law on Youth Care. This would give them the same treatment as Dutch minors at risk.
- **Alternatives to deportation** - Deportation must be used only as a very last resort and only when safeguards have been put in place ensuring the safety of the minor on reaching their destination.

Education

In the Netherlands education at primary, secondary and vocational level is free and compulsory for all between the ages of 5 and 16. Children are obliged to attend and absence without consent can lead to parents being reprimanded and/or fined. After a student has reached the age of 16 there is a partial attendance obligation, i.e. two days per week or, for those that have acquired an apprenticeship, one day a week.

Primary education is from the age of 5 until 11. The controversial issue in its delivery is the large numbers of children attending special schools, of which there are 15 types. The number of children in special education is an indication of a systematic rejection of those unable to achieve near to the average level of mainstream schools. Children often spend a long time in special education before finding the right situation for them, compounding their knowledge deficit in comparison with their mainstream peers. Children in this situation can become outsiders, and this increases the risk of their needing further assistance from social services.

The principle behind the relationship between mainstream primary schools and special schools is that the former have responsibility for all children, but the latter have responsibility for those who cannot be educated in the mainstream. A new law concerning primary education will seek to include a clearer definition of this relationship. The general policy of the Government is to provide a greater breadth of care in mainstream schooling.

Secondary education is from the age of 12 to 18 and consists of the following categories: junior general secondary, general secondary, pre-vocational and pre-university senior. From the age of 16 the parents of children at secondary, vocational or special schools must pay tuition fees. Assistance is provided in the form of an allowance which gives more to lower income groups and less to higher income groups. In recent times there has been a special focus on those struggling in secondary education, to help them achieve at least an initial qualification to be ready for the labour market. Extra study guidance and assistance are available, as is special help for those for whom Dutch is a second language.

GOVERNMENT ACTION AND POLICY

Primary, secondary and special education have a number of basic criteria and objectives laid down by law. Education must be organised in a way that provides continuous development for the pupil, with emotional and intellectual needs given equal status. Social, cultural and physical skills are cited as essential, as is the need to help children be part of a multicultural society. Criteria are laid down for these objectives and attainment targets set.

The school drop-out rate is a continuing and seemingly intractable problem. Each municipality has an officer designated to monitor the problem and each school is obliged to indicate what measures it is taking to prevent truancy and permanent absence. A recent initiative has been to set up the Regional Notification and Co-ordination Centre which takes a countrywide approach to identifying and monitoring drop-outs, with a view to encouraging them to return to their studies.

Pupils in primary and special schools have no legal way of representing themselves to school authorities and their parents are expected to do this. Secondary schools have been obliged to establish pupils' statutes which outline the rights and obligations of the students. Pupils' councils are designed to ensure that the students' voices are heard. However, there is evidence that sometimes schools do not take the views expressed very seriously.

RECOMMENDATIONS

- **Plan of action for the development of primary and special schools** - The Government needs to demonstrate how it will address the situation concerning primary and special schools. A plan of action needs to discussed and piloted so that improvements can be made.
- **Increased funding of the education sector** - There is a definite need for more resources in the education sector and the Government should facilitate this.
- **Codes of conduct to tackle bullying and suspected child abuse** - The Government needs to do more to promote codes of conduct to fight bullying and racism in primary schools. It needs to produce clear guidelines on how to act in cases of suspected child abuse.
- **Student participation** - The Government needs to make sure that the voices of pupils are taken seriously and treated with respect by those who manage the schools.

*'My **dream** is to become a teacher and to create a **new generation** for the **future**'.*

Hussein Abu Shakra, age 14 - Lebanon

New Zealand

THE NEW ZEALAND GOVERNMENT AND THE CRC

The New Zealand Government ratified the Convention on 23 March 1993, however, it did so with three reservations, on:

- **immigration status;**
- **child labour;**
- **the detention of juveniles and adults in the same institution.**

Prior to ratification, the Government had already established the Ministry of Youth Affairs (MYA) in 1989. Its functions include: representing the youth of New Zealand (defined as ages 12 to 25); ensuring that the concerns of youth are heard by policy-makers, service providers, drafters of legislation; allowing young people to make a contribution to New Zealand's cultural, social and economic development. At the time of ratification of the Convention, the Ministry was given responsibility for preparation of the periodic reports to the Committee on the Rights of the Child.

In 1989 the Children, Young Persons and their Families Act was adopted. This Act, which establishes the principles and operational framework for a care and protection system, applies to all children and young persons up to the age of 17. This Act created the Commissioner for Children. The principal aim of the Commissioner is to promote and protect the interests of young people.

Since adoption of the Convention in 1993, there has been some training in relation to the CRC, for example with regard to teacher trainees and police youth aid officers. Unfortunately, this has not been formalised and is carried out in a rather ad hoc fashion. The MYA publishes a youth magazine, and both the MYA and the Office of the Commissioner for Children publish information about the CRC.

At the time of ratification, the Government started from the premise that New Zealand's laws, policies and practices were in full conformity with the CRC except in respect of the three reservations. These assumptions have been challenged, and are not yet proven.

Recent research for UNICEF stated that some government departments are taking no action and no responsibility for commitment to the CRC; there is no formal mechanism for checking that government ministries have structures in place; their work in the area of children's rights is limited by lack of funding and is low on their political agenda.

Some examples of the Government's inconsistencies in relation to the Convention since 1997 include:

- introducing a set of regulations in 1997 which contained stringent new search and seizure powers in respect of children in residential care;

- setting up a working party in 1999 to consider whether the age of criminal responsibility should be lowered;
- when considering amendments to education legislation in 1998, not accepting amendments proposed by the Commissioner for Children, which would have assured school students of rights established by the CRC.

In its first report to the Committee on the Rights of the Child, the Government noted that the Human Rights Commission (HRC) was reviewing all laws and government policies and practices to assess whether they were consistent with the Human Rights Act. The Committee asked that this be extended to cover a review of the CRC. This was not done, and the HRC review has since been halted.

Historically, New Zealand has a proud record of caring for its children. However, there is a widespread community perception that over the past ten or more years, economic and social policies have had a harmful impact on the lives of children. The United Nations Committee urged the Government to measure the impact of economic reform on the country's children.

Some limited progress was made towards developing a National Plan of Action for children, as required by undertakings given at the World Summit on Children. The first stage was a report, which focused on areas in which New Zealand is doing well, while acknowledging that there is work to be done. However, the Government has not followed through with stage two, developing a plan of action.

At the time of the Government's first report to the UN Committee on the Rights of the Child, NGOs prepared their own report, 'Action for Children in Aotearoa'. In preparing the second report (due in March 2000), the Ministry of Youth Affairs appears to be following a more inclusive reporting process, including dialogue with NGOs. At the same time the Ministry acknowledges and respects the right of NGOs to prepare their own report.

It appears that New Zealand Governments have done little to address the recommendations of the UN Committee, or their obligations after ratification. Baseline actions such as reviewing existing laws, policies and practices, and developing a plan of action have not yet been completed. Legislation has not yet been reviewed to see that it is consistent with the CRC and, as yet, the Convention has not been incorporated into domestic legislation, either in whole or in part. The Commissioner for Children remains without any statutory links with, or responsibilities under, the CRC.

The reality *against* the rhetoric

Sexual exploitation

The extent of the commercial sexual exploitation of children is unknown in New Zealand. There is little relevant research on its prevalence or circumstances influencing commercial exploitation. However the research available does indicate that child abuse, including sexual abuse and exploitation, is a serious issue with legislative and policy implications. In 1997/98 the Children, Young Persons and their Families Agency (CYPFA) received 18,378 notifications of sexual abuse that required some intervention by social workers (in a total population of a little over 3.7 million). There is a common public perception that sexual abuse is more common in certain ethnic groups, however, there is no clear evidence to support this.This perception may be symptomatic of a general prejudice in society against ethnic minorities.

Anecdotal evidence from the New Zealand Prostitutes Collective (an NGO funded by government to provide HIV/AIDS and STD prevention programmes for sex workers) indicates that a small number of sex workers are aged between 14 and 17. Factors which contribute to the involvement of children and youth in prostitution in New Zealand include: poverty; increasingly restrictive access to income support from government agencies; unemployment or underemployment for early school leavers; drug and/or alcohol dependency and other related issues; mental health issues for the young person or his or her family; and poor support systems.

Increasing access to, and use of, the Internet are widening the opportunities for children to be exposed to and used for pornographic material.

GOVERNMENT ACTION AND POLICY

New Zealand has not yet developed a plan of action agreed to at the World Congress Against Commercial Sexual Exploitation of Children.

The Victims of Offences Act 1987 entitles victims of sexual offences to counselling services paid for by the Accident Compensation Corporation (ACC), and such claims are dealt with by the Sensitive Claims Unit. An amendment to the Crimes Act 1961 makes it an offence for a New Zealand citizen or resident to engage in sexual activity with children overseas, or to promote or assist other people to travel overseas where one of the purposes of the trip is to engage in sexual activity with children.

The Massage Parlours Act 1978 is designed to prevent people under the age of 18 from working in parlours (where prostitution is often rife), although this is difficult to enforce. There is no such legislation for escort agencies, and it is thought that many of the under-age prostitutes work on the streets.

The Children, Young Persons and their Families Act (1989) provides a mechanism for identifying, monitoring and protecting children at risk. CYPFA works both with children and young people who have been sexually abused, and with those who are offenders. Since 1995 CYPFA and the police have operated a joint protocol for the investigation of sexual abuse, making it a care and protection matter as well as a criminal justice matter. As part of this, the Department for Internal Affairs initiated a programme in 1997, which works closely with children and young people involved in prostitution in Christchurch.

RECOMMENDATIONS

- **Policy to address commercial sexual exploitation** - Policy needs to be developed to improve the recognition of, and response to, commercial sexual exploitation of children.
- **Extension of current programmes targeted at young people involved in prostitution across the country.**
- **Reforms in the prostitution law**- Currently some NGOs are promoting a Prostitution Reform Bill, which recognises the need to change current law on prostitution. The proposed Bill includes stronger measures to protect children up to the age of 18 from sexual exploitation or sexual abuse associated with prostitution.

Juvenile justice

Juvenile offenders in New Zealand are those under 17 years old. Children under the age of ten cannot be charged with any offence. Those between 10 and 13 can only be charged with murder, manslaughter or minor traffic infringements. They can also be brought before the Family Court on the grounds of concern that they are at risk. Young people aged 14-16 can be charged with any criminal offence but will be dealt with initially in a separate youth court. In the case of serious offending, any juvenile over the age of 15 can be ordered to appear before the District Court for sentence. Seventeen year olds are treated as adults and dealt with in adult courts.

In 1996, children aged 10 to 13 accounted for six per cent of the offenders apprehended by police, although none were prosecuted. Offenders aged 14 to 16 (approximately 5.5 per cent of the New Zealand population) accounted for 16 per cent of those apprehended by police, and three per cent of the prosecutions in 1996 (2,728 persons). People aged 17 to 19 accounted for 21.2 per cent of police prosecutions in 1996 (17,597 persons). Figures for under eighteens serving sentences of imprisonment in adult facilities are hard to confirm, but it has been estimated by the Youth Law Project that there are approximately 130 persons in this category. The number of cases involving 14 to 16 year olds increased by 45 per cent between 1990 and 1997. Maori and Pacific Island people are over-represented in criminal justice statistics relative to the size of their population.

There is concern over the number of young men (aged 16 to 18) committing suicide when remanded or sentenced to prison. In a 1998 discussion paper 'Getting Kids Out of Adult Prisons', the Minister of Corrections states, 'Adult prisons are no place for vulnerable teenagers. They are subject to abuse and stand-over tactics. There is a high risk of suicide and self-harm. Gang recruitment occurs frequently and contributes to appalling rates of re-offending.' The Government is currently considering public submissions to a discussion paper on serious young offenders in custody.

GOVERNMENT ACTION AND POLICY

New Zealand has a separate youth justice system established under the Children, Young Persons and their Families Act (1989). This emphasises the rights of children and young people to due process and respect, and the involvement of families in decisions about their children and young people who have offended. The Act applies to children (under 14) and young persons (over 14 and under 17). The New Zealand Bill of Rights 1990 affirms the right of a child to be dealt with in a manner that takes account of the child's age.

There is a separate youth aid section in each police district with specialist police officers. The Children, Young Persons and their Families Act requires that all juveniles are entitled to special protection during police investigations. Other features of this Act are that juveniles should be kept within the community wherever possible; any sanction imposed on a juvenile should be the least restrictive possible; and court proceedings should not be instituted against a juvenile if there is some alternative means of dealing with the matter.

All juveniles charged with a criminal offence are allocated a youth advocate (a lawyer) to represent them. There is also provision for a lay advocate from the juvenile's own culture. There are concerns expressed in some areas about how effectively these provisions are working for the offenders and victims.

When ratifying the Convention, the New Zealand Government noted:
The Government of New Zealand reserves the right not to apply Article 37(c) in circumstances where the shortage of suitable facilities makes the mixing of juveniles and adults unavoidable; and further reserves the right not to apply Article 37(c) where the interests of other juveniles in an establishment require the removal of a particular juvenile offender or where mixing is considered to be of benefit to the persons concerned.

RECOMMENDATIONS

- **Improved detention facilities for juveniles -** There is a lack of residential accommodation for young offenders, which has led to young people being held in police cells for more than brief periods. The Commissioner for Children, among others, has concluded that holding juveniles in police cells is in serious breach of New Zealand's obligations under the Convention and other human rights instruments. Better detention facilities need to be established.

- **Extension of the jurisdiction of the Commissioner for Children** - The Children, Young Persons and their Families Act applies only to those under 17 years old. The jurisdiction of the Commissioner for Children is also restricted to those under 17. These should be amended to meet the CRC definition of children which includes 17 year-olds.
- **Maintenance of the age of criminal responsibility** - Current moves to lower the age of criminal responsibility would appear to be in breach of the Convention. The regulations on search and seizure related to children in care also appear to be in breach of the Convention. The Government needs to reconsider its position on these issues.

Displacement

In comparison to other developed countries there are relatively few refugees in New Zealand and there are no internally displaced children. Refugee children are usually admitted as part of a family group. Refugees, including children, may be admitted to New Zealand under the New Zealand Refugee Quota Programme or may be granted asylum.

Detailed statistics on numbers and nature of refugees in the country are not readily available.

GOVERNMENT ACTION AND POLICY

Government policy accepts single children under the age of 16. As there is no benefit provision directly accessible for these children, they would be placed with a care-giver and an 'Unsupported Child Benefit' applied for. In recent years there have been only one or two children in this situation, and obtaining the benefit was very slow and difficult.

If, after arrival, an 'adopted' child wanted to separate from the family they arrived with, then Refugee and Migrant Services (a New Zealand NGO) would involve the Children and Young Persons Service, Open Home Foundation and the local ethnic community in organising this.

In practice, refugee and migrant children enjoy the same rights as New Zealand citizens regarding access to education, health facilities, protection etc. If a child arrives using the papers of another child, which happens from time to time, then permanent residency is not initially granted and benefits including health benefits are void. Family tracing efforts are undertaken by the New Zealand Red Cross Society.

New Zealand's ratification of the CRC included the reservation:
Nothing in this Convention shall affect the right of the Government of New Zealand to continue to distinguish as it considers appropriate in its law and practice between persons according to the nature of their authority to be in New Zealand including but not limited to their entitlement to benefits and other protections described in the Convention, and the Government of New Zealand reserves the right to interpret and apply the Convention accordingly.

The Committee on the Rights of the Child raised concerns related to this area.

RECOMMENDATIONS

- **New legislation and co-ordinated service delivery** - Currently efforts are being made to lobby for a national resettlement policy for refugees, which will ensure comprehensive and co-ordinated service delivery. The current approach is piecemeal and there are a number of gaps which Government needs to address.

Education

Primary education has been compulsory and free (in state schools) since the 1877 Education Act. Statistics show that 100 per cent of children aged between 5 and 15 are enrolled in schools (this age range also covers the early secondary years). Although education is compulsory until age 16, there are provisions which enable some children aged 15 to leave school. There has been a steady increase in school enrolments during the past five years, which reflects increasing population numbers in the 5 to 16 age range, rather than an increase in the percentage enrolled.

There are signs that distance may be creating a barrier to school attendance for children in remote areas. As the population drops in remote rural areas, small schools are being closed or amalgamated with other schools. Some primary age children are being transferred to the Correspondence School rather than travelling to the nearest school, because of distance or difficult roads.

Few students would be unable to get access to a secondary school. Secondary school rolls are expected to increase steadily until at least 2004. This reflects the number of children currently enrolled in primary schools and early childhood education. Students appear to be staying at school longer, partly as a response to the changes in employment opportunities and increasing levels of unemployment.

For both primary and secondary schools, there is a movement from rural to urban schools, and from south to north, which reflects the general demographic trend within New Zealand. As at 1 July 1997, almost 20 per cent of all students enrolled at a school were identified as being Maori, 7 per cent were identified as being of Pacific Islands ethnicity, and five per cent were identified as being Asian. The remaining 68 per cent are classed as NZ European/Pakeha (some of these students may be from one of the other groups, but have not chosen to be identified as such).

New Zealand does not experience a high drop-out rate under the age of 15, although there are increasing numbers at age 15. There is an increasing need to provide alternatives for alienated students (for example those who have been suspended from their schools). The Commissioner for Children and his staff have an important advocacy role in ensuring that children and young person's rights are upheld in the education system.

The National Curriculum Framework states, 'All young people in New Zealand have the right to gain, through the state schooling system, a broad, balanced education that prepares them for effective participation in society'. This aim is addressed in the 'essential skills, attitudes and values' sections of each curriculum. There is a growing number of state-funded Kura Kaupapa Maori schools, where the teaching medium is the Maori language. There is also a number of Kohanga Reo (Maori-language), and some Pacific Islands-language pre-schools.

GOVERNMENT ACTION AND POLICY

Education is compulsory from six to 16, and free in the state system. The Government has taken a number of steps to try and ensure that all children have equal access to school and are not barred for socio-economic reasons. There is a differential funding system in place to provide additional resources for schools catering for lower socio-economic areas; boarding bursaries are available for rural students; and scholarships to specialist Maori boarding schools.

The rights of school students are addressed in legislation including the Education Acts of 1989, and 1998; Children, Young Persons and the Families Act 1989; New Zealand Bill of Rights 1990; Human Rights Act 1993; Privacy Act 1993.

Vocational opportunities are available to all students. All school curricula include practical or vocational elements; career/guidance counselling services are provided in schools; there are increasing numbers of non-academic programmes at senior as well as junior secondary level; work-experience courses are available (usually for the less able students); and joint enrolment with school and polytechnics is becoming more common. There is also a Special Education Service which provides support, within the school system, for students with special learning needs.

The Ministry of Education has three programmes in place to address problems of drop-outs and non-attendees. The nation-wide District Truancy Service is contracted to work with schools and communities to address the problem of children not attending school. The Non-Enrolment Truancy Service is tasked with finding children who have moved from one school and not enrolled in another, or have been suspended and not re-enrolled with another school. There is also a counselling programme in schools to encourage students to remain within the school system. Many schools have expressed concern that these programmes are not effective in contacting all children.

Higher education is widely available, and the number of students has increased in the past ten years. This may reflect growth in this section of the population, as well as the changed employment market. There is now an increased 'user-pays' element in higher education, which students can fund through accessing student loans. There is public concern about the user-pays principle in education and some aspects of this student loan-scheme.

RECOMMENDATIONS

- **Alternative education programmes for children with behavioural difficulties** - There is concern within the Ministry of Education, and from the Commissioner for Children, over the increasing number of students being suspended from school. Efforts are being made to address this through alternative education programmes, and by looking for alternatives to suspension. Bullying is a common problem in schools. Responses by schools to this problem vary widely and no clear standard has yet emerged. Government needs to develop some clear standards and alternatives.
- **Raised general literacy and numeracy levels.** There is a concern among educationalists that literacy and numeracy rates of students have dropped in comparison with other OECD members, and the Ministry is currently considering ways to address this problem. Government needs to ensure that action is taken.

The Commissioner for Children, teacher associations, boards of trustees and ministry officials need to continue joint efforts to address these concerns.

*‘Even though I was **pregnant** I had to **fight** the **enemy**’.*

Maria, age 16, a former child soldier - Colombia

Norway

THE NORWEGIAN GOVERNMENT AND THE CRC

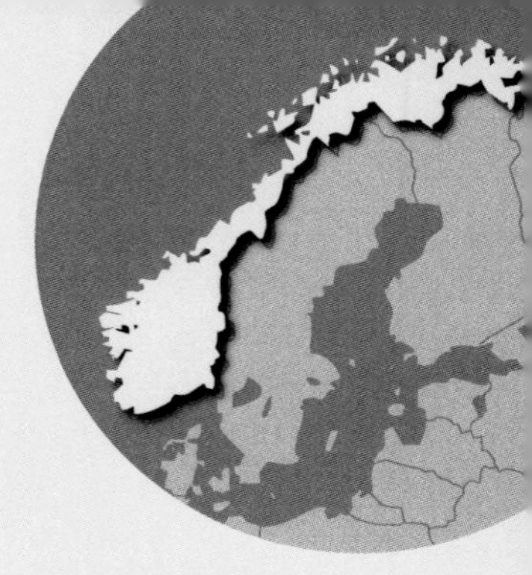

The Norwegian Government ratified the United Nations Convention on the Rights of the Child (CRC) on 8 January 1991 and since then it has taken a number of steps to fulfil its obligations.

Generally, Norwegian legislation is in compliance with the CRC but at present, when the CRC contravenes domestic law, it is the latter that prevails. There is currently a white paper proposing that three main human rights conventions be adopted as national law. Whilst the CRC is not included in this paper, there does seem to be a political will to implement it as domestic law within the next few years.

In the same year as becoming a states party, the Government established a Ministry for Children and Family Affairs to raise awareness of the need to improve children's quality of life. Amongst other things, the Ministry contributed financially towards the distribution by non-governmental organisations (NGOs) of information materials, education programmes, books, magazines and a television series promoting the CRC. The resources, however, failed to relate sufficiently to the CRC, and the objective - to increase the general population's awareness and understanding of the principles and provisions of the CRC was not fully achieved.

It has taken time for the value and relevance of the CRC to be recognised. However, awareness of the CRC and its use as a reference point are on the increase. At Government level, in a bid to show financial commitment, ministries each have a specific amount within their annual budgets earmarked for 'child-related concerns'. Similarly the Ombudsman for Children, set up in 1981, now relies heavily on the guidelines laid out by the CRC, so much so, that in 1998 a reference to the CRC was included in the Ombudsman's Act.

Whilst there has been no systematic approach by the Government to follow up on all the CRC provisions, there have been some minor changes to improve the rights of children since the ratification of CRC. The following issues still need to be addressed:

- the right of a child, conceived from a sperm donation, to know the identity of his/her biological father;
- the low level of knowledge of the CRC amongst the general public;
- unaccompanied children seeking asylum in Norway live in unsatisfactory conditions with limited guidance and protection;
- many children in single-parent families live well below the poverty line;
- school environments are below standard;
- sexually abused children do not receive necessary rehabilitation soon enough. Many of the cases are dismissed and there is a low level of competence amongst the police service and other professionals investigating the cases;
- whether or not school children should be afforded the right to be exempt from religious education.

The reality *against* the rhetoric

Sexual exploitation

Traditional opinions about 'private' family matters and male sexual rights mean that child sexual abuse within the family, the local community and the church is seldom reacted upon and often ignored by society in Norway. Few abusers are ever convicted, most cases are shelved and the compensation to victims is extremely small. As little is being done to change these traditional opinions, the focus tends to rest on the rehabilitation of abusers rather than the prevention of abuse. The mass media provides extensive coverage of sexual abuse cases, especially those involving paedophiles. However their reports tend to sensationalise the details rather than focus on the needs of the victim.

Two years after Norway ratified the CRC in 1991, the country was embroiled in a long and painful debate after the parents of 11 kindergarten pupils claimed their children had been sexually abused by adults working at the school (the Bjugn case). The court could not find enough evidence to prove the case and the parents, witnesses and representatives from the social services were accused of making false claims and of attacking and destroying innocent people. The Bjugn case has had an enormous long-term impact on sexual abuse issues in Norway with the result that few are willing to risk similar stigmatisation and put their credibility on trial. Psychologists and researchers in the field have documented an increased hostility to anyone working on issues involving sexual abuse and the child welfare system is aware that few victims report their cases to them.

Recent estimates suggest that the percentage who have suffered from 'repeated sexual abuse at a serious level' stands at five per cent compared to 14 per cent in the mid-1980s. Comparison is difficult as a much narrower definition of sexual abuse was used in the more recent survey. Even so, if the 1986 definition was narrowed down to include only those who had endured physical contact, the figure would still stand at 10 to 11 per cent. There is an urgent need to provide a working definition of what constitutes abuse as the debate often clouds the fact that there is an extensive lack of respect concerning children's sexual integrity.

There is insufficient data about the extent of child prostitution and pornography in Norway, although it is known that children under the age of 12 are rarely involved. It is not known how many victims of child prostitution come into contact with welfare services nor is it known who their clients are. Save the Children Norway (Redd Barna) initiated a project on the Internet in 1996 in an attempt to combat child pornography. This has involved a confidential service to report child pornography sites on the Internet and aims to collect information and co-operate with authorities at an international level, and it has met with success. In 1998 there were 5,417 e-mail messages from Norway and other countries providing information on illegal sites displaying child pornography. Much of this information was passed over to the Norwegian police authorities for further investigation.

GOVERNMENT ACTION AND POLICY

The Norwegian Government has made some social and legal provisions to protect children from sexual abuse since ratification of the CRC in 1991. In particular the following steps have been taken:

- Civil servants and relevant professional groups, as well as private organisations and individuals, who work for the state, the county or the municipal authorities, have a statutory duty to report to the Child Welfare Service any suspicion of abuse or neglect.

- A National Resource Centre for Sexually Abused Children has been established.
- Under the Day Care Institutions Act (1995), a certificate of good conduct, issued by the police, is now necessary for anyone employed in a day-care centre. Persons who have been charged with, prosecuted for or sentenced for sexual violations against children are prohibited from working in day-care centres.
- The Government has attempted to strengthen children's legal protection against sexual abuse by promoting early intervention by the Child Welfare Service, by promoting greater expertise amongst investigators and by allowing video and/or audio-taped evidence to be admissible in court.
- Confidential telephone helplines have been organised for children who want to talk about or report abuse and neglect - although they are underfunded and generally rely on volunteers.

Norway is developing measures against the sexual exploitation of children for commercial purposes at the regional, national and international levels. This work is in response to initiatives and resolutions made by the UN, the European Council, the Nordic Council, the Council of the Baltic Sea States and NGOs, concerning child pornography, prostitution and trafficking. The police are also collaborating internationally, through Interpol, to combat the sexual abuse of children and other crimes against minors.

The Government has recently made public its plan of action, as called for by the 1996 World Congress Against Commercial Sexual Exploitation of Children held in Stockholm. This concentrates on increasing knowledge and statistical data about the commercial sexual exploitation of children in Norway. Emphasis is also put on the need to collaborate closely with NGOs in tackling these crimes. The Ministry of Children and Family Affairs has already established a network of ministries, NGOs and official institutions to co-operate in this area. The Ministry sees the prevention of such crime as a major aim and advocates appropriate services and assistance for all those who have been exploited and more education and co-operation for all those involved with victims of commercial sexual abuse.

Although measures have been taken to improve the social and legal provisions as set out in the CRC, it is evident that the Bjugn case has had a lasting negative effect which continues to stigmatise those involved in subsequent child sexual abuse cases. The problem is exacerbated by the fact that the National Resource Centre for Sexually Abused Children does not have permanent funding and that many critical issues can be raised concerning current legal procedures. For instance, a child should be questioned by experts as early as possible, certainly within two weeks, when a case of sexual abuse is reported to the police. Research from 1998 shows that many victims waited up to a year before they were interviewed, often by inexperienced policewomen with no relevant training. Worse still, many psychiatric institutions refuse to treat victims before they have been questioned, which means that the children, in many cases, do not get necessary treatment for up to twelve months after they have reported the abuse.

On a positive note, the CRC has ensured a focus on the right of children to be heard and has shown signs of success in Norway as the public is now more aware of the risks of sexual abuse.

RECOMMENDATIONS

- **Training** - A greater level of education and training should be provided for staff in the child welfare system, the police, the prosecuting authority and all other relevant professions.
- **Co-operation** - There should be greater collaboration and co-operation between institutions involved in child crises. Crisis teams should be built at county level.
- **Prevention and follow up** - Practices for the

prevention of sexual abuse must be more widely emphasised and child and youth health institutions must receive better instruction on following up the needs of the victims.

- **Permanent funding** - The National Resource Centre for Sexually Abused Children should receive permanent funding.
- **Good conduct** - People who want to work in NGOs for children should first be cleared by the police and have a certificate of good conduct.
- **Research** - Research and the reliable collection of statistics must be promoted.
- **Enhanced investigation techniques** - Methods used by the police to investigate child pornography cases must be examined. The police are currently not able to infiltrate or collect evidence regarding Internet service providers whose legal status is also unclear.

Juvenile justice

Under the Norwegian legal system, no one under the age of 15 can be prosecuted although the police may still investigate the crimes. In 1997, the legal system dealt with 2,141 juvenile offenders aged between 5 and 13 and 7,855 in the 14-17 age group. Prison for the offenders is considered a last resort and young criminals are, instead, usually put in contact with the Child Welfare Services. In 1996, only 93 adolescents between the ages of 15 and 17 were imprisoned for crimes such as theft, assault and robbery. The reason for this is the great importance Norway attaches to the rehabilitation and social reintegration of young criminals.

GOVERNMENT ACTION AND POLICY

Under the Norwegian criminal penal code all young offenders are fully accorded their rights as outlined in Article 40.2 (a) and (b). Persons between 15 and 18 years of age are dealt with in the adult courts. Certain additional rules exist to protect the rights of juvenile criminals.

- The police must immediately notify the Child Welfare Services when an investigation is initiated. The Child Welfare Services shall, if possible, be present at the interview and express their views before any decision is made with regard to indictment.
- Persons under 18 years of age shall not be arrested or remanded in custody unless special circumstances so warrant.
- The legal guardian should be given an opportunity to be present during the interview and has party rights in addition to the adolescent. The legal guardian has the decisive word with regard to the choice of defence counsel.
- For those under the age of 18 the maximum term of imprisonment is 15 years. In certain circumstances the minimum penalty allowable by law may be reduced for minors.

Norwegian criminal policy is based upon the belief that, given the right conditions, youths can correct their errant behaviour. Previously prisons were believed to be the place to provide such an opportunity; however, recent experiences indicate that imprisonment is more likely to turn juveniles into hardened criminals. As a result, prison for offenders under the age of 18 is now used as a last resort. Those that are detained are kept alongside adult prisoners - although the juveniles may be sent to local and smaller jails so that they can maintain greater contact with their families. A prison has the authority to transfer a juvenile from jail to an institution for treatment or to an open institution.

In accordance with Article 40.3 (b) of the CRC, there are alternative systems to judicial proceedings for juveniles. A prosecutor can either decide to waive the prosecution or transfer the case to a mediation board. The boards usually make financial compensation payable or provide work placements. As an alternative to detention courts can give suspended sentences or up to 360 hours of community service.

As it is accepted that it is in the best interests of the children to remain with their family, the Child Welfare Service provides support to the families of young offenders. This support can range from advice, counselling and leisure activities to training, employment, supervision for the child or financial support.

In the case of serious behavioural problems, juveniles can be placed in an institution for examination and treatment for up to 26 months without consent. This issue was widely debated when the existing child welfare law was adopted in 1992 and it is still unclear whether the ruling has been effective. The decision to place a youth in such an institution is made by the County Social Welfare Board comprising one lawyer, two child experts and two ordinary members.

RECOMMENDATIONS

There are no specific recommendations in the area of juvenile justice other than for the Government and society to keep its focus on the rehabilitation and re-integration of offenders.

Displacement

Between 1993 and 1995 a great number of child refugees arrived in Norway, mainly due to the war in Bosnia. The number declined in the following two years but has since increased dramatically again, rising from 412 children in 1996 to 2,240 in 1998. A large proportion of these refugees are from Somalia and Sri Lanka, followed by Iraq, Iran, Poland and, recently, Croatia and the states of former Yugoslavia. Many of the children from Somalia and Sri Lanka have arrived unaccompanied.

GOVERNMENT ACTION AND POLICY

A major failing of the Government is the time taken for an asylum application to be considered. After refugees are given residence permits, large periods of time are wasted before they are settled into a community. Often refugees have been in asylum centres for more than a year, some up to four years, before they are finally allowed to settle. This is because Norwegian municipalities are under no obligation to receive refugees and few are willing to take responsibility for them. By the beginning of 1999, more than 2,000 refugees were waiting to be assigned to a municipality. For a child, this means an important time in their development is marked by unpredictability. Many refugees who have had their applications denied still reside in the centres as conditions in their country of origin prevent their return.

The Government Aliens Office is under obligation to consider information, collected through police interview, about every person applying for asylum before it reaches a decision. Save the Children Norway (Redd Barna) found that children were, in most cases, denied this right as they had not been interviewed by police and their applications were then considered on the basis of insufficient evidence.

The strain created by increasing numbers of refugees results in too many municipalities not being able to organise adequate school services or Norwegian-language training for the children. Indeed, refugee children do not have an automatic right to education whilst in transit camps; any schooling they have is often within the centres themselves. The fact that children often spend over a year in asylum centres isolated from natural living conditions, with limited education and social and cultural interaction, is of great concern.

All refugees undergo a health check on arrival to Norway, involving a physical examination. Refugees receive few mental health checks or psychological/counselling services. Reports and examinations show that many refugee children struggle with the after-effects of stress. Immediately after arrival in Norway, unaccompanied child refugees should be appointed a legal guardian. However, it appears that there are too few responsible adults willing to take on this task and the network that supports them is inadequate. Many children never have a legal guardian appointed or even receive information about one. This endangers their protection, particularly as police use the same criteria to interview unaccompanied children as they do adult refugees.

Where parents are missing, most of the information collated comes from the children themselves. The process of establishing contact with the parents is often complicated as children sometimes do not know their parents' location, or perceive it as too dangerous to give details of their parents whereabouts. Save the Children Norway has found that children who harbour such secrets about family information are under enormous strain. The Red Cross is involved in helping children trace their parents, although this is rarely successful.

Many unaccompanied children are unaware of the opportunity to apply for a family reunion. For those who have applied, the process is lengthy and, in many cases, the results are negative. Surveys show that the majority of Somalian children, the largest separated group, have not been granted a family reunion in Norway for the last three years. Norwegian authorities are so concerned that the stated parents are not, in fact, the biological parents that they are considering using DNA tests to establish true family relations. Children of other nationalities are more readily granted family reunions in Norway.

RECOMMENDATIONS

Whilst positive action has been taken to adhere to Article 22 of the CRC, there remain a number of key concerns which give rise to the following recommendations.

- **Child experts** - To ensure a child's rights are fully recognised, it is essential to have highly trained professionals, with insight into children's needs and development, to interview children seeking asylum, to consider their applications and to provide psychological and counselling services
- **Accelerated application process** - Because of a child's need for predictability and routine, the time spent waiting in asylum centres needs to be reduced.
- **Appointment of legal guardians** - Unaccompanied children must, by law, be secured legal guardians. Although failure to do so has been known for some time, no action has been taken. Authorities responsible for the oversight should be sanctioned if necessary.
- **Tracing parents** - An increased effort to trace parents must be made. At the same time unaccompanied children need to receive greater assurances on the possibility of reunion with their parents in Norway.

Education

Primary education in Norway has been compulsory for more than 250 years and today all children have to complete at least ten years of basic education. Attendance at primary level is virtually 100 per cent. At secondary school, attendance levels begin to show some geographical disparities. Oslo and the three most northern counties have the lowest attendance rate - about 85 per cent - mainly due to the high number of immigrant children in the area who tend to work for their parents' rather than attend school. In addition, many adolescent boys become involved in fishing from an early age as it provides a reasonable salary and is often seen as entry into adulthood.

The last 25 years have seen a dramatic increase in the number of students who have continued their education beyond the statutory ten years. Currently around 93 per cent of all Norwegian youngsters go on to upper secondary education which is available to all and offers three-year courses in a broad range of subjects. In 1970, 27 per cent of men and 21 per cent of women had a secondary school certificate and nine per cent of men and five per cent of women were university or college graduates. In 1996, 50 per cent of men and 43 per cent of women had secondary school certificates while 21 per cent of men and 19 per cent of women were university or college graduates. These figures show a clear elevation of the educational standard of the population in general, and a diminishing educational gap between the genders.

Attendance at higher education institutions is concentrated in the more urban areas of the country where the universities are located. A recent higher education reform has recommended that 26 National College Centres for higher learning should be established all over the country to create greater access for all.

In 1973 a law was passed securing children with disabilities the right to education in ordinary schools whenever possible. Around 33,800 children (70 per cent boys, 30 per cent girls) are given such education and today only 2,300 attend special schools.

The number of children who do not have Norwegian as a first language has increased from 7,100 in 1984/85 to 33,100 in 1997/98 (6 per cent of the total compulsory school age population). Urdu accounts for the largest group (4,590 pupils), while those whose first language is Vietnamese, English or Spanish number around 2,000.

Another widely debated topic has been the re-introduction of a subject called 'Christian belief and other religions and world views' to the national curriculum. The right to be exempt from these classes has been discussed publicly with much fervour, with a legal commission advising 'that it be better to allow exemption'. The issue has been forwarded to the International Court of Human Rights in the Hague by representatives of the Norwegian Foundation of Human Ethics.

GOVERNMENT ACTION AND POLICY

Almost all political parties in Norway are united on educational policy which aims to provide education for all. Over the last century the labour movement has fought hard for all groups to have access to education regardless of gender or social or cultural background. However, with the demise of the labour party and left-wing political dominance in Norwegian politics, there are concerns that cost-cutting exercises will have repercussions on education and other public social services.

Another issue, currently receiving much media attention, is the rapidly growing number of untrained teachers providing basic education in schools. They amount to six per cent of the total staff, although in parts of the country they account for as much as 30 per cent of the staff, provoking concern at ministry and union level. Concern is also expressed at the accelerated rate that trained teachers are leaving the profession.

RECOMMENDATIONS

There are currently no specific recommendations in relation to the education system in Norway.

'I wish that every child should be equal'.

Abubakar, age 12 - Ghana

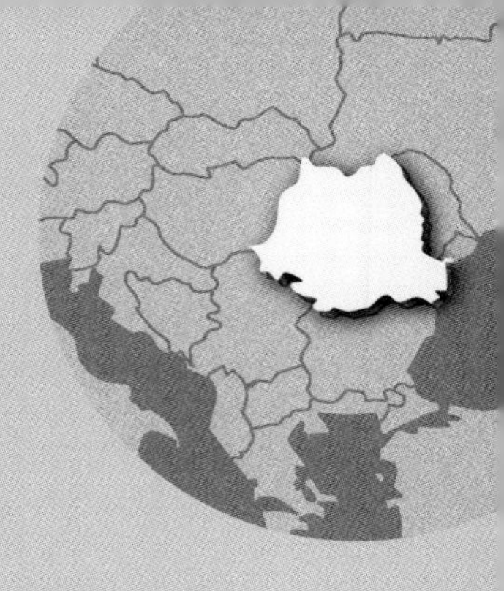

Romania

THE ROMANIAN GOVERNMENT AND THE CRC

Romania ratified the UN Convention on the Rights of the Child on 28 September 1990. All international treaties ratified by the Romanian Parliament are part of domestic law.

In March 1993 the Ministry of Foreign Affairs sent the initial report on the implementation of the CRC to the UN Committee on the Rights of the Child. It carried out a consultation process with the Romanian National Committee of UNICEF.

After the initial report, the National Committee for Child Protection took over the co-ordination role in developing strategies for implementation. Romania's report was debated in a public sitting during the session in January 1994 of the UN Committee on the Rights of the Child.
Key suggestions and recommendations made to the Romanian Government include:

- Follow up the impact of the Structural Adjustment Programmes upon children and take the adequate measures for their protection.
- Ensure better coordination between different mechanisms and institutions involved in child protection. Establish adequate structures at local level and co-ordinate the efforts made at local and national level.
- Ensure total compliance of existing laws with CRC provisions, paying special attention to the principles referring to non-discrimination, the best interests of the child and the respect for his her opinions.
- Analyse issues of child abuse and the neglect issue within the family.
- Re-train staff working with children, including social workers.
- Continue public education with regard to children with special needs and provide extra help for their parents.
- Juvenile justice administration should take into account Articles 37 and 40 of the CRC, as well as the relevant international standards, Beijing Regulations, Riyadh Directions and the Regulations for the protection of young people deprived of liberty. Train judges and officials in justice and administration in this respect.
- Adopt an active, non-discrimination policy regarding the children of minority groups, with a special reference to Roma children.
- Disseminate the Report, additional materials and the remarks of the UN Committee to a wider audience.

Following the establishment of a governmental framework to implement these recommendations, there have been a number of developments, two of which have been particularly important: the adoption of the National Plan for Action in Favour of the Child and a law regarding the organisation and running of the office of the Ombudsman. Further to this the Department for Child Protection has overall responsibility for examining government legislation and ensuring its compliance with the CRC, developing strategies for promoting the

CRC and writing new legislation directly concerning children in Romania.

The Government has made significant progress in putting the provisions of the CRC into practice - mainly by drafting laws and establishing structures. These operate both at the national and county/sector level of government. The main area of criticism for the Government is a question of resources. It seems that budgetary decisions regarding education, health and social protection are not made to the advantage of children and their rights. There is special concern for the most vulnerable children in society - those with special needs, in institutions, street children, those suffering abuse and families in crisis situations. These children are suffering from a serious shortfall in the delivery of their rights. A key problem here is that staff working in social services are not selected on criteria of competence and suitable motivation. It is generally accepted that the non-governmental organisation (NGO) sector has made a positive contribution to governmental efforts, although at the same time the government has reduced support for these organisations.

The reality *against* the rhetoric

Sexual exploitation

The sexual abuse of children and their exploitation is a 'new' issue in Romania. That is not to say that it has suddenly begun - rather it is something that is only now beginning to be considered. Romanian society is focused on adults and the family is seen as a closed space, with any abuse concealed under a heavy veil of silence. The Government itself cannot see this problem and there is no coherent system for the protection of the sexually abused child (no juridical definition and procedure for intervention nor professional standards).

Statistical information is therefore very difficult to use with any degree of certainty that it represents even a pointer towards the real level of sexual exploitation in Romania. Information regarding the exploitative use of children in pornography or prostitution is practically non-existent. The data that does exist shows that sexual offences against children have increased in the period 1995-98 and that most of these offences were rapes carried out against girls.

Studies have been carried out in an attempt uncover the factors which lead to abuse and some of these are the lack of education and information about abuse and poverty. Children who have a low level of education, those that live on the street and those who have alcohol or drug addictions are seen as particularly vulnerable, although it may be that these groups are simply more visible.

GOVERNMENT ACTION AND POLICY

At a policy level, Romanian legislation does not explicitly deal with notions of child sexual abuse and exploitation, but the criminal law contains some measures that increase penalties for those who offend against the young, the latter being split into two age groups, 0 to 4 and 14 to 18. The main offences dealt with in this way are rape, sexual perversion and corruption and the supply of prostitutes. An exception is pornography which, despite being illegal, is generally tolerated by the police. There is no specific law against the involvement of children in the production and dissemination of pornography. Although the Government was represented at the 1996 Congress on Commercial Sexual Exploitation in Stockholm it has not yet produced a plan of action in response.

A recent initiative is attempting to identify those children at risk of abuse - abuse, that is, in the general sense. It is not specifically designed to identify risk of sexual abuse. There is hope that data from this initiative will at least help to bring the issue into public consciousness. The Government does not yet see this problem as very high on its agenda. There has been no substantial improvement in terms of prevention since the Government signed the CRC.

There are several key areas where the Government is failing to meet the provisions of the CRC. Issues of particular concern are the lack of special provisions to protect children used in the production of pornographic materials, the large number of street children who are particularly vulnerable and the Government failure to identify the problem with the rigour required.

RECOMMENDATIONS

- **Legislative change** - Develop a legal definition of child abuse and appropriate punishments via new legislation.
- **Public education programme** - Produce a public education programme which is centred on the notion that a child's rights do not stop when the door to the family home is shut.
- **Policy of intervention** - Establish a policy of intervention where abuse has been identified and develop the competence of the institutions and their responsibilities in intervention.
- **Specialist training** - Develop training for specialist social workers, psychologists, educators, policemen, lawyers.
- **Support network for victims** - Develop a support system (intervention teams, child and family education teams, therapy, rehabilitation and emergency shelters) for children who have suffered abuse.
- **Inter-agency co-operation** - Establish multi-disciplinary co-operation between the Child Protection Department, police, law courts and the Prosecutor's Office. Establish definite duties for each of their responsibilities.

Juvenile justice

According to the Penal Code, children under the age of 14 cannot be prosecuted in a criminal court. Children under 16 are seen as juvenile offenders where it is proven they committed an unlawful action with full knowledge of their act. After the age of 16 juveniles are treated in court as adults in terms of criminal prosecution. The punishment, however, for minor offences is less severe.

Since 1989, the number of child offenders has increased and the types of crime they have committed have broadened in scope and show a trend towards becoming more serious. The growth of juvenile crime has mainly echoed that of all offenders, with juveniles being responsible for approximately 10 per cent of all crimes. The rate of recidivism, although low at eight per cent, has in fact doubled in the period 1993-98. More than 50 per cent of offenders come from a violent family background where over 90 per cent of parents had a low educational level of achievement. In the period 1993-98 approximately 55-60 per cent of the parents of child offenders were unemployed.

GOVERNMENT ACTION AND POLICY

Government policy is centred around a social rather than a juridical approach. However, if a child is sentenced to detention he or she will be sent to one of five institutions where there are 2,705 places. In 1997, 1,130 children were being detained. Recent policy has, to a large degree, been concerned with 'educational measures for children who have committed felonies but do not have penal responsibility'. The Child Protection Commission is responsible for deciding which measure should be applied in each case, and the physical, intellectual and social development of the child.

Not all of the provisions of Article 40 of the CRC are available to children and juveniles in Romania. There is particular concern about the length and conditions of remand for the 16-18 age group. There is a growing tendency to use imprisonment, in spite of the fact that its use in Europe in general is in decline. Forty-nine per cent of those aged 16-18 who were convicted were sent to prison whilst 35 per cent of the 18+ age group were incarcerated.

RECOMMENDATIONS

- **Special courts** - Special courts for children should be set up, with special prosecutors who have a wide knowledge of the effects of any decision they make on the child's potential for re-integration into society.
- **Juvenile crime prevention strategy** - A strategy should be developed to reduce the incidence of juvenile crime. It should work not only at the legislative level but 'on the ground' involviing the ministries of Home Affairs, Education and Work and Social Protection, the courts, Child Protection Commissions, the General Office of Prisons and NGOs.
- **Street children programme** - Reduce the number of street children as they are disproportionately responsible for juvenile crime.
- **Improved re-integration facilities** - The re-education centres need to be adapted to meet the needs of the children better and the education programmes improved to further the goal of societal re-integration.
- **Measures to prevent children falling into crime** - Greater punitive measures are needed for those adults who involve children in crime.
- **Measures to combat habitual crime** - Although recidivism is low, its rapid rate of increase must be addressed as a matter of urgency.
- **Separate juvenile detention facilities** - If juveniles aged 16-18 must be imprisoned they should be housed separately from adult inmates.

Displacement

It is a new experience for Romania to have refugees within its borders and therefore there is little statistical information available from the state. In 1998 there were 267 refugee children in Romania, all of them accompanied by their families.

GOVERNMENT ACTION AND POLICY

In policy terms, the Romanian state, by acceding to further UN conventions regarding the status of refugees as well as the CRC, provides all the appropriate conditions for survival and development of refugees and displaced persons. For children, this means that they have the same rights as local national children to education, health facilities and protection from abuse. Children cannot be summarily expelled or returned to their country of origin and they cannot be sent to territories where their life or freedom would be endangered on the grounds of race, religion, nationality or any of the other provisions of Article 15 of the CRC.

In practice, refugee children have the same rights as Romanian children. The low numbers of refugees make provision for them possible with little extra need for new resources. For most refugee families, Romania is not seen as a final destination and therefore their children sometimes miss out on education and social contact as it is not seen as worthwhile by the family.

RECOMMENDATIONS

- **Accelerated application procedures** - In order to speed processing of refugee families more officers are needed in the refugee office. Although it is a new issue, there is an urgent need to keep up with the steadily increasing numbers.
- **Increased support to refugee families** - General support to refugee families needs to be increased so that they can supply the minimum conditions necessary for child development needs.
- **Greater access to social services** - Increase access to social services for all refugees.

Education

Primary education in Romania covers the age range 7-15 and is split into two grades, first grade 7-10 and second grade 10-15. Since 1865 it has been both free and compulsory. In 1998, 96 per cent of children were enrolled, an increase from 90 per cent in 1991. Attendance is slightly higher in grade one than grade two. Overall attendance is very high; an important reason for this is the monthly allowance that each child in Romania receives, which is dependent on school attendance. The falling birth-rate in Romania means that the total number of children in education is decreasing at the moment.

These statistics conceal the fact that in rural areas attendance can be much lower due to the distance of some schools from their pupils. It may also be difficult to find teachers willing to teach in these districts, agriculture, at certain times of the year, will keep children from school and the weather can make already difficult journeys impossible.

Attendance by children from the Roma population is much lower than for the population as a whole, with some 30 per cent of these children in the 7-10 age group not going to school. In the 10-15 age group the situation is a little better. Overall 20 per cent of Roma children do not receive any education. Poverty is one reason why these children do not attend, but they also have to endure the 'stigma' of being part of the Roma population.

Before 1989, secondary education in Romania was compulsory until the age of 16. There has been a marked decrease in enrolment since then. In 1992 enrolment was 76 per cent; by 1998 it had fallen to 61 per cent. It is likely that these percentages are over-optimistic - separate figures supplied by the Ministry of Education indicate that approximately one-third of children do not progress from primary to secondary education.

The vast majority of secondary schools (85%) are in urban environments. It is likely that very few of the rural students who had trouble travelling to their primary schools will have the ability to travel to secondary school.

There is little statistical information regarding Roma children in secondary school. It is known that by the time they reach secondary-school age over half of them will have permanently dropped out.

Before 1989 children did drop out of school but teachers were forced to hide the phenomenon, as official policy did not allow drop-out to occur. The drop-out rate has remained fairly constant for the last three years for which statistics are available. About 1 per cent of primary-school children leave and do not return and 4.5 per cent of secondary-school children do the same. In absolute numbers this is quite a problem; in 1997/98, 19,291 primary-school pupils dropped out as did 31,974 secondary-school pupils. There are also a number of children who attend school only to satisfy the attendance requirements for the child allowance, and these may be seen as having functionally dropped out.

Dropping-out is caused by a number of factors, social, educational and psychological. Poverty is the main social cause, with some families needing their children for work immediately after the end of compulsory education. Families may not have enough money to provide clothes or shoes for their children and some may be only able to afford these for some of their children. In this scenario it is usually girls who go without education. Educational factors that contribute to the drop-out rate include the unsuitability of the curriculum for some geographical areas - rural areas need different education from urban areas and at different times. The Government has taken steps recently to begin to address this problem. Psychological factors include the diminishing status of acquiring a degree, and the incongruence between the value of further education as opposed to the alternatives.

GOVERNMENT ACTION AND POLICY

Education in Romania is undergoing a huge change from a centralised, explicitly didactic curriculum to one that is more focused on the needs of individual pupils and their communities. There have been recent legislative changes to the curriculum to encourage students' individuality, autonomy and creativity. There have also been recent attempts to encourage multicultural education. The state has developed some counselling services to address some of the factors which contribute to drop-out. Some schools have parent-student programmes and others are providing extra-curricular activities. At times the state has played its part in these endeavours and at others they are more the direct result of NGO involvement.

Some government support is available for the very poorest - generally the provision of clothing, food and school supplies. This is not enough to address the inequality in Romanian society and must be seen in the context of educational expenditure, which is only around the $100 US per child per year at secondary level.

At secondary-school level there are a number of vocational opportunities and these manifest themselves in the 18 different types of high school, covering a wide range of both academic and vocational studies including: industry, agriculture, forestry, economics, administration, information technology, teaching, arts, music, sports and physical education, military studies, theology, and high schools for children with special needs. The pre-1989 education system was designed to cater for both academic and vocational needs and to a large degree this system remains in place.

Theoretically there are no obstacles for a student from any socio-economic background gaining admission to higher education. In practice, secondary education fails to prepare the students for the tough admission exams of the state universities and extra private tuition is required to be successful. Additional tuition fees can only be afforded by the minority. If admission is gained, there are some scholarships for support but these are generally at a level below what a student needs to live on, and without independent support, students need to take a job. Private universities' fees are generally very high in relation to the average salary. This makes university attendance very difficult for most students without family support.

Despite this, there has been a significant increase in the number of students attending university, with approximately one-fifth of those completing secondary education going on to tertiary study in 1997 - double the number since 1990. Most private initiatives in education have been in the tertiary sector contributing to this expansion.

RECOMMENDATIONS

It is not possible to list all the failings of Romanian education and suggested solutions. However the main points, include:

- **Increase in state funding** - The current budget of 3.3 per cent of GDP is insufficient to create an education system that truly delivers the ideals as presented in the CRC. Too much of the current budget is consumed by personnel costs (which are very low in any case) for any new initiatives to be considered.
- **Curriculum development** - Much of what is taught serves neither the child nor society but new materials would be required for curriculum changes. Counselling services, extra-curricular activities and community initiatives in all schools should be developed.
- **Improvement of the literacy rates in schools** - Improve rates of juvenile illiteracy and school drop-out by analysing and then addressing the questions posed by socio-economic, psychological and educational factors.
- **Child rights education** - Work to promote the notion of rights: for children, for society and for members of other societies.
- **Reduction of violence and discrimination in schools** - Twenty-one per cent of children surveyed by Save the Children Romania describe their school as violent and eight per cent said they were scared of making mistakes as this resulted in physical chastisement by their teachers. Violence in schools needs to be addressed. Discrimination in the school environment, especially with regard to the Roma population, also needs to be combated.
- **Support for children from poorer backgrounds** - Children from poorer backgrounds need greater systematic help to realise their full potential at primary, secondary and tertiary levels. A whole range of social services need to be developed to help children and their families where the children can demonstrate an ability to take their education further.

'I wish that I can finish my **studies** *so that I can* **help** *my parents and we will always have* **food to eat**'.

Bernard Satparam, age 7 - Quezon City, The Philippines

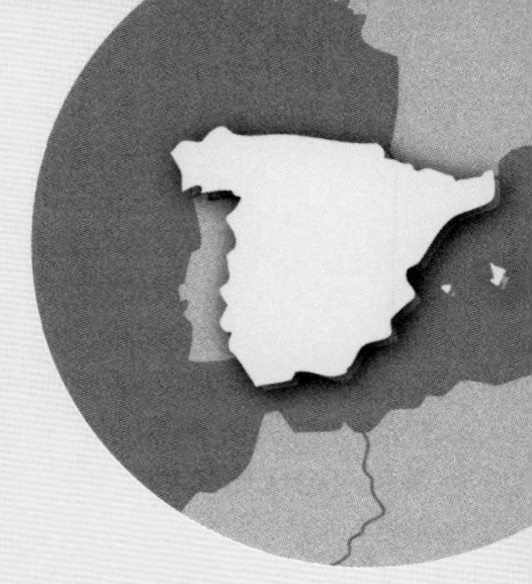

Spain

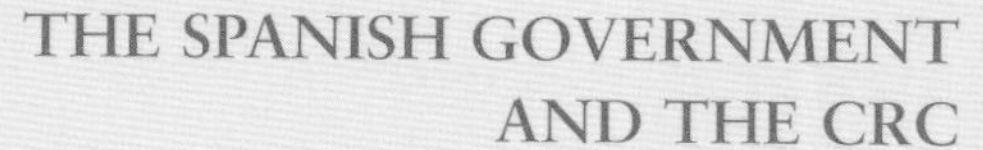

THE SPANISH GOVERNMENT AND THE CRC

The UN Convention on the Rights of the Child (CRC) was ratified by the Spanish Parliament on 30 November 1990 and came into force on 6 January 1991, when it went on to the statute book.

From the end of the 1970s to the first part of the present decade, Spain experienced deep political, social and cultural changes. These radically transformed society as a whole and changed the way in which institutions are structured and run.

In this climate of transformation, the role of children in Spanish society has acquired a new importance. As greater attention has been focused on child development, there has been a growing consensus that minors have rights. As a result, children's issues have had an increasingly important place in policy development, both at national and at local government level, and within the Autonomous Communities.

Two positive initiatives are the drawing up of the National Action Plan for children (although it has not yet been budgeted for) and the consolidation of the social care system for children. Significantly, both recognise the concept of children as social beings with rights.

At the same time, some children's organisations have decided to set up a platform, at present chaired by Save the Children, which is committed to promoting the adoption of general and sector-level policies that will improve children's well-being.

Despite efforts by the government, local authorities and local organisations, work still needs to be done to increase awareness of children's rights among institutions and politicians and to banish the idea that children are second-rate citizens. Information campaigns, also need to be targeted at children and adolescents themselves.

Co-ordination between the different services and sectors working with children is essential and the current level of co-operation needs to be improved. A cross-sector approach would undoubtedly facilitate the implementation of all children's programmes.

One priority is to step up prevention programmes aimed at reducing and preventing violent and criminal behaviour, as well as discrimination directed against particular minority groups.

The Government has not managed to set up an information system to provide a general overview of the situation in the country and give a complete, multi-disciplinary assessment of what progress has been made and what problems there are in applying the Convention. It is essential to develop such a system if policies are to be geared towards efficient implementation of the Convention. It would also enable different social administrative bodies and organisations to share reliable information.

Although progress has been made, insufficient resources have been allocated to children's issues. This means that, despite a nominal commitment, in practice, children's rights have tended to be overshadowed.

The reality *against* the rhetoric

Sexual exploitation

In Spain, it is currently estimated that 23 per cent of girls and 15 per cent of boys suffer from some form of sexual abuse before they are 17 years old. This data includes misconduct with or without minimal physical contact, suich as indecent exposure and touching. One in four cases of sexual abuse of children involves very intimate and coercive acts, such as vaginal or anal sex, oral sex and masturbation.

GOVERNMENT ACTION AND POLICY

In recent years, the General Directorate for Social Action, Minors and the Family, which comes under the Ministry of Labour and Social Affairs, together with the Autonomous Communities, has been organising a programme to improve the system of social protection for children. Within this framework, from 1991 onwards, an action plan involving a series of projects was implemented. The aim of the plan was to formulate well-founded and effective prevention and intervention strategies for dealing with the ill-treatment of children.

It is clear that, particularly since the Stockholm Congress, the Government has been keen to stamp out the sexual abuse of minors, especially given the alarming statistics which have emerged concerning the frequency of abuse. In October 1996, a seminar was held in Madrid to publicise the declaration and action plan that the Congress produced, to examine them in the context of Spain and to identify strategies to raise public awareness of the nature of the problem.

Spanish domestic legislation already includes provisions for assistance to victims of violent crimes and sexual abuse. It includes provisions for victim support offices in courts and for prosecuting officers to provide psychological and social help that may be required.

In May 1997, the plenary of the Congress of Deputies also passed a bill on the sexual exploitation of children. They agreed, among other things, to urge the Government to continue to push for co-operation within the European Union to put an end to the sexual exploitation of children and to ensure that the recommendations of the Stockholm Congress are implemented.

To tackle these crimes in large cities, specific groups, such as the Minors' Group, have been set up within the police force. The Spanish police also participate in permanent working groups set up under the auspices of Interpol to look at crimes affecting minors, especially prostitution and child pornography.

Despite all this, shortcomings remain and a range of basic actions should be implemented to ensure that the provisions protecting children from sexual abuse and exploitation are improved.

RECOMMENDATIONS

- **Prevention programmes** - There is a lack of prevention programmes giving a positive view of children's sexuality, and aimed specifically at minors at high risk. More attention should, therefore, be given to developing work aimed at preventing sexual abuse.
- **Inter-agency co-ordination of services** - There is an urgent need to provide integrated treatment for victims. The absence of any co-ordination between professional services causes unnecessary delays in criminal investigations and psychological rehabilitation. Save the Children Spain calls for the establishment of formal agreements - similar to those which already exist in Cataluña and in some provinces, such as Ciudad Real - which are aimed at simplifying procedures to ensure a speedy and co-ordinated response from the different authorities likely to be involved (health workers, teachers, prosecutors, judges, police, etc).
- **Improved provisions for both juvenile sex offenders and victims of sexual abuse** - In the case of juvenile sex offenders, plans need to be drawn up regarding their schooling to make it possible for them to be integrated back into society. Mental health professionals need to be trained about these issues. Psychotherapy should be available for minors who are victims of sexual abuse to ensure their full recovery.
- **Training of professionals and specialist units** - Professionals working with minors who are victims of sexual abuse should receive specialist training, and mechanisms to evaluate the results of these programmes should be introduced. Within the police force, special minors' units (GRUME) should be set up in all provincial capitals.
- **Review of criminal procedures** - There should be an urgent review of criminal procedures to ensure that they are appropriate for minors who are the victims of sexual abuse. Save the Children Spain has drawn up a series of proposals to amend the Law of Criminal Procedure to avoid the victimisation that children suffer when they turn to the law for protection. Effective procedures need to be established through which the reliability of a child's account can be assessed on the basis of a single statement. Face-to-face confrontations between the victim and the alleged assailant should be expressly prohibited.
- **Improved reporting process** - The way in which these crimes are portrayed by the media moulds the public view. Guidelines should be provided to all journalists with the aim of ensuring that minors' right to privacy is respected and that the issues involved are treated more seriously. Save the Children Spain has drawn up the first-ever guide for the media on this subject. News about the Sexual Abuse of Minors attempts to provide journalists with the necessary information to improve the way in which they report such cases, encouraging them to break the silence about the issue and to handle media coverage in a sensitive and responsible manner.

Juvenile justice

Generally, most juvenile crime is committed by young boys. Figures from 1997 clearly illustrate this, which show that 2,460 boys under 14 were detained by State Social Security Authorities, compared to 295 girls. Similarly, in the age group 14-15 3,793 boys were detained compared to only 435 girls. In the young adult age group 16-17 this trend is reversed only 92 boys were detained compared to 435 girls.

Of the juvenile proceedings instituted, generally only a third receive a decision with an accompanying measure. According to the Annual Report of the State Public Prosecutor's Office of the 15,481 proceedings instituted in 1997 only 4,952 received a sentence.

GOVERNMENT ACTION AND POLICY

On 14 February 1991, the Constitutional Court ruled that the procedures followed by juvenile courts (relating to the 1948 legislation) were unconstitutional. The judgment quoted Article 40.2 (b) of the Convention in its entirety and concluded that the fundamental rights contained in the Constitution should also be respected in criminal proceedings against minors.

The importance of this judgment and various other reports compiled by the Ombudsperson led to the passing of Organic Law 4/1992, 5 June, regulating the jurisdiction of juvenile courts and the procedures they should follow. This law sets the age at which children are criminally liable at between 12 and 16 years. Jurisdiction in such cases and, where appropriate, decisions regarding rehabilitation measures are the responsibility of specialised judicial bodies, known as Minors' Courts. These courts follow special procedures different from those used in adult courts.

Minors under 12 are not deemed to be criminally liable. Should it become necessary to adopt some kind of protective measure with regard to a child under 12, then it is the responsibility of the minors' protection services to do so.

Protection of minors' rights in the context of the justice system, which is guaranteed in the Constitution, has been further strengthened as a result of procedural guidelines prepared by the Attorney General's office.

Offences allegedly committed by a child over 16, on the other hand, fall under the jurisdiction of the ordinary criminal courts.

Organic Law 4/1992 was an interim measure and, almost from the moment it was drafted, a comprehensive reform of the juvenile justice system has been under way. At the same time, Article 19 of the existing Penal Code raised the age of criminal liability to 18, bringing it into line with the age of majority and establishing that minors responsible for committing an offence should be dealt with under the law governing criminal responsibility for minors. (But, given that such a law does not yet exist, Article 19 has not so far come into effect.)

It is important, however, to point out that Parliament is currently debating the proposed law governing criminal liability for minors. Since 1992, several different proposals and Bills have been put forward. The delay in reaching agreement is due to the complexity of the issue and the significant costs that would be involved in implementing a law that establishes measures of a fundamentally punitive but, at the same time, educational nature and that takes into account the interests of the child. The Bill currently under discussion regulates the types of sanctions which can be imposed on young people between 13 and 18 years old, thereby raising the minimum age at which sanctions can be imposed to 13. It also extends the range of possible sanctions for criminal behaviour (they now number 14), with socialising measures taking precedence over detention and the main aim being to rehabilitate the young person concerned.

RECOMMENDATIONS

- **Preventive action** - Priority is not being given to preventive action, and the risk factors leading to marginalisation and delinquency are not being assessed. There is a need for a juvenile justice policy to be introduced. To prevent juvenile crime, it is necessary to develop specific programmes and policies at all levels, in areas ranging from community health to education and services providing assistance to families. Activities which help minors to become integrated into society are not being encouraged. In order for this to happen, the public social services system needs to improve support for teachers working in the community and with families, as well as for other services or system providers who are involved in the care of minors.

- **Increased resources** - Human resources and facilities need to be boosted to implement the measures decided by the courts. The overcrowding in some centres can make the process of rehabilitation more difficult for young people, and may even make their situation worse. There is a tendency to send them to detention centres rather than apply measures which can be implemented in a non-custodial environment, such as community service or probation. In cases where minors are interned in closed centres, every endeavour should be made to ensure that the centre is as near as possible to the minor's home to aid visiting families with limited financial resources.
- **Law for minors** - The law governing criminal liability for minors should be passed as soon as possible. It is also essential for it to be accompanied by a detailed account of the financial resources that will be made available to put the measures into practice. In addition, the higher the minimum age (proposed as 13), the better.
  In order for it to be consistent with the legal order, it should not be lower than 14 since, under Spanish law, that is the age at which a young person can get married and make a will. The judicial system as a whole needs to be brought into line.
  It is of paramount importance that the final approved text takes into account that:
  - the interests of the minor have primacy over others;
  - the possible sanctions are of an educational and socialising nature;
  - detention is used only as a last resort;
  - legal proceedings are as brief as possible and involve as few procedures as possible;
  - sanctions are applied with the greatest possible flexibility.

Displacement

There are many children seeking asylum each year in Spain and many come with their families. However, there are also many unaccompanied minors, who, for the most part come from North Africa. Most of these undertake often hazardous journeys to cross the Mediterranean to Spain where they hope to enjoy a better life in continental Europe. In 1997 there were 60 registered unaccompanied children, 36 coming from Africa and 18 from Eastern Europe. The remaining six came from South America and Asia. Once these unaccompanied minors are located by the police they are transferred to reception centres. As they are minors their rights are provided for under the CRC. Out of the 60 unaccompanied minors arriving in 1997, only 12 obtained full refugee status, 11 obtained exceptional leave to remain, while the remaining 37 have received nothing at all.

Most unaccompanied minors enter Spain for economic reasons in search of a better life. Often they escape from the reception centres preferring to chance their luck on the streets and find work where they can. This leaves them very vulnerable. This is currently having strong social repercussions and has provoked much public and political debate.

GOVERNMENT ACTION AND POLICY

Spanish domestic legislation expressly recognises the need for foreign or stateless minors to be treated in accordance with the terms of the Convention - that their rights are protected and that they are not discriminated against. It spells out that, in accordance with the terms of the Convention, they have the right to education, healthcare and other social services.

Foreign minors who have been abandoned have the following rights:

- they will be entrusted to the care of the minors' protection services in the appropriate Autonomous Community;
- they are exempt from the provisions of the immigration law regarding possible expulsion;
- they are entitled to residence permits and, if they have none, they are to be provided with any necessary documentation.

(Before the current regulations were introduced, abandoned minors often found themselves in illegal situations under Spanish law.)

But perhaps the most important aspect of the current legislation seeking to ensure the integration of foreigners into Spanish society is the introduction of 'permanent' residence permits. The following standards are applicable to foreign minors seeking asylum:

- the Convention relating to the Status of Refugees of 28 July 1951 and the Protocol relating to the Status of Refugees of 31 January 1967;
- the European Agreement on the Abolition of Visas for Refugees of 20 April 1959;
- the Dublin Convention of 15 June 1990 determining the state responsible for examining applications for asylum lodged in one of the member states of the European Communities;
- the United Nations Convention on the Rights of the Child.

When minors arrive on Spanish territory in the company of one or both parents, domestic regulations stipulate that their asylum claim is dealt with as part of the family group. This means that, in cases where they are included in their parents' asylum claim, they are automatically entitled to temporary leave to remain in the country, and the fundamental right not to be returned or expelled to the country where they are at risk of persecution. In addition, if the parents lack adequate financial resources, the appropriate public authorities should provide the child with the necessary social, educational and health services.

If a minor arrives unaccompanied, he or she is provided for under the general regulations for minors who have been abandoned.

Although asylum procedures provide guarantees to protect the rights of asylum-seekers, they do not adequately address the specific needs of minors. The procedures for dealing with family reunification under Spanish immigration law although recent are unsatisfactory. The rules were drawn upon the assumption that the person seeking reunification was an adult and were designed to restrict the entry of parents still of working age. Spain has had little experience of dealing with minors applying for asylum, and it is only recently that any interest in remedying these deficiencies has been expressed.

Finally, it should be pointed out that Spanish asylum regulations do not satisfy the requirements of Article 22 of the Convention. Because the number of unaccompanied asylum-seekers is very low compared with other countries of Western Europe, the domestic laws have not succeeded in establishing an asylum procedure that addresses the specific needs and rights of child refugees and displaced children. To summarise, the key areas where there are serious shortcomings are:

- the lack of co-ordination between the different services processing asylum requests and looking after minors;
- the shortage of statistical data, such as reasons why they left their country of origin;
- the lack of centralised computer databases and the fact that supporting paperwork is held in many different places;
- weaknesses in the Guardianship Commissions within each Autonomous Community which rarely offer real solutions to the adjustment problems facing child refugees.

RECOMMENDATIONS

- **Codes of practice** - Codes of good practice for working with child refugees should be established and more work should be carried out directly with the children concerned to gear any measures to their needs.
- **Data collection** - Mechanisms for systematically collecting data should be developed.

- **Co-ordination of resources** - The work of the different Autonomous Communities should be co-ordinated.
- **Refugee reception systems** - An appropriate reception system for child refugees, that respects their language and cultural background, should be put in place.

Education

The 1978 Spanish Constitution established basic education as compulsory and free.

Since 1990, ten years of education is guaranteed for all children aged from six up until the age of 14, before this it was only obligatory and free until the age of 14. In addition to traditional subjects, Spanish education includes moral and civic education, health education, equal opportunities, environmental education and road safety.

Although the initial year of primary education is voluntary, however, authorities are obliged to ensure that there are sufficient places for those who request it. Generally, primary education comprises six academic courses for six to twelve year olds and it spans three cycles of two academic courses each. According to the 1998 Report on the State of the World's Children, the level of primary school take-up between 1993 and 1997 was 100 per cent.

Secondary education comprises four academic courses for 12 to 16 year olds, spanning two two-year cycles. The Bachillerato (Secondary School Certificate) forms part of secondary education and can be taken by any pupil who has passed the secondary education exams.

Bachillerato courses are provided free in public institutions and grants are available to cover the cost of study materials for poorer students. According to the 1998 Report on the State of the World's Children, the level of secondary school take-up for 1994 was 82 per cent. Generally, drop-out rates are low and current levels are six points above the level recommended by the OECD (Organisation for Economic Co-operation and Development).

Vocational training, designed to prepare pupils for different trades and professions, is also available. Schools also offer more practical work-experience courses.

Further education is the right of everyone, without being discriminated against on grounds of ability to pay or social status.

GOVERNMENT ACTION AND POLICY

Under Spanish legislation all children on Spanish territory has the right to an education. A Royal Decree prohibits the imposition of corrective measures and protects the physical integrity and personal dignity of each child.

Efforts have been made by the Spanish Government to bring educational provisions in line with the CRC. Recently, particular attention has been given to the educational requirements of children with special needs. In addition, efforts have also been made to redress inequalities and eliminate discrimination. Programmes have been developed, for example, to meet the needs of cultural minorities, the itinerant population, hospitalised children, children with disabilities and children from rural or socially deprived areas.

RECOMMENDATIONS

- **Comprehensive education policy** - Although there are no figures available on levels of absenteeism, it does occur, and is heavily influenced by the economic and social inequalities which exist within certain groups in the country. Numerous immigrant or minority families still live in extreme poverty around large cities and the deprivation they face makes it very difficult for children and young people to attend school. A comprehensive policy to improve their social and financial situation and work opportunities should be adopted, since these are clearly the main obstacles preventing their integration into Spanish society.
- **The right to schooling** - The children of immigrants have the right to schooling that is of a sufficiently high standard, and its availability must be ensured. Specific action should be taken both to help them learn the local language while maintaining their own language and culture.
- **Promotion of children's rights** - The right of children to participate in society is contained in Royal Decree 732/1995 of 5 May (concerning the rights and duties of pupils and citizenship). However, it is not effectively implemented and this needs to be addressed.
- **Specific educational requirements** - Although raising the school leaving age to 16 was an important step towards achieving equality of opportunity, it has also brought new problems. For a variety of reasons (abandonment, parental neglect, violence between parents or siblings, physical or psychological ill-treatment), some children between 13 and 16 years old are falling seriously behind with their schooling, failing to attend regularly or are leaving school completely. There is the political will for the vast majority of the population to be able to achieve the minimum level of secondary school qualifications, but there does not appear to be sufficient flexibility in the system to address the special educational needs of some minors resulting from their social situation. There are also not enough support teachers in the centres that are responsible for reducing such gaps in schooling or learning. The lack of effective alternatives is creating serious tensions in the classroom, including disciplinary problems. Some of these failings could be addressed by adapting to the specific educational requirements of young people with a poor school record, adjusting the curriculum to fit the needs of these groups, providing teachers with additional support in making these adjustments.
- **Vocational training** - This needs greater promotion to overcome prejudice that it is of lesser value than university education. The majority of students, therefore, do not consider it an option, choosing instead to take university courses. Those who choose vocational training are, in the main, young people with limited financial resources or social difficulties. Quality professional training needs to be developed and offered as a viable alternative to university courses.
- **Improved grants payment system** - In recent years there has been a boom in university education in Spain. One reason is the availability of grants which have enabled students with limited financial resources to pursue studies which, up until the 1980s, could only be undertaken by those with their own financial means. Unfortunately, payments often arrive late, causing the students financial problems, and this must be improved. It is also important that university authorities do not allow their educational standards to slip as their year intake grows in size.
- **Rights and resources** - The right to learn and use the language of the relevant Autonomous Community should be guaranteed, and sufficient resources should be made available so that full integration into mainstream education can be achieved.
- **Social equality** - Education to overcome social inequalities must continue to be encouraged and greater financial resources allocated to it.

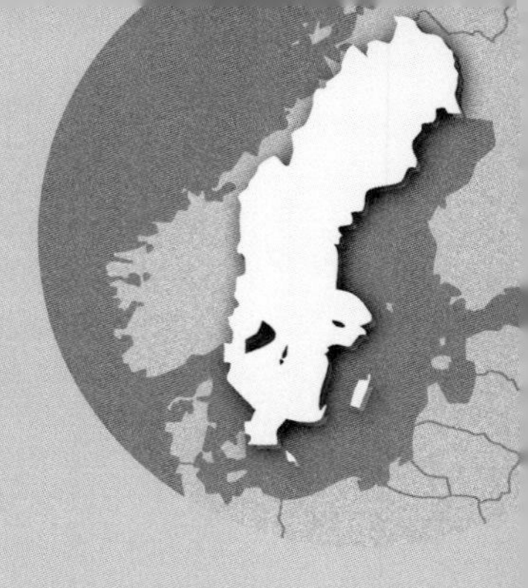

Sweden

THE SWEDISH GOVERNMENT AND THE CRC

The Swedish Government actively participated in the drafting of the CRC from 1979 to 1989 and Save the Children Sweden (Rädda Barnen) played an important role in contributing to this process, as one of the 20 non-governmental organisations (NGOs) which joined the UN Working Group. The Swedish Government signed the CRC, along with 60 countries, in New York on 26 January 1990. Six months later, in June 1990, the Government ratified it without reservation.

The CRC itself cannot directly override Swedish national law. However, domestic law was found to be consistent with the CRC and so there have been no immediate changes to the Swedish constitution as a result of ratification. It serves rather as a guide in interpreting national law and in creating new legislation.

Since ratification there has been a political will in Sweden to promote children's rights. In 1992 Swedish parliamentarians from all seven political parties formed a Network for Children's Rights to express joint concern, draft joint motions and bills, and initiate debates in Parliament to promote children's issues. In keeping with the spirit of the CRC, a Children's Ombudsman was established in July 1993. Accompanying this, a total of 50 million Swedish krona was committed between 1990 and 1997, enabling state and NGO institutions to undertake public awareness campaigns and to ensure good dissemination of the provisions and principles of the Convention (in accordance with Article 42). Sweden was the first country to submit its report to the UN Committee on the CRC in September 1992, and submitted its second report in 1997. Save the Children Sweden (Rädda Barnen) and the NGO Network for the Rights of the Child submitted their reports in 1993 and 1998.

In response to strong pressure from NGOs, the Swedish Government, on 1 February 1996, appointed a Parliamentary Committee for the Rights of the Child, comprising parliamentarians from seven political parties, experts and a reference group from NGOs. The Committee's remit was threefold:

- to conduct a broad review of how Swedish legislation and practice in relation to the provisions of the Convention;
- to create greater clarity and an increased measure of agreement as regards the meaning and concept of 'the best interests of the child' in the Convention and Swedish law, and to analyse any particular conflicts of objectives;
- as a matter of priority, to deal with the issue of the status of the child in matters under the Aliens Act to resolve, among other things, expulsions and extradition involving children.

The main report of this Committee was

submitted in August 1997, following which 115 organisations in Sweden were invited to comment.

The principle recommendations of the UN Committee in 1999 focus upon the care of immigrant and stateless children. More information regarding the CRC needs to be disseminated in different languages for those children who may not speak Swedish. Indeed, a major concern is that racism is pervasive and creates discrimination against stateless, asylum-seeking and refugee children living and hiding in Sweden, who are therefore not benefiting from all state provisions. Similar concerns are expressed about the day care of children of unemployed parents who cannot benefit fully from state provision. In an attempt to address these concerns there is a need to delegate power from central state control to municipalities to ensure that services and provisions are readily and equally available throughout the country.

In response to these concerns the Swedish Government has renewed its commitment to ensure that the provisions of the CRC become a reality. In 1998, eight years after ratification, the Government launched a three year review of Swedish development co-operation. The aim is to ensure that the best interests of the child permeate all of Sweden's international development programmes. In addition to this, the Prime Minister's statement to Parliament pledged that 'the Convention on the Rights of the Child will be observed and all relevant political decisions will be analysed on the basis of how they affect the situation of children. Abuse, sexual exploitation and other violations against children must be forcefully combated.' In March 1999, Parliament formally adopted the strategy for the implementation of the Convention. Sweden is the first country to have taken this action, but in reality, it has taken nearly ten years to develop a coherent policy. This positive attitude of the Swedish Government is commendable, but in terms of implementation it is clear that there is still a long way to go to ensure that the Convention is threaded through all policy-making and legislation.

The reality *against* the rhetoric

Sexual exploitation

The reported frequency of unlawful activities in Sweden has gradually increased over the last ten years with greater public awareness of the problems of child abuse and sexual exploitation. In 1988 there were 1,563 reported cases, this rose to a peak in 1993 with 3,038 reported crimes and has since dropped to 2,443 cases in 1998. However, still only about ten per cent of reported crimes actually lead to a conviction.

The production and proliferation of child pornography has been a crime in Sweden since 1980, however, the incidence of reported cases has been low with less than ten cases in ten years. Since 1990, and the advent of the Internet, the number of reported cases has increased hugely. In 1998 alone the Swedish police dealt with 42 separate cases of child pornography leading to the discovery of thousands of pictures involving over 100 children. It has been found that collectors of child pornography are invariably involved in other serious crimes such as sexual abuse and rape. In an attempt to combat this insidious form of sexual exploitation and to protect children, since the 1 January 1999 it has been a crime to possess child pornography.

With regard to child prostitution, there is very little official information detailing the extent of the problem in Sweden. There is anecdotal evidence, which suggests the existence of young male prostitutes. There is legislation against the 'seduction of youth' - the payment for sexual services from someone between the ages of 15 and 18. The number of reported cases has varied over the years from between 10 and 40 cases per year.

A complex set of socio-economic factors lead to the sexual exploitation of children in its various forms and it is difficult to sum these up succinctly. One underlying and pervasive factor is the imbalance of power in society where children are not accorded the same rights as adults. Their participation in decisions is not required as a matter of course; their testimonies are often dismissed and they are still, even in a progressive secular society such as Sweden, often seen as objects under adult control. Evidence shows that girls and children from lower socio-economic groups are more at risk.

GOVERNMENT ACTION AND POLICY

The Swedish Government is endeavouring to tackle the problems of sexual exploitation of children and to offer better protection to children at risk through preventive action. This involves the identification of vulnerable children and the introduction of measures of protection, which includes support and assistance to both the victims and the perpetrators of these crimes.

- Sexual abuse of children has been a crime in Sweden for many years punishable by between two and ten years' imprisonment. This is specifically to protect all children.
- Since the World Congress against Commercial Exploitation of Children, the Swedish Government has legislated that not only the production and circulation of pornographic materials are criminal offences but so, too, is possession. Further to this a National Plan of Action was published on 2 July, 1998.
- In addition to this, new social legislation makes it a mandatory duty of all childcare personnel to report any suspicion of sexual abuse to the social welfare authorities. This acts as a monitoring mechanism with the day-to-day care of children. Throughout their school years, all children receive regular health checks which is an effective mechanism of identifying children at risk.
- Sexual advice centres are available in big cities and children are introduced to them during their ninth year in school.
- A Swedish NGO, BRIS, has set up a confidential telephone helpline for children.
- The Government is also looking at a strategy for investigating potential childcare workers, youth workers and teachers, before they are employed, to prevent paedophiles from securing employment with children. The principal mechanism currently under discussion is allowing reference to police records as a standard check before employment.

There have certainly been improvements in the protection from and prevention of child sexual exploitation. The media and awareness campaigns have made what was once a taboo subject into a more topical issue and a more widely acknowledged problem.

Prevention is now being examined in more depth. There is an attempt by the Government to address the whole problem by looking at the therapeutic needs, not only of the victims, but also of the offenders, in order to try to prevent further offences and to break the cycle of what is often recurring abuse. This is a positive move forward, but it still meets opposition and requires considerably more research to ensure that offenders receive the requisite treatment to help them with their problem.

One of the greatest concerns remaining is that it too often proves difficult to convict offenders for their crime. Investigation into suspected cases of abuse or exploitation and the questioning of children are often delayed, severely undermining the effectiveness of any action taken. In addition to this, police officers responsible for the interviewing of children rarely receive specialist training to carry out this task. Indeed, at all levels of the legal system, it is found that there are insufficient special provisions made to develop expertise. Lawyers and judges receive no training to deal with children who are victims of abuse or exploitation or to prepare them adequately for the children's behaviour which results from their experiences.

A final key concern is the question of custody of the children of a suspected sexual offender. A sexual offender who has not been convicted still has the right to care for his or her own children even though the children may be frightened and continued abuse suspected. Although social services can provide counselling to address children's fears, there is currently no way to guarantee protection for children in such cases.

RECOMMENDATIONS

While positive action has been taken, there remain a number of key concerns - and the provisions of Article 34 are in reality not being fully realised. However, from the concerns which arise come a number of clear recommendations:

- **Provision of training** - It is essential that all professionals involved in the legal process receive proper training in how to listen to, understand and handle children who are victims of such forms of exploitation.
- **Immediate investigation and acceleration of legal process** - Sexual crimes against children need to be responded to as soon as they are reported. It is essential that the legal process is accelerated. Children's accounts of abuse must be taken extremely seriously. Once they have gathered the courage to discuss their experiences they should be responded to quickly and effectively to ensure that lengthy legal proceedings do not exacerbate the situation and increase the child's distress and alienation. Currently, police resources in Sweden have neither the expertise nor the resources to do this effectively; methods directed towards children have to be developed.
- **Develop preventive action** - Amongst a number of key measures which can be taken to prevent sexual exploitation, is the need to address the needs and problems of the offenders. More research has to be carried out on how best to rehabilitate habitual offenders and thereby protect children.
- **Protection** - Steps are being considered by the Government to prevent sexual offenders from working with groups of children, but more protective measures must be developed. The suggested routine checking of police reports is a start but is insufficient. This suggested measure does not extend to voluntary organisations nor recreation centres and sports clubs frequented by older children. In addition to this, police records only contain information on convicted offenders; checking records will do nothing to protect children from those who have never been convicted. More sophisticated screening mechanisms and routine checking need to be developed to ensure that such methods of protection are effective.

Juvenile justice

Under the Swedish legal system, all children below the age of 18 are defined as juveniles. However, they are regarded as being an adult, for the purposes of prosecution, at the age of 15.

Special provisions for young offenders up to the age of 21 are in place to ensure that they are protected throughout the legal process. Young offenders under the age of 15 are dealt with under the social service system.

The majority of young offenders in Sweden are male.

Young offenders convicted in Sweden in 1997

Age group	Males	Females	Total
15-17 years	11,435	3,512	14, 947
18-20 years	9,420	1,812	11,232

Source: Criminal Statistics, Official Statistics of Sweden - National Council for Crime Prevention

GOVERNMENT ACTION AND POLICY

The issue of juvenile justice is widely debated within Sweden, the general view is that all young offenders should be treated within the social welfare system, based on their individual needs, instead of within the criminal correctional system.

Under the Swedish criminal penal code all young offenders are fully accorded their rights as outlined in Articles 40.1 and 40.2 of the Convention. Since January 1999 the National Board for Institutional Care (Statens Institutionsstyrelse (SiS)) has been made responsible for the care and treatment of young people with serious social problems and criminal behaviour, establishing a specific body and a separate mechanism to deal with juvenile offenders.

Under this new system young people (aged 15 to 17) who have committed serious crimes can be sentenced to secure institutional treatment in 32 special facilities throughout Sweden, under the SiS. This is regulated by the Care of Young Persons Act, a law with special provisions regarding the care of young people between the age of 13 and 20. Cases are tried every six months by the local social authority who also decide when the juvenile can be released.

The aim of this reform is to counteract psychological harm which can result from a stay in prison. The new sanction is for a fixed period of time (from 14 days to four years) and the length of sentence is determined by the nature of the crime. Efforts are made to integrate these young offenders into the regular activities of the SiS, which operates under the auspices of the municipal social services. The rationale is to provide each child with the most appropriate form of rehabilitation available, and to place offenders as near to their homes as possible. SiS tries to work co-operatively with social services so that continuous care is provided. Such advanced co-operation with social services, families and voluntary services is essential for the creation of an effective chain of care comprising investigation, treatment, discharge and after-care.

Crime prevention work in Sweden focuses on combating crime and drugs. Sweden is comparatively progressive in its approach to juvenile correction and offers a range of alternatives. A network of parents, police, social services and educational establishments has been set up in most municipalities to work with young people to prevent them from falling into drug-taking and other criminal habits. Alternative approaches are being explored, such as mediation between young offenders and the victims of their crimes, and family consultations where the whole family is involved in identifying the possible causes of delinquent behaviour and the best means of treatment. The family consultation initiative comes from social services. Through this, the young offender and their family (together with social services) draw up a plan of correction and rehabilitation. The benefits of these alternative methods have not yet been assessed but they are to be reviewed in the middle of 2000.

RECOMMENDATIONS

Overall it is felt that the Swedish Government is implementing all aspects of Article 40. A range of special provisions for juvenile offenders exists, and the best interests of young people are in the mind of the Government when drawing up new legislation and mechanisms for dealing with juvenile offenders.

That said, there remain a number of areas of concern where changes could improve implementation:

- **Provide alternative juvenile detention facilities during investigation** - Currently there are few special provisions for young offenders whilst they are under detention. They are currently held in custody along with adults. The Swedish Government should ensure that alternative custody arrangements are available for children below the age of 18.
- **Develop a more coherent and comprehensive prevention strategy** - It is felt that social services need to take more action towards crime prevention amongst juveniles.

A more coherent and comprehensive prevention strategy needs to be developed.

- **Increase social services capacity** - Overall responsibility for children in conflict with the law lies with the social welfare system in Sweden. Concerns exist that the social welfare system does not always have the capacity to respond fully to all juvenile offenders, and when it is unable to meet the demands, young offenders fall under the normal criminal penal system and are not accorded the special provisions which should be available. This situation needs to be examined closely and more resources committed to the social services to cope with all young offenders.

Displacement

In 1998 12,844 asylum-seekers came to Sweden, including 3, 606 children under the age of 18. Of these children 291 were unaccompanied. The majority of asylum-seekers come from the former Yugoslavia, Iraq, Somalia, Turkey, Colombia and the former Soviet states.

GOVERNMENT ACTION AND POLICY

The Swedish Immigration Board is responsible for the reception of asylum-seekers. Unaccompanied minors are either placed with relatives, if they can be traced, or cared for in special homes. Whilst their primary needs are provided for, concern is expressed over the capacity of social services to provide the necessary psycho-social care.

In principle, asylum-seeking children have the same right to education, health facilities and protection as national children. However, those aged between 16 and 18 do not have the same rights of access to upper secondary education as national children. The Immigration Board is responsible for arranging alternative educational and training opportunities. The reality, of course, is that these are not always put into practice.

For unaccompanied children, the Immigration Board immediately starts to trace their family, in co-operation with the Red Cross. The policy of the Swedish Government is that the children should be reunited with their families in the country in which their family are found to be. This naturally causes problems where the family is at risk from war or persecution. Recently the Swedish Government has started to award temporary resident permits to separated children while their family is being traced.

RECOMMENDATIONS

Two years ago (1997), the Swedish Aliens Act was modified to better accommodate the provisions of the CRC. The principle of the 'best interests of the child' is incorporated into the very first paragraph of the law, and the right to be heard is now clearly stipulated in the text.

The question remains whether these are translated into practice, and a number of criticisms and concerns are raised which call for further steps to be taken.

- **Focus upon assessment of the best interests of the child** - Many concerns are voiced over the way in which the best interests of the child and their need for protection are assessed. Better methods for interviewing children need to be developed, and for interpreting the often conflicting and confused information that unaccompanied children may provide. Many of these children have undergone extreme trauma, the effects of which need to be fully understood.
- **Reassess criteria for family reunion** - The criteria for family reunion in Sweden are strict and often criticised as overly severe. The process is also lengthy and time-consuming. The Immigration Board needs to look at ways of accelerating the process, particularly where unaccompanied minors are involved. It is felt that the situation, falls short of current Article 10 of the CRC which states that all applications for

family reunion should be dealt with by in a 'positive, humane and expeditious manner'.

Education

It was 1842 when the principle of compulsory education was established in Sweden. At this time, children were obliged to begin some form of education before reaching the age of ten. In 1936 this became more formalised and education provided by the state was expanded to cover a four-year period. Since 1962 Swedish children have benefited from nine years of state education (only seven per cent of students attend independent schools). This is provided for children between the ages of seven and sixteen and, as of the 1997/98 academic year, all primary schools must now offer a preliminary year of kindergarten for six-year-olds.

Special education facilities are available for children with special needs ranging from learning difficulties to disabilities such as visual and aural impairment. An additional year of education is offered to handicapped children at special schools in addition to the mandatory provisions of the education system.

Upper secondary school (gymnasium) is not compulsory, but is free and available to all. The senior secondary curriculum is extremely broad to cater for the needs of all teenagers preparing for their adult life. Sixteen different three-year courses are offered, two of which are designed to prepare for higher education, whilst the remaining 14 offer vocational training. Entrance to the gymnasium is high and each year an average of 97 per cent of students completing secondary school go on to start senior secondary courses.

Whilst school attendance on the whole is high, the numbers of those leaving secondary school before completing their final exams appear to be on the increase. Overall girls tend to achieve slightly better results than boys with 87 per cent graduating with complete grades, compared to 80 per cent for boys. The number of students leaving school without graduating with any final grades has increased in the last decade from 0.8 per cent to 1.3 per cent. At the senior secondary school level the drop-out rates are even higher. Here the drop-out rate for children with parents born outside Sweden differs significantly from native Swedish children. Forty-five per cent of non-ethnic Swedes leave before completing their studies, a stark contrast to four per cent of Swedish students.

GOVERNMENT ACTION AND POLICY

The Swedish Government has set out national goals for the education system in Sweden. These are based on the Education Law, which emphasisies democratic values and these should be at the heart of education and teaching in Sweden. Together with families and the community, schools are charged with raising independent, tolerant and responsible citizens who respect and value their fellow citizens.
In principle, children are treated as equals involved in resolving difficult problems which impact on them through open discussion; the underlying ethos is that children will treat others as they are treated themselves.

Despite these aims, discipline within schools is an increasing concern and violence is a growing problem. Statistics reveal that between eight and ten per cent of children in state education have in some way been exposed to mobbing and bullying. One of the contributing factors to this is the decreasing ratio of full-time teaching staff to students. In 1994/95 there were 8.1 teachers per 100 children. This has decreased to 7.5 teachers per 100 students in the last academic year (1997/98).

Since the early 1990s the Swedish Government has sought to decentralise the education system, devolving greater autonomy and responsibility to the municipalities. The aim has been to encourage municipalities to become more proactive in developing local education provision. The desire has also been to ensure: greater local participation with parents; students and teachers involved in the development of extra-curricular activities; alternative teaching methodologies and strategies for addressing problems such as non-attendance and bullying.

While this strategy has been successful in some regions, an unfortunate outcome has been that discrepancies have developed between municipalities, and considerable differences have emerged in the quality of service provision, facilities available and the general standards of education. Although funds are received from central government municipalities have different demands on their education budgets for each year. For example, a high incidence of immigrant children necessitates a range of special provisions, which draw funds from the central budget, effectively reducing the overall budget available for other services.

Of major concern are the increased levels of non-attendance and drop-out rates. An alarming number of students leave school without completing their final exams and with no formal qualifications. It has been claimed that this is, in part, caused by the low status of teachers in Sweden. Salaries are comparatively low, graduates are deterred from entering the teaching profession and the level of resources committed to education seems to diminish each year. There is a shortage of well qualified teachers (particularly science teachers) and the shortage is geographically concentrated in areas of low social status. Thus opportunities and services offered to children, particularly those with special needs, are outstripped by demand.

RECOMMENDATIONS

- **Prioritise education and raise the profile of teaching** - The profile of teaching and the level of resources made available by central government need to be raised. Education budgets tend to be at the top of the casualty list for public spending cuts. Education needs to be prioritised and subsidies provided to schools with pupils who have special needs. All schools have to be adequately resourced to meet the needs of the pupils and provide them with the proper level of support they require.
- **Improved learning environment** - Excessive levels of violence and delinquent behaviour create a poor social and learning environment and impact on the whole school community including teachers, pupils, parents and the community at large. To develop effective and conducive working and learning environments, which motivate and interest young people, schools need to address the nature of the whole school environment. This will involve a whole range of strategies and interventions. One method of tackling the increasing problem of violence and bullying in schools is to place greater emphasis on the pedagogical education of all teachers. Interventions are also needed to combat discrimination and to ensure that children with special needs have their rights fulfilled.
- **Increased participation by children** - In particular school children, but also parents and teachers, should have a greater influence in the school environment and the development of strategies to combat problems such as non-attendance and bullying.
- **Reduce non-attendance and drop-out rates** - The problem with non-attendance and drop-outs is, in part, a result of the new theoretical approach within all programmes in upper secondary school and the problem of unemployment. This directs almost all children to remain in school, committing themselves to a basic education of 12 years, not necessarily out of their own choice but as a result of the lack of alternative opportunities. The upper secondary school system is currently under review to try and identify a solution to improve the opportunities and facilities offered.

United Kingdom

THE UK GOVERNMENT AND THE CRC

The UK Government ratified the Convention on the Rights of the Child in 1991. Having done so it then took the view that no detailed scrutiny of legislation, policy or practice was necessary as it perceived itself as already fully compliant with the Convention's principles and standards. As a result of this, therefore, no legislative or other changes were introduced in order to promote compliance, nor were any government structures introduced to ensure that the Convention was effectively monitored. In reality, the only action taken by the Government was to commission a non-governmental organisation (NGO) to draft a leaflet on the Convention, published by the Department of Health. Available free of charge, it was targeted at an adult audience with no information made available for children.

Despite lobbying from NGOs, the Government failed to consult them in the preparation of its Initial Report to the Committee on the Rights of the Child. The Children's Rights Development Unit, an NGO working in collaboration with over 180 other NGOs and 45 groups of children submitted an alternative report to the Committee. The Committee examined the UK Government delegation in January 1995 and made concluding observations critical of many aspects of government policy.

They expressed particular concern about:

- the evidence of growing inequality and child poverty in UK society;
- the continued legitimacy of physical punishment of children;
- the low age of criminal responsibility;
- the introduction of 'child prisons' for 12 to 14 year olds;
- the failure to implement the underlying principles of the Convention;
- the operation of the youth justice system in Northern Ireland and the impact of the emergency legislation.

It also expressed regret at the reservations entered by the Government and the lack of any co-ordinating mechanisms or independent monitoring body to promote implementation.

In spite of the Committee's concluding observations, no government action followed.

In 1997, the new Labour Government took office. Like the previous government it, too, has failed to introduce mechanisms to ensure consistent scrutiny of its obligations, nor has it given proper regard to the Convention rights in its legislative programme. However it did adopt a more open approach to the reporting obligation. An illustration of this was the January 1998 conference to launch the process of preparing its report. It agreed to establish an Advisory Group comprising representatives from all key government departments, and representative NGOs from England, Wales, Scotland and Northern Ireland, it also agreed to consult children and young people as part of the process. The report was due to be submitted in January 1999, but was eventually published in August 1999.

The Government has so far refused to consider establishing a statutory Children's Rights Commissioner. It has no national strategy for implementation, nor an inter-departmental forum for promoting or monitoring implementation (although discussions are currently taking place within the Department of Health to explore the potential of such a forum). Draft Bills and proposed policy are not systematically assessed to ensure compliance. There are a number of current key concerns where the Government is clearly failing to implement the Convention, for example:

- the age of criminal responsibility (ten in England, Wales and Northern Ireland and eight in Scotland) remains one of the lowest in Europe;
- the UK locks up more and more children convicted of criminal offences;
- the conditions under which many children are held are deplorable;
- the Government has legislated to empower local authorities to introduce curfews on younger children (see section 2.1, Articles 15 and 16);
- corporal punishment remains lawful for parents;
- the rights of asylum-seekers are being significantly eroded.

There are other areas where the Government is genuinely seeking to achieve change but, to date, the problems for children persist. These include: extensive child poverty; high numbers of school exclusions; widespread racism and racial harassment; high levels of teenage pregnancy; very high levels of mental illness amongst young people coupled with poor adolescent mental health services; very poor social and educational outcomes for children in public care; and a lack of consistent measures to respect the right of children to express their views.

The reality *against* the rhetoric

Sexual exploitation

Quite how widespread the problem of sexual exploitation is remains unclear, however it is a cause for concern. There is a distinct lack of accurate statistical information on sexual offences against children, and estimates are correspondingly diverse. The Home Office estimates that between 3,500 and 72,600 children are sexually abused in England and Wales each year. According to the 1996 report of the National Commission of Inquiry into the Prevention of Child Abuse, each year up to 100,000 children in the UK are estimated to have a potentially harmful sexual experience.

However clear evidence exists of a growing industry in child prostitution and pornography. Latest figures for England and Wales show that in 1996, 288 young people were cautioned and 210 convicted for offences related to prostitution, a rise of 85 per cent and 75 per cent respectively in ten years. The number of people convicted for taking, distributing or publishing indecent photographs of children more than doubled in the ten years to 1995. The increasing use of modern technology in widening the distribution of child pornography is also a grave concern. It is widely accepted that the numbers of children involved in prostitution and pornography are in reality far higher than official data suggests.

Homeless young people and runaway children are particularly vulnerable to drifting into prostitution as a means to survive. In addition children are experiencing abuse in some children's homes - being more susceptible to exploitation by paedophiles and individuals who target children's homes in order to recruit child prostitutes.

GOVERNMENT ACTION AND POLICY

Articles 19 and 34 - the right to protection from abuse, neglect and sexual exploitation, including prostitution and involvement in pornography.

Since the UK's ratification of the CRC in 1991 there has been a resurgence of concern about child sexual exploitation, due in part to successful campaigning and an increased awareness of the existence of child prostitution and child pornography. Despite some government action, there remain clear gaps where the Government is failing to meet the provision of Articles 19 and 34 of the Convention.

Overall, policy-making to prevent the sexual exploitation of children has not been founded on the perspective of a young person. For example, in relation to prostitution, the Street Offences Act 1959 makes no distinction between adults, young people or children. But, following lobbying, the Government has shifted its view of child prostitution, with guidelines published in December 1998 recommending that children under 18 should be treated as victims of crimes rather than offenders. As a result of this change, the number of convictions for child prostitution is likely to fall. There has been some argument that this guidance does not go far enough and that child prostitution should be decriminalised altogether.

Unlike some other European countries, possession of child pornography is an offence in Britain. The 1991 Criminal Justice Act made possession a serious arrestable offence with a possible upper penalty of six months' imprisonment. So far this has had minimal impact on the possession and distribution of child pornography. The Act also increased powers to search for and seize computer pornography but there remains a loophole in the law both regarding material accessed via bulletin boards and also in relation to the use of encryption to hide computer pornography.

Since the 1996 World Congress against Commercial Sexual Exploitation of Children in Stockholm in August 1996, some progress has been made on legislation relating to sex tourism. The Sexual Offences (Conspiracy and Incitement) Act 1996 gave UK courts jurisdiction to deal with those who conspire or incite others in this country to commit sexual acts against children abroad. The 1997 Sexual Offences Act made it possible to prosecute UK citizens for sexual offences against children committed outside the UK.

In recent years government action has largely centred on attempting to break the cycle of re-offending among all those convicted for sexual offences. Measures have been taken to extend supervision to sex offenders after they are released from prison. The 1991 Criminal Justice Act extended supervision, the Sex Offenders Act of 1997 created a register of sex offenders and the 1998 Crime and Disorder Act introduced sex offender orders to help police manage sex offenders in the community.

Recent government action demonstrates an increased focus on preventive measures. Firstly, guidance for inter-agency co-operation to safeguard children from abuse has been reviewed and updated reflecting a shift towards identifying children and families in need and providing early intervention and support. Secondly, a three-year programme, 'Quality Protects', was launched in 1999. It aims to improve the management of children's services and tackle issues such as reducing the incidence of runaway children, which has been so closely linked to the increase in sexual exploitation. Thirdly, legislation passed in 1999 allows for the establishment of a central register of those who are unsuitable to work with children and the government has promised further legislation to ensure heavy fines or prison sentences are given to those individuals who break a ban on working with children.

RECOMMENDATIONS

- **Decriminalise soliciting for young girls** - Decriminalise loitering and soliciting for young girls under 16.
- **Change in criminal legislation** - Create a statutory offence for someone to encourage or procure any young person under 16 to engage in sexual activity, regardless of whether or not the young person has been involved in prostitution.
- **Improved analysis** - Improve data collection and statistical analysis of the situation for children in the UK in respect of abuse and exploitation.
- **Mechanisms for combating computer porn** - Strengthen legislation to prosecute those accessing computer porn via bulletin boards and close the loophole enabling individuals subject to a search warrant to use encryption to hide computer porn.

Juvenile justice

As an issue of much public concern, juvenile crime has attracted much political attention. An estimated seven million offences are committed by under 18s each year (10 to 15 year olds account for 14 per cent of convicted offenders and 10 to 17 year olds account for around 25 per cent). Despite a general fall in the offending rate among 10 to 17 year olds during the past decade (with the exception of certain crimes such as robbery and drug-related offences), a growing anxiety in the early 1990s has led to the abandonment of commitments to base youth justice upon principles of diversion and minimum, but appropriate, intervention. In their place, more punitive approaches based on a greater use of custody have been introduced.

GOVERNMENT ACTION AND POLICY

Article 40.3(a) - the age of criminal responsibility

Compared with most European neighbours, the age of criminal responsibility in the UK is very low - ten in England and Wales, eight in Scotland. This was to some extent mitigated by the principle of doli incapax, which required that when prosecuting a child between the ages of 10 and 14, the prosecution must demonstrate that the child understood that what he or she had done was seriously wrong. However, in recent legislation (the Crime and Disorder Act 1998), the Government has abolished this principle. This means that children as young as ten are held to be fully accountable for their actions in exactly the same way as adults. This reduction in the age of criminal responsibility has been introduced despite the fact that one of the recommendations from the Committee on the Rights of the Child in 1995 was for the UK Government to give serious consideration to raising the age.

Article 37(b) - detention must be used only as a measure of last resort and for the shortest appropriate period of time
The Criminal Justice and Public Order Act 1994 increased the maximum length of time 15 to 17 year old children could spend in custody from 12 to 24 months. It also gave the courts powers to convict a child aged 10 to 14 years of a 'grave offence'. Previously children under 14 could not be convicted of a grave offence unless it was homicide. This results in younger children being convicted of a wider range of offences and thereby given longer sentences.

The legislation also provided for the establishment of 'secure training centres' - prisons for 12 to 14 year olds. The Committee on the Rights of the Child expressed concern in 1995 that these centres would not be compliant with the Convention. Nevertheless, the first centre opened in April 1998 and four more are planned for the future. The first centre encountered an extremely troubled start with inexperienced staff trying to handle a group of highly challenging and disruptive children. There was a high staff turnover, significant evidence of inappropriate control and restraint techniques being used, unsatisfactory education provision, and inadequate competence in managing situations where bullying, self-harm and attempted suicide occurred. These conditions are not compatible with the right of a child to promotion of their best interests, as well as the obligations under Article 37(b).

The UK locks up proportionally more children than other European countries, and the numbers have been rising. Since 1995, the number of children serving custodial sentences increased by 17 per cent from 4,671 during 1995, to 5,617 in 1997. The number of girls given custodial sentences increased by 45 per cent between 1995 and 1997. Article 37(b) requires that imprisonment is only used as a last resort and for the shortest period of time. It is known that locking up children does not work and produces a recidivist rate of at least 80 per cent.

Article 37(c) - the right of children deprived of liberty to be treated with humanity and respect for their dignity
The conditions under which many children are held are dire and cannot be accepted. Recent reports from Her Majesty's Chief Inspector of Prisons make sobering reading. In one young offender institution, he describes the reception arrangements as appalling and the level of overcrowding unacceptable; children are forced to eat in their cells which are little more than lavatories, they are given very limited time out of their cells, and (he goes on to observe), 'I have not come across such totally deliberate and unnecessary impoverishment of children anywhere'. Even more recently in his report on the Feltham Young Offender Institution, a large prison servicing the London area, he describes the conditions he found as 'unacceptable in a civilised country'. His concerns included inmates being locked up for 22 hours a day, in cold, dirty and dilapidated cells, with a lack of opportunities for exercise, unwashed linen and pitifully inadequate provision of personal clothing. He commented that the conditions in which many children are held fall far below the minimum conditions required by the Convention on the Rights of the Child.

Articles 15 and 16 - the right to freedom of association, to privacy and respect for family life
The Crime and Disorder Act 1998 introduces powers for local authorities to impose curfews for children under the age of ten years. Once imposed these will deny young children the right to be out even though they have committed no offence nor have even been identified as at risk of committing an offence. Such curfews amount to a blanket ban on a child's freedom. The Government has failed to produce any evidence that such a measure is justified either in terms of children's protection or to reduce criminal activity amongst this age group. The Police Federation have stated that, in their view, the under-tens do not pose a problem. Curfews will, in effect, criminalise young children and

their parents, create a presumption that children are unacceptable in public arenas, and potentially expose to greater risk children who spend time outside their home to escape abuse.

RECOMMENDATIONS

- **Reduction of numbers held in custody** - Reduce the numbers of young people held in custody and introduce more community-based dispositions.
- **Improvement of conditions for custody** - Substantially improve the conditions under which children are held in custody.
- **Secure training centres** - Reconsider the plans to retain and expand the use of secure training centres.
- **Curfew powers** - Repeal the powers to impose curfews on young children.
- **Age of criminal responsibility** - Raise the age of criminal responsibility.

Displacement

The number of applications for refugee status in the UK stands currently at around 20,000 a year. The number of unaccompanied children arriving in the UK seeking asylum is increasing (1,105 in 1997) and they represent 5 per cent of the total applications. The main countries from which they arrive are Kosovo, Turkey, Afghanistan, Uganda and Somalia. The war in the Balkans dramatically increased the numbers of refugees from Kosovo.

GOVERNMENT ACTION AND POLICY

Article 3, 37, and 40 - rights to promotion of best interests, to detention only as a last resort and to respect for the child's dignity

While it is stated government policy that children seeking asylum are not held in detention, in practice a number are so held. Since 1994, over 153 young people have been detained, some as young as 13 years. Over 50 per cent were held for more than one month. The experience of detention for a child is immensely traumatic. Recent research highlighted their fear and bewilderment, their experience of racism from staff, the poor physical conditions and the onset of ill health. These practices, in respect of children who have committed no offences, would appear to breach Article 37 and 40 as well as Article 3.

Articles 26 and 27 - the right to benefit from social security and to an adequate standard of living

At the time of writing the Immigration and Asylum Bill is progressing through the UK Parliament and will introduce measures which result in children in families who are seeking asylum being afforded fewer rights than other children in respect of Articles 26 and 27. For example, it will remove the right to cash benefits and replace them with vouchers - a system which causes hardship, promotes social exclusion, reduces independence and imposes a loss of dignity. Furthermore, the value of these vouchers (with respect to adults) is lower in real terms than that available to other families dependent on state support. This means that asylum-seeking families will be entitled to less than the minimum income identified by government as sufficient to live on. In view of the fact that such families usually arrive in this country with no resources whatsoever, this will cause more detrimental hardship.

Articles 2, 3 and 22 - the right to non-discrimination, to promotion of best interests and to protection and humanitarian assistance for refugees

The Bill also proposes to 'disperse' asylum seekers throughout the country in order to spread the load on local authorities. Asylum seeking families will have no choice as to where they are sent, which may expose them to social isolation, a lack of community support, exposure to racism and a lack of specialist and informed support services.

RECOMMENDATIONS

- **Amendments to Immigration and Asylum Bill** - Amend the following measures proposed in the Immigration and Asylum Bill:
- **The introduction of vouchers as substitutes for cash benefits;**
- **Introduce an element of choice in the dispersal of asylum seeking families;**
- **The withdrawal of responsibilities for children of asylum-seeking families who are destitute.**
- **No detention of unaccompanied children** - End the detention of unaccompanied asylum-seeking children.
- **Funding for representation** - Provide adequate funding to ensure that all unaccompanied asylum-seeking children have access to proper support and representation.

Education

Free, compulsory, full-time education in the UK extends to all children from 5 to 16 years. Enrolment is virtually universal.

GOVERNMENT ACTION AND POLICY

Article 12 - the right to be listened to and taken seriously
The principle that children are entitled to express their views on all matters of concern to them has not been incorporated into the education system. There is no legal requirement to hold school councils and, where they exist, they tend to deal with the most peripheral issues on the school agenda. There is no right for children to make representations or appeal if they are excluded from school. There are rarely any clearly defined complaints procedures in the event of a pupil experiencing abuse, discrimination or injustice.

In a number of recent consultations with children and young people concerning respect for their rights, education consistently arises as the most significant source of dissatisfaction. The most common complaints relate to unfair treatment by teachers, widespread violence and bullying, failure to listen to children, irrelevant and boring lessons, failure to prepare them for adult life and the imposition of unnecessary, petty or inappropriate rules.

Article 28 - the right of all children to education on the basis of equality of opportunity
There is a significant and growing problem of truancy and exclusion from schools. It is estimated that in the UK at least one million children play truant each year and 100,000 are temporarily excluded. Permanent exclusions have increased very rapidly. In 1991, around 3,000 children were permanently excluded from schools in England and Wales and by 1995, the figure had risen to 13,000. Afro-Caribbean boys, children in public care and those with special educational needs make up the highest proportion of excluded children. The causes of the problem are complex, but, from the perspective of the child, major factors cited include poor relationships with teachers, bullying, irrelevance of the curriculum, and control and discipline in the classroom. Additional relevant factors include the introduction by the Government of published performance league tables of schools, which provide an incentive for schools to exclude children not likely to achieve well.

The Government has acknowledged the extent of the problem and established a Social Exclusion Unit, whose remit includes the development of measures to address pupil disaffection. Accordingly, a range of new measures are being introduced through legislation and guidance to promote social inclusion. The most significant failure in these changes is the inadequate recognition of the need for schools to change to accommodate the concerns of children. The measures focus exclusively on strategies to change the behaviour of individual children exhibiting problems.

At no time has the Government given any proper consideration to the implications of Article 12 in addressing disaffection.

Articles 2 and 23 - the right to non-discrimination and to the fullest possible social integration for disabled children

The majority of disabled children and children with special educational needs are educated within the mainstream system, but around 1 to 2 per cent are educated in special day or residential schools. The law provides for parents to state a preference as to which school their child attends, but in respect of disabled children, the local authority can determine that a child attends a special school regardless of the views of the parent or the child. The right to inclusive education is a fundamental human right and as it currently stands, the law discriminates against these children, in breach of Articles 2 and 23.

RECOMMENDATIONS

- **Criteria for exclusion** - Introduce statutory criteria for school exclusions.
- **Appeal mechanism against exclusion** - Introduce a right of appeal for pupils against permanent exclusion.
- **School councils** - Introduce a requirement for schools to introduce school councils which are effective in introducing more democratic structures to schools.
- **Commitment to a forum for children's views** - Introduce a commitment to promoting respect for the right of children to express their views on all aspects of the education system.
- **Teacher training** - Introduce training for teachers on the CRC.
- **A rights approach in schools** - Human rights principles should underpin the philosophy of schools in the UK.
- **End to compulsory segregation of disabled children** - Bring an end to compulsory segregation of some disabled children into special schools and make a long-term commitment to include all children fully.

The USA

THE USA GOVERNMENT AND THE CRC

The United States signed the UN Convention on the Rights of the Child (CRC) in February 1995. Although President Clinton pledged to work toward the Convention's formal ratification, he has not sent the treaty to the US Senate for debate, nor made its ratification a priority during his presidency.

The CRC is not well known in the United States. Relatively few Americans are familiar with its purpose, the specific rights outlined, or its provisions for implementation. Although the United States typically implements international treaties through separate national legislation, opponents of the CRC contend that this United Nations treaty poses a threat to US sovereignty. Further opposition comes from those who regard the CRC as an assault on the integrity of the family by threatening its right to make decisions about raising and disciplining children and by offering children the opportunity to participate fully in family and community life.

There currently is little consensus regarding the rights of children as outlined in the CRC among US government officials, nor the will to move the debate forward. Unfortunately, there is little chance that Congress will bring the CRC ratification vote forward before the next presidential election in 2000. Its future remains unclear after that as well, as Senator Helms, chair of the Senate Committee on Foreign Relations, has promised to block debate if the treaty is submitted for consideration.

For children in the United States, the major consequence of the failure to ratify the CRC lies in the lack of a centralised system to assess their status and oversee their conditions. Without a framework to protect children's rights and develop appropriate policies to ensure this protection, it is difficult to document whether children's rights are safeguarded, their basic needs are met and equal opportunities for full development and participation are available to all children. Save the Children would advise that the development of this framework involve government agencies, non-profit organisations and the private sector.

Regardless of the current ratification status of the CRC, there is much the United States can do to improve conditions for children that would be in accordance with the spirit and principles of the treaty.

In the area of education, the US must create and support programmes that narrow the gap between rich and poor and reduce racial and ethnic discrimination in order to improve the quality of education that children receive and the level of performance they are able to achieve.

Refugee children in the US are often lost in the cracks of our educational, health and economic systems and should be afforded added protection and services to help them and their families cope with resettlement and adaptation to a new culture. Although legislation protecting children from sexual abuse and punishing sex offenders is in place, more preventive programmes are needed to ensure that more children are safe from this type of exploitation. Young offenders are particularly in need of protection from abuse and neglect as our juvenile justice system increasingly focuses on punishment rather than rehabilitation for violent offenders. Moreover, the US must increase to 18 years the age at which offenders can receive the death penalty.

The reality *against* the rhetoric

Sexual exploitation

In 1998, according to the Children's Bureau (a government agency within the Administration for Children and Families, US Department of Health and Human Services), approximately one million children were victims of substantiated or suspected child abuse and neglect. Of these, 119,397 were victims of sexual abuse. Several recent studies suggest, however, that maltreatment of children, including sexual abuse and exploitation, is under-reported, leading experts to believe that millions of cases are undetected each year.

GOVERNMENT ACTION AND POLICY

Children in the US are protected from sexual abuse by both civil and criminal statutes.

- ***Civil statutes*** provide child protection by mandating various professionals to report known or suspected cases of abuse; and ensure that they are investigated by state child protection agencies.

- ***Criminal statutes***, covered by federal and state laws, prohibit certain sexual acts and specify penalties for offenders. Varying from state to state, penalties are related to the age of the child, the presence of force, the relationship between child and offender, and the nature of the sexual act.

In order to qualify for federal funding, states must have a child-protection system that addresses sexual abuse as part of their child abuse and neglect programme. Although state systems aim to protect children from abuse, limited funding for caseworkers and resources affect services for troubled families and at-risk children.

Child pornography

There are numerous federal laws prohibiting child pornography. The 1977 Sexual Exploitation of Children Act prohibits the use of children in the production of pornographic materials and the circulation of materials advertising child pornography. The development of the Internet offers very easy access to pornographic material involving children; provisions of the Act extend to the transfer or receipt of child pornography by any interstate means, including computer. The Child Pornography Prevention Act of 1996 amends the definition of child pornography to include depictions of sexual conduct of real minor children and those that appear to be depictions, but may well be images that have been altered to look like children.

Today, every state has enacted statutes that specifically address the problem of child pornography. Unfortunately, whereas all states impose criminal liability on producers and distributors, there are seven states that have not yet established laws prohibiting the possession of child pornography.

Child prostitution
Child-advocacy groups estimate that there are 100,000 to 300,000 children, ranging in age from as young as 11 up to 17, who are sexually exploited through prostitution and pornography in the United States. Many have been victims of sexual abuse as children, with most children younger than 11 exploited by their caregivers. A large proportion of child prostitutes make up the 1.5 million young people who run away from home each year, many from physically or sexually abusive families, and survive by trading sex for money, shelter, food and drugs.

There are numerous federal and state laws prohibiting child prostitution. The primary federal law prohibiting child prostitution is the 'Mann Act', which provides federal protection to all youth under the age of 18.

It is estimated that tens of thousands, perhaps as many as 50,000, women and children are trafficked into the US each year, primarily from Latin America, the former Soviet Union and South-East Asia. In response, the Freedom from Sexual Trafficking Act of 1999 has been drafted, which aims to provide protection and assistance to victims and seeks to eliminate sexual trafficking by imposing severe penalties on those convicted.

Further government action is expected from President Clinton's endorsement of the International Labour Organization's (ILO) Worst Forms of Child Labour Convention 1999, which defines and imposes penalties for some of the worst labour violations, including use of children for prostitution and pornography. President Clinton has promised to bring this Convention before the US Congress for ratification.

Two key strategies for preventing child sexual abuse and exploitation include strengthening families and public education. The Federal Government provides grants through the US Department of Health and Human Services' Administration for Children and Families to non-governmental organisations (NGOs) for outreach and education and support services for runaway, homeless and street children at risk of sexual abuse.

RECOMMENDATIONS

- **Increased funding levels** - Increase federal and state funding to reduce caseloads of child-protection staff and other professionals, including social workers and teachers. Improve training opportunities to increase the number of victimised children identified, protected and treated.
- **Acceleration of new legislation** - Immediate passage of the Freedom from Sexual Trafficking Act of 1999 to protect children from forced prostitution and sexual slavery and to punish perpetrators of these crimes.
- **Ratification of Worst Forms of Child Labour Convention 1999.**
- **Awareness programmes** - At the local level, provide children and families with the skills and resources they need to prevent and recognise sexual abuse, as well as treatment opportunities to cope with the short-term and long-term effects of abuse.
- **Research funding** - Federal funding for research in the field of sexual abuse, including best interview practices and treatment outcome studies, to improve services to victims and detection of sexual abuse.
- **Legislation to police the Internet** - Strengthen legislation protecting children from predators on the Internet.

Juvenile justice

In 1997, an estimated 2.8 million juveniles were arrested for criminal activity in the United States. Around 28 per cent of these involved serious crimes, including murder, manslaughter, rape,

assault, burglary, larceny and arson.
The majority of crimes committed by juveniles, however, are those considered less serious, such as vandalism, prostitution and status crimes (offences specific to juveniles that would not be considered crimes if committed by adults, e.g. running away, truancy and curfew violations).

After a decade of rising crime, the number of juveniles arrested for violent crimes peaked in 1993 and has declined each year since. Nevertheless, concerns about juvenile crime, coupled with numerous highly publicised school shootings in the 1990s, have intensified national debate about youth crime and led to changes in state laws for violent or serious juvenile crimes. These make it easier to transfer jurisdiction to adult courts, introduce tougher sentencing, reduce the level of confidentiality of juvenile records and proceedings and increase the rights of victims of juvenile crimes to be involved in court proceedings.

There is great concern among child advocates that the current trend in juvenile justice legislation may well dismantle a fairly successful system whose goal, historically, has been to rehabilitate juveniles and steer them back on the right path instead of deeper into criminal activities.

Although female juvenile crime has risen dramatically during the last decade, arrests of males still exceed those of females by five to one. Minority youth, especially African-American and Hispanic youth, are vastly over-represented in the justice system: while approximately 32 per cent of youth aged 10 to 17 were classified as minorities in 1995, they made up more than half of those arrested. Minorities are also over-represented in detention populations, accounting for over two-thirds of all juveniles in custody in public facilities and just under half of those in private facilities. The Federal Government requires states to implement policies that reduce minority over-representation in the juvenile justice system.

GOVERNMENT ACTION AND POLICY

Since the passage of the Juvenile Justice Court Act in 1899 establishing a juvenile justice system, the United States has treated children (youth under the age of 18 or the age of maturity as determined by individual states) who have committed crimes differently from adults. This is guided by the philosophy that juveniles have not reached their full level of social, cognitive and emotional maturity and cannot be considered responsible for their behaviour in the same way as adults. Since its inception, the goal of the juvenile justice system has been to help children through treatment or rehabilitation rather than punishment, providing them confidentiality, separate courts and detention or treatment facilities and after-care programming.

The primary federal agency charged with overseeing children involved in the justice system is the Office of Juvenile Justice and Delinquency Prevention (OJJDP) of the US Department of Justice, established in 1974 under the Juvenile Justice and Prevention Act. The Act provides for the evaluation of federally assisted programmes and the development of national standards.
It prohibits the incarceration in secure facilities of juveniles who have committed status offences and the confinement of juvenile offenders in adult facilities.

Although guided by OJJDP, federal legislation and the United States Constitution, individual states have broad legislative power to pass additional statutes. Since the early 1990s, nearly every state has enacted tougher juvenile crime legislation, particularly in the areas of jurisdictional authority and sentencing. Virtually all states have passed provisions allowing juveniles who have committed serious and violent offences to be dealt with under the criminal (adult) court prosecution, and many have lowered the minimum age of juvenile court jurisdiction and given the courts stricter sentencing options. These, and other changes to state juvenile justice systems, reflect a dramatic shift away from policies that aim to protect the rights of juvenile offenders and provide treatment and rehabilitation, towards those that regard juveniles as adults, fully responsible for their actions and deserving of adult court proceedings and punishment.

Despite this trend, the number of juvenile cases transferred to criminal courts remains fairly small, accounting for 1.4 per cent of all delinquency cases, with the vast majority involving youth aged 16 years and older. According to OJJDP, the latest available data from 1995 shows that 9,700 juveniles were tried as adults in that year.

Juveniles in confinement

With rising numbers of youth being held in juvenile facilities each year (reaching more than 100,000 in 1997) the problem of overcrowding has become critical. Children in overcrowded facilities receive fewer services and supervision; personal safety and physical and emotional well-being are severely compromised. Recent studies show that many children in confinement lack basic care and supervision, are victims of verbal and physical abuse by staff and receive inadequate educational, training and counselling services.

Additional reports show that juveniles confined in adult facilities are eight times more likely to commit suicide, five times more likely to be assaulted and twice as likely to be assaulted by staff as those in juvenile facilities.

Children and the death penalty

The United State's policy on the death penalty is one of the most debated and contentious issues relating to children's rights and the juvenile justice system. The United States' history of sentencing juveniles to death dates back to 1642 and since then, 357 offenders have been executed for crimes committed when they were younger than 18 years old, accounting for about 1.8 per cent of the 19,200 people executed in the US during this time.

Since the US Supreme Court allowed states to re-institute capital punishment in 1973, courts have issued death sentences to 130 people who were younger than 18 at the time of their crimes. Of these, 13 executions have taken place and, currently 70 juveniles remain on death row.

The US policy of allowing states to impose the death penalty on offenders under the age of 18 is in clear violation of the Convention on the Rights of the Child.

RECOMMENDATIONS

- **Prohibit the death penalty for juvenile offenders** - The US must cease the practice of imposing the death penalty on children under the age of 18 through federal legislation or constitutional amendment.
- **Create a national monitoring system** - Under the supervision of the OJJDP, this system would help ensure that children in public and private detention facilities are not mistreated and receive proper educational, vocational and therapeutic services.
- **Increase funding for crime prevention** - Increase federal and state resources for mentoring, after-school programmes and youth development.
- **Increase funding for diversion programmes** - Increase federal and state resources to divert more youth offenders from the juvenile justice system to counselling, community service, employment and educational programmes.
- **Separate juvenile facilities** - Make federal funding contingent upon state compliance with federal regulations that prohibit placing juveniles alleged to be delinquent or status offenders in facilities in which they have any contact with adult offenders.

Displacement

Since 1975, the United States has admitted more than 2 million refugees. In the fiscal year 1997, the US admitted 70,085 refugees and hosted nearly 400,00 asylum seekers. The Government has set a ceiling for refugee admissions in the fiscal year 1998 at 83,000. The US hosts refugees from a variety of backgrounds, cultures and personal experiences.

GOVERNMENT ACTION AND POLICY

Refugees and asylum seekers in the US come under the legal jurisdiction of the US Immigration and Naturalization Service (INS), part of the US Department of Justice. National policies relating to refugees, migration and the US refugee assistance and admittance programmes are developed and administered by the Bureau of Population, Refugees and Migration (BPRM), an agency within the US State Department.

State agencies and national and local NGOs provide a variety of services to refugee children and their families, such as housing and financial assistance and legal aid. These social services are designed to aid refugees' integration into the community, help them achieve self-reliance and preserve cultural norms and family integrity.

Refugees are guaranteed state public assistance, including financial grants and Medicaid benefits for health-care for a period of eight months. They are also eligible to apply for food stamps and Supplemental Security Income for those with physical or emotional disabilities. Although these safety nets provide refugees with some support, the amount of monthly grants is quite small. As a result, most refugees live at or below the poverty level at least for a period of time. Refugees have the same rights as citizens to education and to the rights guaranteed in the US Constitution. After a year in the US, refugees may apply for permanent residency status and after five years may apply for US citizenship.

Many children enter the US without their families and outside the legal refugee process and, as a result, often are apprehended by federal and state authorities. The Immigration and Naturalization Services reports a five-fold increase in the number of unaccompanied minors entering the country illegally over the last five years. In 1998, the agency apprehended 4,284 such children, most between the ages of 15 and 18.

Some unaccompanied children are seeking asylum in the United States, a procedure that grants applicants temporary protected status. Guidelines were developed in December 1998 to improve the care provided to children seeking asylum, offering child-friendly and sensitive procedures to enable INS officers to better interact with children during asylum or refugee interviews.

Most children arrested by the INS are either released to family or deported within a few days. Some, however, are detained for longer periods while their cases are pending. Generally, there are several hundred children in long-term INS custody at any one time. Unaccompanied children are among the most vulnerable refugees; with little or no English, financial resources, or family support, they often are detained in restrictive settings and receive little information about their situation or future. With limited access to legal recourse to change their status, many remain in detention for months.

Human Rights Watch asserts that, although conditions for children in INS detention can vary according to the region, most are very poor. The organisation reports that conditions of facilities examined in Los Angeles and Arizona in 1996 violate the principles of the CRC, US statutory provisions and INS regulations. Many children, for instance, are housed with the general prison population, a clear violation of US and international standards.

The children in the custody of INS represent only a fraction of the number who enter the United

States undetected each year to escape a variety of hardships and in search of a better life. Their journeys to the United States are invariably arduous and fraught with danger. Once in the US, many find work, either illegally or with the help of forged immigration documents, and as they live in fear of deportation, a good number are exploited by unscrupulous employers and work long hours in unsafe conditions. The National Child Labor Committee in New York estimates 120,000 undocumented children may be working in illegal and dangerous situations in the US.

RECOMMENDATIONS

- **National register of refugee children** - Establish a national tracking and monitoring system to better evaluate the status of refugee children and to ensure that they are receiving the care they need and the rights to which they are entitled.
- **Better treatment for unaccompanied minors** - The INS should comply with international standards regarding detained refugee children. Specifically, unaccompanied minors should not be detained except as a measure of last resort. If detention is necessary, INS must provide children with legal representation, timely information about their status and their right to contact the UNHCR and translations of all relevant documents. INS should increase its capacity and commitment to family reunification efforts.
- **Improved approach to detention** - Unaccompanied refugee children should be supervised by care-giving agencies rather than detention and prosecution services. Appoint a watch-keeping agency to ensure that all detained children receive adequate care, including counselling and education, and protection, such as legal assistance.
- **Increased funding of social provisions for refugee children** - The Federal Government should increase funding to voluntary private organisations for additional counselling, tutoring and vocational services.
- **Language and training services for refugee children and their families** - Increase financial assistance, English language training, counselling and educational and employment services to refugee parents so they can more quickly achieve self-sufficiency and better care for themselves and their children.

Education

Public education is free to all Americans and compulsory to age 16. The majority of American youth attend public institutions, which are funded primarily by the state and local communities.

The standard of education is high and over the past decade, there has been progress in improving proficiency scores in three of the major subject areas, reading, mathematics and science. Unfortunately, there still remain wide racial and ethnic gaps in proficiency test scores. In reading scores, for example, Black, American Indian and Hispanic students lagged behind their White and Asian peers. Improvements in proficiency tests, however, do not necessarily mean that students themselves have increased in proficiency. Fourth-grade reading scores, for instance, have improved over the past decade, but today 40 per cent of fourth-graders cannot read at a basic level.

Over the past thirty years, overall school drop-out rates have decreased. In 1997, the overall drop-out rate for students aged 16-24 was 11 per cent, compared to 27.2 per cent in 1960 and 14.1 per cent in 1980. However, little progress has been made in the last five years to reduce the number of students who do not finish school. In the nation's 20 largest urban school districts, more than half of all students never complete high school.

Many schools in the US are in disrepair, with those in impoverished communities in the worst condition. According to the General Accounting Office, about 14 million children attend schools that need extensive repairs. The Department of Education has linked school achievement with physical surroundings, finding poorer academic skills associated with overcrowded buildings, substandard science facilities, faulty air conditioning and high noise levels.

GOVERNMENT ACTION AND POLICY

The US Department of Education oversees the national education system. It provides funding and national leadership to improve the quality of education in each state. The Department produces and funds a variety of research, helps families with college costs, assists local communities in meeting the needs of its students and helps students prepare for employment. The Department also enforces federal statutes prohibiting discrimination based on race, colour, national origin, gender and disability.

Although the Federal Government provides some funding and establishes guidelines to enhance student and teacher performance, individual states are primarily responsible for budgeting and programming for public schools within their jurisdiction. Much school funding comes from town and city tax bases, including property and corporate taxes. This causes wide disparities in funds available for teachers' salaries, school supplies and educational, social and recreational services for students. The nation's richest school districts spend 56 per cent more per pupil than the poorest districts.

Although schools in poor communities are eligible for federal and state assistance, they still provide most of the cost of educating their students. Poor school districts inevitably have fewer resources available than wealthier towns, while often serving a higher number of at-risk students who have a variety of special needs. These factors combine to have a negative effect on students' performance, drop-out rates, safety, well-being and future opportunities.

Although the US provides all children with an opportunity to receive an education, the quality of this education varies considerably throughout the country. What is needed is additional help to communities to strengthen families, provide after-school tutoring and supervision and provide additional support to special-needs students

RECOMMENDATIONS

- **More equitable resource provision** - Establish minimum funding levels to local schools to achieve greater equity in educational opportunities and resources.
- **Better pre-school facilities** - Increase funding for, and availability of, quality early childhood education programmes to better prepare young children for school.
- **School nutrition programmes** - Expand nutritional programmes for children in school, such as school lunches and breakfasts, as well as summer food programmes to help low-income communities.
- **National standards** - Create a national system of accountability and standards for teachers, administrators and students to make more equal the quality of education in the US
- **Increase after-school activities** - Increase funding for community after-school and in-school programmes for elementary and middle-school students to keep children safe, supervised and learning throughout the year.
- **Create national academic goals** - Building upon the successful 'America Reads' model, create additional targets for academic excellence in the areas of maths and science.

Emerging themes

Despite the range of analysis contained in these country reports, a number of shared recommendations emerge, and common conclusions can be drawn. These should be used as a basis around which governments, NGOs and community organisations develop their own agendas for action.

SEXUAL EXPLOITATION

More effective awareness campaigns must be developed

Children should be made more aware of issues about their individual sexuality and the community at large should be more aware of issues of sexual abuse and exploitation. Children need to be better equipped to protect themselves and communities need to break down the taboos around sexual exploitation so that children at risk can ultimately be better protected. The development of more effective research into, and monitoring of, child sexual exploitation is an essential feature for promoting public awareness of this issue.

Develop improved strategies for the protection of children at risk

More effective mechanisms are needed for identifying and protecting children at risk, which should include a variety of strategies and involve close inter-agency co-operation. Preventive programmes should also be developed, including registers of sex offenders, better screening of people working with children (both professionally and voluntarily), supervision of places where children are at risk and the development of effective mechanisms of intervention. The wider social factors which force children into prostitution, such as limited financial resources, family breakdown, abandonment of children and low levels of schooling need also to be addressed. Social welfare systems addressing many of these problems must be strengthened. The sexual abuse or exploitation of a child is publicly condemned by all societies but it remains all too commonplace. Sanctions for these crimes must be stricter to act as a strong deterrent.

All of these strategies should fall within or complement national Plans of Action as called for by the World Congress Against Commercial Sexual Exploitation of Children held in Stockholm in 1996. Countries which have not as yet developed a Plan of Action must do so as a matter of the utmost priority.

A need to develop codes of good practice for intervention
All professionals working with children from pre-shool staff to personnel working in the judiciary and law enforcement services should receive specialist training. Codes of good practice for protection, intervention and investigation should be developed. This is important in ensuring that children receive the appropriate level of protection and that their experiences are not compounded through insensitive handling.

Development of appropriate legal provisions
In many countries, where commercial sexual exploitation is a growing problem, adequate legal provisions need to be put in place for the proper protection of children involved in commercial sexual activities. All too often children involved in prostitution are treated as criminals rather than vulnerable individuals in need of support and protection.

JUVENILE JUSTICE

The co-ordination of all service provision to juvenile offenders must be improved
The liaison between the police, the courts, social services and all other institutions caring for juvenile offenders needs to be improved, so that their care can be comprehensive and consistent.

Reinforcement of the juvenile justice system and child-focused specialist provisions
The majority of juvenile crime must be dealt with through a specialist juvenile system, which is child-focused and promotes the best interests of each individual child. When juveniles have to be detained, they should be kept in facilities separate from adult offenders. A code of good practice for the interrogation, detention and rehabilitation of juvenile offenders must be developed.

Prevention and rehabilitation programmes must be improved
The focus of juvenile justice systems should be on the correction and prevention of criminal behaviour. This requires the concerted efforts of law enforcement agencies, social services and the juvenile courts. Prevention has to include attempts to address some of the many social factors which lead to juvenile delinquency while rehabilitation should concentrate on specialist detention facilities, alternative measures for first-time offenders and programmes for social reintegration.

DISPLACEMENT

Better provision is needed for refugee and displaced children

To realise the principle of non-discrimination fully, all asylum-seeking or refugee children should receive the same rights and treatment as national children, regardless of their status. All too often, where full provision is not provided, vulnerable children are openly discriminated against. Efforts must also be made to work with community health and social services and schools to mitigate the effects of further discrimination. This should involve close inter-agency co-operation to ensure the comprehensive and co-ordinated delivery of services.

Improved legal representation and acceleration of asylum procedures

Asylum-seeking children and their families should be provided with adequate information on application procedures, and all children should receive proper legal representation. Every effort should be made to make the application process as efficient as possible.

Better family reunification facilities

In the case of unaccompanied minors, the tracing of children's families must be made a priority. Thereafter children should be reunited with their families as soon as possible.

EDUCATION

Increased investment in education

Many countries fail to fulfil the educational provisions of the CRC because of the level of resources they have committed to education. To ensure that children's developmental needs are being met, proper levels of funding and resources should be dedicated to developing broad and flexible education programmes which are able to meet the diversity of children's needs.

Broader based curricula to accommodate the needs of all children

Educational curricula needs to be relevant, inclusive and developmental. Curricula need to address the growth of the whole child, to provide the development of essential skills, effective social education, vocational training and to meet any specialist needs which they may have. Inevitably this will require significant investment and staff commitment.

Create improved learning environments
Effective and conducive learning environments are essential to ensure that children are able to learn and benefit from educational services provided so that education programmes achieve their objectives. Violence and bullying remains a problem in many schools and there are too many examples in all countries of disaffected pupils. Few children are really involved in the decision-making processes of their schools. Concerted efforts need to be made by all governments to ensure that the correct learning environments can be provided which ensure a child's safety, are free from prejudice and violence and offer children the maximum levels of participation to ensure their proper development.

Incorporation of the CRC into all education curricula
The underlying principles and the basic provisions of the CRC should be an essential feature of all education curricula. Failure to do this is a fundamental contradiction to the CRC itself.

'My name is Khalid Hussain.

I am 15 years old *and come from Sialkot in Pakistan. I've been stitching footballs for the last four years, and I'm also going to school. I like stitching footballs because I like* studying *and my parents can't afford the* costs *of my* education. *If I* study *I can become an office manager and* earn good money. *The* people *who want to* ban *child labour - do they know the conditions we live in? Most of the people in my village stitch footballs. If there were a ban, people would go* hungry *they would die of hunger'.*

Khalid Hussain, age 15 - Pakistan

PART IV
Conclusion

'I hope there will be a solution to our problems'.

Hussein, age 14 - Lebanon

Chapter 6

Challenges Ahead

Reality Check

The International Save the Children Alliance's main concern in this publication is to gauge the difference between the full vision of the CRC and the reality for children. It seeks to note the achievements of the Convention while identifying the failures of national governments and the international community to implement its provisions and improve children's lives.

Have children's lives changed for the better since the adoption of the CRC? Ten years on, there is too little evidence that the provisions of the Convention really are filtering down to reach children and bring actual positive change to their lives. The full vision of the CRC, promising a better world for children, remains as yet unrealised. Although some children have benefited, too many children remain excluded through discrimination, and too many of the basic principles of the CRC remain, in reality, forgotten. The recurrent conclusion in the preceding chapters and country reports is that there has been a consistent failure on the part of governments to implement the Convention's provisions to the full. After ten years, ratification of the CRC is no longer good enough and we must demand more.

The undoubted successes

The CRC is a seminal piece of international legislation. It is the most widely ratified human rights convention in history. It is the first instrument to cover the full rights of an individual, creating the potential for radically changing the way in which children are viewed. Through this it has engendered a global sense of responsibility towards the promotion and protection of children's rights.

In creating a common legal framework, the CRC has increased levels of governmental accountability, bringing about legislative and institutional reform and establishing a precedent for international co-operation. While it may be 'soft law', lacking the authority to bind governments legally to its provisions, it carries a moral authority and leverage, which obliges governments to work towards the fulfilment of children's rights.

Children's rights are certainly more visible now and more practised as a result of the Convention. Some progress has been made towards a global children's community, with the strengthening of

Chris Eldridge / Save The Children

inter-community coalitions in support of child welfare. Awareness of children's rights, in some sectors of society, is growing and children have begun to participate in debates which affect them, although this is still little more than tokenism.

The fundamental failings

Undeniable though this progress is, the evidence of this report has shown that there are still enormous gaps between the full vision of children's rights espoused in the CRC and the quality of life for children today across the world.

Central to this disparity is the consistent failure by national governments to develop an explicit strategy for the implementation of the Convention. The CRC has great potential but without effective action its provisions remain little more than rhetoric. Remarkably, despite the fact that 191 nations have ratified the

Most countries still lack the correct framework for enabling the advancement of children's rights.

There is a general failure to disseminate adequate information about the CRC, and there are consequently serious gaps in public awareness.

How can children actively enjoy the fulfilment of their rights when they do not even know what they are?

Convention, only one - Sweden - has an explicit strategy for its implementation, and this was only introduced early in 1999, taking nearly a decade to develop. Most countries still lack the correct framework for enabling the advancement of children's rights and, as seen in the country reports, implementation remains weak. While there may be commitment to the CRC on paper, a distinct lack of political will to further children's rights is apparent in most countries. Following ratification of the CRC in the UK, for example, the government made no legislative, institutional or policy changes as it believed that it fully complied with the provisions of the Convention. The recent response of Save the Children UK to their government's second periodic report to the UN Committee on the Rights of the Child condemns it for failing to implement the CRC comprehensively. Minority children remain neglected and the government still lacks a clear vision for making a reality of children's rights.

There is a general failure to disseminate adequate information about the CRC, and there are consequently serious gaps in public awareness. Efforts to disseminate information about the Convention have been made in some countries, but to limited effect. Generally, there is an alarming ignorance of what the Convention is and what it means. In particular, the vision of the CRC is failing to filter down from central to local government, and this failure is critical, given that local authorities are the primary providers of services to children in many countries. This is substantiated by the findings of the recent study,[1] published by Save the Children Sweden (Rädda Barnen). The study examined the implementation of the CRC in six countries, and identified a considerable difference between awareness at the national and local government levels. Effective implementation is impossible without a sound understanding of the provisions of the CRC. Information dissemination is therefore vital. It is worrying then to find such ignorance in most municipal agencies. It is also cause for concern that in most countries the CRC is not yet a mandatory part of educational curricula. This seems to contradict the very spirit of the CRC. How can children actively enjoy the fulfilment of their rights when they do not even know what they are? Similarly, how can we expect state bodies, civil servants and other professionals to realise these rights if they are not aware of what they are? The media in all its forms should be harnessed as a primary dissemination tool and non-governmental organisations (NGOs) should be playing an important role in addressing this.

1 Lisa Woll, 1999, The Convention on the Rights of the Child Impact Study, Rädda Barnen, Stockholm.

An associated problem is the paucity of accurate data on child welfare available in some countries. As borne out by the country reports, social research in some countries makes no distinction between adults and children. Access to data also varies from country to country. In some cases, even when official data is compiled, it can be difficult to obtain. It is vital that more in-depth and reliable sources of data are developed and made easily accessible. In order to look beyond the rhetoric of each nation's efforts a system of monitoring needs to be devised for the CRC. Possibly using measurable indicators akin to those developed for the Human Development Index, would urge nations to adopt a series of statistical conventions to produce data at regular periods in easily comparable forms to establish a systematic monitoring mechanism.[2]

One of the most serious violations of the provisions of the CRC is the consistent failure on the part of governments to uphold one of its key principles, that of non-discrimination and its vision of universality.

Perhaps one of the most serious violations of the provisions of the CRC is the consistent failure on the part of governments to uphold one of its key principles; that of non-discrimination and its vision of universality. The Convention specifically aimed to protect all children regardless of race, creed, socio-economic group or nationality. Yet this principle is regularly being ignored around the world and the rights of the most vulnerable children (such as the disabled, the homeless, refugees, ethnic minorities and the socially deprived) are repeatedly neglected. The CRC and its potential benefits are simply failing to reach every child - undermining its strength and utility, diminishing its ability to improve children's lives.

The CRC has been radical in seeking to change the way in which children are viewed. Yet in reality the notion of children as individuals in their own right is still largely unrealised.

The CRC has been radical in seeking to change the way in which children are viewed. Yet in reality the notion of children as individuals in their own right is still largely unrealised. A range of social and cultural factors make it difficult for many to accept children as rights-bearers. Children are rarely seen as individuals, with their identities distinct from their families' and, in practice, they are seldom consulted as individuals. NGOs and the media must work to bring about change in social attitudes. A central tenet of the CRC is that children should be heard (Article 12) and involved in all decision-making processes which affect them. However, where children are still not recognised as the holders of rights this is not possible. While there are exceptions to this, the majority of efforts to include children in decision-making and to give them a voice (such as children's parliaments) have been little more than gestures. There are, as yet, few examples of coherent or consistent policies to give children the platform and level of participation desired.

2 See Chris Smith "The field trial of policy analysis for the Convention on the Rights of the Child". The International Journal of Children's Rights. 6: 407-431, 1998.

Tamara Wyss / Loud Minority / Save The Children

This situation is made worse by the fact that children tend to be put into categories and there is an ongoing failure to address children's needs holistically. Despite the CRC, children are viewed not as complete individuals, but as victims in need of protection, juvenile offenders in need of constraint and correction, or pupil, patient or charge. As children come into contact with various professional groups, they tend to be looked at from isolated perspectives: of schools, of social and health services or of the juvenile justice system. As children are categorised, so are their needs. Too often these needs are dealt with discretely by separate service providers and, as a result, only partial support is provided, and the full range of a child's needs tends to be neglected. The challenge is a complex one, but it is imperative that children are viewed as complete individuals with a diversity of needs. What is required is better liaison between the whole range of public and private institutions and NGOs working with children to ensure full provision of care.

The very essence of the Convention is that the rights of children should be embedded within society.

Overall, there are evidently fundamental failings on the part of civil society to recognise its collective responsibility for the protection and promotion of children's rights. The very essence of the Convention is that the rights of children should be embedded within society. This cannot simply be the responsibility of individual national governments. There is a larger collective responsibility which has to be shared by the whole of society. As yet this is not being recognised. In virtually every country considered in this report, service provision remains piecemeal and inconsistent, often provided in isolation and ignoring the wider context of the CRC. As a result there is an inevitable failure to address the broader needs and rights of children.

In the light of this, it is encouraging that some countries have established designated child institutions, such as a national committee for children, and introduced special children's codes and provisions. However, this is not without risks of its own. Experience suggests that once specialist children's institutions are developed there is a tendency for children's issues to be dealt with by them in isolation, with little liaison with, or reference to, other institutions. As a result, children's issues continue to be marginalised and are not embedded in the decision-making processes of the broader aspects of society, such as health education, housing or transport. Again this runs contrary to the vision of the Convention.

In reality there are many stakeholders in the promotion of children's rights, from the individual parent to the neighbour and the larger community, and from the local municipality to the national government and beyond this to the wider international community. There is clearly a profound need for inter-agency co-operation and liaison in the provision of services for children and in the promotion of children's rights.

In reality there are many stakeholders in the promotion of children's rights, from the individual parent to the neighbour and the larger community, and from the local municipality to the national government and beyond this to the wider international community.

The new global environment

It would be impossible to evaluate implementation of the CRC without considering the broader socio-economic context. The last ten years have seen profound changes; the impact of increasing globalisation means that international economic systems, trade and financial policies are impacting on individual states as never before. An overall increase in global wealth is characterised by extreme polarisation, with an ever-widening gap between the rich and the poor. While there has been a decline in the overall percentage of people living in poverty, the real numbers are increasing. This trend of economic polarisation is not unique to developing or transitional economies. Poverty is expanding rapidly in industrialised countries even as they become richer overall. Far from a situation of economic growth, the global picture at the end of the 1990s, depicted by The World Bank Development Report[3], is one of stalled progress in which the number of children being born and raised in poverty is increasing.

The last ten years have seen profound changes; the impact of increasing globalisation mean that international economic systems, trade and financial policies are impacting on individual states as never before.

The global concentration of wealth is now so acute that the assets of 358 billionaires (in US dollars) surpass the combined incomes of poor countries containing 45% of the world's population. The UNDP Poverty Report 1999[4] concludes that globalisation is increasing the gap between the rich and the poor, highlighting the concentration of wealth in the industrialised countries. This has involved a massively expanded private sector of enormous economic power. Indeed, of the 100 largest economies in the world, 49 are international corporations. The annual sales of General Motors, for example, are larger than

3 The World Bank 1999, The World Bank Development Report 1999/2000 - Entering the 21st Century: The Changing Development Landscape, Washington.

4 United Nations Development Report (UNDP) The UNDP Development Report 1999, OUP, New York.

the GDPs of Thailand or Norway and the annual revenues of Ford surpass those of the oil-rich Saudi Arabia. The new international environment is therefore one of diminishing state power in the face of an increasingly powerful private sector.

A different approach will be needed which recognises the broader roles of the private sector, international organisations, including the large financial institutions, and the wider civil society to protect and promote children's rights.

This poses a range of challenges. The global markets of production, marketing and finance exert enormous impact on national governments who have a growing sense of political disempowerment and loss of sovereignty. Increasingly national governments find themselves sharing power with other forces. The private sector and international organisations such as the International Monetary Fund, the World Bank, regional banks and trading associations, dictate the terms of the global economy and have a growing influence over state economic practice. By extension, these same supranational organisations have an increasing influence over, and responsibility for, the conditions under which children grow up, influencing national budgets for health, education, welfare assistance and other basic services critical for children's well-being.

How far then is the framework of the CRC, as an international instrument, appropriate in this new global environment? Responsibility for the implementation of the CRC currently rests in the state, whilst globalisation and free-market enthusiasm are severely limiting the mandate and power of the state to intervene in social and economic affairs. Many governments simply do not play the roles or possess the resources compatible with the responsibilities they are charged with under the CRC. A different approach will therefore be needed which recognises the broader roles of the private sector, international organisations, including the large financial institutions, and the wider civil society to protect and promote children's rights.

The challenges ahead

In the new global environment, NGOs and other civil organisations have a critical role to play. They can represent a powerful political force - their role in overthrowing apartheid in South Africa and communism in Eastern Europe bears witness to this. Increasingly, NGOs and civil society organisations are assuming roles and tasks that have formerly been the remit of governments. Such groups - often with the support of other international organisations - can be extremely powerful advocates, capable of appealing to the public over the head of governments. All current indicators suggest that NGOs and pressure groups will continue to grow in number and become increasingly influential as we move into the next decade. The role of NGOs in the promotion and protection of children's rights and welfare in this new global arena will be significant.

It is clear that the actual provisions of the CRC and the subject of children's rights have not been fully understood or implemented either by government or the public. The issue still rests very much with a small group of child rights advocates. The time has now come for children's issues to be made far more visible and recognised as a collective responsibility of the whole international community. The International Save the Children Alliance, UNICEF and other children's rights agencies must bring this about. They have to capitalise on their growing strength and seize the opportunity to advance children's rights, positioning them at the heart of the public domain.

Howard Davies / Save The Children

The UN Committee on the Rights of the Child was designed to provide a co-operative, non-confrontational mechanism with which to monitor governmental implementation of the Convention and its provisions. However, it has not had the impact that was envisaged. The reporting mechanism is lengthy and the Committee is unable to process reports efficiently or make observations expediently. In such a situation, it is inevitable that it has only had limited effect in enforcing compliance among countries signatory to the Convention.

NGOs have to capitalise on their growing strength and seize the opportunity to advance children's rights, positioning them at the heart of the public domain.

It is left to the NGOs, then, to put the Convention to the test and formally call governments to account for violations of its provisions. Many northern governments, for example, are both signatories to the CRC and part of the executive of the World Bank. There is an opportunity here for NGOs to lobby these governments to ensure that a children's rights approach is adopted in all the decision-making processes of the World Bank.

NGOs must strengthen their work to liaise with the government, the private sector, international donors, financial institutions and other organisations to ensure that the CRC has a place on all political agendas. The challenge is to develop dynamic and flexible programmes which mobilise different quarters of the international community to work in close co-operation to advance children's rights. Agencies will need to develop better mechanisms for co-operation and broader advocacy strategies; to possess the ability to communicate more effectively with donors and the public; and to demonstrate high degrees of competence, innovation and efficiency.

The challenge is to develop dynamic and flexible programmes which mobilise different quarters of the international community to work in close co-operation to advance children's rights.

Beyond the rhetoric

The evidence of this report demonstrates that the international community can allow itself no room for complacency. The last ten years have shown that the articulation of children's rights in the CRC - despite its near universal ratification - is simply not enough. Governments may be signatories to the Convention, legislation, mechanisms and institutions may be in place, but while children remain victims of discrimination and while their basic rights are still not being assured, it is clear that the full vision of the CRC is not being realised. Ratification is only the beginning, and the real work of implementation remains to be done.

Sarah Muscroft / Save The Children

In the first decade of its existence, the CRC has established the legal framework and laid down the basic foundations upon which to build a practical strategy for change. The challenge now is to harness the spirit of the Convention and the profound common desire to achieve a better world for children, and to translate its provisions into practice. This will help to bring about an important shift in the way children are viewed. As Professor Karl-Eric Knutsson argues, children should not be seen as noble causes requiring rescue through the intervention of adults; they are worthy citizens, reasonable and capable individuals, fully competent participants in defending their own rights.[5] Tomorrow's challenges have to be met by today's children. To prepare them for this, we must treat them as respected citizens, letting them learn leadership, democracy and collective responsibility, as children learn best, through doing. The responsibility for this does not lie with any single institution; governments and civil society must work hand in hand if we are to create a world where children are truly seen and heard.

Tomorrow's challenges have to be met by today's children.

Governments and civil society must work hand in hand if we are to create a world where children are truly seen and heard.

5 Professor Knutsson is an eminent Swedish anthropologist. He was a former official of UNICEF and Assistant Secretary-General of the United Nations. He is also a former Board member of Save the Children Sweden (Rädda Barnen).

Annexes

Annex 1 The UN Convention on the Rights of the Child

Annex 2 Background information on Save The Children

Annex I

Convention on the Rights of the Child,

Adopted by the United Nations General Assembly on 20 November 1989 and entered into a force on 2 September 1990.

PREAMBLE

The States Parties to the present Convention,

Considering that, in accordance with the principles proclaimed in the Charter of the United Nations, recognition of the inherent dignity and of the equal and inalienable rights of all members of the human family is the foundation of freedom, justice and peace in the world,

Bearing in mind that the peoples of the United Nations have, in the Charter, reaffirmed their faith in fundamental human rights and in the dignity and worth of the human person, and have determined to promote social progress and better standards of life in larger freedom,

Recognizing that the United Nations has, in the Universal Declaration of Human Rights and in the International Covenants on Human Rights, proclaimed and agreed that everyone is entitled to all the rights and freedoms set forth therein, without distinction of any kind, such as race, colour, sex, language, religion, political or other opinion, national or social origin, property, birth or other status,

Recalling that, in the Universal Declaration of Human Rights, the United Nations has proclaimed that childhood is entitled to special care and assistance,

Convinced that the family, as the fundamental group of society and the natural environment for the growth and well-being of all its members and particularly children, should be afforded the necessary protection and assistance so that it can fully assume its responsibilities within the community,

Recognizing that the child, for the full and harmonious development of his or her personality, should grow up in a family environment, in an atmosphere of happiness, love and understanding,

Considering that the child should be fully prepared to live an individual life in society, and brought up in the spirit of the ideals proclaimed in the Charter of the United Nations, and in particular in the spirit of peace, dignity, tolerance, freedom,equality and solidarity,

Bearing in mind that the need to extend particular care to the child has been stated in the Geneva Declaration of the Rights of the Child of 1924 and in the Declaration of the Rights of the Child adopted by the General Assembly on 20 November 1959 and recognized in the Universal Declaration of Human Rights, in the International Covenant on Civil and Political Rights (in particular in articles 23 and 24), in the International Covenant on Economic, Social and Cultural Rights (in particular in article 10) and in the statutes and relevant instruments of specialized agencies and international organizations concerned with the welfare of children,

Bearing in mind that, as indicated in the Declaration of the Rights of the Child, "the child, by reason of his physical and mental immaturity, needs special safeguards and care, including appropriate legal protection, before as well as after birth",

Recalling the provisions of the Declaration on Social and Legal Principles relating to the Protection and Welfare of Children, with Special Reference to Foster Placement and Adoption Nationally and Internationally; the United Nations Standard Minimum Rules for the Administration of Juvenile Justice (The Beijing Rules); and the Declaration on the Protection of Women and Children in Emergency and Armed Conflict,

Recognizing that, in all countries in the world, there are children living in exceptionally difficult conditions, and that such children need special consideration,

Taking due account of the importance of the traditions and cultural values of each people for the protection and harmonious development of the child,

Recognizing the importance of international co-operation for improving the living conditions of children in every country, in particular in the developing countries, have agreed as follows:

PART I

Article 1 - Definition of a child

For the purposes of the present Convention, a child means every human being below the age of eighteen years unless under the law applicable to the child, majority is attained earlier.

Article 2 - Non-discrimination

1. States Parties shall respect and ensure the rights set forth in the present Convention to each child within their jurisdiction without discrimination of any kind, irrespective of the child's or his or her parent's or legal guardian's race, colour, sex, language, religion, political or other opinion, national, ethnic or social origin, property, disability, birth or other status
2. States Parties shall take all appropriate measures to ensurethat the child is protected against all forms of discrimination or punishment on the basis of the status, activities, expressed opinions, or beliefs of the child's parents, legal guardians, or family members.

Article 3 - Best interests of the child

1. In all actions concerning children, whether undertaken by public or private social welfare institutions, courts of law, administrative authorities or legislative bodies, the best interests of the child shall be a primary consider.ation.
2. States Parties undertake to ensure the child such protection and care as is necessary for his or her well-being, taking into

account the rights and duties of his or her parents, legal guardians, or other individuals legally responsible for him or her, and, to this end, shall take all appropriate legislative and administrative measures.

3. States Parties shall ensure that the institutions, services and facilities responsible for the care or protection of childrenshall conform with the standards established by competent authorities, particularly in the areas of safety, health, in the number and suitability of their staff, as well as competent supervision.

Article 4 - Implementation of rights

States Parties shall undertake all appropriate legislative, administrative, and other measures for the implementation of the rights recognized in the present Convention. With regard to economic, social and cultural rights, States Parties shall undertake such measures to the maximum extent of their available resources and, where needed, within the framework of international co-operation.

Article 5 - Parental guidance and the child's evolving capacities

States Parties shall respect the responsibilities, rights and duties of parents or, where applicable, the members of the extended family or community as provided for by local custom, legal guardian or other persons legally responsible for the child, to provide, in a manner consistent with the evolving capacities of the child, appropriate direction and guidance in the exercise by the child of the rights recognized in the present Convention.

Article 6 - Survival and development

1. States Parties recognize that every child has the inherent right to life.
2. States Parties shall ensure to the maximum extent possible the survival and development of the child.

Article 7 - Name and nationality

1. The child shall be registered immediately after birth and shall have the right from birth to a name, the right to acquire a nationality and. as far as possible, the right to know and be cared for by his or her parents.
2. States Parties shall ensure the implementation of these rights in accordance with their national law and their obligations under the relevant international instruments in this field, in particular where the child would otherwise be stateless.

Article 8 - Preservation of identity

1. States Parties undertake to respect the right of the child to preserve his or her identity, including nationality, name and family relations as recognized by law without unlawful interference.
2. Where a child is illegally deprived of some or all of the elements of his or her identity, States Parties shall provide appropriate assistance and protection, with a view to re-establishing speedily his or her identity.

Article 9 - Separation from parents

1. States Parties shall ensure that a child shall not be separated from his or her parents against their will, except when competent authorities subject to judicial review determine, in accordance with applicable law and procedures, that such separation is necessary for the best interests of the child. Such determination may be necessary in a particular case such as one involving abuse or neglect of the child by the parents, or one where the parents are living separately and a decision must be made as to the child's place of residence.

2. In any proceedings pursuant to paragraph 1 of the present article, all interested parties shall be given an opportunity to participate in the proceedings and make their views known.
3. States Parties shall respect the right of the child who is separated from one or both parents to maintain personal relations and direct contact with both parents on a regular basis, except if it is contrary to the child's best interests.
4. Where such separation results from any action initiated by a State Party, such as the detention, imprisonment, exile, deportation or death (including death arising from any cause while the person is in the custody of the State) of one or both parents or of the child, that State Party shall, upon request, provide the parents, the child or, if appropriate, another member of the family with the essential information concerning the whereabouts of the absent member(s) of the family unless the provision of the information would be detrimental to the well-being of the child. States Parties shall further ensure that the submission of such a request shall of itself entail no adverse consequences for the person(s) concerned.

Article 10 Family reunification

1. In accordance with the obligation of States Parties under article 9, paragraph 1, applications by a child or his or her parents to enter or leave a State Party for the purpose of family reunification shall be dealt with by States Parties in a positive, humane and expeditious manner. States Parties shall further ensure that the submission of such a request shall entail no adverse consequences for the applicants and for the members of their family.
2. A child whose parents reside in different States shall have the right to maintain on a regular basis, save in exceptional circumstances personal relations and direct contacts with both parents. Towards that end and in accordance with the obligation of States Parties under article 9, paragraph 1, States Parties shall respect the right of the child and his or her parents to leave any country, including their own, and to enter their own country. The right to leave any country shall be subject only to such restrictions as are prescribed by law and which are necessary to protect the national security, public order (ordre public), public health or morals or the rights and freedoms of others and are consistent with the other rights recognized in the present Convention.

Article 11 - Illicit transfer and non-return

1. States Parties shall take measures to combat the illicit transfer and non-return of children abroad.
2. To this end, States Parties shall promote the conclusion of bilateral or multilateral agreements or accession to existing agreements.

Article 12 - The child's opinion

1. States Parties shall assure to the child who is capable of forming his or her own views the right to express those views freely in all matters affecting the child, the views of the child being given due weight in accordance with the age and maturity of the child.
2. For this purpose, the child shall in particular be provided the opportunity to be heard in any judicial and administrative proceedings affecting the child, either directly, or through a representative or an appropriate body, in a manner consistent with the procedural rules of national law.

Article 13 - Freedom of expression

1. The child shall have the right to freedom of expression; this right shall include freedom to seek, receive and impart information and ideas of all kinds, regardless of frontiers, either orally, in writing or in print, in the form of art, or through any other media of the child's choice.
2. The exercise of this right may be subject to certain restrictions, but these shall only be such as are provided by law and are necessary:
   (a) For respect of the rights or reputations of others; or
   (b) For the protection of national security or of public order (ordre public), or of public health or morals.

Article 14 - Freedom of thought, conscience and religion

1. States Parties shall respect the right of the child to freedom of thought, conscience and religion.
2. States Parties shall respect the rights and duties of the parents and, when applicable, legal guardians, to provide direction to the child in the exercise of his or her right in a manner consistent with the evolving capacities of the child.
3. Freedom to manifest one's religion or beliefs may be subject only to such limitations as are prescribed by law and are necessary to protect public safety, order, health or morals, or the fundamental rights and freedoms of others.

Article 15 - Freedom of association

1. States Parties recognize the rights of the child to freedom of association and to freedom of peaceful assembly.
2. No restrictions may be placed on the exercise of these rights other than those imposed in conformity with the law and which are necessary in a democratic society in the interests of national security or public safety, public order (ordre public), the protection of public health or morals or the protection of the rights and freedoms of others.

Article 16 - Protection of privacy

1. No child shall be subjected to arbitrary or unlawful interference with his or her privacy, family, home or correspondence, nor to unlawful attacks on his or her honour and reputation.
2. The child has the right to the protection of the law against such interference or attacks.

Article 17 - Access to appropriate information

States Parties recognize the important function performed by the mass media and shall ensure that the child has access to information and material from a diversity of national and international sources, especially those aimed at the promotion of his or her social, spiritual and moral well-being and physical and mental health. To this end, States Parties shall:

(a) Encourage the mass media to disseminate information and material of social and cultural benefit to the child and in accordance with the spirit of article 29;

(b) Encourage international co-operation in the production, exchange and dissemination of such information and material from a diversity of cultural, national and international sources;

(c) Encourage the production and dissemination of children's books;

(d) Encourage the mass media to have particular regard to the linguistic needs of the child who belongs to a minority groupor who is indigenous;

(e) Encourage the development of appropriate guidelines for the protection of the child from information and material injurious to his or her well-being, bearing in mind the provisions of articles 13 and 18.

Article 18 - Parental responsibilities

1. States Parties shall use their best efforts to ensure recognition of the principle that both parents have common responsibilities for the upbringing and development of the child. Parents or, as the case may be, legal guardians, have the primary responsibility for the upbringing and development of the child. The best interests of the child will be their basic concern.
2. For the purpose of guaranteeing and promoting the rights set forth in the present Convention, States Parties shall render appropriate assistance to parents and legal guardians in the performance of their child-rearing responsibilities and shall ensure the development of institutions, facilities and services for the care of children.
3. States Parties shall take all appropriate measures to ensure that children of working parents have the right to benefit from child-care services and facilities for which they are eligible.

Article 19 - Protection from abuse and neglect

1. States Parties shall take all appropriate legislative, administrative, social and educational measures to protect the child from all forms of physical or mental violence, injury or abuse, neglect or negligent treatment, maltreatment or exploitation, including sexual abuse, while in the care of parent(s), legal guardian(s) or any other person who has the care of the child.
2. Such protective measures should, as appropriate, include effective procedures for the establishment of social programmesto provide necessary support for the child and for those who have the care of the child, as well as for other forms of prevention and for identification, reporting, referral, investigation, treatment and follow-up of instances of child maltreatment described heretofore, and, as appropriate, for judicial involvement.

Article 20 - Protection of children without families

1. A child temporarily or permanently deprived of his or her family environment, or in whose own best interests cannot be allowed to remain in that environment, shall be entitled to special protection and assistance provided by the State.
2. States Parties shall in accordance with their national laws ensure alternative care for such a child.
3. Such care could include, inter alia, foster placement, kafalah of Islamic law, adoption or if necessary placement in suitable institutions for the care of children. When considering solutions, due regard shall be paid to the desirability of continuity in a child's upbringing and to the child's ethnic, religious, cultural and linguistic background.

Article 21 - Adoption

States Parties that recognize and/or permit the system of adoption shall ensure that the best interests of the child shall be the paramount consideration and they shall:

(a) Ensure that the adoption of a child is authorized only by competent authorities who determine, in accordance with applicable law and procedures and on the basis of all pertinent and reliable information, that the adoption is permissible in view of the child's status concerning parents, relatives and legal guardians and that, if required, the persons concerned have given their informed consent to the adoption on the basis of such counselling as may be necessary;

(b) Recognize that inter-country adoption may be considered as an alternative means of child's care, if the child cannot be placed in a foster or an adoptive family or cannot in any suitable manner be cared for in the child's country of origin;

(c) Ensure that the child concerned by inter-country adoption enjoys safeguards and standards equivalent to those existing in the case of national adoption;

(d) Take all appropriate measures to ensure that, in inter-country adoption, the placement does not result in improper financial gain for those involved in it;

(e) Promote, where appropriate, the objectives of the present article by concluding bilateral or multilateral arrangements or agreements, and endeavour, within this framework, to ensure that the placement of the child in another country is carried out by competent authorities or organs.

Article 22 - Refugee children

1. States Parties shall take appropriate measures to ensure that a child who is seeking refugee status or who is considered a refugee in accordance with applicable international or domestic law and procedures shall, whether unaccompanied or accompanied by his or her parents or by any other person, receive appropriate protection and humanitarian assistance in the enjoyment of applicable rights set forth in the present Convention and in other international human rights or humanitarian instruments to which the said States are Parties.
2. For this purpose, States Parties shall provide, as they consider appropriate, co-operation in any efforts by the United Nations and other competent intergovernmental organizations or non-governmental organizations co-operating with the United Nation to protect and assist such a child and to trace the parents or other members of the family of any refugee child in order to obtain information necessary for reunification with his or her family. In cases where no parents or other members of the family can be found, the child shall be accorded the same protection as any other child permanently or temporarily deprived of his or her family environment for any reason , as set forth in the present Convention.

Article 23 - Handicapped children

1. States Parties recognize that a mentally or physically disabled child should enjoy a full and decent life, in conditions which ensure dignity, promote self-reliance and facilitate the child's active participation in the community.
2. States Parties recognize the right of the disabled child to special care and shall encourage and ensure the extension, subject to available resources, to the eligible child and those responsible for his or her care, of assistance for which application is made and which is appropriate to the child's condition and to the circumstances of the parents or others caring for the child.
3. Recognizing the special needs of a disabled child, assistance extended in accordance with paragraph 2 of the present article shall be provided free of charge, whenever possible, taking into account the financial resources of the parents or others caring for the child, and shall be designed to ensure that the disabled child has effective access to and receives education, training, health care services, rehabilitation services, preparation for employment and recreation opportunities in a manner conducive to the child's achieving the fullest possible social integration and individual development, including his or her cultural and spiritual development
4. States Parties shall promote, in the spirit of international cooperation, the exchange of appropriate information in the field of preventive health care and of medical, psychological and functional treatment of disabled children, including dissemination of and access to information concerning methods of rehabilitation, education and vocational services, with the aim of enabling States Parties to improve their capabilities and skills and to widen their experience in these areas. In this regard, particular account shall be taken of the needs of developing countries.

Article 24 - Health and health services

1. States Parties recognize the right of the child to the enjoyment of the highest attainable standard of health and to facilities for the treatment of illness and rehabilitation of health. States Parties shall strive to ensure that no child is deprived of his or her right of access to such health care services.
2. States Parties shall pursue full implementation of this right and, in particular, shall take appropriate measures:
   (a) To diminish infant and child mortality;
   (b) To ensure the provision of necessary medical assistance and health care to all children with emphasis on the development of primary health care;
   (c) To combat disease and malnutrition, including within the framework of primary health care, through, inter alia, the application of readily available technology and through the provision of adequate nutritious foods and clean drinking-water, taking into consideration the dangers and risks of environmental pollution;
   (d) To ensure appropriate pre-natal and post-natal health care for mothers;
   (e) To ensure that all segments of society, in particular parentsand children, are informed, have access to education and are supported in the use of basic knowledge of child health and nutrition, the advantages of breastfeeding, hygiene and environmental sanitation and the prevention of accidents;
   (f) To develop preventive health care, guidance for parents and family planning education and services.
3. States Parties shall take all effective and appropriate measures with a view to abolishing traditional practices prejudicial to the health of children.
4. States Parties undertake to promote and encourage international co-operation with a view to achieving progressively the full realization of the right recognized in the present article. In this regard, particular account shall be taken of the needs of developing countries.

Article 25 Periodic review of placement

States Parties recognize the right of a child who has been placed by the competent authorities for the purposes of care, protection or treatment of his or her physical or mental health, to a periodic review of the treatment provided to the child and all other circumstances relevant to his or her placement.

Article 26 - Social security

1. States Parties shall recognize for every child the right to benefit from social security, including social insurance, and shall take the necessary measures to achieve the full realization of this right in accordance with their national law.
2. The benefits should, where appropriate, be granted, taking into account the resources and the circumstances of the child and persons having responsibility for the maintenance of the child,as well as any other consideration relevant to an application for benefits made by or on behalf of the child.

Article 27 - Standard of living

1. States Parties recognize the right of every child to a standard of living adequate for the child's physical, mental, spiritual, moral and social development.
2. The parent(s) or others responsible for the child have the primary responsibility to secure, within their abilities and financial capacities, the conditions of living necessary for the child's development.

3. States Parties, in accordance with national conditions and within their means, shall take appropriate measures to assist parents and others responsible for the child to implement this right and shall in case of need provide material assistance and support programmes, particularly with regard to nutrition, clothing and housing.
4. States Parties shall take all appropriate measures to secure the recovery of maintenance for the child from the parents or other persons having financial responsibility for the child, both within the State Party and from abroad. In particular, where the person having financial responsibility for the child lives in a State different from that of the child, States Parties shall promote the accession to international agreements or the conclusion of such agreements, as well as the making of other appropriate arrangements.

Article 28 Education

1. States Parties recognize the right of the child to education, and with a view to achieving this right progressively and on the basis of equal opportunity, they shall, in particular:
   (a) Make primary education compulsory and available free to all;
   (b) Encourage the development of different forms of secondary education, including general and vocational education, make them available and accessible to every child, and take appropriate measures such as the introduction of free education and offerin financial assistance in case of need;
   (c) Make higher education accessible to all on the basis of capacity by every appropriate means;
   (d) Make educational and vocational information and guidance available and accessible to all children;
   (e) Take measures to encourage regular attendance at schools and the reduction of drop-out rates.
2. States Parties shall take all appropriate measures to ensure that school discipline is administered in a manner consistent with the child's human dignity and in conformity with the present Convention.
3. States Parties shall promote and encourage international cooperation in matters relating to education, in particular witha view to contributing to the elimination of ignorance and illiteracy throughout the world and facilitating access to scientific and technical knowledge and modern teaching methods. In this regard, particular account shall be taken of the needs of developing countries.

Article 29 - Aims of education

1. States Parties agree that the education of the child shall be directed to:
   (a) The development of the child's personality, talents and mental and physical abilities to their fullest potential;
   (b) The development of respect for human rights and fundamental freedoms, and for the principles enshrined in the Charter of the United Nations;
   (c) The development of respect for the child's parents, his or her own cultural identity, language and values, for the national values of the country in which the child is living, the country from which he or she may originate, and for civilizations different from his or her own;
   (d) The preparation of the child for responsible life in a free society, in the spirit of understanding, peace, tolerance, equality of sexes, and friendship among all peoples, ethnic, national and religious groups and persons of indigenous origin;
   (e) The development of respect for the natural environment.

2. No part of the present article or article 28 shall be construed so as to interfere with the liberty of individuals and bodies to establish and direct educational institutions, subject always to the observance of the principle set forth in paragraph 1 of the present article and to the requirements that the education given in such institutions shall conform to such minimum standards as may be laid down by the State.

Article 30 - Children of minorities or of indigenous peoples

In those States in which ethnic, religious or linguistic minorities or persons of indigenous origin exist, a child belonging to such a minority or who is indigenous shall not be denied the right, in community with other members of his or her group, to enjoy his or her own culture, to profess and practise his or her own religion, or to use his or her own language.

Article 31 - Leisure, recreation and cultural activities

1. States Parties recognize the right of the child to rest and leisure, to engage in play and recreational activities appropriat to the age of the child and to participate freely in cultural life and the arts. 2. States Parties shall respect and promote the right of the child to participate fully in cultural and artistic life and shall encourage the provision of appropriate and equal opportunities for cultural, artistic, recreational and leisure activity.

Article 32 - Child labour

1. States Parties recognize the right of the child to be protected from economic exploitation and from performing any work that is likely to be hazardous or to interfere with the child's education, or to be harmful to the child's health or physical, mental, spiritual, moral or social development.
2. States Parties shall take legislative, administrative, social and educational measures to ensure the implementation of the present article. To this end, and having regard to the relevant provisions of other international instruments, States Parties shall in particular:
   (a) Provide for a minimum age or minimum ages for admission to employment;
   (b) Provide for appropriate regulation of the hours and conditions of employment;
   (c) Provide for appropriate penalties or other sanctions to ensure the effective enforcement of the present article.

Article 33 - Drug abuse

States Parties shall take all appropriate measures, including legislative, administrative, social and educational measures, to protect children from the illicit use of narcotic drugs and psychotropic substances as defined in the relevant international treaties, and to prevent the use of children in the illicit production and trafficking of such substances.

Article 34 - Sexual exploitation

States Parties undertake to protect the child from all forms of sexual exploitation and sexual abuse. For these purposes, States Parties shall in particular take all appropriate national, bilateral and multilateral measures to prevent:

(a) The inducement or coercion of a child to engage in any unlawful sexual activity;
(b) The exploitative use of children in prostitution or other unlawful sexual practices;
(c) The exploitative use of children in pornographic performances and materials.

Article 3 - Sale, trafficking and abduction

States Parties shall take all appropriate national, bilateral and multilateral measures to prevent the abduction of, the sale of or traffic in children for any purpose or in any form.

Article 36 - Other forms of exploitation

States Parties shall protect the child against all other forms of exploitation prejudicial to any aspects of the child's welfare.

Article 37 - Torture and deprivation of liberty

States Parties shall ensure that:

(a) No child shall be subjected to torture or other cruel, inhuman or degrading treatment or punishment. Neither capital punishment nor life imprisonment without possibility of releaseshall be imposed for offences committed by persons below eighteen years of age;

(b) No child shall be deprived of his or her liberty unlawfully or arbitrarily. The arrest, detention or imprisonment of a child shall be in conformity with the law and shall be used only as a measure of last resort and for the shortest appropriate period of time;

(c) Every child deprived of liberty shall be treated with humanity and respect for the inherent dignity of the human person, and in a manner which takes into account the needs of persons of his or her age. In particular, every child deprived of liberty shall be separated from adults unless it is considered in the child's best interest not to do so and shall have the right to maintain contact with his or her family through correspondence and visits, save in exceptional circumstances;

(d) Every child deprived of his or her liberty shall have the right to prompt access to legal and other appropriate assistance,as well as the right to challenge the legality of the deprivation of his or her liberty before a court or other competent, independent and impartial authority, and to a prompt decision on any such action.

Article 38 - Armed conflict

1. States Parties undertake to respect and to ensure respect for rules of international humanitarian law applicable to them in armed conflicts which are relevant to the child.
2. States Parties shall take all feasible measures to ensure that persons who have not attained the age of fifteen years do not take a direct part in hostilities.
3. States Parties shall refrain from recruiting any person who has not attained the age of fifteen years into their armed forces. In recruiting among those persons who have attained the age of fifteen years but who have not attained the age of eighteen years, States Parties shall endeavour to give priority to those who are oldest.
4. In accordance with their obligations under international humanitarian law to protect the civilian population in armed conflicts, States Parties shall take all feasible measures to ensure protection and care of children who are affected by an armed conflict.

Article 39 - Rehabilitative care

States Parties shall take all appropriate measures to promote physical and psychological recovery and social reintegration of a child victim of: any form of neglect, exploitation, or abuse; torture or any other form of cruel, inhuman or degrading treatment or punishment; or armed conflicts. Such recovery and reintegration shall take place in an environment which fosters the health, self-respect and dignity of the child.

Article 40 - Administration of juvenile justice

1. States Parties recognize the right of every child alleged as, accused of, or recognized as having infringed the penal law to be treated in a manner consistent with the promotion of the child's sense of dignity and worth, which reinforces the child's respect for the human rights and fundamental freedoms of others and which takes into account the child's age and the desirability of promoting the child's reintegration and the child's assuming a constructive role in society.
2. To this end, and having regard to the relevant provisions of international instruments, States Parties shall, in particular, ensure that:
   (a) No child shall be alleged as, be accused of, or recognized as having infringed the penal law by reason of acts or omissions that were not prohibited by national or international law at the time they were committed;
   (b) Every child alleged as or accused of having infringed the penal law has at least the following guarantees:
      (i) To be presumed innocent until proven guilty according to law;
      (ii) To be informed promptly and directly of the charges against him or her, and, if appropriate, through his or her parents or legal guardians, and to have legal or other appropriate assistance in the preparation and presentation of his or her defence;
      (iii) To have the matter determined without delay by a competent, independent and impartial authority or judicial body in a fair hearing according to law, in the presence of legal or other appropriate assistance and, unless it is considered not to be in the best interest of the child, in particular, taking into account his or her age or situation, his or her parents or legal guardians;
      (iv) Not to be compelled to give testimony or to confess guilt; to examine or have examined adverse witnesses and to obtain the participation and examination of witnesses on his or her behalf under conditions of equality;
      (v) If considered to have infringed the penal law, to have this decision and any measures imposed in consequence thereof reviewed by a higher competent, independent and impartial authority or judicial body according to law;
      (vi) To have the free assistance of an interpreter if the child cannot understand or speak the language used;
      (vii) To have his or her privacy fully respected at all stages of the proceedings. 3. States Parties shall seek to promote the establishment of laws, procedures, authorities and institutions specifically applicable to children alleged as, accused of, or recognized as having infringed the penal law, and, in particular:
   (a) The establishment of a minimum age below which children shall be presumed not to have the capacity to infringe the penal law;
   (b) Whenever appropriate and desirable, measures for dealing with such children without resorting to judicial proceedings, providing that human rights and legal safeguards are fully respected.
4. A variety of dispositions, such as care, guidance and supervision orders; counselling; probation; foster care; education and vocational training programmes and other alternatives to institutional care shall be available to ensure that children are dealt with in a manner appropriate to their well-being and proportionate both to their circumstances and the offence.

Article 41 - Respect of existing standards

Nothing in the present Convention shall affect any provisions which are more conducive to the realization of the rights of the child and which may be contained in:

(a) The law of a State party; or

(b) International law in force for that State.

PART II

Article 42 - Implementation and entry into force

States Parties undertake to make the principles and provisions of the Convention widely known, by appropriate and active means, to adults and children alike.

Article 43

1. For the purpose of examining the progress made by States Parties in achieving the realization of the obligations undertaken in the present Convention, there shall be established a Committee on the Rights of the Child, which shall carry out the functions hereinafter provided.
2. The Committee shall consist of ten experts of high moral standing and recognized competence in the field covered by this Convention. The members of the Committee shall be elected by States Parties from among their nationals and shall serve in their personal capacity, consideration being given to equitable geographical distribution, as well as to the principal legal systems.
3. The members of the Committee shall be elected by secret ballot from a list of persons nominated by States Parties. Each State Party may nominate one person from among its own nationals.
4. The initial election to the Committee shall be held no later than six months after the date of the entry into force of the present Convention and thereafter every second year. At least four months before the date of each election, the Secretary-General of the United Nations shall address a letter to States Parties inviting them to submit their nominations within two months. The Secretary-General shall subsequently prepare a list in alphabetical order of all persons thus nominated, indicating States Parties which have nominated them, and shall submit it to the States Parties to the present Convention.
5. The elections shall be held at meetings of States Parties convened by the Secretary-General at United Nations Headquarters. At those meetings, for which two thirds of States Parties shall constitute a quorum, the persons elected to the Committee shall be those who obtain the largest number of votes and an absolute majority of the votes of the representatives of States Parties present and voting.
6. The members of the Committee shall be elected for a term of four years. They shall be eligible for re-election if renominated. The term of five of the members elected at the first election shall expire at the end of two years; immediately after the first election, the names of these five members shall be chosen by lot by the Chairman of the meeting.
7. If a member of the Committee dies or resigns or declares that for any other cause he or she can no longer perform the duties of the Committee, the State Party which nominated the member shall appoint another expert from among its nationals to serve for the remainder of the term, subject to the approval of the Committee.
8. The Committee shall establish its own rules of procedure.

9. The Committee shall elect its officers for a period of two years.
10. The meetings of the Committee shall normally be held at United Nations Headquarters or at any other convenient place as determined by the Committee. The Committee shall normally meet annually. The duration of the meetings of the Committee shall be determined, and reviewed, if necessary, by a meeting of the States Parties to the present Convention, subject to the approval of the General Assembly.
11. The Secretary-General of the United Nations shall provide the necessary staff and facilities for the effective performance of the functions of the Committee under the present Convention.
12. With the approval of the General Assembly, the members of the Committee established under the present Convention shall receive emoluments from United Nations resources on such terms and conditions as the Assembly may decide.

Article 44

1. States Parties undertake to submit to the Committee, through the Secretary-General of the United Nations, reports on the measures they have adopted which give effect to the rights recognized herein and on the progress made on the enjoyment of those rights:
   (a) Within two years of the entry into force of the Convention for the State Party concerned;
   (b) Thereafter every five years.
2. Reports made under the present article shall indicate factors and difficulties, if any, affecting the degree of fulfilment of the obligations under the present Convention. Reports shall also contain sufficient information to provide the Committee with a comprehensive understanding of the implementation of the Convention in the country concerned.
3. A State Party which has submitted a comprehensive initial report to the Committee need not, in its subsequent reports submitted in accordance with paragraph 1 (b) of the present article, repeat basic information previously provided.
4. The Committee may request from States Parties further information relevant to the implementation of the Convention.
5. The Committee shall submit to the General Assembly, through the Economic and Social Council, every two years, reports on its activities.
6. States Parties shall make their reports widely available to the public in their own countries.

Article 45

In order to foster the effective implementation of the Convention and to encourage international co-operation in the field covered by the Convention:

(a) The specialized agencies, the United Nations Children's Fund, and other United Nations organs shall be entitled to be represented at the consideration of the implementation of such provisions of the present Convention as fall within the scope of their mandate. The Committee may invite the specialized agencies, the United Nations Children's Fund and other competent bodies as it may consider appropriate to provide expert advice on the implementation of the Convention in areas falling within the scope of their respective mandates. The Committee may invite the specialized agencies, the United Nations Children's Fund, and other United Nations organs to submit reports on the implementation of the Convention in areas falling within the scope of their activities;

(b) The Committee shall transmit, as it may consider appropriate, to the specialized agencies, the United Nations Children's Fund and other competent bodies, any reports from States Parties that contain a request, or indicate a need, for technical advice or assistance, along with the Committee's observations and suggestions, if any, on these requests or indications;

(c) The Committee may recommend to the General Assembly to request the Secretary-General to undertake on its behalf studies on specific issues relating to the rights of the child;

(d) The Committee may make suggestions and general recommendations based on information received pursuant to articles 44 and 45 of the present Convention. Such suggestions and general recommendations shall be transmitted to any State Party concerned and reported to the General Assembly, together with comments, if any, from States Parties.

PART III

Article 46

The present Convention shall be open for signature by all States.

Article 47

The present Convention is subject to ratification. Instruments of ratification shall be deposited with the Secretary-General of the United Nations.

Article 48

The present Convention shall remain open for accession by any State. The instruments of accession shall be deposited with the Secretary-General of the United Nations.

Article 49

1. The present Convention shall enter into force on the thirtieth day following the date of deposit with the Secretary-General of the United Nations of the twentieth instrument of ratification or accession.
2. For each State ratifying or acceding to the Convention after the deposit of the twentieth instrument of ratification or accession the Convention shall enter into force on the thirtieth day after the deposit by such State of its instrument of ratification or accession.

Article 50

1. Any State Party may propose an amendment and file it with the Secretary-General of the United Nations. The Secretary-General shall thereupon communicate the proposed amendment to States Parties, with a request that they indicate whether they favour a conference of States Parties for the purpose of considering and voting upon the proposals. In the event that, within four months from the date of such communication, at least one third of the States Parties favour such a conference, the Secretary-General shall convene the conference under the auspices of the United Nations. Any amendment adopted by a majority of States Parties present and voting at the conference shall be submitted to the General Assembly for approval.
2. An amendment adopted in accordance with paragraph 1 of the present article shall enter into force when it has been approved by the General Assembly of the United Nations and accepted by a two-thirds majority of States Parties.
3. When an amendment enters into force, it shall be binding on those States Parties which have accepted it, other States Parties still being bound by the provisions of the present Convention and any earlier amendments which they have accepted.

Article 51

1. The Secretary-General of the United Nations shall receive and circulate to all States the text of reservations made by States at the time of ratification or accession.
2. A reservation incompatible with the object and purpose of the present Convention shall not be permitted.
3. Reservations may be withdrawn at any time by notification to that effect addressed to the Secretary-General of the United Nations, who shall then inform all States. Such notification shall take effect on the date on which it is received by the Secretary-General

Article 52

A State Party may denounce the present Convention by written notification to the Secretary-General of the United Nations. Denunciation becomes effective one year after the date of receipt of the notification by the Secretary-General.

Article 53

The Secretary-General of the United Nations is designated as the depositary of the present Convention.

Article 54

The original of the present Convention, of which the Arabic, Chinese, English, French, Russian and Spanish texts are equally authentic, shall be deposited with the Secretary-General of the United Nations.

Annex 2

THE WORK OF SAVE THE CHILDREN

The International Save the Children Alliance comprises 26 member organisations working in over 100 countries around the world. They all share a common vision of a world which respects and values each child, which listens to children and learns, and where all children have hope and opportunity. Its work is based on the rights of the child, first advocated by the founders of Save the Children and expressed today in the United Nations Convention on the Rights of the Child.

The International Save the Children Alliance provides both emergency relief and long term development assistance, wherever possible working closely with local partners who firmly believe in providing their children with the best possible start in life.

In its work to tackle emergency situations which threaten children's survival and development, Save the Children provides material assistance for immediate relief, protection to children caught up in conflict (including reunification of thousands of children separated from their families) and assists with the rebuilding of foundations for a secure future.

Save the Children also runs major programmes of work to secure the rights of children by bringing about sustainable and equitable development. Poverty and inequality are the root causes of many of the obstacles preventing the fulfilment of children's rights, and their eradication is a fundamental aim of Save the Children's programmes. In the programmes themselves, particular fields of expertise include health, education, disability, child labour, nutrition and juvenile justice. In recent years the Alliance has also responded to the emergence of the HIV/AIDS epidemic and has developed a range of innovative programmes designed to increase the protection of children from the virus itself and from the impact of the loss of parents or other carers.

Equally importantly, Save the Children focuses on the research and advocacy which brings the lack of recognition of children's rights to the attention of decision makers, politicians and opinion formers across the world. This work has focused on:

- raising awareness of the UN Convention on the Rights of the Child
- encouraging the practical implementation of the Convention, globally
- supporting the monitoring mechanisms established by the Convention

Its achievements in leading the fight for recognition of children's rights have been substantial. To mention just a few examples, these include:

- the development of the International Save the Children Alliance training kit on the Convention which has been translated into many different languages
- offering capacity building and other support to national groupings and coalitions who are responsible for monitoring the implementation of the Convention by States Parties. This includes assistance in the preparation of alternative NGO reports for submission to the UN Committee on the Rights of the Child as well as funding NGO representatives to attend pre-sessional hearings of the UN committee
- providing training on the convention and children's rights with a wide range of groups, including children, parents,

teachers, health care workers, planners, judges, the police, UN peacekeepers, journalists, politicians and policy makers

- preparing a variety of different information and resource materials on the Convention, including versions of the Convention prepared by children themselves, to increase awareness and understanding of children's rights
- assisting governments in amending domestic legislation to bring it into conformity with the Convention, or developing child care law within the framework of the Convention
- piloting and supporting the development of independent watchdogs who oversee the protection of children's rights such as ombudsmen or children's commissioners
- developing practical ways in which children can participate in decisions made about them or which concern them, including schools councils, children's parliaments, children's press bureaux, children's hearings and children-led organisations
- pioneering methods through which children have become active participants in research on children's lives to give them more control over research carried out about them
- offering financial and practical support to the creation of the Children's Rights Information Network (CRIN) in 1995. This provides a central focus and mechanism for sharing information on children's rights through a newsletter, a website, theme desks and an E-mail list. Over 800 organisations worldwide are now members of CRIN.
- Giving training and support groups of children to become more actively involved in international conferences discussing their lives and situation. For example, Save the Children enabled children to attend the 1996 Stockholm conference on the commercial sexual exploitation of children and working children to then present their views to the ILO Oslo Child Labour Conference in 1998

The statistics speak for themselves. Half the world's poor are now children. There are more children living in poverty than ever before in history. Each year 12 million children under five years of age die unnecessarily of easily preventable diseases, and millions of others are ill because of unsafe drinking water and poor sanitation. More than 8 million children have lost their mothers or both parents as a result of the AIDS epidemic. 130 million children of primary school age are not in school and an estimated 250 million children are now working worldwide, often in dangerous and exploitative conditions.

Ten Years ago, the UN Convention on the Rights of the Child inspired a renewed commitment to make adults and adult institutions much more accountable for what they do for children, and to address the stark reality that these statistics portray. But clearly, what the Convention has achieved lacks the drama and visibility of immediate success.
Only fundamental changes to attitudes, behaviour and overall commitment to children will ultimately protect them from horrors of wars, poverty, exploitation and abuse. The Members of the International Save the Children Alliance see it as their role to continue the fight to keep this enormous challenge in the hearts and minds of everyone who can bring about benefits in the lives of children.

The Members of the International Save the Children Alliance are listed below.

Australia
Save the Children Australia
mail address:
P.O. Box 1281, Collingwood, Victoria 3066, Australia
office address:
66 Sackville Street, Collingwood, Victoria 3066, Australia
Tel +61 3 94 17 76 62
Fax +61 3 94 19 95 18
E-mail scfa@scfa.asn.au

Canada
Save the Children Canada
office address:
4141 Yonge Street
Suite 300, Toronto, Ontario M2P 2A8, Canada
Tel +1 416 221 55 01
Fax +1 416 221 82 14
E-mail sccan@savethechildren.ca
Website www.savethechildren.ca

Denmark
Save the Children Denmark
(Red Barnet)
office address:
Rantzausgade 60,
DK-2200 Copenhagen, N.Denmark
Tel +45 70 20 61 20
Fax +45 70 20 62 20
E-mail redbarnet@redbarnet.dk
Website www.redbarnet.dk

Dominican Republic
Fundacion Para El Desarrollo Comunitario
mail address:
EPS #X-10397 FUDECO, P.O Box 02-5261, Miami, Florida 33102-5261, USA
office address:
Calle Jacinto Mañón 32 Ensanche Paraíso
Santo Domingo, Dominican Republic
Tel +1 809-567 3351/542 5403
Fax +1 809-566 82 97
E-mail fudeco@codetel.net.do
Website http://fudeco.com/indexs.html

Egypt
Egyptian Save the Children
mail address:
P.O. Box 5854
Heliopolis West
11771 Cairo, Egypt
office address:
21 Abu Bakr El Seddik Mahkama Square, Heliopolis, Cairo
Tel +202 248 67 64
Fax +202 249 4602

Faroe Islands
Barnabati
office address: Margarinfabrikkin
Magnus Heinsonargöta 12, Postboks 1052, FR-110 Torshavn, Faroe Islands
Tel +298 373 007
Fax +298 374 045

Finland
Save the Children Finland
(Pelastakaa Lapset Ry)
mail address:
P.O. Box 177, 00181
Helsinki, Finland
office address:
Lapinrinne 2, 00180
Helsinki, Finland
Tel +358 9 4135 5400
Fax +358 9 4135 5444
E-mail eija.kemppi@pela.fi
Website www.pela.fi

France
Save the Children France
(Enfants et Développement)
office address:
13 rue Jules Simon,
F-75015 Paris, France
Tel +33 1 53 68 98 20
Fax +33 1 53 68 98 29
E-mail eedparis@worldnet.fr

Greece
Save the Children Greece
office address:
54 Papadiamandopoulou Street, GR-157 71
Zografou - Athens, Greece
Tel +30 1 775 87 32
Fax/Tel +30 1 779 94 81
E-mail stc@nyx.gr

Guatemala
Save the Children Guatemala
(Alianza Para El Desarrollo Juvenil Comunitario)
mail address:
1era Avenida 9-33
Zona 9, Apdo Postal 2903, Guatemala City, Guatemala
Tel +502 332 62 12, 339 42 31-3
Fax +502 334 23 38, 360 62 42
E-mail adejucsc@infovia.com.gt

Honduras
Save the Children Honduras
(Asociacion Salvemos Los Niños de Honduras)
mail address:
Apartado Postal 333 Tegucigalpa, M.D.C, Honduras, Central America
Tel +504 239 5051/9212/0158
Fax +50 42 32 58 69
E-mail director@asch1.sdnhon.org.hn

Iceland
Save the Children Iceland
(Barnaheill)
office address:
Laugavegur 7
101 Reykjavik, Iceland
Tel +354 561 05 45
Fax +354 552 2721
E-mail barnaheill@barnaheill.is
Website www.barnaheill.is

Japan
Save the Children Japan
office address:
Daisaku Am Bldg 8F
11-11 Sugahara-Cho,
Kita-Ku Osaka,
530-0046 Japan
Tel +81 66 361 5695
Fax +81 66 361 5698
E-mail info@savechildren.or.jp

Jordan
Jordanian Save the Children
mail address:
Jabal Al-Nuzha Princess Basma Center for Social Development, P.O. Box 927370, Amman, Jordan
Tel. +962 6 567 0241
Fax +962 6 568 7718